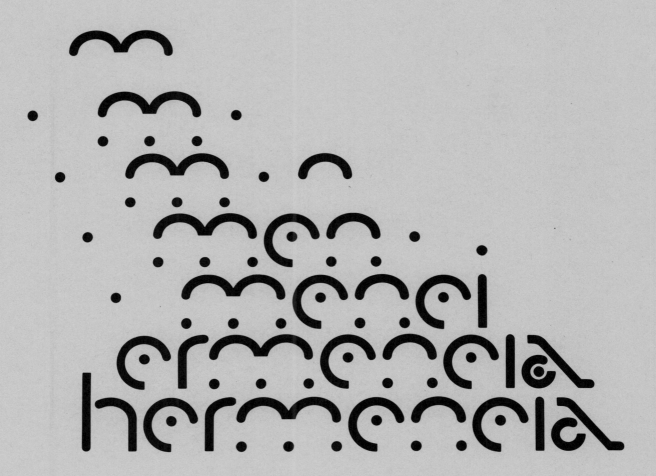

**Hermeneia
—A Critical
and Historical
Commentary
on the Bible**

The Pastoral Epistles

A Commentary on
the Pastoral Epistles

by Martin Dibelius †
and Hans Conzelmann

Translated by
Philip Buttolph and
Adela Yarbro

Edited by
Helmut Koester

Fortress
Press   Philadelphia

Translated from the German *Die Pastoralbriefe* by
Martin Dibelius†; fourth, revised edition by Hans
Conzelmann. Handbuch zum Neuen Testament
begründet von Hans Lietzmann in Verbindung mit
Fachgenossen, herausgegeben von Günther Born-
kamm, 13, 1966. © J. C. B. Mohr (Paul Siebeck),
Tübingen, 1955.

Library of Congress Catalog Card Number 71-157549
ISBN-0-8006-6002-1

20–6002 Printed in the United States of America

Type set by Maurice Jacobs, Inc., Philadelphia

Martin Dibelius, 1881–1947, was for thirty-two years
Professor of New Testament Exegesis and Criticism at the
University of Heidelberg, Germany. A contributor to
both the *Handbuch zum Neuen Testament* and the *Meyer
Kommentar*, he is remembered for his contributions to the
Formgeschichtliche studies. His major work, *From Tradition
to Gospel*, appeared in English in 1935.

Hans Conzelmann, born in 1915, served on the theological faculties at Tübingen, Heidelberg, and Zürich
before assuming his present position in the theological
faculty at Göttingen. He is well known in English for *The
Theology of St. Luke* (1960) and *An Outline of the Theology
of the New Testament* (1969). He has also contributed to
Kittel's *Theological Dictionary of the New Testament*, *Religion
in Geschichte und Gegenwart*, *Das Neue Testament Deutsch*, the
Handbuch zum Neuen Testament and the *Meyer Kommentar*.

Contents

The name *Hermeneia*, Greek ἑρμηνεία, has been chosen as the title of the commentary series to which this volume belongs. The word *Hermeneia* has a rich background in the history of biblical interpretation as a term used in the ancient Greek-speaking world for the detailed, systematic exposition of a scriptural work. It is hoped that the series, like its name, will carry forward this old and venerable tradition. A second, entirely practical reason for selecting the name lay in the desire to avoid a long descriptive title and its inevitable acronym, or worse, an unpronounceable abbreviation.

The series is designed to be a critical and historical commentary to the Bible without arbitrary limits in size or scope. It will utilize the full range of philological and historical tools including textual criticism (often ignored in modern commentaries), the methods of the history of tradition (including genre and prosodic analysis), and the history of religion.

Hermeneia is designed for the serious student of the Bible. It will make full use of ancient Semitic and classical languages; at the same time, English translations of all comparative materials—Greek, Latin, Canaanite, or Akkadian—will be supplied alongside the citation of the source in its original language. Insofar as possible, the aim is to provide the student or scholar with full critical discussion of each problem of interpretation and with the primary data upon which the discussion is based.

Hermeneia is designed to be international and interconfessional in the selection of its authors; its editorial boards were also formed with this end in view. Occasionally the series will offer translations of distinguished commentaries which originally appeared in languages other than English. Published volumes of the series will be revised continually, and, eventually, new commentaries will replace older works in order to preserve the currency of the series. Commentaries are also being assigned for important literary works in the categories of apocryphal and pseudepigraphical works of the Old and New Testaments, including some of Essene or Gnostic authorship.

The editors of *Hermeneia* impose no systematic-theological perspective upon the series (directly, or indirectly by its selection of authors). It is expected that authors will struggle to lay bare the ancient meaning of a biblical work or pericope. In this way the text's human relevance should become transparent, as is always the case in competent historical discourse. However, the series eschews for itself homiletical translation of the Bible.

The editors are heavily indebted to Fortress Press for its energy and courage in taking up an expensive, long-term project, the rewards of which will accrue chiefly to the field of biblical scholarship.

We are grateful to Philip Buttolph for a first draft of the translation of this volume. Adela Yarbro of Harvard University and the Volume Editor are responsible for the final version of the text here presented. Professor John Strugnell of Harvard University gave valuable help and advice in the translation of the often difficult Greek texts. Miss Yarbro, untiring in her efforts, also assisted in the editing of the manuscript. We are indebted to Professor Hans Conzelmann, who provided a list of corrections and addenda and permitted us to incorporate the notes from his personal copy of the last German edition of this commentary. Judith Dollenmayer undertook the meticulous task of copyediting with her usual skill and tact. The editors wish to acknowledge that only the help and cooperation of these and many other persons has made it possible to produce this English edition of a book which is and will continue to be a classic of biblical interpretation and, at the same time, an up-to-date commentary on a group of closely related New Testament writings.

The editor responsible for this volume is Helmut Koester of Harvard University.

January 1972

Frank Moore Cross, Jr.
For the Old Testament
Editorial Board

Helmut Koester
For the New Testament
Editorial Board

Martin Dibelius, who died in 1947, left behind almost no preparations for the revision of his commentary on the Pastoral Epistles. The undersigned is solely responsible, therefore, for changes from the preceding, second edition, which had been published in 1931 (a few exceptions involve additions to the bibliographical materials). It is my hope that the unity of the interpretation has been preserved. In view of Dibelius' masterly accomplishment, I have been as careful as possible with his text. Nevertheless, the changes are, of course, numerous, for the revision could not be limited to including the voluminous literature which has appeared in the meantime. Increased attention has been given to historical and theological matters (see especially the Introduction). Yet the character of a "handbook" has been retained consciously. The scope of the work has grown; condensations were possible in only a few places (for example, in the excursus on "The Imagery of the Military Service of the Pious," because the newly revised excursus on Eph 6:10ff is now available for reference). In the most important instances divergences in judgment from the second edition have been indicated.

I would like to thank the editor (Professor Günther Bornkamm) for much valuable help. A fruitful exchange of ideas with him has, here and there, found its way into the text. I was allowed to use the library of the Seminar in Ancient Philology at Heidelberg, and I am indebted to Dr. Walter Bauhuis, Bibliotheksrat in Heidelberg, for his valuable assistance in the often difficult task of procuring the needed literature. Dr. Wolfgang Nauck, Privatdozent in Tübingen, permitted me to use his unpublished dissertation. Dr. Helmut Koester, while Assistant in Heidelberg, undertook the task of proofreading. I am indebted to my colleague here, Hans Wildberger, for the rendering of a difficult text from the Qumran scrolls.

Hans Conzelmann
Pfaffhausen bei Zürich

23 May 1955

1. Sources and General Abbreviations

Abbreviations used in this volume for sources and literature from antiquity are the same as those used in the *Theological Dictionary of the New Testament*, ed. Gerhard Kittel, tr. Geoffrey W. Bromiley, vol. 1 (Grand Rapids, Michigan, and London: Eerdmans, 1964), xvi–xl. Some abbreviations are adapted from that list and can be easily identified.

In addition, the following abbreviations have been used:

ad loc.	*ad locum*, at the place or passage discussed
Ambst.	Ambrosiaster
ARW	*Archiv für Religionswissenschaft*, 1898ff
Asc. Isa.	Ascension of Isaiah
b. Ber.	Babylonian Talmud, tractate Berakoth
b. Yoma	Babylonian Talmud, tractate Yoma
BFTh	Beiträge zur Förderung der christlichen Theologie
BHTh	Beiträge zur historischen Theologie
BWANT	Beiträge zur Wissenschaft vom Alten und Neuen Testament
BZNW	Beihefte zur Zeitschrift für die neutestamentliche Wissenschaft und die Kunde der älteren Kirche
CD	The Cairo Genizah *Damascus Document*
cf.	*confer*, compare with
CII	*Corpus Inscriptionum Iudaicarum*, ed. J. B. Frey (City of the Vatican: Rome's Pontifical Institute of Christian Archaeology, 1936–52)
col.	column(s)
Con. Neot.	*Coniectanea Neotestamentica*
ed.	editor, edited by
[Ed.]	Editor of this volume of Hermeneia
ET	English translation
EThR	*Etudes théologiques et religieuses*, 1926ff
ExpT	*The Expository Times*, 1900ff
FGRH	*Die Fragmente der griechischen Historiker*, ed. Felix Jacoby (Leiden: E. J. Brill, 1957–58)
FRLANT	Forschungen zur Religion und Literatur des Alten und Neuen Testaments
GCS	Die griechischen christlichen Schriftsteller der ersten drei Jahrhunderte (Leipzig and Berlin: Hinrichs and Akademie–Verlag, 1897ff)
Gen. Rabba	The midrash *Genesis Rabba*
GGA	*Göttingische Gelehrte Anzeigen*, 1839ff
HAT	Handbuch zum Alten Testament, ed. O. Eissfeldt
HNT	Handbuch zum Neuen Testament, ed. Hans Lietzmann and Günther Bornkamm
HUCA	*Hebrew Union College Annual*, 1924ff
ICC	International Critical Commentary, ed. S. R. Driver, A. Plummer, C. A. Briggs
idem	the same (person)
Iren.	
Adv. haer.	Irenaeus, *Adversus haereses*
item	also, in addition
JBL	*Journal of Biblical Literature*, 1881ff
KD	*Kerygma und Dogma: Zeitschrift für theologische Forschung und kirchliche Lehre*, 1955ff
KEK	Kritisch–exegetischer Kommentar über das Neue Testament begründet von Heinrich August Wilhelm Meyer
KlT	Kleine Texte für Vorlesungen und Übungen, ed. Hans Lietzmann
Loeb	The Loeb Classical Library, founded by James Loeb, ed. E. H. Warmington (Cambridge, Mass., and London: Harvard University Press and Heinemann, 1912ff)
MPG	Patrologia, Series Graeca, ed. J. P. Migne
n.	note
NF	Neutestamentliche Forschungen
NGG	Nachrichten von der königlichen Gesellschaft der Wissenschaften zu Göttingen, Philologisch–historische Klasse
N.S.	New Series
NTAbh	Neutestamentliche Abhandlungen
NTD	Das Neue Testament Deutsch, ed. Paul Althaus and Gerhard Friedrich
NTS	*New Testament Studies*, 1954ff
p. (pp.)	page(s)
P. Grenf.	I, *An Alexandrian Erotic Fragment and Other Greek Papyri, chiefly Ptolemaic*, ed. B. P. Grenfell (Oxford: Clarendon Press, 1896). II, *New Classical Fragments*, ed. B. P. Grenfell and A. S. Hunt (Oxford: Clarendon Press, 1897)

P. Reinach	*Papyrus grecs et démotiques recueillis en Egypte*, ed. Théodore Reinach (Paris: Leroux, 1905–40)	TS	Texts and Studies; Contributions to Biblical and Patristic Literature
P. Strassb.	*Der Griechische Papyrus der Kaiserlichen Universitäts- und Landesbibliothek zu Strassburg*, ed. Friedrich Preisigke, vol. 1, 2 (Leipzig: Hinrichs, 1906–20)	TU	Texte und Untersuchungen zur Geschichte der altchristlichen Literatur
		TWNT	*Theologisches Wörterbuch zum Neuen Testament*, ed. Gerhard Kittel and Gerhard Friedrich, vol. 1–9 (Stuttgart: Kohlhammer, 1933–71)
Pauly-Wissowa	Real-Encyclopädie der classischen Altertumswissenschaften, ed. A. Pauly, G. Wissowa, etc. (1893ff)	v (vss)	verse(s)
Q	Qumran documents:	*v.l.*	*varia lectio*, variant reading
		vol.	volume(s)
1 Q27	The Book of Mysteries	WMANT	Wissenschaftliche Monographien zum Alten und Neuen Testament
1 QpHab	Pesher Habakkuk, the Commentary on Habakkuk	*ZDMG*	*Zeitschrift der deutschen morgenländischen Gesellschaft*, 1847ff
1 QS	Serek hay-yaḥad, the Rule of the Community	*ZKG*	*Zeitschrift für Kirchengeschichte*, 1877ff
RAC	*Reallexikon für Antike und Christentum*, ed. Theodor Klauser, vol. 1–7 (Stuttgart: Hiersemann, 1950)	*ZNW*	*Zeitschrift für die neutestamentliche Wissenschaft und die Kunde der älteren Kirche*, 1900ff
RB	*Revue Biblique* 1892ff, N.S. 1904ff	*ZSTh*	*Zeitschrift für systematische Theologie*, 1923ff
RechSR	*Recherches de science religieuse*, 1910ff		
rev.	revised by	*ZThK*	*Zeitschrift für Theologie und Kirche*, 1891–1917; N.S. 1920ff
RevSR	*Revue des sciences religieuses*, 1921ff		
RHPR	*Revue d'histoire et de philosophie religieuses*, 1921ff	*ZWTh*	*Zeitschrift für wissenschaftliche Theologie*, 1858–1914
RSPT	*Revue des sciences philosophiques et théologiques*, 1907ff		
RSV	Revised Standard Version of the Bible		
SAH	Sitzungsberichte der Heidelberger Akademie der Wissenschaften, Philologisch-historische Klasse		
SAQ	Sammlung ausgewählter kirchen- und dogmengeschichtlicher Quellenschriften		
SBT	Studies in Biblical Theology		
SJT	*Scottish Journal of Theology*, 1948ff		
ST	*Studia Theologica*		
s.v.	*sub verbo* or *sub voce*, under the word (entry)		
SVF	*Stoicorum veterum fragmenta*, ed. H. F. A. von Arnim (Leipzig: Teubner, 1903–24)		
TDNT	*Theological Dictionary of the New Testament*, ed. Gerhard Kittel and Gerhard Friedrich, tr. and ed. Geoffrey Bromiley, vols. 1–6 (Grand Rapids, Mich.: Eerdmans, 1964–68)		
ThLZ	*Theologische Literaturzeitung*, 1876ff		
ThR	*Theologische Rundschau*, 1898–1917; N.S. 1929ff		
ThStKr	*Theologische Studien und Kritiken*, 1828–1942		
ThZ	*Theologische Zeitschrift der theologischen Fakultät der Universität Basel*, 1945ff		
tr.	translator, translated by, translation		
[Trans.]	Translator of this volume of Hermeneia		
[trans. by Ed.]	Translated by editor of this volume of Hermeneia		

2. Short Titles of Frequently Cited Literature

Abramowski, "Der Christus der Salomooden"
R. Abramowski, "Der Christus der Salomooden,"
ZNW 35 (1936): 44–69.

Almqvist, *Plutarch und das NT*
Helge Almqvist, *Plutarch und das Neue Testament;
ein Beitrag zum Corpus Hellenisticum Novi Testamenti*
(Uppsala: Appelberg, 1946).

Ante–Nicene Christian Library
Alexander Roberts and James Donaldson, ed.,
Ante–Nicene Christian Library 1–24 (Edinburgh:
T. & T. Clark, 1867–72).

Asting, *Verkündigung*
Ragnar Asting, *Die Verkündigung des Wortes Gottes
im Urchristentum* (Stuttgart: Kohlhammer, 1939).

Baldensperger, " 'Il a rendu témoignage' "
G. Baldensperger, " 'Il a rendu témoignage devant Ponce Pilate,' " *RHPR* 2 (1922): 1–25.

Bartsch, *Anfänge*
Hans Werner Bartsch, *Die Anfänge urchristlicher
Rechtsbildungen: Studien zu den Pastoralbriefen* (Ham-
burg: Herbert Reich, 1965).

Bauer
Walter Bauer, *A Greek–English Lexicon*, tr. William
F. Arndt and F. Wilbur Gingrich (Chicago: Uni-
versity of Chicago Press, 1957, 1965).

Bauer, *Johannesevangelium*
Walter Bauer, *Das Johannesevangelium erklärt*, HNT
6 (Tübingen: J. C. B. Mohr [Paul Siebeck],
³1933).

Bauer, *Orthodoxy and Heresy*
Walter Bauer, *Orthodoxy and Heresy in Earliest
Christianity*, tr. by the Philadelphia Seminar on
Christian Origins (Philadelphia, Pa.: Fortress
Press, 1971).

Bauer, *Der Wortgottesdienst*
Walter Bauer, *Der Wortgottesdienst der ältesten
Christen* (Tübingen: J. C. B. Mohr [Paul Siebeck],
1930).

Baur, *Die sogenannten Pastoralbriefe*
Ferdinand Christian Baur, *Die sogenannten Pastoral-
briefe des Apostels Paulus aufs neue kritisch untersucht*
(Stuttgart and Tübingen: Cotta, 1835).

Behm, *Handauflegung*
Johannes Behm, *Die Handauflegung im Urchristentum*
(Leipzig: A. Deichert, 1911).

Bell, *Jews and Christians in Egypt*
Harold Idris Bell ed., *Jews and Christians in Egypt:
the Jewish Troubles in Alexandria and the Athanasian
Controversy. Illustrated by Texts from Greek Papyri in
the British Museum* (London: Quaritch, 1924).

Belser
J. E. Belser, *Die Briefe des Apostel Paulus an Timo-
theus und Titus übersetzt und erklärt* (Freiburg i.B.:
Herder, 1907).

Billerbeck
Hermann Strack and Paul Billerbeck, *Kommentar
zum Neuen Testament aus Talmud und Midrasch* 1–4
(München: Beck, 1954–61).

Blass–Debrunner
F. Blass and A. Debrunner, *A Greek Grammar of the
New Testament and other Early Christian Literature*,
tr. and rev. Robert W. Funk (Chicago: University
of Chicago Press, 1961) [This work is cited by
section numbers].

Bornkamm, *Early Christian Experience*
Günther Bornkamm, *Early Christian Experience*, tr.
Paul Hammer (London: SCM Press, 1969).

Bornkamm, "Häresie des Kolosserbriefes"
Günther Bornkamm, "Die Häresie des Kolosserbriefes" in *Das Ende des Gesetzes: Paulusstudien*,
Gesammelte Aufsätze 1, Beiträge zur evangelischen Theologie 16 (München: Chr. Kaiser,
⁶1966), 139–56.

Bornkamm, "Homologia"
Günther Bornkamm, "Homologia" in *Geschichte
und Glaube* 1, Gesammelte Aufsätze 3, Beiträge zur
evangelischen Theologie 48 (München: Chr.
Kaiser, 1968), 140–56.

Bousset, *Die Religion des Judentums*
Wilhelm Bousset, *Die Religion des Judentums im
späthellenistischen Zeitalter*, ed. Hugo Gressmann
(Tübingen: J. C. B. Mohr [Paul Siebeck], ⁴1966).

Bover, " 'Fidelis Sermo' "
José M. Bover, " 'Fidelis Sermo,' " *Biblica* 19
(1938): 74–9.

Bruston, "De la date"
Ch. Bruston, "De la date de la première Épître de
Paul à Timothée," *EThR* 5 (1930): 272–76.

Bultmann, review of Cullmann, *Les premières confessions de foi chrétiennes*
Rudolf Bultmann, review of Oscar Cullmann,
Les premières confessions de foi chrétiennes, *ThLZ* 74
(1949): 40–2.

Bultmann, *Theology*
Rudolf Bultmann, *Theology of the New Testament*,
vol. 1, tr. Kendrick Grobel (New York: Charles
Scribner's Sons, 1951); vol. 2, tr. Kendrick Grobel
(New York: Charles Scribner's Sons, 1955).

Bultmann, "Untersuchungen zum Johannesevangelium"
Rudolf Bultmann, "Untersuchungen zum Johannesevangelium" in *Exegetica: Aufsätze zur Erforschung des Neuen Testaments* (Tübingen: J. C. B.
Mohr [Paul Siebeck], 1967), 124–97.

von Campenhausen, "Asceticism"
Hans von Campenhausen, "Early Christian Asceticism," in *Tradition and Life in the Church: Essays
and Lectures in Church History*, tr. A. V. Littledale
(Philadelphia, Pa.: Fortress Press, 1968), 99–122.

von Campenhausen, *Ecclesiastical Authority*
Hans von Campenhausen, *Ecclesiastical Authority
and Spiritual Power*, tr. J. A. Baker (Stanford,
Calif.: Stanford University Press, 1969).

von Campenhausen, "Polykarp"
Hans von Campenhausen, "Polykarp von Smyrna
und die Pastoralbriefe," in *Aus der Frühzeit des*

Christentums (Tübingen: J. C. B. Mohr [Paul Siebeck], 1963), 197–252.

Charles, *APOT*
R. H. Charles, ed., *The Apocrypha and Pseudepigrapha of the Old Testament in English, with Introductions and Critical and Explanatory Notes to the Several Books*, vol. 1 and 2 (Oxford: Clarendon Press, 1913; reprint 1965).

Conzelmann, *Luke*
Hans Conzelmann, *The Theology of St. Luke*, tr. Geoffrey Buswell (London: Faber & Faber, 1960).

Cramer, *Catene*
John A. Cramer, *Catene in Sancti Pauli: Epistolas ad Timotheum, Titum, Philemona et ad Hebraeos*, Catenae Graecorum Patrum in Novum Testamentum 7 (Oxford: Clarendon Press, 1843).

Cullmann, *Confessions*
Oscar Cullmann, *The Earliest Christian Confessions*, tr. J. K. S. Reid (London: Lutterworth Press, 1949).

Dahl, "Formgeschichtliche Beobachtungen"
Nils Alstrup Dahl, "Formgeschichtliche Beobachtungen zur Christusverkündigung," in *NT Studien für Bultmann*, pp. 3–9.

Deissmann, *Bible Studies*
Adolf Deissmann, *Bible Studies*, tr. A. Grieve (Edinburgh: T.&T. Clark, 1901).

Deissmann, *LAE*
Adolf Deissmann, *Light from the Ancient East, the New Testament Illustrated by Recently Discovered Texts of the Graeco–Roman World*, tr. Lionel R. M. Strachan (New York: George H. Doran, 1927).

Delling, *Stellung des Paulus zu Frau und Ehe*
Gerhard Delling, *Die Stellung des Paulus zu Frau und Ehe* (Stuttgart: Kohlhammer, 1931).

Dey, ΠΑΛΙΓΓΕΝΕΣΙΑ
Joseph Dey, ΠΑΛΙΓΓΕΝΕΣΙΑ: *Ein Beitrag zur Klärung der religionsgeschichtlichen Bedeutung von Tit 3, 5*, NTAbh 17, 5 (Münster: Aschendorff, 1937).

Dibelius, *Geisterwelt*
Martin Dibelius, *Die Geisterwelt im Glauben des Paulus* (Göttingen: Vandenhoeck & Ruprecht, 1909).

Dibelius, *Der Hirt des Hermas*
Martin Dibelius, *Der Hirt des Hermas*, HNT, Ergängungsband 4 (Tübingen: J. C. B. Mohr [Paul Siebeck], 1923).

Dibelius–Greeven, *Kolosser, Epheser, Philemon*
Martin Dibelius and Heinrich Greeven, *An die Kolosser, Epheser, An Philemon*, HNT 12 (Tübingen: J. C. B. Mohr [Paul Siebeck], ³1953).

Dibelius, "Rom und die Christen"
Martin Dibelius, "Rom und die Christen im ersten Jahrhundert," *Botschaft und Geschichte* 2 (Tübingen: J. C. B. Mohr [Paul Siebeck], 1956), 177–228.

Dibelius, *Thessalonicher, Philipper*
Martin Dibelius, *An die Thessalonicher I, II, An die Philipper*, HNT 11 (Tübingen: J. C. B. Mohr

[Paul Siebeck], ³1937).

von Dobschütz, *Die urchristlichen Gemeinden*
Ernst von Dobschütz, *Die urchristlichen Gemeinden* (Leipzig: Hinrichs, 1902).

Dölger, *Ichthys*
Franz Dölger, *Ichthys* (Freiburg i.B.: Herder, 1910).

Dupont–Sommer, *Essene Writings*
A. Dupont–Sommer, *The Essene Writings from Qumran*, tr. G. Vermes (Cleveland, Ohio and New York: The World Publishing Co., 1962).

Easton
Burton Scott Easton, *The Pastoral Epistles* (London: SCM Press, 1948).

Elliger, *Habakuk–Kommentar*
Karl Elliger, *Studien zum Habakuk–Kommentar vom Toten Meer*, BHTh 15 (Tübingen: J. C. B. Mohr [Paul Siebeck], 1953).

Erbes, "Zeit und Ziel"
K. Erbes, "Zeit und Ziel der Grüsse Röm. 16, 3–15 und der Mitteilungen 2 Tim. 4, 9–21," *ZNW* 10 (1909): 207ff.

Falconer
Robert Falconer, *The Pastoral Epistles* (Oxford: Clarendon Press, 1937).

Gerhard, *Phoinix*
Gustav Gerhard, *Phoinix von Kolophon* (Leipzig and Berlin: Teubner, 1909).

Gerlach, *Griechische Ehreninschriften*
Günther Gerlach, *Griechische Ehreninschriften* (Halle: Niemeyer, 1908).

Gressmann, *Altorientalische Texte*
Hugo Gressmann, Arthur Ungnad and Hermann Ranke, *Altorientalische Texte und Bilder zum Alten Testamente* (Tübingen: J. C. B. Mohr [Paul Siebeck], 1909).

Haerens, "ΣΩΤΗΡ et ΣΩΤΗΡΙΑ"
H. Haerens, "ΣΩΤΗΡ et ΣΩΤΗΡΙΑ," *Studia Hellenistica* 5 (1948): 57–68.

von Harnack, *Chronologie*
Adolf von Harnack, *Geschichte der altchristlichen Literatur* vol. 2: *Die Chronologie* (Leipzig: Hinrichs, ²1958).

von Harnack, *Constitution*
Adolf von Harnack, *The Constitution and Law of the Church in the First Two Centuries*, tr. F. L. Pogson, ed. H. D. A. Major (New York: G. P. Putnam's Sons, 1910).

von Harnack, *Expansion of Christianity*
Adolf von Harnack, *The Expansion of Christianity in the First Three Centuries*, tr. and ed. James Moffatt (New York: G. P. Putnam's Sons, 1904); republished as *The Mission and Expansion of Christianity in the First Three Centuries* (New York: Harper's, 1962).

von Harnack, *Marcion*
Adolf von Harnack, *Marcion: das Evangelium vom fremden Gott, eine Monographie zur Geschichte der Grundlegung der katholischen Kirche* (Leipzig: J. C.

Hinrichs, ²1924; reprinted 1960).

Harris–Mingana, *Odes and Psalms of Solomon*
(James) Rendel Harris and Alphonse Mingana,
ed., *The Odes and Psalms of Solomon* vol. 2 (Manchester: The University Press, 1920).

Harrison, *The Problem*
P. N. Harrison, *The Problem of the Pastoral Epistles*
(London: Oxford University Press, 1921).

Hatch, *Organization*
Edwin Hatch, *The Organization of the Early Chris-
tian Churches* (London and New York: Longmans,
Green & Co., ⁴1892).

Hennecke–Schneemelcher 1, 2
Edgar Hennecke, *New Testament Apocrypha*, ed.
Wilhelm Schneemelcher, tr. and ed. R. McL.
Wilson (Philadelphia, Pa.: Westminster Press,
1963–1965).

Holtzmann, *Die Pastoralbriefe*
Heinrich Julius Holtzmann, *Die Pastoralbriefe
kritisch und exegetisch bearbeitet* (Leipzig: Wilhelm
Engelmann, 1880).

Holzmeister, "Si quis episcopatum desiderat"
U. Holzmeister, "Si quis episcopatum desiderat,
bonum opus desiderat," *Biblica* 12 (1931): 41–69.

Jentsch, *Urchristliches Erziehungsdenken*
Werner Jentsch, *Urchristliches Erziehungsdenken*
(Gütersloh: Bertelsmann, 1951).

Jeremias
Joachim Jeremias and Hermann Strathmann,
*Die Briefe an Timotheus und Titus. Der Brief an die
Hebräer*, NTD 9 (Göttingen: Vandenhoeck &
Ruprecht, ⁸1963).

Jeremias, *Infant Baptism*
Joachim Jeremias, *Infant Baptism in the First Four
Centuries*, tr. David Cairns (Philadelphia, Pa.:
Westminster Press, 1961).

Jeremias, *Jerusalem in the Time of Jesus*
Joachim Jeremias, *Jerusalem in the Time of Jesus;
an Investigation into Economic and Social Conditions
during the New Testament Period*, tr. F. H. and C. H.
Cave (Philadelphia, Pa.: Fortress Press, 1969).

Kaerst, *Geschichte des Hellenismus*
Julius Kaerst, *Geschichte des Hellenismus* (Leipzig:
Teubner, ² 1926).

Käsemann, "Formular"
Ernst Käsemann, "Das Formular einer neutestamentlichen Ordinationsparänese," *NT Studien
für Bultmann*, pp. 261–68.

Käsemann, *Das wandernde Gottesvolk*
Ernst Käsemann, *Das wandernde Gottesvolk*
FRLANT 55 (Göttingen: Vandenhoeck &
Ruprecht, ⁴1961).

Klostermann, *Apocrypha 1*
Erich Klostermann, *Apocrypha 1. Reste des Petrus-
evangeliums, der Petrusapokalypse und des Kerygma
Petri*, KlT 3 (Berlin: De Gruyter, 1933).

Knopf, *Lehre der Zwölf Apostel, Clemensbriefe*
Rudolf Knopf, *Die Lehre der Zwölf Apostel, Die
zwei Clemensbriefe*, HNT, Ergänzungsband 1

(Tübingen: J. C. B. Mohr [Paul Siebeck], 1920).

Knopf, *Das nachapostolische Zeitalter*
Rudolf Knopf, *Das nachapostolische Zeitalter:
Geschichte der christlichen Gemeinden vom Beginn der
Flavierdynastie bis zum Ende Hadrians* (Tübingen:
J. C. B. Mohr [Paul Siebeck], 1905).

Kühl, *Gemeindeordnung*
E. Kühl, *Die Gemeindeordnung in den Pastoralbriefen*
(Berlin: Besser'sche Buchhandlung, 1885).

Kuhn, "Die in Palästina gefundenen hebräischen
Texte"
Karl–Georg Kuhn, "Die in Palästina gefundenen
hebräischen Texte und das Neue Testament,"
ZThK 47 (1950): 192–211.

Lietzmann–Kümmel, *Korinther*
Hans Lietzmann and Werner Georg Kümmel,
An die Korinther, I, II, HNT 9 (Tübingen: J. C. B.
Mohr [Paul Siebeck], ⁵1969).

Lietzmann, *Römer*
Hans Lietzmann, *An die Römer*, HNT 8 (Tübingen: J. C. B. Mohr [Paul Siebeck], ⁴1933).

Lietzmann, "Symbolstudien" (1)
Hans Lietzmann, "Symbolstudien," *ZNW* 21
(1922): 1–34.

Lietzmann, "Symbolstudien" (2)
Hans Lietzmann, "Symbolstudien (Fortsetzung)," *ZNW* 22 (1923): 257–79.

Lietzmann, "Verfassungsgeschichte"
Hans Lietzmann, "Zur altchristlichen Verfassungsgeschichte," *ZWTh* 55 (1914): 97–153.

Lietzmann, *Der Weltheiland*
Hans Lietzmann, *Der Weltheiland* (Bonn: Marcus
& Weber, 1909).

Lipsius–Bonnet,
Richardus Adelbertus Lipsius and Maximilianus
Bonnet, *Acta Apostolorum Apocrypha*, 3 vol. (Darm-
stadt: Wissenschaftliche Buchgesellschaft, 1959).

Lock
Walter Lock, *A Critical and Exegetical Commentary
on the Pastoral Epistles*, ICC (Edinburgh and New
York: T. & T. Clark, 1924).

Lohmeyer, *Christuskult und Kaiserkult*
Ernst Lohmeyer, *Christuskult und Kaiserkult*
(Tübingen: J. C. B. Mohr [Paul Siebeck], 1919).

Lohse, *Colossians and Philemon*
Eduard Lohse, *Colossians and Philemon*, Hermeneia
(Philadelphia, Pa.: Fortress Press, 1971).

Lührmann, *Das Offenbarungsverständnis*
Dieter Lührmann, *Das Offenbarungsverständnis bei
Paulus und in den paulinischen Gemeinden*, WMANT
16 (Neukirchen–Vluyn: Neukirchen, 1965).

Lütgert, *Irrlehrer*
Wilhelm Lütgert, *Die Irrlehrer der Pastoralbriefe*,
BFTh 13, 3 (Gütersloh: Bertelsmann, 1909).

Magie, *De iuris*
David Magie, *De Romanorum iuris publici sacrique
vocabulis sollemnibus in Graecum sermonem conversis*
(Leipzig: Teubner, 1905).

Meyer, *Ursprung und Anfänge des Christentums*

Eduard Meyer, *Ursprung und Anfänge des Christentums, 3: Apostelgeschichte* (Stuttgart: Cotta, 1923).

Michaelis, *Echtheitsfrage*
Wilhelm Michaelis, *Pastoralbriefe und Gefangenschaftsbriefe. Zur Echtheitsfrage der Pastoralbriefe,* NF 1, 6 (Gütersloh: Bertelsmann, 1930).

Michaelis, *Einleitung*
Wilhelm Michaelis, *Einleitung in das Neue Testament* (Bern: Berchthold Haller, ³1961).

Michel, "Grundfragen"
Otto Michel, "Grundfragen der Pastoralbriefe" in *Auf dem Grunde der Apostel und Propheten, Festgabe für Theophil Wurm,* ed. Max Loeser (Stuttgart: Quell–Verlag, 1948), 83–99.

Moulton–Howard
James Hope Moulton and Wilbert Francis Howard, *A Grammar of New Testament Greek 2: Accidence and Word–Formation with an Appendix on Semitisms in the New Testament* (Edinburgh: T. & T. Clark, 1929).

Moulton, *Prolegomena*
James Hope Moulton, *A Grammar of New Testament Greek 1: Prolegomena* (Edinburgh: T. & T. Clark, ³1919, London: The Epworth Press, ⁴1952).

Munck, "Discours d'adieu"
Johannes Munck, "Discours d'adieu dans le Nouveau Testament et dans la littérature biblique," in *Aux sources de la tradition chrétienne* (Neuchatel and Paris: Delachaux & Niestle, S.A., 1950).

Nägeli, *Wortschatz*
Theodor Nägeli, *Der Wortschatz des Apostel Paulus* (Göttingen: Vandenhoeck & Ruprecht, 1905).

Nauck, *Die Herkunft*
Wolfgang Nauck, *Die Herkunft des Verfassers der Pastoralbriefe,* Unpub. Diss. (Göttingen: 1950).

Norden, *Agnostos Theos*
Eduard Norden, *Agnostos Theos: Untersuchungen zur Formengeschichte religiöser Rede* (Leipzig: Teubner, 1913 = Darmstadt: ⁴1956).

Norden, *Geburt des Kindes*
Eduard Norden, *Die Geburt des Kindes: Geschichte einer religiösen Idee* (Leipzig: Teubner, 1924; reprint 1958).

NT Studien für Bultmann
Neutestamentliche Studien für Rudolf Bultmann, ed. Walther Eltester, BZNW 21 (Berlin: Töpelmann, 1954).

Pohlenz, "Paulus und die Stoa"
Max Pohlenz, "Paulus und die Stoa," *ZNW* 42 (1949): 66–104.

Pohlenz, *Die Stoa*
Max Pohlenz, *Die Stoa,* 2 vol. (Göttingen: Vandenhoeck & Ruprecht, 1948f).

Poland, *Griechisches Vereinswesen*
Franz Poland, *Geschichte des griechischen Vereinswesens* (Leipzig: Teubner, 1909).

Preisigke
Friedrich Preisigke, *Wörterbuch der griechischen Papyrusurkunden mit Einschluss der griechischen usw. . . . Ägypten,* vollendet und herausgegeben von Emil Kiessling (Berlin: 1914–27).

Prümm, "Herrscherkult"
Karl Prümm, "Der Herrscherkult im Neuen Testament," *Biblica* 9 (1928): 1ff.

Preis. *Zaub.*
Karl Preisendanz, *Papyri Graecae Magicae: Die griechischen Zauberpapyri,* 1, 2 (Leipzig and Berlin: Teubner, 1931).

Radermacher, *Grammatik*
Ludwig Radermacher, *Neutestamentliche Grammatik, Das Griechische des Neuen Testaments im Zusammenhang mit der Volkssprache,* HNT 1, 1 (Tübingen: J. C. B. Mohr [Paul Siebeck], ²1925).

Reitzenstein, *Mysterienreligionen*
Richard Reitzenstein, *Die hellenistischen Mysterienreligionen* (Leipzig: Teubner, ³1927; reprinted 1956).

Rohde, *Psyche*
Erwin Rohde, *Psyche; the Cult of Souls and Belief in Immortality among the Greeks* (New York: Harcourt, Brace & Co., 1925).

Roller, *Das Formular*
Otto Roller, *Das Formular der paulinischen Briefe,* BWANT 4, 6 (Stuttgart: Kohlhammer, 1933).

Schermann, *Griechische Zauberpapyri*
Theodor Schermann, *Griechische Zauberpapyri und das Gemeinde– und Dankgebet im ersten Klemensbrief* (Leipzig: Hinrichs, 1909).

Schlatter
Adolf Schlatter, *Die Kirche der Griechen im Urteil des Paulus: Eine Auslegung seiner Briefe an Timotheus und Titus* (Stuttgart: Calwer Verlag, ²1958).

Schlatter, *Theologie des Judentums*
Adolf Schlatter, *Die Theologie des Judentums nach dem Bericht des Josephus* (Gütersloh: Bertelsmann, 1932).

Schleiermacher, *Sendschreiben*
Friedrich Schleiermacher, *Sendschreiben an J. C. Gaß: Über den sogenannten ersten Brief des Paulos an den Timotheos* (Berlin: Realschulbuchhandlung, 1807); reprinted in *idem, Sämtliche Werke,* I, 1, (1836), pp. 221ff.

Schürer, *Geschichte des jüdischen Volkes*
Emil Schürer, *Geschichte des jüdischen Volkes im Zeitalter Jesu Christi* 1, 2, 3 (Leipzig: Hinrichs, ³,⁴1901, 1907, 1909).

Schürer, *A History of the Jewish People in the Time of Jesus Christ,* vol. 1¹⁻² tr. John MacPherson, vol. 2¹⁻³ tr. Sophia Taylor and Peter Christie (Edinburgh: T. & T. Clark, 1885–90).

Schweizer, *Church Order*
Eduard Schweizer, *Church Order in the New Testament* (Naperville, Ill.: Alec R. Allenson, 1961).

Schweizer, *Erniedrigung und Erhöhung*
Eduard Schweizer, *Erniedrigung und Erhöhung bei Jesus und seinen Nachfolgern* (Zürich: Zwingli–Verlag, 1955).

Schweizer, *Lordship and Discipleship*
Eduard Schweizer, *Lordship and Discipleship* (Naperville, Ill.: Alec R. Allenson, 1960).

Scott
Ernest Findlay Scott, *The Pastoral Epistles*, The Moffatt NT Commentary (London: Hodder & Stoughton, 1936).

Seeberg, *Katechismus*
Alfred Seeberg, *Der Katechismus der Urchristenheit* (Leipzig: A. Deichert, ²1913; reprint 1966).

von Soden
H(ermann) von Soden, *Die Briefe an die Kolosser, Epheser, Philemon, Die Pastoralbriefe, etc.* in Handcommentar zum Neuen Testament 3 (Freiburg i.B. and Leipzig: J. C. B. Mohr [Paul Siebeck], ²1893).

Spicq, *Agape*
Ceslaus Spicq, *Agape in the New Testament*, tr. Marie Aquinas McNamara and Mary Honoria Richter, 1–3 (St. Louis, Mo.: Herder, 1963–66).

Spicq
Ceslaus Spicq, *Saint Paul: Les Épîtres Pastorales*, Études Bibliques (Paris: Gabalda, ⁴1969).

Staerk, *Soter*
Willy Staerk, *Soter 1* (Gütersloh: Bertelsmann, 1933).

Strack, *Introduction*
Hermann Strack, *Introduction to the Talmud and Midrash*, authorized tr. (Philadelphia, Pa.: Jewish Publication Society of America, 1931).

Strack, "Müllerinnung"
Max L. Strack, "Die Müllerinnung in Alexandrien," *ZNW* 4 (1903): 213–34.

Thieme, *Inschriften von Magnesia*
Gottfried Thieme, *Die Inschriften von Magnesia am Mäander und das Neue Testament* (Göttingen: Vandenhoeck & Ruprecht, 1906).

Vielhauer, *Oikodome*
Philipp Vielhauer, *Oikodome; das Bild vom Bau in der christlichen Literatur vom Neuen Testament bis Clemens Alexandrinus* (Karlsruhe–Durlach: G. Tron, 1940).

Vögtle, *Tugend– und Lasterkataloge*
Anton Vögtle, *Die Tugend– und Lasterkataloge im Neuen Testament*, NTAbh 16, 4/5 (Münster i.W.: Aschendorff, 1936).

Weber, *Hadrianus*
Wilhelm Weber, *Untersuchungen zur Geschichte des Kaisers Hadrians* (Leipzig: Teubner, 1907).

Weidinger, *Die Haustafeln*
Karl Weidinger, *Die Haustafeln: Ein Stück urchristlicher Paränese*, Untersuchungen zum Neuen Testament 14 (Leipzig: Hinrichs, 1928).

B. Weiss
Bernhard Weiss, *Die Briefe Pauli an Timotheus und Titus*, KEK 11 (Göttingen: Vandenhoeck & Ruprecht, ⁷1902).

Wendland, *Hellenistische Kultur*
Paul Wendland, *Die hellenistisch–römische Kultur in* ihren Beziehungen zu Judentum und Christentum, Die urchristlichen Literaturformen, HNT I, 2, 3 (Tübingen: J. C. B. Mohr [Paul Siebeck], ²,³1912).

Wendland, "Philo und die kynisch–stoische Diatribe"
Paul Wendland, "Philo und die kynisch–stoische Diatribe," in Paul Wendland and Otto Kern, *Beiträge zur Geschichte der griechischen Philosophie und Religion* (Berlin: Reimer, 1895), 1–75.

Wettstein, *Novum Testamentum Graecum*
Joannes Jacobus Wetstenius, *Novum Testamentum Graecum etc.* 1–2 (Amsterdam: Ex Officina Dommeriana, 1751, 1752).

Wilhelm, *Beiträge*
Adolf Wilhelm, *Beiträge zur griechischen Inschriftenkunde* (Wien: Hölder, 1909).

Windisch, *Hebräerbrief*
Hans Windisch, *Der Hebräerbrief*, HNT 14 (Tübingen: J. C. B. Mohr [Paul Siebeck], ²1931).

Windisch–Preisker, *Katholische Briefe*
Hans Windisch and Herbert Preisker, *Die katholischen Briefe*, HNT 15 (Tübingen: J. C. B. Mohr [Paul Siebeck], ³1951).

Windisch, "Zur Christologie"
Hans Windisch, "Zur Christologie der Pastoralbriefe," *ZNW* 34 (1935): 213–38.

Winer-Schmiedel
G. B. Winer, *Grammatik des neutestamentlichen Sprachidioms*, 1867; rev. P. Schmiedel, 1894ff.

Wohlenberg
Gustav Wohlenberg, *Die Pastoralbriefe etc.*, Zahn's Kommentar zum Neuen Testament 13 (Leipzig: Deichert, ⁴1923).

Zahn, *Apostelgeschichte*
Theodor Zahn, *Die Apostelgeschichte des Lukas*, Kommentar zum Neuen Testament 5; 1, 2 (Leipzig and Erlangen: Deichert, 1922, 1927).

Zahn, *Introduction*
Theodor Zahn, *Introduction to the New Testament*, tr. and ed. Melanchthon Williams Jacobus and Charles Snow Thayer (New York: Charles Scribner's Sons, ³1917).

Ziebarth, *Das griechische Vereinswesen*
Erich Ziebarth, *Das griechische Vereinswesen* (Leipzig: Teubner, 1896).

Zscharnack, *Der Dienst der Frau*
Leopold Zscharnack, *Der Dienst der Frau im Neuen Testament* (Göttingen: Vandenhoeck & Ruprecht, 1902).

The English translation of the Greek text of the Pastoral Epistles printed in this volume was made by the editor on the basis of the Greek text. It reflects the author's exegetical decisions throughout. The German translation of the author was consulted in each instance.

Translators and editor are responsible for all translations of other Biblical texts, but they have followed the *Revised Standard Version* wherever possible.

Translations of ancient Greek and Latin texts are taken from *Loeb Classical Library* in all instances in which no particular source for the translation is identified. In all other cases, the source of the translation is given in brackets [ ]; or it is noted that the translator or the editor has rendered the text into English: [Trans.] or [trans. by Ed.].

Whenever available, recent scholarly works are cited in their published English versions. Quotations from literature not available in English translation have been rendered by the translators.

With respect to all scholarly publications which are available in English language, we have not preserved the author's references to the original publications in other languages, except in the Bibliography. Though it seemed desirable to maintain such references, it would have overburdened the footnotes considerably.

The Bibliography has been supplemented by a few additional entries which have appeared since 1966.

The front endpaper of this volume shows a stretching frame used for the restoration of ancient papyri. It is reproduced with the permission of the publisher from H. J. M. Milne and T. C. Skeat, *Scribes and Correctors of the Codex Sinaiticus* (London, The British Museum, 1938). The second endpaper is Plate LXXVI (2 Timothy 2:19–3:5) from W. H. P. Hatch, *The Greek Manuscripts of the New Testament at Mount Sinai* (Paris, Librairie Orientaliste Paul Geuthner, 1932). The plate reproduced on p. v is a fragment from Titus (3:8–9, 14–15); it is Plate 6 (5.151–72) found in L. Casson and E. L. Hettich, *The Literary Papyri*, Excavations at Nessana, Vol. II (Copyright 1950 by the Princeton University Press), and is reproduced here through the courtesy of the publisher.

1. The Question of Authenticity

Any judgment as to what the Pastorals are and intend to be depends in great measure upon the question of authorship. The person who considers them to be genuine Pauline epistles must understand them as portions of Paul's correspondence. In that case, 2 Tim best fits our accustomed picture of the Pauline letter because 1) in 2 Tim, especially in the last chapter, the personal element is strongly emphasized, and 2) because the exhortations in the epistle really apply to the addressee and therefore can well be accounted "correspondence." Finally, the letter displays a very loose train of thought, something which is characteristic of parenesis as a whole and thus also of the parenesis of Paul (cf. Rom 12; Col 3 and 4).

1 Tim, on the other hand, affords the most difficulties. For here, personal elements fade into the background, and the letter's primary purpose is to transmit regulations (see 1 Tim 2, 3, and 5) which are not intended for the addressee, but for other people. Timothy's duty could have been merely to pass them on—but that explanation is odd, for in such situations Paul was accustomed to write to the congregations themselves.

Here, as with respect to other questions, Tit holds a median position: the fact that the regulations are addressed to the apostle's disciple seems more justified in this case, since in Crete the foundation for church organization had yet to be laid. Furthermore, the epistle, with its concern for the special circumstances of the local situation (see below on Tit 1:10ff), contains more "correspondence" than 1 Tim.

Whoever regards the Pastoral Epistles as *pseudonymous* will draw his conclusions concerning the literary character of all three writings from those sections in which the features of letter-writing play a less prominent role—sections dealing with instructions and congregational rules—also taking into consideration the way in which kerygmatic and liturgical traditions are employed. From this perspective, 2 Tim poses a special problem, for a motive underlying its composition is not readily apparent, and the prominence of its epistolary character protects it, in the opinion of many, from the charge of pseudonymity. It follows from all of this that one cannot discuss the question of authenticity without investigating the literary character of the letters. In case they are spurious, it is not only the writer's immediate purpose that is characteristic; the couching of the letters as epistles of Paul is itself symptomatic for the development of the concept of tradition, and reflects the basic problem of the second and third generation. How did the kerygma become a "deposit" ($\pi\alpha\rho\alpha\theta\dot{\eta}\kappa\eta$)?

This transformation cannot be explained simply by reference to the fact that the apostle has become an authority, for it is not merely a question of "development" in a straight line. Rather, the transformation results from a considered change of position. The question is how and in what sense the kerygma of the apostles, during the course of transmission, *becomes* doctrinal authority. The self-understanding of this generation becomes objectified in a particular image of the apostle and a specific understanding of doctrine. In this process, two turning points can be observed: one in the transition to the second generation, the other in the transition to the third. At the latter point, the figure of the apostle's disciple plays a role; it is he who guarantees the genuineness of the tradition, but, on the other hand, he stands on the same level as those who received the tradition, inasmuch as he himself is already a recipient. (In the Pastorals the apostle himself never stands on the level of the recipient within a chain of tradition—in contrast to 1 Cor 11:23; 15:3.) In this case the Pastorals would represent one of the first attempts to assess the new ecclesiastical situation, and in this connection it should be noted that the concept of tradition was not yet bound up with a concept of succession. The disciple of the apostle is not yet a link in a rigid chain of succession in which an office is transmitted. The process of contemplation does not go beyond the elaboration of its own position, which is determined by the possession of right doctrine. This distinguishes the Pastorals from Irenaeus, for example, who also points out the mediating role of the second generation (so that he is able to link himself—via Polycarp—with the earliest possible point in the chain); but with him the idea of succession is already constitutive.

The judgment concerning the Pastoral Epistles depends less on a single argument than on the convergence of a whole series of arguments:[1]

a) The testimony of the early Church: it is not very strong. Literary dependence of Ignatius and Polycarp

---

1   See Hans von Campenhausen, "Polykarp von Smyrna und die Pastoralbriefe" in *Aus der Frühzeit des Christentums* (Tübingen: J. C. B. Mohr [Paul Siebeck], 1963), 200; Burton Scott Easton, *The Pastoral Epistles* (London: SCM Press, 1948), p. 15.

cannot be proven.[2] The Pastorals are absent in the canon of Marcion; whether he did not know them or was not willing to include them is debatable.[3] Tatian rejected 1 and 2 Tim but not Tit.[4] The letters are also absent in the Chester Beatty Papyri (P 46).[5] 2 Tim 2:19 appears to be quoted in a fragment from the beginning of the 3rd century.[6]

b) The polemic against heretics. We would be able to arrive at a decision regarding the question of authenticity and also at a fixed date for the Pastorals, if the thesis to which Walter Bauer and Hans von Campenhausen have again called attention were substantiated: namely, the thesis that the Pastorals were written against Marcion (or even that they were compiled by Polycarp). In that case, by the production of the Pastorals, Paul would be snatched away from the heretics once and for all, and made chief witness for the orthodoxy which was being formed. In fact the literary style is related to that of Polycarp's *Epistle to the Philippians*, as is the theological and ecclesiastical attitude. But neither the argument of literary dependence nor that of the author's identity is needed to explain these agreements.[7] It is more probable that they emerge from a common milieu. The specific details of Marcion's teaching cannot be recognized in the heresy which is being attacked. The Old Testament is not in contention; in fact, the opposing side seems to work with it, while the author of the Pastorals is reserved in its use. But while a reference to Marcion cannot be proved, the style of the polemic against heresy provides a clue for evaluating the authenticity of the Pastorals. The tone and manner are very different from the polemical style of the genuine Pauline epistles (cf. the excursus to 1 Tim 4:15). The writer does not argue with his opponents.[8] The "false teaching" is simply contrasted with the "correct teaching"; the fact that the opponents "deny" ($\dot{\alpha}\rho\nu\epsilon\hat{\iota}\sigma\theta\alpha\iota$), i.e. they depart from orthodoxy, is simply stated in a formal manner; the writer's own correct teaching is not presented but taken for granted and quoted in fixed formulations.[9] Hence a picture of the opponents can hardly be reconstructed.[10] The assertion that there is a connection between false teaching and immorality is a characteristic feature of this style of polemic. It is not just a personal mannerism of the author, but rather part of the fixed style of the heresy battle in its nascent stages, the style of what was becoming orthodoxy.[11]

Another typical feature of this style is the presentation of examples. If one contends that a relation exists between teaching and morality, he can see in the background the Jewish view that godlessness (the heathen) produces immorality (cf. Wisd Sol)—a theme which is

2   About Polycarp see the comments below on 1 Tim 6:7, 10.
3   On the question of whether the Pastorals were later accepted by the Marcionites cf. E. C. Blackman, *Marcion and His Influence* (London: S.P.C.K., 1948), 52ff; von Campenhausen, "Polykarp," 204.
4   See Adolf von Harnack, *Marcion: das Evangelium vom fremden Gott* (Leipzig: J. C. Hinrichs, ²1924; reprinted 1960), 150 *f, 237 *f.
5   See F. G. Kenyon, *The Chester Beatty Biblical Papyri* (London: E. Walker, Ltd., Fasc. III, Suppl. 1936), pp. viii ff. But cf. M. J. Lagrange, "Les Papyrus Chester Beatty pour les Épîtres de S. Paul et l'Apocalypse," *RB* 43 (1934): 481–93; P. Benoit, "Le Codex paulinien Chester Beatty," *RB* 46 (1937): 58–82; also Joachim Jeremias and Hermann Strathmann, *Die Briefe an Timotheus und Titus*, NTD 9 (Göttingen: Vandenhoeck & Ruprecht, ⁸1963), p. 4.
6   See Idris Bell and T. C. Skeat, *Fragments of an Unknown Gospel* (London: Trustees of the British Museum, 1935), pp. 48, 44; cf. Wilhelm Michaelis, *Einleitung in das Neue Testament* (Bern: Berchtold Haller, ³1961), 238.
7   Cf. Ernst Käsemann, "Ein neutestamentlicher Überblick," *Verkündigung und Forschung* (1949–50): 215. Polycarp quotes constantly; he appeals to Paul directly as his authority; this makes him unsuitable as a pseudonymous writer. Between them also exist characteristic divergences in style.
8   Cf. his own statements to this effect 1 Tim 6:20; 2 Tim 2:16, 23; Tit 3:9.
9   Cf. the schematic expressions, as in 1 Tim 4:6f; 6:3; 2 Tim 2:14; Tit 3:8, and the contrasts: 1 Tim 6:4; 2 Tim 3:10, 14; and Tit 2:1; etc.
10 In contrast cf. the way in which the Epistle to the Colossians deals with the opponents. See Günther Bornkamm, "Die Häresie des Kolosserbriefes," *ThLZ* 73 (1948): 11ff; reprinted in *Das Ende des Gesetzes* (München: Kaiser, ⁶1966), 139–56.
11 Cf. the treatment in the Epistle of Jude, the Second Epistle of Peter, Acts 20:29ff, and the book of Revelation. On the whole question see Walter Bauer, *Orthodoxy and Heresy in Earliest Christianity*, tr. by the Philadelphia Seminar on Christian Origins (Philadelphia, Pa.: Fortress Press, 1971).

taken up and elaborated theologically in Paul's Letter to the Romans. The Pastorals are satisfied with the bare assertion and apply it to groups within the Church; what is new, in comparison with Paul's situation, is the phenomenon of heresy. The little that can be known definitely about the opponents points not to the great Gnostic systems, but rather to a kind of Judaizing Gnosticism (with speculation and observance of the Law) as is to be found elsewhere (Col and Ign.).

c) Situations. The situations presupposed in the Pastoral Epistles are discussed in the excursus on 1 Tim 1:3; 2 Tim 4:21 and Tit 3:14. It is hard for us to find a place for them within the portion of Paul's life known to us; only for Tit is there at least some possibility of doing so. Advocates of the Pastorals' authenticity can try to place them within the time between a first and an assumed second or during such a second imprisonment, which would have to be inferred primarily from *1 Clem.* 5.7. But *1 Clem.* does not present a pertinent biographical orientation. It is concerned with the idea of the mission to the uttermost parts of the earth, as in Acts, except that the goal in the latter is Rome, in the former perhaps (?) Spain. But *1 Clem.* and Acts agree that the goal is achieved *before* (or in Acts precisely *during*) the one and only imprisonment of Paul. *1 Clem.* knows nothing about a release from such imprisonment.[12]

But in this point *1 Clem.* also agrees with the conception of the Pastorals, which likewise know of only *one* imprisonment.[13] Thus 1 Tim and Tit simply presuppose the situation of the mission (known from Acts), and 2 Tim that of the (Roman? Caesarean?) imprisonment; therefore, any divergences from the real historical situation result from the fact of a literary fiction.[14] Again, in another connection, the closer scrutiny of the situations results in a strong argument against the authenticity of

the Pastorals: the extensive detail of the regulations, which are by no means emergency measures for the present, but rather orders for a considerable length of time—all this contradicts the assertion of the Pastorals that Paul has not been gone very long from the place in question, and that he is not going to be away from the addressee for very long (cf. the excursus on 1 Tim 1:3 and Tit 3:14). So the Pastorals give the impression of being occasional letters, but really are not, as is shown by the artificial statement of purpose in 1 Tim 3:14f.

d) The vocabulary of the Pastorals appears to diverge markedly from that of the other Pauline epistles. Heinrich Julius Holtzmann counts 171 "new" words. But recent debate has shown that the method of arguing against authenticity on the basis of statistics is inadequate. The value of word statistics is diminished from the start, because they ignore the fact that divergences are partially conditioned by adoption of traditional material. It would therefore be meaningful to use such statistics only in conjunction with a more comprehensive linguistic and form–critical investigation. Further, even the other Pauline epistles vary widely from each other in vocabulary.[15] To be sure, the Pastorals seem to have the largest percentage of divergences;[16] but the comparative figures of each individual epistle give an essentially different picture from that of the three Pastorals taken together.[17] Much more important than bare statistics is the fact that the Pastorals' vocabulary, inasmuch as it differs from the vocabulary of the Pauline epistles, belongs mainly to the higher Koine. Therefore, when compared with the whole of Hellenistic Greek it appears to be less peculiar than the vocabulary of the rest of the NT.[18] This fact argues strongly against the authenticity of the Pastorals. The force of this argument can be diminished, to be sure through certain observations—for example the

---

12 Karl Holl, "Der Kirchenbegriff des Paulus in seinem Verhältnis zu dem der Urgemeinde," in *Gesammelte Aufsätze zur Kirchengeschichte* (Tübingen: J. C. B. Mohr [Paul Siebeck], 1927–28; reprinted 1964), II: p. 65, n. 2.

13 See the excursus mentioned above. Even 2 Tim 4:16 is not looking back to an earlier imprisonment.

14 Christian Maurer undertakes a more detailed attempt to explain how the pseudonymous writer may have envisaged the situation; see his article, "Eine Textvariante klärt die Entstehung der Pastoralbriefe auf," *ThZ* (1947): 321–37. A criticism of the article appears in Michaelis, *Einleitung*, 250ff. See

also Hans Conzelmann, "Miszelle zu Act 20.4f," *ZNW* 45 (1954): 266.

15 See F. Torm, "Über die Sprache in den Pastoralbriefen," *ZNW* 18 (1917–18): 225–43.

16 The most detailed account is found in P. N. Harrison, *The Problem of the Pastoral Epistles* (London: Oxford University Press, 1921).

17 On the computations of Otto Roller, *Das Formular der paulinischen Briefe* (Stuttgart: W. Kohlhammer, 1933), see Wilhelm Michaelis, "Pastoralbriefe und Wortstatistik," *ZNW* 28 (1929): 69–76, and *idem*, *Einleitung*, 240.

18 See Theodor Nägeli, *Der Wortschatz des Apostel Paulus*

consideration that the anti–Gnostic polemic provides new linguistic material—or through hypotheses which at any rate are somewhat risky: e.g., the effect of the writer's advanced age or the influence of Hellenistic secular literature. But the argument cannot be entirely nullified, especially since the writer has not absorbed and utilized the concepts and terminology of his opponents. Above all, one fact cannot be simply wished away: in place of definite expressions with religious significance, expressions which have already become "set" in Paul's language, the Pastorals employ different terms; what is more, they use the vernacular designations instead of the original Pauline words.[19] This is substantiated in the excursus to 1 Tim 1:5 (Good Conscience), 1:10 (The Terms "To Be Sound," etc.), and to Tit 2:14 (Soteriological Terminology of Tit, section 3). Whoever wishes to derive from Paul the words and sentences which are investigated in these instances must bear the burden of proof.

e) Hans von Campenhausen has provided a new viewpoint in his demonstration of the un–Pauline character of the church order in the Pastorals.[20] From the standpoint of the history of development of church constitution the epistles belong to the time of the turn of the century (or even later?).

f) In connection with these arguments still other observations gain added weight: many passages give the impression of imitation.[21] Further, it is difficult to deny the impression that the Pastorals know the book of the Acts of the Apostles. One must be cautious, however, in comparing the Christology of the Pastorals with that found in Paul. For in both instances one can discern formulas which have been borrowed from the tradition; in each case the traditional formulas are quite disparate in content and terminology. The difference could simply be attributed to the traditional source which is cited. But a difference must be noted in the way in which traditional materials are used. Paul appropriates and interprets the tradition; in the Pastorals it is not theologically appropriated but learned, like a lesson.

The linguistic arguments can be partially evaded by resorting to the *fragment hypothesis* and the *secretary hypothesis*. The former regards especially the personal statements at the end of 2 Tim as a fragment of a genuine Pauline letter. In recent times it has been most thoroughly presented by P. N. Harrison (cf. also Robert Falconer).[22] Harrison attempts, by means of word statistics (see above), to prove the authenticity of five small epistles or fragments.[23] One must recognize from the outset, however, that the personal statements are likely to contain fewer peculiar expressions than the other parts of the Pastorals. But even apart from the fanciful partition of 2 Tim 4, the strongest doubts must be raised against such an hypothesis. We can scarcely assume that a stray fragment of a Pauline letter has *accidentally* found its way into one of the Pastorals![24] For even if the prescript and the conclusion of such a letter had been damaged, it still would have possessed, in the address on the other

(Göttingen: Vandenhoeck und Ruprecht, 1905), 85ff; Adolf Bonhöffer, *Epiktet und das Neue Testament* (Berlin: Töpelmann, 1911; reprint 1964), 201ff; Gottfried Thieme, *Die Inschriften von Magnesia am Mäander und das Neue Testament* (Göttingen: Vandenhoeck & Ruprecht, 1906), 33ff; Paul Wendland, *Die hellenistisch-römische Kultur in ihren Beziehungen zu Judentum und Christentum, Die urchristlichen Literaturformen*, HNT I, 2 and 3 (Tübingen: J. C. B. Mohr [Paul Siebeck], ³1912), p. 364, n. 5; K. Grayston and G. Herdan, "The Authorship of the Pastorals in the Light of Statistical Linguistics," *NTS* 6 (1959–1960): 1–15.

19 On the attempt by Gösta Thörnell, *Pastoralbrevens Äkthet*, Svenskt arkiv för humanistika avhandlingar (Göteborg: Eranos' Förlag, 1931), to prove the authenticity of the Pastorals by means of a collection of stylistic parallels, cf. Hans Lietzmann, "Notizen,"

ZNW 31 (1932): 90, and Ernst von Dobschütz, "Die Pastoralbriefe (zu Gösta Thörnell, Pastoralbrevens Äkthet)," *ThStKr* 104 (1932): 121–123.

20 See his *Ecclesiastical Authority and Spiritual Power*, translated by J. A. Baker (Stanford, Calif.: Stanford University Press, 1969), especially 106–19.

21 For example, 1 Tim 1:12–16; cf. Gal 1:13–16 and 1 Cor 15:9f; 2 Tim 1:3–5; cf. Rom 1:8–11. See Rudolf Bultmann, "Pastoralbriefe," *RGG*², 4:994.

22 Robert Falconer, *The Pastoral Epistles* (Oxford: Clarendon Press, 1937), 1–30, especially 13–7.

23 Tit 3:12–15; 2 Tim 4:13–15, 20, 21a; 2 Tim 4:16–18a; 2 Tim 4:9–12, 22b; 2 Tim 1:16–18; 3:10f; 4:1, 2a, 5b, 6–8, 18b, 19, 21b, and 22a.

24 See Hans Lietzmann and Werner Georg Kümmel, *An die Korinther I–II*, HNT 9 (Tübingen: J. C. B. Mohr [Paul Siebeck], ⁵1969), on 2 Cor 7:1.

side, an indication of its independent status as a letter.[25] Thus, it would have been the pseudonymous "Paul" after all who copied, for his own purposes, pieces from Pauline letters which are unknown to us. The fragment hypothesis owes its popularity to interpreters who wish to avoid the conclusion that the wonderful ethos of 2 Tim 4 is the product of a "pseudonymous writer." But the fragment hypothesis does not exonerate the "pseudonymous writer," but only ascribes to him a different method (cf. further the commentary below on 2 Tim 4:8). The difficulty of taking the personal remarks as simply a part of the epistolary frame seems in itself to have led many exegetes to adopt the fragment hypothesis; but even this difficulty is not as great as is often assumed, as will be shown below.[26]

The secretary hypothesis has recently been set upon a new foundation by Roller. The rich diplomatic material, however, which he adduces proves no more in favor of this hypothesis than his computations of the ancient writing speed.[27] Roller's attempt to prove authenticity by reference to the development of the Pauline letter formula[28] is likewise unsuccessful, inasmuch as he presupposes what is still to be demonstrated: the authenticity of all the canonical Pauline epistles. The secretary hypothesis and the fragment hypothesis are nothing but modifications of the declaration of inauthenticity. The relationship to the remaining Pauline epistles turns into an even greater puzzle; the situation of the origin of the Pastorals is not clarified at any point.

2. The Literary Character of the Pastoral Epistles

Whoever decides for these reasons to assume inauthenticity of the Pastorals must explain the existence and genre of these pseudo–Pauline letters. In the light of this assumption, the personal sections of all three Epistles at once fade into the background; their primary purpose is, at any rate, to demonstrate the authorship of Paul. What the author himself wanted to say is to be inferred first of all from passages with a different content.

a) 1 Tim and Tit are of an essentially similar literary character. The core of the epistle to Titus is Tit 2, resembling the "rules for the household" (*Haustafel*) which give instructions to the individual members of the family, including the slaves. To this passage belong the verses in the first chapter which deal with the "Bishop" (ἐπίσκοπος, Tit 1:7–9) and the first verses of the third chapter, which may be regarded as the conclusion of these rules for the household. We cannot with equal certainty identify a basic body of materials in 1 Tim. For there the interest is directed to two main points: church order and the refutation of heretics (in this regard cf. also Tit 1:10ff and 3:9ff—but this is in no sense the main concern in Tit). But even apart from this twofold interest, the character of the church order materials themselves does not seem uniform. First of all, their arrangement is by no means clear: 1 Tim 2:1ff deals with the worship service; 3:1ff with bishops and deacons; 5:3ff with widows; 5:17ff with presbyters; and 6:1f with slaves. Moreover, not all the regulations appear to have been formulated for the situations into which they have here been placed. Thus the argument in 1 Tim 2:13–15 applies not to the conduct of women in the worship service, but rather to the position of women in general; and even the instructions in 2:9–12 seem, in part at least, not to apply exclusively to the worship service. The parallel to 2:9f, 1 Petr 3:3ff, is found in a table of rules for the household! Even in the rules concerning widows, some passages sound more like exhortations which we are accustomed to find in rules for the household (cf. 1 Tim 5:5, 6). All these observations justify the hypothesis that the regulations in 1 Tim are not a uniform piece, but rather represent a collection of various materials.

b) A good object of comparison is offered by the corresponding regulations in the *Teaching of the Twelve Apostles* (*Didache*). There the regulations regarding the worship and organization of the congregation (*Did.* 7–10, 14, 15)—regulations which form the main struc-

---

25 Perhaps also in the vertical covering which served as a binding and which is only partially separated from the papyrus. See Hugo Ibscher, "Beobachtungen bei der Papyrusaufrollung," *Archiv für Papyrusforschung und verwandte Gebiete*, 5(1913): 192f.

26 Cf. below pp. 127f, the excursus on 2 Tim 4:21; also Wendland, *Hellenistische Kultur*, 367. As an example of personal references in pseudonymous writings, cf. the 13th Pseudo–Platonic Epistle.

27 Cf. the critique by Ernst Percy, *Die Probleme der Kolosser– und Epheserbriefe* (Lund: C. W. K. Gleerup, 1946; [Koebenhavn, Villadsen og Christensen, 1964, photomechanischer Neudruck]), 10ff, and Michaelis, *Einleitung*, 242ff.

28 Especially in his *Das Formular*, 92ff; cf. also the footnotes to these pages.

ture of the second part of the book—are interrupted by a passage of more pressing importance, dealing with apostles and prophets (*Did.* 11–13), in short, rules which seem to be of a later date than the regulations about worship and church organization. We can accordingly conclude, from the Pastorals as well as from the *Did.*, that the core of these materials was a church order. This may have been fixed in writing or in oral form and was stated with different nuances according to particular needs. It must have been formed within the Christian communities and was concerned firstly with the worship service, and secondly with the organization of the congregation. (Cf. especially the relationship between *Did.* 14 and 1 Tim 2:8; see below *ad loc.*). Tit 1:7–9 would be very well explained as a quotation from such a church order, because in this case the exegetical difficulty of the passage, which had led to the hypothesis of an interpolation, would be resolved (see below on Tit 1:7ff). Thus the following schema would result:

Did. 7–10 Baptism, Fasting, Prayer, Eucharistic Prayers	1 Tim 2:1 Prayers, especially for those in authority	
Did. 14 Ethical requirements of the worship service	1 Tim 2:8 Ethical requirements of the worship service	
Did. 15:1, 2 Bishops and deacons	1 Tim 3:1 Bishops and deacons	Tit 1:7–9 Bishops
	1 Tim 5:3ff Widows	
	1 Tim 5:17 Presbyters	

If the remaining regulations in 1 Tim and Tit are gathered, the results would fit into a table of rules for the household (with minor necessary changes):

1 Tim 2:8 Men and women	Tit 2:1–6 Old men; old women; young women; young men
(? 1 Tim 5:1, 2 Behavior of the leader of the congregation over against the different age groups)	(? Tit 2:7f The leader of the congregation as example)
(? 1 Tim 5:5f Ethical behavior of widows)	
1 Tim 6:1ff Slaves	Tit 2:9f Slaves

The resulting amalgamation of church order and rules for the household has but *one* parallel: Polycarp's *Epistle to the Philippians*. Otherwise the rules for the household deal exclusively with natural "classes." Here, on the contrary, they are applied to the "house of God" (1 Tim 3:15).[29]

c) These rules and orders are applied to actual situations in a twofold connection in 1 Tim and Tit. First, they are presented as instructions of the apostle to his assistants, and second, they are brought into close connection with the refutation of the heresy. *Did.* 11–13 reveals an analogous contemporary application within a church order. But in the Pastorals the contemporaneity is more strongly emphasized because of the epistolary form of the external frame. In Tit 1:9f the connection between the refutation of the heretics and church organization is clearly observable; but also in 1 Tim the proem 1:3ff and several details in the regulations reveal more or less clearly the position of the "front line." In the second excursus on 2 Tim 4:21, the degree to which the reports on individual heretics may serve the same purpose is investigated.[30] Again there is a close correspondence to Polycarp's *Epistle to the Philippians*. It is to be seen in the

29 Cf. von Campenhausen, "Polykarp," 228ff. For further parallels, see Georg Strecker, *Das Judenchristentum in den Pseudoklementinen*, TU 70 (Berlin: Akademie–Verlag, 1958).

30 On the special character of the Cretan heresy, cf. below pp. 152ff the excursus on Tit. 3:14.

combination of church order (of the same type as described here!), polemic against heresy and general parenesis. There is an appeal to tradition, in which a particular picture of the apostle is presumed; the whole is presented in the form of a letter. To be sure, the Pastorals are pseudonymous, while Polycarp writes under his own name. Polycarp, therefore, tries to lend authority to his instructions by copious quotations; the Pastorals, on the other hand, already possess their authority through the name of the writer. Corresponding to the observations regarding the literary character of the Pastorals, the motive for their composition is complex; the concern for fundamental questions and their contemporary application to actual problems cannot be separated. To state the correct teaching is to mark the line of separation from heresy, and conversely, the struggle against heresy leads to the formation of criteria, i.e. to the conscious establishment of orthodoxy.[31] The emphasis upon tradition in the Pastorals means that Paul is being established as the authority for the church. By framing the church order as letters addressed to the disciples of the apostle, two things are accomplished: first, the regulations are transmitted to a large number of churches rather than to a single congregation, because they are addressed to men who are supposed to be in charge of whole provinces and are expected to transmit everything which they receive from the apostle (cf. 2 Tim 2:2). (This in no sense implies a fixed, official designation of a position, e.g., in the sense of a Metropolitan. It is simply a matter of preserving the tradition and seeing that it is applied to the current situations.) Second, the responsibility for the wellbeing of the congregations thus becomes a matter of the education of the individual disposition of the church leader (cf. especially 2 Tim). On the other hand, one must not be deceived by the personal elements in

certain passages of 1 Tim and Tit which are only part of the external frame; thus, 1 Tim 2:8ff is in reality addressed directly to men and women, 1 Tim 3:1ff directly to bishops and deacons.[32]

d) In 2 Tim the personal elements become prominent to a remarkable extent. Not only does the content of the whole letter seem to be a genuine personal communication, even apart from the polemic, which appears here too, but even the loose, unconstrained train of thought (e.g., in 3:10–4:8) and the manner of exhortation (e.g., in 2:3ff) indicate that this piece of writing belongs to the genre of parenesis. Just as Isocrates exhorts his Nicocles, as Pseudo–Isocrates exhorts Demonicus, or as Basil exhorts his son Leon,[33] likewise Paul, as he goes to his death, exhorts his "beloved child Timothy." Indeed, if we change the formulation of the subject matter, we could even say with regard to 2 Tim, as Isocrates (*Ad Nicoclem* 2) says to Nicocles, that it teaches: "what pursuits you should aspire to, and from what you should abstain in order to govern to the best advantage your state and kingdom." ($\pi o \acute{\iota} \omega \nu$ $\dot{\epsilon}\pi\iota\tau\eta\delta\epsilon\upsilon\mu\acute{a}\tau\omega\nu$ $\dot{o}\rho\epsilon$-$\gamma\acute{o}\mu\epsilon\nu o\varsigma$ $\kappa a\grave{\iota}$ $\tau\acute{\iota}\nu\omega\nu$ $\ddot{\epsilon}\rho\gamma\omega\nu$ $\dot{a}\pi\epsilon\chi\acute{o}\mu\epsilon\nu o\varsigma$ $\ddot{a}\rho\iota\sigma\tau'$ $\dot{a}\nu$ $\kappa a\grave{\iota}$ $\tau\grave{\eta}\nu$ $\pi\acute{o}\lambda\iota\nu$ $\kappa a\grave{\iota}$ $\tau\grave{\eta}\nu$ $\beta a\sigma\iota\lambda\epsilon\acute{\iota}a\nu$ $\delta\iota o\iota\kappa o\acute{\iota}\eta\varsigma$). Thus, if 2 Tim is primarily personal parenesis in its content and a letter in its form, it is not surprising that its conclusion contains more personal information than the other Pastorals. The manner in which the pseudonymous author came by this material will be dealt with in the second excursus to 2 Tim 4:21. The motivation for the composition of the "letter," however, seems clear if we consider the content of the parenesis: Paul sets himself up as an example of suffering in order to encourage Timothy to similar endurance.[34] On the other hand, through the exhortation to pass on what has been received (2 Tim 2:2), as well as through the universal application of the

---

31 Cf. the procedure in 1 John, which is in a way analogous. See Hans Conzelmann, " 'Was von Anfang war,' " in *NT Studien für Rudolf Bultmann*, BZNW 21 (Berlin: Töpelmann, 1954), 194–201.

32 Cf. the *Muratorian Canon*, lines 59ff, as reconstructed by Hans Lietzmann, KlT 1, p. 9: verum ad Philemonem unam et ad Titum unam et ad Timotheum duas pro affectu et dilectione, in honorem tamen ecclesiae catholicae in ordinem ecclesiasticae disciplinae sanctificatae sunt. "But he [wrote] one [letter] to Philemon and one to Titus, but two to Timothy for the sake of affection and love. In honor of the General Church, however, they have been sanctified

by an ordination of the ecclesiastical discipline." [Translated by D. J. Theron in: *Evidence of Tradition* (London: Bowes & Bowes, 1957), 111.]

33 Cf. MPG, Vol. 107, pp. 21ff.

34 Cf. the treatment in the second excursus to 2 Tim 4:21, sect. 5, and see below on 2 Tim 1:3–14.

concept of suffering (3:12), the whole letter takes on a significance which goes beyond the personal appeal. The attitude toward the enemy within and without, which Paul recommends and requires of Timothy, i.e. his behavior in the midst of conflict and persecution— this attitude and this behavior become exemplary for all those who, coming after the apostle and the disciple of the apostle, have the responsibility of leadership in the Christian congregations. The theme of the apostle as example is a typical component of the understanding of tradition as it is being formed at this time (cf. again Polycarp). So the Pastoral Epistles, taken together, are all three expressions of one and the same concept.

3. The Theological Character of the Epistles

The historical evaluation of the Pastorals suffers from onesided emphasis upon the question of authenticity. Such an emphasis leads both advocates and critics to a onesided confrontation with Paul and hence to an unhistorical "value judgment" based upon the Pauline theology. The historian must try to understand the Pastorals within the ecclesiastical situation of post– Apostolic times (the inauthenticity of the Pastorals being presupposed). The evaluation of the Epistles cannot be made without taking into consideration the change in the way the Church understood itself, a change which occurred during this epoch.[35] Their concept of "good citizenship" places them beside Luke, *1 Clement*, Polycarp—in short, those writings to which they are closely related in their development of church constitution as well.[36] "Good citizenship," in the actual situation of conflict, proves to be the taking of a position, a mode of acting for the church's consolidation. The church must make adjustments for a prolonged stay in the world in the face of the evolution of both orthodoxy and heresy within the Christian communities. Elements of the concept of "good citizenship" can already be found in the parenesis of Paul. Now they are elaborated and thus the rationale is characteristically changed. In Paul, good citizenship is eschatologically conditioned. It results from the paradox of change in the world and can be observed, for instance, in the dialectical character of the demand to remain in one's "calling" (1 Cor 7:17ff). Good citizenship is the concrete fulfillment of the demand "to serve" ($\delta o\nu$-$\lambda\epsilon\acute{\nu}\epsilon\iota\nu$). The Pastorals, on the other hand, derive it from the order of creation and from the correct teaching in general. To be sure, we cannot simply speak of the loss of a dialectical understanding of existence. Good citizenship does not turn into secular piety; the appeal to the Creator and the order of creation is not developed into a reflection about the world. It appears in a polemical context where the observance of ascetic regulations is being opposed. In such a situation it makes good sense when the wives are required to bear children and when the disciple of the apostle is requested to drink a glass of wine.

One must consider the historical situation in order to understand the particular position which the author assumes with respect to the "tradition." Naturally, our judgment recognizes the fact that the Pastorals are to a great extent concerned with traditional material. (Here we are concerned especially with the "kerygmatic" passages, not with traditions of parenesis or church order.) How was this material assimilated? What is the relation between interpretation and tradition? It is in itself symptomatic that these materials appear in the guise of Pauline epistles (see above), and that their propensity for quoting is quite prominent. The apostle serves directly as example (see above on 2 Tim). In comparison with the later development one is struck again by the reticence: although the picture of the apostle is already that of a later generation, it has not yet been developed in legendary form, and it has not yet become the content of the communication in its own right. Even in 2 Tim it remains related to the particular purpose of the letter. The office of the apostle is not in itself the object of reflection. A general concept of apostolic authority or tradition has not yet been developed. It is only the one man, Paul, who is important. This is consistent with the absence of the concept of succession. (Even the laying on of hands in 2 Tim 1:6 is not elaborated in the sense of a ritual establishment and succession; cf. 1 Tim 4:14).[37] The style is characterized by a combination of the kerygma, which is quoted, and the appeal to Paul

---

35 Rudolf Bultmann, *Theology of the New Testament*, vol. 2, tr. Kendrick Grobel (New York: Charles Scribner's Sons, 1955), pp. 3–92.

36 See von Campenhausen, *Ecclesiastical Authority*.

37 Cf. Hans Windisch, "Zur Christologie der Pastoralbriefe," *ZNW* 34 (1935): 224.

as the guarantor.[38] This combination may cast some light on the function of 2 Tim within the corpus of the Pastorals. Paul appears as the guarantor of the tradition, as the interpreter of the present (1 Tim 4:1ff; 2 Tim 3:1ff) and as an example for life, especially an example of suffering. (1 Tim 1:15 especially demonstrates the validity of the preaching of salvation to sinners, and 1 Tim 2:6 to pagans.) The combination of kerygma and apostle stands in the broader context of the general understanding of revelation. In the passages already mentioned and elsewhere we can discern yet another fixed characteristic: together with the citing of tradition (whether in the form of confessional formulas, hymns, or liturgical pieces) the line is extended into the present. This is done in such a way that two things are explicitly mentioned along with the objective fact of salvation: (1) its proclamation in the present and (2) its contemporary significance. This schema has not been created by the author. It is partly present in the material which he quotes, especially clearly in 1 Tim 3:16 (see below *ad loc.*). Analogies, of course, can also be found outside the Pastorals.[39] But it is especially clearly set forth in the Pastorals (cf., e.g., Tit 1:2f) where the object of the epiphany is the "word" (with the characteristic addition "in the preaching with which I have been entrusted" [ἐν κηρύγματι ὃ ἐπιστεύθην ἐγώ]). In Tit 2:11 "grace, favor" (χάρις) takes on a revelatory character; cf. further Tit 3:4ff and 2 Tim 1:10. The comparison of these passages shows that Tit 1:2f does not intend to hypostatize the "word." The writer is thinking rather of the actual proclamation (personifying expressions such as 2 Tim 2:9 prove nothing about hypostatization). Here we must of course also mention the formula "the word stands firm" (πιστὸς ὁ λόγος, see below, the excursus to 1 Tim 1:15). It serves to document a tendency which runs throughout the Pastorals. The traditional material is not interpreted but inculcated and established as the means of salvation for the present. Once again, it is necessary to make a distinction: the tradition remains

fixed; there is no thought of the evolution of a deposit of faith (*depositum fidei*) in the sense of the Catholic "living tradition" (*traditio viva*). Another critical safeguard exists insofar as the representation of salvation is not transformed into a cultic "mystery." To be sure, the Pastoral Epistles presuppose a liturgy when they cite liturgical pieces; but the liturgy is not the object of reflection and teaching as if it were itself a factor in the process of salvation. Liturgy plays a part only inasmuch as in it the salvation event is recited.[40] In the interests of completeness, it may be added that yet another possibility for the connection of the present with the past is missing in the Pastorals: there is no elaboration of a concept of history of salvation (e.g. in the way in which it is used in Luke). The Pastorals do not reflect upon Israel and its connection with the church (cf. below on 2 Tim 1:5). Even where the "mediator" is mentioned (1 Tim 2:5) this line is not extended; the "covenant" (διαθήκη) is not recalled (although obviously the idea of the covenant is inherent in the material that is used here).

The traditional material which has been taken over by the Pastorals is of a disparate nature, both in form and content. Thus, for example, there is a diversity of Christological perspectives which must not be combined to reconstruct "the" Christology of the Pastorals. The unity does not lie in a particular Christological conception (several types stand side by side with no sign of theological reflection). Rather unity results from the constant emphasis upon the meaning of salvation for the present. This explains the strangely undefined relationship between God and Christ. The latter, on the one hand, appears (on the basis of the tradition) in a subordinate position.[41] On the other hand, however, since there is no metaphysical speculation regarding essence and nature, another viewpoint becomes prominent: from the perspective of their saving activity, God and Christ stand side by side (as seen from the point of view of the community of faith). Thus, the soteriological concepts can be used indiscriminately (and the question can remain open

---

38 Otto Michel, "Grundfragen der Pastoralbriefe" in Max Loeser ed., *Auf dem Grunde der Apostel und Propheten*, *Festgabe für Theophil Wurm* (Stuttgart: Quell–Verlag, 1948), 86. See also 1 Tim 1:15; 2:6; and 2 Tim 2:8ff.

39 For example, Lk 24:47. Cf. Eduard Schweizer, *Lordship and Discipleship*, translated from the German with revisions by the author, SBT 28 (Naperville, Ill.: Alec R. Allenson, 1960), p. 66, n. 2. The con-

stant appeal to the church in the epistle to the Ephesians is a case in point; it occurs together with the references to the mythical salvation event; cf. Eph 1:13, 22f; 3:8ff; cf. further Ign. *Eph.* 19.

40 In contrast cf. Ignatius on the one hand, and the theological interpretation of "homology" in the Epistle to the Hebrews on the other.

41 Cf. Tit 3:4ff, esp. v 6, the concept of the "mediator," and the passive style of 1 Tim 3:16 and 6:15.

whether in Tit 2:13 the divine title refers to Christ, see *ad loc.*). It is consistent with the unspeculative nature of the Pastorals that no interest is shown in developing the idea of pre–existence. The manner in which the soteriological perspective is formulated explains why the delay of the Parousia presents no difficulties. The church has obviously adjusted to the thought of the world's duration and has learned to become at home in it. The presupposition is that salvation has become a reality in the epiphany of the past; salvation in the future appears to be nothing but the shadow of this past epiphany.

This consciousness of salvation forms the ultimate essential presupposition of the attitude toward the world which is expressed in the concept of good citizenship. While the acute eschatological expectation has diminished, the corrective is given, a corrective which forbids the Christian to tread the path of salvation by works that lies to the right, and the way of world–renunciation and speculation that lies to the left.

Outline

Initial greeting (1:1, 2).

Timothy must combat the heretics in Ephesus (1:3–7) in the spirit of the Gospel, as it was entrusted to Paul (1:8–12). For Paul, who was the foremost persecutor, is now an example of God's mercy (1:13–17). In view of the heretics Paul transmits exhortations to Timothy (1:18–20).

Church orders (2:1–3:13): on prayers for all men, especially for those in authority (2:1–7); on the prayer of men (2:8) and women (2:9–15); on the conduct of bishops (3:1–7) and deacons (3:8–13); with a concluding personal word to Timothy concerning the church, to which the great divine secret is entrusted (3:14–16).

Church order: concerning heretics, who recommend abstention from marriage and from certain foods (4:1–5); Timothy should enlighten the brethren on this matter and combat this teaching (4:6–10). Above all, he should be an example in conduct, in leading the congregation, and in his relationships with individual members of the congregation (4:11–5:2).

Church orders: on widows (5:3–16; the true widows [5:3–8]; certain duties of the older widows, the duty of the younger widows to remarry [5:9–16]); on presbyters (5:17–20); on slaves (6:1, 2); with a personal exhortation to Timothy inserted at 5:21–25.

Warnings against false doctrine and against avarice (6:3–10); exhortations to Timothy to fight the battle of faith (6:11–16); parenetic rules for the wealthy (6:17–19). Conclusion, with a final warning against false 'Gnosis' (6:20, 21).

1

Initial Greeting

1　**Paul, Apostle of Christ Jesus by the commission of God our Savior and of Christ Jesus our hope, to Timothy, his true child in faith: 2/ grace, mercy, and peace from God the Father and Christ Jesus our Lord.**

■ 1　The form of the prescript is taken from the Pauline epistles.[1] Genuine Pauline letters also mention in the introduction the commission of God, or of God and Christ (as in Gal). "By the commission etc." ($\kappa\alpha\tau'$ $\epsilon\pi\iota\tau\alpha\gamma\grave{\eta}\nu\ \kappa\tau\lambda$.): this does not express the personal consciousness of holding an office (as, e.g., 1 Cor 9:16); rather it is a formulaic expression (see Bauer, s.v.) which is also found in Tit 1:3 and Rom 16:26 in a schema which will be discussed below. Noteworthy in the rhetorically corresponding titles is the designation of God as "Savior" ($\sigma\omega\tau\acute{\eta}\rho$, see the excursus to 2 Tim 1:10) and the title of Christ as "hope" ($\dot{\epsilon}\lambda\pi\acute{\iota}s$). This latter predicate is used as a formula, as in Ignatius.[2] In this passage the expression stands in the context of the soteriological schema: formerly hidden—now openly preached—a schema which appears frequently in the deutero-Pauline epistles and especially in the Pastorals.[3] On the interpretation of these titles as they are used by the author of the Pastorals, cf. Tit 1:1–3; 3:4–7, where there is reflection upon the relation of God and Christ as "Savior" and exposition of the notion of "hope." The anchoring of the schema in the liturgy is clear from Rom 16:25ff.

■ 2　A "true child" ($\gamma\nu\acute{\eta}\sigma\iota o\nu\ \tau\acute{\epsilon}\kappa\nu o\nu$) is actually the legitimate child, the child born in wedlock. The expression could be meant here as an allusion to what is reported in Acts 16:1ff or 2 Tim 1:6. It would then have to be understood spiritually, as in *Corp. Herm.* 13.3: "Do not refuse me, father; I am (your) true son; explain to me the nature of the rebirth." ($\mu\grave{\eta}\ \phi\theta\acute{o}\nu\epsilon\iota\ \mu o\iota,\ \pi\acute{\alpha}\tau\epsilon\rho\cdot$ $\gamma\nu\acute{\eta}\sigma\iota o s\ \upsilon\acute{\iota}\acute{o}s\ \epsilon\grave{\iota}\mu\iota\cdot\ \delta\iota\acute{\alpha}\phi\rho\alpha\sigma\acute{o}\nu\ \mu o\iota\ \tau\hat{\eta}s\ \pi\alpha\lambda\iota\gamma\gamma\epsilon\nu\epsilon\sigma\acute{\iota}\alpha s$ $\tau\grave{o}\nu\ \tau\rho\acute{o}\pi o\nu$). Cf. the designation of the "mystagogue" ($\mu\upsilon\hat{\omega}\nu$) in the mysteries as "father" ($\pi\alpha\tau\acute{\eta}\rho$).[4] But perhaps "true" ($\gamma\nu\acute{\eta}\sigma\iota o s$) is not used at all technically. Therefore, "true child" is not a fixed expression, but rather a friendly, polite form of address.[5] The formulaic use of the expression "in faith" ($\dot{\epsilon}\nu\ \pi\acute{\iota}\sigma\tau\epsilon\iota$) is not found in the genuine Pauline epistles (1 Cor 16:3; Gal 2:20; 2 Thess 2:13 are not analogous). The usage is characteristic of a later time.[6] The salutation in 1 and 2 Tim (cf. 2 Jn) has a tripartite form which diverges from the introductions of the other Pauline epistles, including Tit. Since in the letter of *2 Bar.* 78.2, a greeting is attested corresponding to the formula "mercy and peace" ($\check{\epsilon}\lambda\epsilon o s$ $\kappa\alpha\grave{\iota}\ \epsilon\grave{\iota}\rho\acute{\eta}\nu\eta$); and, moreover, since the ℵ Text of Tob 7:12,[7] as well as Paul in Gal 6:16, seem to presuppose

1　On the form of the Pauline prescript cf. Ernst Lohmeyer, "Probleme paulinischer Theologie," *ZNW* 26 (1927): 158–73; see also Gerhard Friedrich, "Lohmeyers These über das paulinische Briefpräskript kritisch beleuchtet," *ThLZ* 81 (1956): 343–46. On the form of the prescript of the Pastorals in particular see Roller, *Das Formular*, 147ff.

2　Ign. *Eph.* 21:2; *Mg.* 11; *Tr.* in the salutation and 2:2; *Phld.* 11:2; cf. also Pol. *Phil.* 8:1. In the NT cf. Col 1:27.

3　See Nils A. Dahl, "Formgeschichtliche Beobachtungen zur Christusverkündigung in der Gemeindepredigt" in *NT Studien für Rudolf Bultmann*, BZNW 21 (Berlin: Töpelmann, 1954), 4ff.

4　Cf. the references given in Martin Dibelius and Heinrich Greeven, *An die Kolosser, Epheser, An Philemon*, HNT 12 (Tübingen: J. C. B. Mohr [Paul Siebeck], ³1953), on Phlmn 1:10.

5　See the proof texts given by Martin Dibelius, *An die Thessalonicher I, II. An die Philipper*, HNT 11 (Tübingen: J. C. B. Mohr [Paul Siebeck], ³1937), on Phil 4:3. For an example of both meanings of $\gamma\nu\acute{\eta}$-$\sigma\iota o s$, cf. the following passage (*P. Lips.* 28.17ff): (Adoption) "(the person adopted) whom I feed and clothe nobly and *truly* as my *lawful* and natural son, as one who was born to me" ($\check{o}\nu\pi\epsilon\rho\ \theta\rho\acute{\epsilon}\psi\omega\ \kappa\alpha\grave{\iota}\ \acute{\iota}\mu\alpha$-$\tau\acute{\iota}\zeta\omega\ \epsilon\grave{\upsilon}\gamma\epsilon\nu\hat{\omega}s\ \kappa\alpha\grave{\iota}\ \gamma\nu\eta\sigma\acute{\iota}\omega s\ \acute{\omega}s\ \upsilon\acute{\iota}\grave{o}\nu\ \gamma\nu\acute{\eta}\sigma\iota o\nu\ \kappa\alpha\grave{\iota}$ $\phi\upsilon\sigma\iota\kappa\grave{o}\nu\ \acute{\omega}s\ \grave{\epsilon}\xi\ \grave{\epsilon}[\mu]o\hat{\upsilon}\ \gamma\epsilon\nu\acute{o}\mu\epsilon\nu o\nu$).

6　Bultmann, *Theology* 2, p. 184. Cf. 1 Tim 1:4; Tit 3:15; Jas 1:6; 2:5; Pol. *Phil.* 9:2; 12:2.

7　Tob 7:12: "and grant you mercy and peace" ($\kappa\alpha\grave{\iota}$ $\pi o\iota\hat{\eta}\sigma\alpha\iota\ \grave{\epsilon}\phi'\ \acute{\upsilon}\mu\hat{\alpha}s\ \check{\epsilon}\lambda\epsilon o s\ \kappa\alpha\grave{\iota}\ \epsilon\grave{\iota}\rho\acute{\eta}\nu\eta\nu$).

this formula, we may accordingly regard the tripartite salutation as a combination of Jewish and "Pauline" formulas.[8] A parallel development towards the tripartite form is seen in Jude 2 and in the salutation of *Mart. Pol.*; the keyword "mercy" (ἔλεος) is also found in the salutation of Pol. *Phil.* and in Ign. *Sm.* 12.2. The latter passage shows that the use of the formula cannot be limited to Asia Minor.[9] The additional member "mercy" replaces, in the rhythm of the greeting, the otherwise customary "to you" (plural: ὑμῖν); for "to you" (singular: σοί) would not have been adequate as a rhythmical substitute. One must be careful in drawing conclusions as to authenticity or imitation, since there are no other Pauline letters addressed to a single person (in Phlmn we find the plural "to you" [ὑμῖν]).

---

8   Cf. Wendland, *Hellenistische Kultur*, 413.
9   In this point I disagree with Jeremias, *ad loc.*

1 Combat the Heretics

3   I commanded you to remain in Ephesus, when I travelled to Macedonia, so that you might forbid certain people to proclaim other teachings and to indulge in endless myths about genealogies, 4/ which result more in the racking of one's brain than in godly education leading to salvation in faith. 5/ But the purpose of the instruction is love, (born) of a pure heart, of a good conscience and a sincere faith. 6/ Some have renounced these things to run after foolish talk. 7/ They wish to be teachers of the law and do not know what they are saying, nor to what they are bearing witness.

■ 3 With "as" ($\kappa\alpha\theta\dot\omega\varsigma$, not reproduced in the translation above) begins an anacoluthon, which results from the loose subordination of many clauses introduced by this conjunction. This phenomenon can be observed in other instances.[1] Therefore, in this passage, it is impossible to determine whether the main idea to which "as I have . . ." is to be subordinated must be derived from the prescript ("I am writing to you just as I have previously commanded you"), or from what follows ("as I have previously commanded you, now I give you an order"). Every unprejudiced reader will translate $\pi\rho\sigma$-$\mu\epsilon\hat\iota\nu\alpha\iota\ \dot\epsilon\nu\ ᾿E\phi\dot\epsilon\sigma\omega$ as "remain in Ephesus" and not "stand fast in Ephesus," and will therefore infer that Paul has travelled from Ephesus to Macedonia, and that Timothy has remained in Ephesus. On the basis of 1:20, it is probable that Paul had already been in Ephesus.[2]

The Situation of the Writing of 1 Timothy

Paul traversed the route to Macedonia, which is pre-supposed here, twice during the portion of his life known to us. But, according to Acts 16:11ff, Timothy was among the travelling companions. Furthermore, Paul had probably not yet preached in Ephesus at that time. And, according to Acts 20:1, the apostle had sent ahead his assistant with the intention (according to 19:22) of meeting him again in Macedonia. Acts 19:22, indeed, could be based on an error,[3] and consequently our passage could be a reference to the departure mentioned in Acts 20:1. Whoever assumes a fictitious Pauline framework will recognize this latter situation in 1 Tim 1:3 and will take the reference to Timothy either in Acts or in the Pastorals as a mistake or as a legendary feature. It is not without precedent in legendary stories of the apostles that a well–known situation is alluded to but at the same time modified.[4] A journey such as the one presupposed in this passage could naturally have been made during a time unknown to us; e.g., during the long stay in Ephesus[5] or during the time between the first

---

1. As an example of such relative independence, cf. especially Gal 3:6; 1 Thess 1:5; Eph 1:4; but also 1 Cor 1:6; Phil 1:7; 17:2; and finally the epistolary introductions with "since" ($\dot\epsilon\pi\epsilon\iota$) in Ign *Eph*. 1.3; *Rom*. 1:1.

2. Here I am in disagreement with Wilhelm Michaelis, *Pastoralbriefe und Gefangenschaftsbriefe* and *Zur Echtheitsfrage der Pastoralbriefe* NF 1, 6 (Gütersloh: Bertelsmann, 1930), 137; cf. Ch. Bruston, "De la date de la première Épître de Paul à Tim," *EThR* 5 (1930): 272–76, and Michaelis, *Einleitung*, p. 235.

3. Cf. the statement about Trophimus in Acts 21:29, and see below on 2 Tim 4:20.

4. Cf. *Act. Pl.* (*Martyrdom of Paul* 1, Ricardus Albertus Lipsius and Maximilianus Bonnet, *Acta Apostolorum Apocrypha* [Darmstadt: Wissenschaftliche Buchgesellschaft, 1:59], 1, p. 104) with 2 Tim 4:10f. See also below pp. 126f, the first excursus to 2 Tim 4:21.

5. This stay was interrupted by an "interim visit" in Corinth; but was that not just an excursion overseas?

Roman imprisonment and a second imprisonment in the same place, which would have to be postulated. To be sure, one could hardly appeal to *1 Clem* 5:7, as this passage seems to know of only one imprisonment. But if it should in fact know of two imprisonments, and (what is equally questionable) if it should be reliable, could Paul have visited the East again in the time between these Roman imprisonments?[6] But one decisive objection exists to placing the Pastorals during the time between the two Roman imprisonments. The Pastorals themselves know of only *one* such imprisonment and they themselves claim to be written during the time before or during the first (and only) imprisonment.[7] But we must consider further the reason for which 1 Tim was supposed to have been written. According to 3:14f and 4:13, Paul gives Timothy these directions—both the statutes with more lasting relevancy and the advice given for specific cases—only in case his return to Ephesus should be delayed. One wonders why Paul did not make these arrangements himself in Ephesus and why it is necessary to write them at this time to Timothy, when the apostle's speedy return can still be expected. This consideration takes on special force when we observe that in 1 Tim 3 the writer does not introduce the offices of bishops and deacons, but rather gives an ethical injunction for the officeholders, as though that were something new. Schleiermacher, who inaugurated the criticism of this Epistle[8]—though not of the other two Pastoral Epistles!— emphasized the difficulty which lies in the artificiality of the situation. This difficulty is resolved if the verses in question are literary devices which serve to clothe the work in the guise of a Pauline epistle, and which may be modelled on such passages as 1 Cor 4:19; 11:34; 16:3ff. To be sure, the situation there is entirely different, since Paul had already left Corinth a good while before.[9]

■ **3, 4** What is said here about the "proclaiming other teachings" (ἑτεροδιδασκαλοῦντες, cf. Ign. *Pol.* 3:1)

is not sufficient to identify the doctrine being opposed with any position known to us. This lack of clarity is connected with the whole style of the heresy polemic.[10] The position of the opponents is characterized by the words "myths and genealogies."

Myths and Genealogies

The coupling of the terms *myths* and *genealogies* is already found in Plato and elsewhere.[11] In the passage under discussion the use is, to be sure, not specifically literary. "Myth" (μῦθος) is used here, as is frequently the case elsewhere, to denote false and foolish stories. As a formal parallel, cf. the reproachful question in Epictetus *Diss.* 3.24.18 "And do you take Homer and his *tales* as authority for everything?" (σὺ δ' Ὁμήρῳ πάντα προσέχεις καὶ τοῖς μύθοις αὐτοῦ;),[12] cf. Plut. *Mor.* 348a–b. See also the double meaning of "myth" in Clement of Alexandria, *Quis div. salv.* 42: "Hear a story that is no mere story, but a true account of John the Apostle that has been handed down and preserved in memory" (ἄκουσον μῦθον, οὐ μῦθον, ἀλλὰ ὄντα λόγον περὶ Ἰωάννου τοῦ ἀποστόλου παραδεδομένον καὶ μνήμῃ πεφυλαγμένον). "Endless" (ἀπέραντος) is used in the same sense in the criticism of "those who want to speak at length" (μακρολογεῖν ἐθέλοντες) in Galen (ch. VIII, p. 748.8 [Kühn]). What are we to understand by "genealogies"? Is the commonly heard alternative between Gnostic enumerations of aeons and Jewish, Biblical speculations adequately formulated in this way? Philo (*Vit. Mos.* 2.45–47) designates a portion of the historical presentation of the Pentateuch as "genealogical matters" (γενεαλογικόν): "One division of the historical side deals with the creation of the world, the other with genealogical matters, and this last partly with the punishment of the impious, partly with the honouring of the just." (ἔστιν οὖν τοῦ ἱστορικοῦ τὸ μὲν περὶ τῆς τοῦ κόσμου γενέσεως, τὸ δὲ γενεαλογικόν, τοῦ δὲ γενεαλογικοῦ τὸ μὲν περὶ κολάσεως ἀσεβῶν, τὸ δ' αὖ περὶ τιμῆς δικαίων) [Loeb modified]. The word is not

---

6   See below, pp. 124f, the exursus to 2 Tim 4:21.

7   See Ernst Findlay Scott, *The Pastoral Epistles* (London: Hodder & Stoughton, 1936), p. XX.

8   Friedrich Schleiermacher, *Sendschreiben an J. C. Gass: Über den sog. ersten Brief des Paulos an den Timotheos* (Berlin: Realschulbuchhandlung, 1807); also in his *Sämtliche Werke*, vol. 1, Pt. 2 (1836), pp. 221ff.

9   See the Introduction, Section 2, on the Pastorals as epistles; see also Appendices 1 and 2.

10   See the Introduction, Section 1, and below p. 65, the exursus to 1 Tim 4:5.

11   Plato, *Tim.* 22a; cf. further Polybius 9.2.1 (*FGRH* I:47f).

12   See further 2 Petr 1:16; also Hans Windisch, *Die katholischen Briefe*, HNT 15 (Tübingen: J. C. B. Mohr [Paul Siebeck], ³1951), *ad loc.*; see also *2 Clem.* 13:3 and cf. below on 1 Tim 4:7.

13   This seems to be the opinion of Friedrich Büchsel,

used here to designate a literary genre,[13] but rather refers only to the content. Moreover there is no corresponding "mythological part" (μυθολογικόν)—which is an impossibility for Philo. Since the genealogies are mentioned together with "myths," they cannot, in this passage, refer to the Jewish proof for kinship of Abraham, nor to the demonstration of Israel's historical continuity. Neither Paul nor a pseudo–Paul could mention such things in the same breath with "fables." Kittel has pointed out that in post–exilic Judaism genealogical speculations about Biblical persons led to discussions which could under certain circumstances be regarded as heretical, in view of their criticism of Biblical accounts.[14] That Christians too could be involved in these discussions is shown by *Baba Batra* 91a, where statements are made about the mothers of the men of the OT: "Why does one have to know about that? To answer the *Minim* (that is, the heretics)." To be sure, in the Pastorals it is not a question of debates within the frame of (rabbinic) interpretation of scripture, as the whole controversy shows, but rather of a gnosticizing Judaism. (Cf. Tit 1:14; 3:9 on the one hand; 1 Tim 4:3; 6:20; 2 Tim 2:18; Tit 1:16 on the other.). Gnosticizing interpretations in which Old Testament genealogical registers are understood mythologically (Iren. *Adv. haer.* 1.30.9) and, moreover, mythical speculations about sequences of principalities and aeons are as fundamental to the theology of Gnosticism (see below the excursus to 1 Tim 4:5) as they are destructive to the belief in the divine education for salvation (οἰκονομία) which is held by the writer of the Pastorals. To be sure, Irenaeus and Tertullian are wrong to refer such passages from the Pastorals to the advanced Gnosticism of their time; they naturally took the statements as prophecy. Cf. Iren. *Adv. haer.* 1, Preface 1: "Inasmuch as certain men have set the truth aside, and bring in lying words and vain genealogies, which, as the apostle says, 'minister questions rather than godly edifying which is in faith' . . . 2 . . . I have deemed it my duty (after reading some of the *Commentaries*, as

they call them, of the disciples of Valentinus . . . .)" (ἐπὶ τὴν ἀλήθειαν παραπεμπόμενοί τινες ἐπεισάγουσι λόγους ψευδεῖς καὶ γενεαλογίας ματαίας, αἵτινες ζητήσεις μᾶλλον παρέχουσι, καθὼς ὁ ἀπόστολός φησιν, ἢ οἰκοδομὴν θεοῦ τὴν ἐν πίστει . . . 2 . . . ἀναγκαῖον ἡγησάμην, ἐντυχὼν τοῖς ὑπομνήμασι τῶν, ὡς αὐτοὶ λέγουσιν, Οὐαλεντίνου μαθητῶν). [15] Cf. also Tertullian, *Praescr. haer.* 33. Rather, we must think of early Jewish or Judaizing forms of Gnosticism, which are reflected elsewhere within the horizon of deutero–Pauline literature.[16] Characteristic are: speculations about the elements, but no systematic cosmology; a tendency towards soteriological dualism and the observation of ascetic rules. All this applies to the false teachers opposed by the Pastorals; a similar picture emerges from the epistles of Ignatius. Thus we may view the different reproaches ("teachers of the law," "ritualists," "Jews," "Gnostics," and "speculators") as forming a unified picture. A surprising parallel, which points in the same direction, is found in the *Manual of Discipline* from Qumran: "For the man of understanding, that he instruct and teach all the sons of light concerning the succession of the generations of all the sons of men, all the spirits which they possess with their distinctive characters; their works with classes; and the visitation with which they are smitten, together with the times when they are blessed."[17]

"Speculations" (ἐκζητήσεις or ζητήσεις as MSS D G read) is meant contemptuously: "to rack one's brain." The opposite would be well expressed by "building up" (οἰκοδομήν D* lat Iren Ambst). The more surprising term "economy" (οἰκονομίαν), which is better attested and therefore perhaps preferable, refers either to God's plan of salvation (in contrast to the "myths"), or to the education of men by God for salvation. The latter meaning is attested in Clement of Alexandria and Origen; cf. Clem. Alex. *Paed.* 1.8.69, 3 and 70, 1 (Stählin, *TDNT* IV p. 130): "Through the Prophet Amos, the Word explains His economy

　　　TDNT 1, pp. 665f. See also Jeremias, *ad loc.*
14　Gerhard Kittel, "Die γενεαλογίαι der Pastoralbriefe," *ZNW* 20 (1921): 49–69.
15　Translated by Rev. Alexander Roberts and Rev. W. H. Rambaut, *The Writings of Irenaeus*, vol. 1, in *Ante-Nicene Christian Library*, ed. Alexander Roberts and James Donaldson, vol. 5, (Edinburgh; T. & T. Clark, 1868), pp. 1f.
16　Bornkamm, "Häresie des Kolosserbriefes," 139–56;

on the Jewish origin of early Gnosticism, see Georg Kretschmar, *EvTh* 13 (1953): 354ff.
17　1 QS III, 13–15; adapted from A. Dupont–Sommer, *The Essene Writings from Qumran*, tr. G. Vermes (Cleveland, Ohio, and New York: The World Publishing Company, 1962), 77f. On the history of religions classification of the passage, cf. Karl–Georg Kuhn, "Die in Palästina gefundenen hebräischen

fully: (there follows Amos 4:11); notice how God seeks their conversion in loving kindness and, in the economy itself with which He makes His threats, sweetly reveals the love He has for men." (σαφέστατα γοῦν διὰ τοῦ Ἀμὼς τοῦ προφήτου τὴν οἰκονομίαν μεμήνυκεν ὁ λόγος τὴν ἑαυτοῦ [there follows a citation of Amos 4:11]; ὁρᾶτε πῶς ὁ θεὸς τὴν μετάνοιαν ὑπὸ φιλαγαθίας ζητεῖ ἐνδείκνυταί τε παρὰ τὴν οἰκονομίαν τῆς ἀπειλῆς ἡσυχῇ τὸ φιλάνθρωπον τὸ ἑαυτοῦ.[18] To be sure, this meaning is late and attested in a limited circle of literature, whereas for the earlier time the first meaning is general.[19] The rejection of the myths corresponds to a heightened stress upon terms which express the concept of "history of salvation." "In faith" (ἐν πίστει) is a formulaic expression; "in" (ἐν) is therefore not to be understood as instrumental ("through").

■ 5 "The purpose is" (τέλος ἐστί) corresponds to "result" (παρέχειν) of the preceding clause; τέλος ("purpose" or "goal") is common in Epictetus. Whether it refers to the factual outcome or to the intended purpose depends upon whether one understands "instructions" (παραγγελία) generally as preaching or rather as the special instruction about which v 3 spoke.[20] Since the sentence wants to characterize something in general, and since in these terms of proclamation the notions of promise and exhortation are not sharply distinguished (cf. v 18 and Tit 1:9), the expression seems to refer to the "purpose of the preaching" as opposed to the "racking of one's brain" (ζητήσεις), which is the "outcome" of the activities of the false teachers. Cf. the maxim about καλῶς and πολυτελῶς ζῆν in Epicte-

tus (Schenkl, p. 466, No. 16): "But the purpose of the former (i.e. living well) is the praise of the good, but the outcome of the latter (i.e., living sumptuously) is blame" (τέλος δὲ τοῦ μὲν [scil., καλῶς ζῆν] ἔπαινος ἀληθής, τοῦ δὲ [scil., πολυτελῶς ζῆν] ψόγος) [Trans.]; cf. also Ign. Eph. 14.1. The triad which follows shows the writer's tendency to form triadic expressions and exhibits his inclination to use edifying language. Admittedly Paul could also describe the faith and life of the Christians with a formula (see 1 Thess 1:3). By designating love as the purpose of the preaching, the author adopts a valuable thought of Paul's (see Gal. 5:6). This passage also allows the assumption that "love" (ἀγάπη) means active love: for only in this case is it possible to explain the surprising mention of "faith" (πίστις) together with "heart" (καρδία) and "conscience" (συνείδησις), among the causes of love. The expression "pure heart" (καθαρὰ καρδία) derives from the LXX. The adjective "sincere" (ἀνυπόκριτος) does not fit the Pauline conception of faith.[21] To be sure, even in Paul the use of "faith" (πίστις)shows that the word is not always fixed terminologically, but it never stands in any other triad than the familiar faith–love–hope; one cannot help noticing the transformation of faith into a human attitude.

"Good Conscience"

What the expression "good conscience" means in the Pastorals can be demonstrated in a consideration of the previous history of the word. Three problems confront one in such an attempt.

1. The first is raised by the very appearance of the term

Texte und das NT," ZThK 47 (1950): 192–211; Kurt Schubert, "Der Sektenkanon von En Feschcha und die Anfänge der jüdischen Gnosis," ThLZ 78 (1953): 495–506. Oscar Cullmann, "Die neuentdeckten Qumran–Texte und das Judenchristentum der Pseudoklementinen," in Neutestamentliche Studien für Bultmann, BZNW 21 (Berlin: Töpelmann, 1954). On "genealogies" see Friedrich Büchsel, TDNT 1, pp. 662–65; on "myth" see Gustav Stählin, TDNT 4, pp. 781–92, especially 786–89; Samuel Sandmel, "Myths, Genealogies, and Jewish Myths and the Writing of Gospels," HUCA 27 (1956): 201–11; Olof Linton, Synopsis historiae universalis (København [Lund]; 1957).

18   For further examples see Eduard Schwartz, Tatiani Oratio ad Graecos, TU 4, 1 (Leipzig: Hinrichs, 1888), Index.

19   O. Lillge, Das patristische Wort OIKONOMIA, Un-

pub. Diss. (Erlangen: 1956), and Martin Widmann, Der Begriff OIKONOMIA im Werk des Irenäus und seine Vorgeschichte, Unpub. Diss. (Tübingen: 1956).

20   Adolf Schlatter, Die Kirche der Griechen im Urteil des Paulus (Stuttgart: Calwer Verlag, ²1958) and Ceslaus Spicq, St-Paul: les épîtres pastorales, Études Bibliques (Paris: Gabalda, ⁴1969), ad loc.; Michel, "Grundfragen," p. 88; Otto Schmitz, TDNT 5, p. 764, n. 33.

21   Hermann von Soden, Die Briefe an die Kolosser, Epheser, Philemon. Die Pastoralbriefe etc. in Handcommentar zum NT 3 (Freiburg i. B. and Leipzig: J. C. B. Mohr [Paul Siebeck], ²1893), ad loc., and Bultmann, Theology 2, p. 184.

22   The comparison of the conscience with the Furies is found in Cicero (De legibus 40 and Pro Roscio Amerino 67).

23   The expression "for the sake of conscience" appears

"conscience" in the literature of antiquity. What this term describes has existed ever since the final verdict of guilt was spoken within man himself, when the true Furies were recognized as the consciousness of guilt.[22] But the word "consciousness" (σύνειδός), or "conscience" (συνείδησις), for which there is no corresponding term in the OT, does not become prominent until late, but then it becomes very prominent. It means "consciousness" (as in Josephus *Ant.* 16.100; 2 Petr 2:19; Heb 10:2), but can take on the specialized meaning "what is within man" (as in Eccl 10:20 for מַדָּע). It can also take on the connotation of moral consciousness— at first primarily the consciousness of an evil act. In this meaning, that of the witness and judge of human actions, it is still missing in early Stoicism. It appears perhaps with the Epicurean teaching, which advises against immoral behavior because of its ill effects, even those within man himself. Notably, Stoicism too fails to define the term further, but it appears quite frequently from the first century on, also in formulaic expressions.[23] All these observations suggest that the term derives from the vernacular language and from there was taken up into the language of philosophical ethics.[24] The way in which the term came into Hellenistic Judaism (with the two nuances: consciousness of one's self and a judgmental self–consciousness) is shown by Wisd Sol 17:10 which stands in close proximity to the passage from Josephus *Ant.* 16.103 mentioned above.

2. The expression "good conscience" is even more problematic. The subject matter is present when one speaks of the consciousness of a life lived according to one's destiny (Epict. *Diss.* 3.22.94: τὸ συνειδός) or the consciousness of having fulfilled the Law (Josephus *Ap.* 2.218: τὸ συνειδός). Outside of the NT the expression "good conscience" established itself in Greek only gradually. The sayings which Stobaeus (*Ecl.* 3.24, p. 603f, ed. Hense) ascribes to Bias and Periander which praise the "correct" (ὀρθή) or "good conscience" (ἀγαθὴ συνείδησις) are late. In Philo *Spec. Leg.* 1, 203

someone asserts his innocence "with a pure conscience" (ἐκ καθαροῦ τοῦ συνειδότος). A remark in Seneca (*De tranquillitate animi* 3.4) "secure and free is the blessing of a good conscience" (Quam tutum gratumque sit bona conscientia) can perhaps be attributed to Athenodorus, upon whom this paragraph in Seneca depends. Marcus Aurelius (6.30) says, in commending the Emperor Antoninus as an example, "that you may have as good a conscience, when your last hour comes, as he had" (ἵν' οὕτως εὐσυνειδήτῳ σοι ἐπιστῇ ἡ τελευταία ὥρα, ὡς ἐκείνῳ).[25] The word is also found in Ign. *Mag.* 4; *Phld.* 6.3 and Clem. Alex. *Strom.* 7.83.1. The sparsity of evidence is understandable when one considers the origin of the concept; conscience is first of all accuser and judge. Strangely, "good conscience" is much more frequent in Latin, where it is presupposed as a familiar expression, above all by Seneca.[26] Perhaps the cause lies in the special character of the Latin word *conscientia*, or that of Roman thought, or in the fact that the literary use of the word in Latin is closer to common usage.

3. Especially interesting is the difference in usage among the writings of the NT. In Paul (Rom 2:15) conscience appears as a general human phenomenon. At the basis of this conception lies the anthropology of popular philosophy, which was taken up into Hellenistic Judaism (conscience as self–consciousness, an authority which demands and judges). It is from this background that the nuances of Pauline usage are to be explained.[27] The conscience that judges and convicts also occurs in the Koine-text of the spurious passage John 8:9 and in Heb 9:14 (10:22). But it is necessary to distinguish clearly between this usage and the meaning of the term in the fixed formulaic expression "good conscience" (ἀγαθή, καθαρά, καλή, ἀγνή, ἀπρόσκοπος). The latter is not found in the genuine Pauline epistles (nor in the Gospels). It is only found in that portion of the early Christian literature which, in comparison to the Pauline writings, expresses a thought world both more strongly Hellenistic and closer to the vernacular, espe-

---

in Pseudo Dio Chrysostomus, *Oratio Corinthiaca* 34; Ditt. *Or.*, II, 484.37; Rom 13:5.

24   On the origin of the word in Greek, see Bruno Snell's review of Friedrich Zucker, *Syneidesis–Conscientia*, in *Gnomon* 6 (1930): 21–30.

25   The translation is by G. Long in *The Stoic and Epicurean Philosophers*, ed. W. J. Oates (New York: Random House, 1940).

26   *Epistulae morales* 12.9 and 43.5 (*mala* and *bona conscientia*); cf. *De clementia* 1.1.1; *Epistulae morales* 23.7 and 97.12; *De vita beata* 19.1, among others.

27   Max Pohlenz, "Paulus und die Stoa", *ZNW* 42 (1949): 77ff; Bultmann, *Theology* 1, pp. 216ff.

cially in those instances where one can see the influence of the Hellenistic synagogue and its language.[28] The opposite of "good" conscience is, according to this transformed understanding, no longer a "weak" but rather an "evil" conscience.[29] The term here implies the necessarily binding moral alternative, whereas in Paul it expresses the critical possibility of freedom in relation to the alternatives posed. The Pastorals too belong in the context of this vernacular–ecclesiastical usage of the term (1 Tim 1:5, 19; 3:9; 2 Tim 1:3 and 1 Tim 4:2; Tit 1:15). The term "good conscience" thus proves to be a characteristic sign of a particular understanding of faith which is expressed in the adoption of a typical terminology. It belongs among the qualities which characterize "Christian good citizenship."[30] It is a sign of the transformation of an unbroken eschatological understanding of the world into a view which must reckon with the fact that, for the time being, the world is going to remain as it is (and that the Christians are to exist within it). Furthermore, this view must accordingly work out lasting norms for behavior. To this extent, the critical comparison with Paul is not to be taken as a value judgment. One must bear in mind the comprehensive change in the church's situation. It is only in view of this situation that the adoption of generally acceptable ethical standards becomes understandable.[31] In a passage, which is probably dependent upon Epicurus,[32] Plutarch

praises the "soul free from evil acts and purposes" ($\psi v \chi \grave{\eta} \kappa a \theta a \rho \epsilon \acute{v} o v \sigma a \pi \rho a \gamma \mu \acute{a} \tau \omega \nu \kappa a \grave{\iota} \beta o v \lambda \epsilon v \mu \acute{a} \tau \omega \nu \pi o \nu \eta \rho \hat{\omega} \nu$) as that which "imparts calm and serenity of life" ($\epsilon \grave{v} \delta \acute{\iota} a \nu \pi a \rho \acute{\epsilon} \chi \epsilon \iota \beta \acute{\iota} \omega \kappa a \grave{\iota} \gamma a \lambda \acute{\eta} \nu \eta \nu$, De tranquillitate animi 19, p. 477A). In the same sense, the author of the Pastorals includes a good conscience among fundamental presuppositions of a peaceful Christian life. It is for him the "best pillow," as in the popular German proverb. He also has in mind the goal of a peaceful life in blessedness and respectability which he proclaims in 2:2.[33]

■ 6 "To renounce" ($\grave{a} \sigma \tau o \chi \epsilon \hat{\iota} \nu$) is obviously used in a very active sense.[34] Cf. in biblical usage Sir 7:19 "Do not deprive yourself of a wise and good wife," ($\mu \grave{\eta} \grave{a} \sigma \tau \acute{o} \chi \epsilon \iota \gamma v \nu a \iota \kappa \grave{o} s \sigma o \phi \hat{\eta} s \kappa a \grave{\iota} \grave{a} \gamma a \theta \hat{\eta} s$ see also 8:9?), and as a further example, P. Oxy. II, 291.21 "I am distraught, for my rooster has failed me" ($\grave{o} \gamma \grave{a} \rho \grave{a}[\lambda]\acute{\epsilon} \kappa \tau \omega \rho \grave{\eta} \sigma \tau \acute{o} \chi \eta \kappa \acute{\epsilon} \mu o v$); and Ditt. Syll. II.543.28ff: "They have renounced . . . what benefits the fatherland as well as my own cause" ($\grave{\eta} \sigma \tau o \chi \acute{\eta} \kappa \epsilon \iota \sigma a \nu \ldots \kappa a \grave{\iota} \tau o \hat{v} \sigma v \mu \phi \acute{\epsilon} \rho o \nu \tau o s \tau \hat{\eta} \iota \pi a \tau \rho \acute{\iota} \delta \iota \kappa a \grave{\iota} \tau \hat{\eta} s \grave{\epsilon} \mu \hat{\eta} s \kappa \rho \acute{\iota} \sigma \epsilon \omega s$) "To run after" ($\grave{\epsilon} \kappa \tau \rho \acute{\epsilon} \pi \epsilon \sigma \theta a \iota$) occurs frequently in the Pastorals; see also Philo: "They fail of necessity to see the road before them and wander away into pathless wilds . . ." ($\tau \grave{\eta} \nu \grave{a} \gamma o v \sigma a \nu \grave{o} \delta \grave{o} \nu o \grave{v} \chi \grave{o} \rho \hat{\omega} \nu \tau \epsilon s \epsilon \grave{\iota} s \grave{a} \nu o \delta \acute{\iota} a s \grave{\epsilon} \kappa \tau \rho \acute{\epsilon} \pi o \nu \tau a \iota$, Spec. leg. 2.23). See also Epict. Diss. 1.6.42. The rarity of these words in the NT does not at all correspond

---

28 Acts 23:1; 24:16 (in the speeches of Paul); 1 Petr 3:16, 21; Heb 13:18; then *1 Clem.* 1.3 (in rules for the household: to the women); Pol. *Phil.* 5.3 (in rules for the household: to virgins); *1 Clem.* 41.1; 45.7; *2 Clem.* 16.4; cf. Ign. *Tr.* 7.2.

29 In contrast to this understanding, cf. 1 Cor 8:7; Heb 10:2, 22; *Barn.* 19.12; *Did.* 4.14 and *Herm. mand.* 3.4.

30 See below pp. 39ff, the second excursus to 1 Tim 2:2, and Bultmann, *Theology* 2, pp. 217f.

31 The German original speaks of "bürgerliche Ethik."

32 See section 1 above in the present excursus; the case for dependency is argued by Max Pohlenz in his article, "Plutarchs Schrift ΠΕΡΙ ΕΤΘΥΜΙΑΣ," *Hermes* 40 (1905): 275–300.

33 On conscience cf. the following: Martin Kähler, *Das Gewissen* 1 (Halle: Fricke, 1878); Martin Pohlenz's review of Adolf Bonhöffer, *Epiktet und das Neue Testament*, in *GGA* 11 (Nov. 13, 1913): 633–50; H. Böhlig, "Das Gewissen bei Seneca und Paulus," *ThStKr* 37 (1914): 1ff; Friedrich Zucker, *Syneidesis–Conscientia*, Jenaer Akademische Reden 6 (1928); Bruno Snell's review of Zucker's work in *Gnomon* 6 (1930): 21–30; Gunnar Rudberg, "Ur Samvetets

Historia" in *Studier och tankar tillaegnade J. A. Eklund paa hans sjuttioaarsdag den 7 Januari* 1933 (Stockholm: Svenska Kyrkans Diakonistyrelses Bokförlag, 1933), 165ff; Ceslaus Spicq, "La conscience dans le Nouveau Testament," *RB* 47 (1938): 50–80; Spicq, *ad loc.* excursus II (pp. 29ff); further literature in Spicq, *ad loc.*, and Walter Bauer, *A Greek–English Lexicon*, tr. W. F. Arndt and F. W. Gingrich (Chicago: University of Chicago Press, 1957, 1965), *s.v.*; Johannes Stelzenberger, *Die Beziehungen der frühchristlichen Sittenlehre zur Ethik der Stoa* (München: Hueber, 1933); Jacques Dupont, O.S.B., "Syneideis aux origines de la nation chrétienne de conscience morale," *Studia Hellenistica* 5 (1948): 119–53; Otto Seel, "Zur Vorgeschichte des Gewissen–Begriffs im altgriechischen Denken," *Festschrift Franz Dornseiff* (Leipzig: 1953), 291–319; C. A. Pierce, *Conscience in the New Testament* (London: S. C. M. Press, 1955); Johannes Stelzenberger, *Syneidesis im Neuen Testament* (Paderborn: Schöningh, 1961); Christian Maurer, *TWNT* 7, pp. 897–918.

34 Cf. the use of "to deny" ($\grave{a} \rho \nu \epsilon \hat{\iota} \sigma \theta a \iota$) in 2 Tim 2:12; Tit 1:16 and 2:12; both together in *2 Clem* 17.7.

to their usage in Koine Greek. Rather, the language of the Pastorals has here enriched the NT with good Greek expressions, as it does elsewhere. "Foolish talk" ($\mu\alpha$-$\tau\alpha\iota o\lambda o\gamma\iota\alpha$) and "the foolish talker" ($\mu\alpha\tau\alpha\iota o\lambda\acute{o}\gamma os$, Tit 1:10) also belong to the higher Koine.[35] Note also the widespread usage of the catchword "foolish" ($\mu\acute{\alpha}\tau\alpha\iota os$) in Hellenistic Judaism and Christianity: it is used to characterize idol worship, and thus occurs in connection with conversion (Acts 14:15; 1 Petr 1:18); to describe worldliness (*1 Clem.* 7:2; Pol. *Phil.* 2.1 and 8.2); it is also used in parenesis (Jas 1:26; 2 Petr 2:18).[36] Here, as in 1:4, 7b and 6:20, one feels strongly the difference between the Pastorals and the Pauline epistles in the style of the polemic. The Pastorals almost entirely avoid describing the opponents; they only want to combat them, and indeed with the same reproaches which the popular philosopher directs at his opponent. This fact is fundamental for the evaluation of the anti-heretical purpose of the Pastorals (see below, the excursus to 4:5, section 2), and is also important for the exegesis of the following sentence, verse 7.

■ **7** Fixed forms of polemical style have been developed early. The Pastorals are representative of an early stage of this style. It is characteristic to speak of disloyal and questionable persons as "some" (cf. *1 Clem.* 1.1 and 47.6); this is foreshadowed in Paul (Rom 3:8; 1 Cor 4:18; 5:1, 22; 2 Cor 3:1 etc.). One can see the parenetic char-

acter of this way of speaking in Heb 10:25; from the latter passage the use of this stylistic feature in the heresy polemic can be easily understood (cf. Jude 4). Ignatius offers many parallels.[37] In the Pastoral Epistles, 1 Tim 6:10, 21 should be mentioned in this connection, as well as v 19 in the chapter under discussion, where we also find the giving of examples as a further typical feature of this polemical style (cf. 2 Tim 2:17f). The untenability of the opponents' position is demonstrated by reference to its representatives. We must be cautious, however, in drawing conclusions as to the specifics of their position.[38] It may be assumed that the designation $\nu o\mu o\delta\iota\delta\acute{\alpha}\sigma\kappa\alpha\lambda o\iota$ implies the typical interweaving of speculation and ascetic observance which is related to an appeal to the OT. This is the simplest way of explaining the formulation of the reproach in v 7 and the positive answer in v 8.[39] Although Judaizing demands concerning the law are nowhere attacked, "Jewish myths" and ascetic commands (4:3) are.[40] The meaning of the reproach in v 7b can be derived from v 8; cf. Epict. *Diss.* 2.1.25, where the philosopher calls to the many "who say 'Only the free can be educated' " ($o\acute{\iota}$ $\lambda\acute{\epsilon}\gamma o\upsilon\sigma\iota$ $\mu\acute{o}\nu o\iota s$ $\acute{\epsilon}\xi\epsilon\hat{\iota}\nu\alpha\iota$ $\pi\alpha\iota\delta\epsilon\acute{\upsilon}\epsilon\sigma\theta\alpha\iota$ $\tau o\hat{\iota}s$ $\acute{\epsilon}\lambda\epsilon\upsilon\theta\acute{\epsilon}\rho o\iota s$) in a scornful tone: "How then shall we any longer trust you, O dearest lawgivers?" ($\pi\hat{\omega}s$ $o\hat{\upsilon}\nu$ $\acute{\epsilon}\tau\iota$ $\acute{\upsilon}\mu\hat{\iota}\nu$ $\pi\iota\sigma\tau\epsilon\acute{\upsilon}\sigma o\mu\epsilon\nu$, $\hat{\omega}$ $\phi\acute{\iota}\lambda\tau\alpha\tau o\iota$ $\nu o\mu o\theta\acute{\epsilon}\tau\alpha\iota$).

---

35   See Vettius Valens, ed. Wilhelm Kroll, Index. Cf.
     Corp. Herm. 14.4 (Nock, Vol. II, p. 223): "therefore,
     putting aside all verbosity and vain discourse, we
     must hold to [these two concepts] etc." ($\delta\iota\grave{o}$ $\tau\hat{\eta}s$
     $\pi o\lambda\upsilon\lambda o\gamma\acute{\iota}\alpha s$ $\tau\epsilon$ $\kappa\alpha\grave{\iota}$ $\mu\alpha\tau\alpha\iota o\lambda o\gamma\acute{\iota}\alpha s$ $\acute{\alpha}\pi\alpha\lambda\lambda\alpha\gamma\acute{\epsilon}\nu$-
     $\tau\alpha s$ $\chi\rho\grave{\eta}$ $\nu o\epsilon\hat{\iota}\nu$ $\kappa\tau\lambda$.) [Trans.].
36   See the attestations in Bauer, *s.v.*; Otto Bauernfeind,
     TDNT 4, pp. 519–22.
37   Ign. *Eph.* 7.1; 9.1; *Mag.* 4.1; 8.1; *Tr.* 10.1; *Phld.* 7.1;
     8.2. The last named passage shows, in comparison
     with *Phld.* 2.2, that we may not draw hasty con-
     clusions as to the number of people addressed as
     "some" (cf. Rom 3:3).
38   On the whole question see Bauer, *Orthodoxy and Her-*

     esy; the historical consequences are discussed on
     pp. 61ff.
39   This statement contradicts the 2d German ed. of
     this commentary, where Dibelius wrote: "$\nu o\mu o$-
     $\delta\iota\delta\acute{\alpha}\sigma\kappa\alpha\lambda os$ (teacher of the law) does not mean for
     our author a history–of–religions category, but
     rather a value judgment in Paul's sense. . . ." It also
     contradicts Friedrich Büchsel, *TDNT* 1, pp. 662–
     65, and Karl Heinrich Rengstorf, *TDNT* 2, p. 159.
40   But see below on Tit 1:10ff.

1

The Gospel Entrusted to Paul

8   **But we know: the law is good, if one knows how to use it according to the law (or: appropriately), 9/ that is, in the recognition that the law is not for the righteous, but for people who live without the law and without obedience, impious people and sinners, people who are wicked and godless, patricides and matricides, murderers, 10/ fornicators, pederasts, kidnappers, liars, perjurors— and whatever else goes against the sound teaching. 11/ (Of this we are sure) according to the Gospel of the majesty of the blessed God which has been entrusted to me. 12/ I am thankful to our Lord Jesus Christ, who makes me strong, that he has given me his confidence and designated me for service.**

■ **8**   The author reproduces literally a phrase from Paul's reflections on the law (see Rom 7:16, 12), and introduces it with the phrase "we know" ($o\check{\iota}\delta\alpha\mu\epsilon\nu$) as an acknowledged principle. But the specific Pauline teaching about the law is missing. The law does not serve to disclose the paradoxical situation of man without faith. That the law is good is said unconditionally in Paul, but here only with qualifications. The play on words shows how the understanding of the law has been transformed. There is an order in life, which is a matter of course for decent people; the others rightfully experience it as compulsion. The connection with a view of the state, as presented in Rom 13:1ff, is clear.[1] Taken by itself, a positive exposition of the "lawful use" ($\nu o\mu\acute{\iota}\mu\omega\varsigma\ \chi\rho\tilde{\eta}\sigma\theta\alpha\iota$), as we find it in 2 Tim 3:16f, might have followed.

V 9 introduces instead a further, well-known principle, which implies something entirely different from the preceding clause. The tension results from the fact that, both times, the writer takes up common expressions.

The connecting thought may lie in the allusion to the theory of the state, a new principle found in Stoicism.[2] In the golden age no law was required.[3] The author can now use the content of the law in order to characterize his opponents; at the same time he has safeguarded himself from a possible antinomian misunderstanding.

The analysis of vss 7–9 given here can be challenged from two viewpoints. Whoever considers the Pastorals genuine will evaluate these principles by analogy with other passages in Paul. In the people attacked here he may perhaps even recognize affinities with other opponents of Paul.[4] But whoever sees in the words "the law is good" ($\kappa\alpha\lambda\grave{o}\varsigma\ \acute{o}\ \nu\acute{o}\mu o\varsigma$) an antithesis, will take the position that the opponents are antinomians,[5] The expression "teachers of the law" ($\nu o\mu o\delta\iota\delta\acute{\alpha}\sigma\kappa\alpha\lambda o\iota$) speaks against this assumption, not to mention 1 Tim 4:1ff.

■ **9, 10**   This is a catalogue of vices.[6] In the passage under discussion it is remarkable that only serious and

---

1   On the history of this kind of parenesis and its relation to tradition see Martin Dibelius, "Rom und die Christen im ersten Jahrhundert," *Botschaft und Geschichte* 2 (Tübingen: J. C. B. Mohr [Paul Siebeck], 1956), 178f.

2   Cf. *SVF* 3, p. 519; Max Pohlenz, *Die Stoa* (Göttingen: Vandenhoeck & Ruprecht, 1948f), 1, p. 133, and 2, p. 75.

3   Ovid, *Metamorphoses* 1.89f, and Tacitus, *Annales* 3.26. There is a variation of this theme applied to pre–Mosaic times (Irenaeus *Adv. haer.* 4.16.3).

4   See Wilhelm Lütgert, *Die Irrlehrer der Pastoralbriefe*, BFTh 13, 3 (Gütersloh: Bertelsmann, 1909). Against

this view see section 1 (on the heretics) of the Introduction.

5   Ferdinand Christian Baur, *Die sogenannten Pastoralbriefe des Apostels Paulus aufs neue kritisch untersucht* (Stuttgart and Tübingen: Cotta, 1835), 15.

6   On catalogues of vices in general see the excursus on Rom 1:31 in Hans Lietzmann, *An die Römer*, HNT 8 (Tübingen: J. C. B. Mohr [Paul Siebeck], ⁴1933); Anton Vögtle, *Die Tugend– und Lasterkataloge im Neuen Testament* (Münster i. W.: Aschendorff, 1936).

unusual crimes are mentioned. This is to be explained on the basis of the style of such lists. They are intended to have the effect of posters. [7] For this reason patricides and matricides are mentioned in such catalogues. Since the listing of virtues and vices in tabular form is a widespread form of presentation, one must not see the list as referring to actual contemporary events or as closely related to the historical or fictitious situation of the Epistle. As far as the order is concerned, the linking in this passage of crimes against gods, "wicked and godless people" (ἀνόσιοι, βέβηλοι), with those against parents is consistent with long–established usage. Polygnotus's picture of the descent (κατάβασις) of Odysseus in Delphi represents patricides and temple desecrators (Pausanias 10.28.4f). [8] As in this passage, so also in Plato, murder is added to other crimes named. [9] "Kidnappers" (ἀνδραποδιστής) in the passage under discussion is perhaps to be regarded as a special kind of theft. Notice the parallelism which occurs occasionally between "kidnappers" (ἀνδραποδιστής) and "cloth–stealers" (λωποδύτης), cf. Demosthenes 4.47 and Polybius 13.6.4. Admittedly, the specific form of the catalogue is not to be explained from the lists of crimes given. [10] Beginning with the fourth in the sequence, the list coincides with the Decalogue. [11] The coincidence is even clearer when one bears in mind the rabbinic interpretation of the Eighth Commandment (by rabbinic count) as applied to kidnapping. (See Hermann Strack and Paul Billerbeck, *Kommentar zum Neuen Testament aus Talmud und Midrasch* [Munich: Beck, 1961], vol. 1, pp. 810ff). In addition to the passages from ancient Greek literature cited under "kidnapper" (ἀνδραποδιστής), cf. also the following from the OT and Judaism: Exod. 21:17; Deut. 24:7; Philo (*Spec. leg.* 4.13): "the kidnapper too is a kind of thief who steals the best of all the things that exist on the earth."

(κλέπτης δὲ τίς ἐστι καὶ ὁ ἀνδραποδιστής, ἀλλὰ τοῦ πάντων ἀρίστου, ὅσα ἐπὶ γῆς εἶναι συμβέβηκεν). One must recognize, however, that it is precisely the unique features of this passage which cannot be derived from the Decalogue: the form of a catalogue, the division into four double members and four single members, and the typical catechetical phrase at the end of the list. At the very least we are dealing with a Hellenistic transformation of Jewish ethics; cf. the similar phrases, which only seem to be references to the Decalogue, in the list in Pseudo–Phocylides 3ff: "Not to commit adultery, nor excite a man to love. | Not to contrive plots, nor stain one's hands with blood. | Not to become rich at the expense of justice, but to gain one's livelihood from honest things, | nor to receive a profit or take what belongs to others." (μήτε γαμοκλοπέειν, μητ' ἄρσενα κύπριν ὀρίνειν. | μήτε δόλους ῥάπτειν, μηθ' αἵματι χεῖρα μιαίνειν. | μὴ πλουτεῖν ἀδίκως, ἀλλ' ἐξ ὁσίων βιοτεύειν, | ἀρκεῖσθαι παρεοῦσι καὶ ἀλλοτρίων ἀπέχεσθαι) [Trans.]. That the construction of the Decalogue was not considered normative is also evident from a comparison of LXX Bar 4:17 with 8:5 and 13:4: The order of the commandments is very loose. The catechetical conclusion is also found here (in the NT compare, e.g., Gal 5:21; Rom 13:9 and 1 Petr 5:5). Considered as a whole, the material collected by Lietzmann and Vögtle (see above) indicates that the early Christian catalogues are an adaptation of Hellenistic–Jewish parenesis. The catalogue form is not found in the writings of rabbinic Judaism. This fact makes it even more interesting that a double catalogue also appears in the *Manual of Discipline* from the Dead Sea (1 QS III.15ff). In the clause which rounds out the catalogue in 1 Tim, the term "to be sound," which is so characteristic of the Pastoral Epistles, occurs for the first time.

---

7   Cf. the "Reproach of Ballio the Procurer" in the *Pseudolus* of Plautus (Adolf Deissmann, *Light from the Ancient East*, tr. Lionel R. M. Strachan [New York: George H. Doran, 1927], p. 316f) and Albrecht Dieterich, *Nekyia* (Leipzig: B. G. Teubner, 1893), p. 161.

8   On the connection between worship of gods and parents see Dibelius–Greeven, *Kolosser, Epheser, Philemon*, on Eph 6:1ff.

9   "Sacrilege, murderers, patricides, matricides" (ἱεροσυλία ἀνδροφόνοι πατρολοῖαι μητρολοῖαι) are mentioned in a row (*Phaed.* 113e, 114a). See also the following passage from the *Resp.* (10.615c): "and

he had still greater requitals to tell of piety and impiety towards the gods and parents and of self–slaughter." (εἰς δὲ θεοὺς ἀσεβείας τε καὶ εὐσεβείας καὶ γονέας καὶ αὐτόχειρος φόνου μείζους ἔτι τοὺς μισθοὺς διηγεῖτο).

10   See Vögtle, *Tugend– und Lasterkataloge*, 234f, who, to be sure, attempts to come to an understanding of the form from the context of the epistle. How can this be done?

11   This coincidence has recently been emphasized by Jeremias, *ad loc.*, and Wolfgang Nauck, *Die Herkunft des Verfassers der Pastoralbriefe*, Unpub. Diss. (Göttingen: 1950).

The Terms "To Be Sound" (ὙΓΙΑΙΝΕΙΝ) and "Sound" (ὙΓΙΗΣ)

"To be sound" and "sound" (ὑγιαίνειν, ὑγιής), as terms which characterize the content of Christian preaching, do not occur anywhere else in the NT. In the Pastorals they are frequently used: "sound teaching" (ὑγιαίνουσα διδασκαλία, 1 Tim 1:10; 2 Tim 4:3; Tit 1:9; 2:1), "sound words" (ὑγιαίνοντες λόγοι, 1 Tim 6:3; 2 Tim 1:13), "to be sound in faith" (ὑγιαίνειν [ἐν] τῇ πίστει, Tit 1:13; 2:2), "sound preaching" (λόγος ὑγιής, Tit 2:8). But cf. also Justin, *Dial.* 3.3: "(to be ruled by reason . . .) in order to recognize that the others are in error and that, in their undertakings, they do nothing sound or pleasing to God." (καθορᾶν τὴν τῶν ἄλλων πλάνην καὶ τὰ ἐκείνων ἐπιτηδεύματα, ὡς οὐδὲν ὑγιὲς δρῶσιν οὐδὲ θεῷ φίλον) [trans. by Ed.].

The singular use of these words in the Pauline literature would offer no problem were it a question either of things which had no further importance for the content of the writings in which they occur, or of formulas coined *ad hoc*.

1. The first condition does not apply, for the Pastorals designate with "sound teaching" (ὑγιαίνουσα διδασκαλία) or "sound words" (ὑγιαίνοντες λόγοι) the loftiest and holiest things they know: the true faith, the true message about faith. According to the Pauline use of language one could (e.g. in 1 Tim 6:3) substitute a phrase containing the term "gospel" (εὐαγγέλιον). We must assume that it is highly unlikely that in his old age Paul would have designated his gospel with other formulas—unless he had to formulate new expressions to meet new situations. But the basic terms of the Pastorals are *not* applied to an actual situation.

2. Therefore the second condition is not fulfilled either. Such a use of "to be sound" (ὑγιαίνειν) and its cognates is ancient (ὑγιὴς μῦθος, λόγος occur in Homer and Herodotus) and was widespread in the philosophical terminology of the time. Therefore one must not read into these passages an original poetic viewpoint, e.g. that

the word "sound," "healthy," is intended to describe the power of the gospel to bring healing and life. Nor is it possible to be content with the assumption that the expressions in question were coined for the purposes of the heresy polemic. Rather we must understand them as they must have been understood by the original readers. In referring to the two speeches which say things about Eros which are wrong, Plato writes "for while they were saying nothing sound or true, they put on airs as though they amounted to something" (τὸ μηδὲν ὑγιὲς λέγοντε μηδὲ ἀληθὲς σεμνύνεσθαι ὡς τὶ ὄντε, *Phaedr.* 242e). In Epictetus the adjective and adverb "sound" (ὑγιής, ὑγιῶς) designate the correct, because reasonable opinion.[12] The phrase "nothing sound" (οὐδὲν ὑγιές) is common in the writings of Lucian.[13] In his usage, the term means "nothing that makes any sense." Cf. also "(the grain) is correctly deposited into the earth" (καταθήσεται εἰς τὴν γῆν ὑγιῶς *P. Oxy.* 1024.33); ". . . the truth and the sound teaching, and virtue, and the knowledge of the righteous law" (. . . ἀλήθειάν γε καὶ ὑγιῆ λόγον, καὶ ἀρετήν, καὶ γνῶσιν νόμου δίκης Maximus of Tyre 16.3f) [trans. by Ed.]; "but the standards you use are not sound" (σὺ δὲ κριτηρίοις χρώμενος οὐχ ὑγιέσιν, Philo *Cher.* 36) [trans. by Ed.]; ". . . had you with a healthy resolve come to be trained" (εἰ ἀπὸ γνώμης ὑγιοῦς ἐπὶ τὴν ἄσκησιν ἦλθες, Philo, *Det. pot. ins.* 10); "These opinions . . . do not belong to sound doctrine" (ταῦτα τὰ δόγματα . . . οὐκ ἔστιν ὑγιοῦς γνώμης, Irenaeus, *ad Florinus*, in Eusebius, *Hist. eccl.* 5.20.4); "For people of sound judgment were very glad about the generosity of the Romans" (οἱ μὲν γὰρ ὑγιαίνοντες περιχαρεῖς ἦσαν ἐπὶ τῇ φιλανθρωπίᾳ τῶν Ῥωμαίων, Polybius 28.17.12) [trans. by Ed.]; "For these are the sound and true opinions about the gods" (αὗται γάρ εἰσιν ὑγιαίνουσαι περὶ θεῶν δόξαι καὶ ἀληθεῖς, Plutarch, *Aud. poet.* 4) [trans. by Ed.]; "That it is no sound inference to infer . . . that our hero was a wizard . . ." (ὅτι τοῖς γόητα τὸν ἄνδρα ἡγουμένοις οὐχ ὑγιαίνει ὁ λόγος, Philostratus, *Vit. Ap.* 5.12); "It is

---

12 Cf. e.g. Epict., *Diss.* 1.11.28 "if indeed what is said by the philosophers is sound" (εἴπερ ὑγιές ἐστι τὸ ὑπὸ τῶν φιλοσόφων λεγόμενον); 2.15.2 "but first what is judged ought to be sound [or reasonable]" (ἀλλὰ πρῶτον ὑγιὲς εἶναι δεῖ τὸ κεκριμένον); 3.9.5 "Do we therefore all have sound opinions, including you and your opponent?" (ἆρ' οὖν πάντες ἔχομεν ὑγιῆ δόγματα καὶ σὺ καὶ ὁ ἀντίδικός

σου;) [trans. by Ed.].

13 See The *Index* of Lucianus Samosatensis, *Opera*, 3 vol., ed. by Carl Jacobitz (Leipzig: Teubner, 1874–77).

necessary to treat (those of the female sex) rationally and not to allow oneself to become engaged in a quarrel" (δέον δ' ἐστὶ κατὰ τὸ ὑγιὲς χρῆσθαι καὶ μὴ πρὸς ἔριν ἀντιπράσσειν, *Ep. Ar.* 250) [Trans.]. There are some passages which contrast the "healthy" opinion with "sick" views, thus retaining the original vividness of the imagery: "to follow impulses which were healthy and did not cause disease" (ὑγιαινούσαις καὶ ἀνόσοις ὁρμαῖς ἐπακολουθῆσαι, Philo, *Abr.* 275) [trans. by Ed.]; "the passions and diseases still prevailed over the healthy principles" (ἔτι τῶν παθῶν καὶ νοσημάτων παρευημερούντων τοὺς ὑγιαίνοντας λόγους, Philo, *Abr.* 223) [Loeb modified]. Therefore, if the Pastoral Epistles were Paul's work, Paul would have had to use these common expressions designating rational speech and opinions with reference to his gospel. That is very improbable, since nothing of the sort appears in the genuine epistles.

3. This point is related to a third observation. The "sound teaching" (ὑγιαίνουσα διδασκαλία) is foreign, not only to Paul's language but also to his Christianity. To be sure, elements of rational argumentation, "natural" theology and ethics are found also in Paul (Rom 1:19ff and Phil 4:8). But this does not alter the fact that rationality does not provide the primary structure for his Christian thinking; on the contrary, his Christianity is pneumatic throughout—so that he can contrast it to wisdom as foolishness and base his ethics upon the revelatory character of the commandment (cf. Rom 13:9 with this passage), elaborating obedience as a structural element of faith.[14] Anyone who wishes the Pastorals to be regarded as Pauline epistles must ask himself seriously whether he is not paying too high a price for the assumption of authenticity, if this implies mitigating or eliminating an essential element in the thinking of the true Paul in order to adjust Paul's image to that of the Pastorals.

4. On the other hand one cannot quite ascribe "rationalism" to the Pastorals. The formal designation of the teaching as "sound" is made concrete by the ideal which applies in each case.[15] In the passage 1 Tim 1:10, the next verse provides the concrete criterion: the gospel which is a firm part of the church's teaching tradition. There is some shift toward rationalism, inasmuch as the gospel has become a principle which can be applied. It is the kind of rationalism which is widely documented in the post–Apostolic literature.[16] The dialectic of wisdom and foolishness has been replaced by the correspondence of mystery and proclamation.

■ **11** is a clause which rounds out the passage (like Rom 2:16) and provides a transition to the personal reference (as in Eph 3:7); the Pastorals repeat such expressions frequently.[17] That "majesty" (δόξα) is the content of Paul's gospel is also said in 2 Cor 4:4, 6 and Col 1:27. This usage apparently reflects liturgical style.[18] "Blessed" (μακάριος) is here (as in 1 Tim 6:15) a predicate of the deity; it designates the sphere of the divine "incorruptibility" (ἀφθαρσία) and "true happiness" (εὐδαιμονία)[19] and may be regarded—even in Jewish writings —as a Greek admixture. Cf. the Stoic expression in Philo, "when I made its spirit my own in all its beauty and loveliness and true blessedness . . ." (τὸν καλὸν καὶ περιπόθητον καὶ μακάριον ὄντως νοῦν ἐκαρπούμην *Spec. leg.* 3.1). Cf. further "But the nature of God is without grief or fear and wholly exempt from passion of any kind, and alone partakes of perfect happiness and bliss" (ἄλυπος δὲ καὶ ἄφοβος καὶ παντὸς πάθους ἀμέτοχος ἡ τοῦ θεοῦ φύσις εὐδαιμονίας καὶ μακαριότητος παντελοῦς μόνη μετέχουσα *Abr.* 202); "For God is good, He is the maker and begetter of the universe and His providence is over what He has begotten; He is a saviour and a benefactor, and has the plenitude of all blessedness and all happiness" (ὁ γὰρ θεὸς ἀγαθός τέ ἐστι καὶ ποιητὴς καὶ γεννητὴς τῶν ὅλων καὶ προνοητικὸς ὧν ἐγέννησε, σωτήρ τε καὶ εὐεργέτης, μακαριότητος καὶ πάσης εὐδαιμονίας ἀνάπλεως *Spec. leg.* 1.209); "For God alone is happy and blessed" (μόνος

---

14 Max Pohlenz, "Paulus und die Stoa," *ZNW* 42 (1949): 77ff.
15 Cf. the passages cited above, and, as a Jewish example, Prov 31:8f.
16 See Bultmann, *Theology* 2, p. 53.
17 Cf. 1 Tim 1:15; 2:7; 2 Tim 1:11; 2:8f; Tit 1:3.
18 Note the double genitive; cf. Johannes Schneider *Doxa* (Gütersloh: Bertelsmann, 1932), 112.
19 Cf. Epicurus as cited in Diogenes Laertius 10.123 (cited at 1:17 below).

γὰρ εὐδαίμων καὶ μακάριος *Spec. leg.* 2.53); "the Imperishable Blessed One" (ὁ ἄφθαρτος καὶ μακάριος *Deus imm.* 26); "(which may truly be called) better than the good, more excellent than the excellent, more blessed than blessedness, more happy than happiness itself, and any perfection there may be, greater than these" (τὸ κρεῖττον μὲν ἀγαθοῦ, κάλλιον δὲ καλοῦ, καὶ μακαριότητος μὲν μακαριώτερος, εὐδαιμονίας δὲ αὐτῆς εὐδαιμονέστερον, καὶ εἰ δή τι τῶν εἰρημένων τελειότερον, *Leg. Gaj.* 5). See also in Josephus: "that the universe is directed by a blessed and immortal Being, to the end that the whole of it may endure" (ὑπὸ τῆς μακαρίας καὶ ἀφθάρτου πρὸς διαμονὴν τῶν ὅλων οὐσίας κυβερνᾶσθαι τὰ σύμπαντα *Ant.* 10.278); "the universe is in God's hands; perfect and blessed" (ὁ θεὸς ἔχει τὰ σύμπαντα, παντελὴς καὶ μακάριος Josephus, *Ap.* 2.190). Thus the gifts of the Divinity are also called "blessed gifts" (μακάρια δῶρα *1 Clem.* 35.1), and "blessed" (μακάριος) can also be used to refer to the "hope" (ἐλπίς Tit 2:13).

■ 12 "I am thankful" (χάριν ἔχω) is a phrase that belongs to epistolary style; but it does not occur in the genuine Pauline epistles known to us.[20] The second half of the verse is reminiscent of 1 Cor 7:25. "Who has received confidence" (πιστός) takes up "it has been entrusted to me" (ἐπιστεύθην).[21] It is not only a question of being taken into service in general, but rather of the special calling to serve as an apostle.[22] Indeed the following statements are based on this concept. The mention of the event of revelation (see the following vss) and of the apostolic office, together form a fixed context in the Pastorals (cf. 1 Tim 2:7 and Tit 1:2f).

---

20 But cf. 2 Tim 1:3 and *P. Oxy.* I.113.13: "I am thankful to all the gods, knowing etc." (χάριν ἔχω θεοῖς πᾶσιν γινώσκων κτλ.); see also *Corp. Herm.* 6.4. [Nock, I, p. 74].

21 On the meaning "trusted person" or "delegate" see Lietzmann–Kümmel, *Korinther*, on 1 Cor. 7:25, and Bauer, *s.v.*

22 See Eduard Schweizer, *Church Order in the New Testament*, tr. Frank Clarke, STB 32 (Naperville, Ill.: Alec R. Allenson, 1961), 179.

1   **Paul, Example of God's Mercy**

13   **I, who once was a blasphemer, persecutor, and evil-doer; but I have received mercy, because I acted from ignorance in unbelief. 14/ Indeed, the grace of our Lord has been abundantly rich with faith and love in Christ Jesus. 15/ The word stands firm and deserves all recognition: "Christ Jesus came into the world, in order to save sinners." 16/ I am the first one among them. But it is precisely for this reason that I received mercy, so that Jesus Christ could show through me, as the first one, the whole extent of his forbearance, (that I might become) a prototype for all those who will in the future attain faith through fellowship with him for eternal life. 17/ But (to him), to the king of the universe, to the immortal, invisible, one God, to him be honor and glory for all eternity! Amen.**

■ **13, 14** As in 1 Cor 15:9f and Gal 1:13ff, the pre–Christian period in the life of Paul is contrasted with the Christian period. Neither in the genuine Pauline epistles nor in the Pastorals is there any interest in a psychological process. The conversion is seen exclusively from the viewpoint of contrast and from the perspective of receiving mercy.[1] The clause "because I acted etc." (ὅτι κτλ.) explains the possibility of such a pardon. This explanation is to be understood in connection with a widespread early Christian conception. The pagans are already for Paul those who "do not know God" (1 Thess 4:5).[2] Likewise, "to know God" (γινώσκειν τὸν θεόν) can designate conversion (*1 Clem.* 59.3; *2 Clem.* 17.1 and *Herm. sim.* 9.18.1). The theoretical element of knowing and the practical element of acknowledgement and moral fulfillment are combined in this terminology;[3] it originates in Hellenistic Judaism. The statement about "ignorance" (ἄγνοια) can, however, be applied in two ways: a) ignorance is guilt (cf. Acts 13:27ff); or

b) ignorance offers a relative excuse (as in Acts 27:30 and in this passage of the Pastorals). Both aspects can be combined; cf. Acts 3:17 and the interesting attempt to reconcile both aspects in Wisd Sol 13:1ff, 6ff. One must also bear in mind the common Jewish distinction between conscious and unconscious transgressions (see Billerbeck, 2, 264). It plays a major role in the *Manual of Discipline* of the sect of Qumran. See also Josephus, where the distinction is made between sinning "out of ignorance" (κατὰ ἄγνοιαν) and sinning "consciously and intentionally" (ἑαυτῷ συνειδώς, *Ant.* 3.231f). Naturally the Christians soon began to apply this characterization to Judaism. Concepts of the Greek natural theology form the ultimate background for this terminology.[4] But early Christianity did not receive these concepts directly from Hellenism, but mediated through Judaism. The explanation which the author of the Pastorals thus gives for the possibility of pardon does not mean that he denies the role of grace in the conversion. On the contrary:

---

1   On "to receive mercy," cf. Rudolf Bultmann, *TDNT* 2, pp. 477f.

2   Cf. the later stereotyped characterization of paganism as "ignorance" (ἄγνοια) in Eph 4:18; 1 Petr 1:14; Acts 17:23, 30 ("the time of ignorance" [ἄγνοια] in an absolute sense); Aristides, *Apol.* 17.3; Justin Martyr, *Apol.* 1.12.11; Athenagoras, *Suppl.* 28.2; *Kg. Pt.* 4; *Act. Pt.* 2 [Lipsius–Bonnet, 1, p. 47].

3   Bultmann, *TDNT* 1, pp. 704–08. Cf. the analogous use of "truth" (ἀλήθεια) and "error" (πλάνη), respectively.

4   See Günther Bornkamm, "The Revelation of God's Wrath," *Early Christian Experience*, tr. Paul Hammer (London: S. C. M. Press, 1969), 50ff.

"grace has been abundantly rich" ($\upsilon\pi\epsilon\rho\epsilon\pi\lambda\epsilon\acute{o}\nu\alpha\sigma\epsilon\nu$), cf. 1 Cor 15:10. Paul also likes to emphasize that grace is incommensurable, surpassing all computation and expectation.[5] Occasionally in the Pastorals (though not in Tit 2:2), "faith" ($\pi\acute{\iota}\sigma\tau\iota s$) and "love" ($\mathring{\alpha}\gamma\acute{\alpha}\pi\eta$) take the place of the early Christian triad (faith, love, hope)[6] in the depiction of the Christian's status. Such a dual formula is already indicated in Phlmn 5; Eph 1:15: 3:17; 6:23; cf. 2 Tim 1:13. There as well as here the formulaic character of the words stands out clearly, so that one must not place special stress upon the preposition "with" ($\mu\epsilon\tau\acute{\alpha}$) which connects "faith and love" with the rest of the sentence. What is meant is that grace made Paul a person who had faith and love. Faith and love have become attributes of the Christian.

The Portrayal of Paul's Conversion

The portrayal of Paul's conversion does not have a biographical effect, but rather constitutes an illustration of the well-known, edifying, preaching schema: "Once/But Now."[7] In v 13 we encounter words belonging to the common catalogue of vices;[8] only the designation "persecutor" ($\delta\iota\acute{\omega}\kappa\tau\eta s$) applies to the specific case of Paul. In view of Phil 3:4ff, it is inconceivable that the terms "blasphemer" and "evil-doer" could have been used by Paul in describing his past. 1 Tim presents a portrayal of Paul from post-apostolic times, stylized for use as a missionary paradigm.[9] Here, as in 2:7, a secondary picture of Paul is connected in a characteristic manner with the formulation of the kerygma. Two motifs intersect: a) the *typical* character of the conversion, from which even the worst of sinners may take hope, and b) the *unique* position of the apostle (cf. the following verses).

■ **15** The interpretation of this verse depends upon the understanding of its introductory phrase.

"The Word Stands Firm" (ΠΙΣΤΟΣ 'Ο ΛΟΓΟΣ)

The phrase "the word stands firm" ($\pi\iota\sigma\tau\grave{o}s$ $\acute{o}$ $\lambda\acute{o}\gamma os$) appears five times in the Pastoral Epistles: 1 Tim 1:15; 3:1; 4:9; 2 Tim 2:11; Tit 3:8 (not Tit 1:9, where $\lambda\acute{o}\gamma os$

is conditioned by $\kappa\alpha\tau\grave{\alpha}$ $\tau\grave{\eta}\nu$ $\delta\iota\delta\alpha\chi\acute{\eta}\nu$). Since "word" ($\lambda\acute{o}\gamma os$) is used in these five passages without a recognizable referent, it must mean "word," not "preaching," and $\pi\iota\sigma\tau\acute{o}s$ characterizes this word as "trustworthy." Moreover, in this passage and in 4:9 this meaning is confirmed by the parallel expression, "it deserves all recognition" ($\pi\acute{\alpha}\sigma\eta s$ $\mathring{\alpha}\pi o\delta o\chi\mathring{\eta}s$ $\mathring{\alpha}\xi\iota os$). Cf. the attestations below. The phrase therefore receives its referent only from the context; it is followed or preceded by the particular "word" ($\lambda\acute{o}\gamma os$) to which it refers. The reliability of that "word" is established by the formula "the word stands firm" ($\pi\iota\sigma\tau\grave{o}s$ $\acute{o}$ $\lambda\acute{o}\gamma os$); for a short expression like this one, so often repeated and so self-contained, must be regarded as a formula. Admittedly the question remains whether we have a quotation formula or a formula of affirmation.[10] As a rule, this formula is either preceded or followed by a clause whose content goes beyond the particular context. Almost always of more general significance, this clause shows an especially fixed character; for example, the fragment (possibly of a hymn) 2 Tim 2:11–13 which is constructed in parallelisms, or the faith-formula which follows the passage under discussion, or the aphorism preceding 1 Tim 4:8. In Tit 3:8 one can debate the extent of the quotation. But it seems credible that a quotation is contained in the section beginning with 3:3 (first person plural! see below *ad loc.*), a passage which accords completely with the parenetic tradition. It seems evident that the Pastorals already cite Christian texts in other instances, texts pertaining to the cult (1 Tim 1:17; 3:16; 6:13, 15f) and to church law (see the Introduction above, sections 2 and 3). This indicates that the Pastorals stem from a Christianity which has already found its mould. It is typical of this Christianity that it quotes truths about salvation and presents them as proven. To be sure, this does not in itself demonstrate that this formula is to be designated as a quotation-formula in the strict sense. Above all, 1 Tim 3:1 causes difficulties. It would be artificial to connect the formula with the following piece, which has to do with church law (a passage which surely comes from the tradition). Since the formula is always found in connection with statements about salvation (or faith), it probably refers to what goes before (see

5   See Gilles P:son Wetter, *Der Vergeltungsgedanke bei Paulus* (Göttingen: Vandenhoeck & Ruprecht, 1912), 126f, 155.
6   Cf. Dibelius, *Thessalonicher, Philipper*, on 1 Thess 1:3.
7   Bultmann, *Theology* 1, pp. 105f.
8   See the materials in Bauer, *s.v.*, and in the Index in Vögtle, *Tugend- und Lasterkataloge*.
9   Cf. Michel, "Grundfragen," 86.

below *ad loc.*). One would do better, therefore, to understand the formula as an affirmation: when the Pastorals
speak in coined expressions about salvation, they consistently combine this with an application to the present.
In this context a remark is added to edify and to confirm: the word is true and does not deceive. In this way
we can explain why the formula occurs in the context
of fixed tradition (likewise the unique passage Tit 1:9).
Not all quotations in the Pastorals are marked in this
way, by any means. Only a few pointed connections
between tradition and present–day application are high-
lighted in this fashion, with the encouragement of the
apostolic word.

"Trustworthy, firm" ($\pi\iota\sigma\tau\acute{o}s$) is frequently used with
"word" ($\lambda\acute{o}\gamma os$): see Rev 21:5; 22:6 (with "true"
$\dot{a}\lambda\eta\theta\iota\nu\acute{o}s$); Plato, *Tim.* 49b "to use a word that is trust-
worthy and firm" ($\pi\iota\sigma\tau\hat{\omega}\ \kappa\alpha\grave{\iota}\ \beta\epsilon\beta\alpha\acute{\iota}\omega\ \chi\rho\acute{\eta}\sigma\alpha\sigma\theta\alpha\iota$
$\lambda\acute{o}\gamma\omega$).[11] Perhaps even Jewish formulas are compar-
able; namely, expressions of affirmation. To be sure, there
is no exact corresponding expression. Cf., for example,
the prayer following the *Shema*: "true and firm, established and enduring, right, and faithful, beloved and
precious, desirable and pleasant, revered and mighty,
well–ordered and acceptable, good and beautiful is
this thy word unto us for ever and ever." (*The Authorized
Daily Prayer Book*, ed. Joseph H. Hertz [New York: Bloch
Publishing Company, 1948], p. 127). A passage from a
fragment from Qumran comes even closer: "This word is
certain to come to pass and this oracle is truth. And by
this it may be known to you that it is beyond recall."

(1 Q 27, I, 8) [Trans. from Dupont–Sommer, *Essene
Writings*, p. 327]. "Recognition" ($\dot{a}\pi o\delta o\chi\acute{\eta}$) took on a
positive nuance in the Koine. It designates the recogni-
tion which someone or something has been accorded.[12]
One must, therefore, not regard the phrase "to receive
the word" ($\dot{a}\pi o\delta\acute{\epsilon}\chi\epsilon\sigma\theta\alpha\iota\ \tau\grave{o}\nu\ \lambda\acute{o}\gamma o\nu$) as an expression
for the acceptance of the gospel (Acts 2:41; cf. Enoch
94:1), because we are dealing with common "fixed"
expressions. The double expression shows that the faith
which is the object of belief (*fides quae*) and the faith
which believes (*fides qua creditur*) are more definitely
separated than in Paul and must be brought together
again afterward.[13] From the verses which follow, one
cannot assume that the author used Gospel writings, but
rather that he is passing on phrases from the tradition
of the community. The expression "he came into the
world" ($\mathring{\eta}\lambda\theta\epsilon\nu\ \epsilon\mathring{\iota}s\ \tau\grave{o}\nu\ \kappa\acute{o}\sigma\mu o\nu$) by no means contains
the conception of preexistence, although this conception
can also be easily and naturally connected with it (3:17).
We must also count on the possibility that the author
understands it differently from the way it was originally
intended. Only other passages can give us information
about the Christology of the Pastorals. The relative
clause ("I am the first among them") forms the bridge
to the theme "Paul," which is connected with the reference to the tradition and its application (see above).

■ **16** Why Paul is represented as the "first" of the sinners

10 J. M. Bover, " 'Fidelis sermo,' " *Biblica* 19 (1938):
74–9; Nauck, *Die Herkunft*, and cf. Gerhard Kittel,
TDNT, 4, pp. 100–43, esp. pp. 117f.
11 Dionysius of Halicarnassus, *Ant. Roma.* 3.23.17; Dio
Chrys. 25.3.
12 Thus in *Inscr. Priene* 108.311 (cf. also 109.233ff) it
designates the honor that is conferred: "in order that,
henceforth, those who see that men of this sort have
come into the highest recognition, might also render
themselves eager for the well-being of the city" ($\mathring{\iota}\nu\alpha$
$[\kappa]\alpha\grave{\iota}\ o\mathring{\iota}\ \mu\epsilon\tau\grave{\alpha}\ \tau\alpha\hat{\upsilon}\tau\alpha\ \theta\epsilon\omega|\rho o\hat{\upsilon}\nu\tau\epsilon s\ \dot{\epsilon}\nu\ \dot{a}\pi o\delta o\chi\hat{\eta}\iota\ \tau\hat{\eta}\iota$
$\mu\epsilon\gamma\acute{\iota}\sigma\tau\eta\iota\ \gamma\iota\nu o\mu\acute{\epsilon}\nu o\upsilon s\ \tau o[\grave{\upsilon}s\ \tau o\iota o\acute{\upsilon}]\tau o\upsilon s|\mathring{a}\nu\delta\rho\alpha s$
$\pi\rho o\theta\acute{\upsilon}\mu o\upsilon s\ \dot{\epsilon}\alpha\upsilon\tau o\grave{\upsilon}s\ \pi\alpha\rho\alpha\sigma\kappa\epsilon\upsilon\acute{a}\zeta[\omega]\sigma\iota\nu\ \epsilon\mathring{\iota}s\ \tau\grave{\alpha}\ \tau\hat{\eta}[\iota$
$\pi\acute{o}\lambda\epsilon\iota]|\sigma\upsilon\mu\phi\acute{\epsilon}\rho o\nu\tau\alpha$) [trans. by Ed.]; cf. *ibid.*
109.170; Ditt. *Syll.* II, 799.29; 867.21 (2d century
A.D.), where the expression has the same form as
in the passage under discussion: ". . . of a man of
sincerity and worthy of all honor and recognition"
($\dot{a}\nu\delta\rho\grave{o}s\ \delta o\kappa\iota\mu\omega\tau\acute{a}\tau o\upsilon\ \kappa\alpha\grave{\iota}\ \pi\acute{a}\sigma\eta s\ \tau\iota\mu\hat{\eta}s\ \kappa\alpha\grave{\iota}\ \dot{a}\pi o\delta o$-
$\chi\hat{\eta}s\ \dot{a}\xi\acute{\iota}o\upsilon$). Philo, *Praem. Poen.* 13: "He alone
is worthy of approval who has placed his hope in
God" ($\mu\acute{o}\nu os\ \delta'\ \dot{a}\pi o\delta o\chi\hat{\eta}s\ \mathring{a}\xi\iota os\ \dot{o}\ \dot{a}\nu\alpha\theta\epsilon\grave{\iota}s\ \tau\grave{\eta}\nu$
$\dot{\epsilon}\lambda\pi\acute{\iota}\delta\alpha\ \theta\epsilon\hat{\omega}$); Ditt. *Or.* I.339.13f; *Ep.Ar.* 257.308;
Hierocles in Stob., *Ecl.* 4.27.20 (p. 662, ed. Hense):
"A man's work is worthy of great recognition, when
it has (been able to) temper a stupid and clumsy
man by means of those who are acting for him"
($\dot{a}\nu\delta\rho\grave{o}s\ \mathring{\epsilon}\rho\gamma o\nu\ \kappa\alpha\grave{\iota}\ \pi o\lambda\lambda\hat{\eta}s\ \mathring{a}\xi\iota o\nu\ \dot{a}\pi o\delta o\chi\hat{\eta}s,\ \tau\grave{o}\nu$
$\dot{a}\beta\acute{\epsilon}\lambda\tau\epsilon\rho o\nu\ \kappa\alpha\grave{\iota}\ \sigma\kappa\alpha\iota\grave{o}\nu\ \pi\rho\alpha\hat{\upsilon}\nu\alpha\iota\ \tau o\hat{\iota}s\ \dot{\epsilon}s\ \alpha\dot{\upsilon}\tau\grave{o}\nu\ \pi\rho\alpha\tau$-
$\tau o\mu\acute{\epsilon}\nu o\iota s$) [trans. by Ed.]; Diog. L. 5.64 "a man . . .
worthy of great recognition" ($\dot{a}\nu\grave{\eta}\rho\ .\ .\ .\ \pi o\lambda\lambda\hat{\eta}s\ \tau\hat{\eta}s$
$\dot{a}\pi o\delta o\chi\hat{\eta}s\ \mathring{a}\xi\iota os$) [trans. by Ed.]; see also 5.37.
13 See Ragnar Asting, *Die Verkündigung des Wortes Got-
tes im Urchristentum* (Stuttgart: Kohlhammer, 1939),
pp. 189ff.

is to be learned from v 16.[14] His conversion seems to have no other purpose than to serve as a "prototype" ($\upsilon\pi o\tau\upsilon\pi\omega\sigma\iota\varsigma$, not "example" as in 2 Petr 2:4). As "the first," Paul is the typical representative of those who have received the mercy which the sinner can experience. The interest lies not in the historical or individual case, but rather in the edifying application.[15] A parallel is offered in the custom, widespread in the literary "world" of the time, of arranging and presenting the "life" ($\beta\iota o\varsigma$) of the hero to fit into the pattern of instruction in virtue.[16] "Forbearance" ($\mu\alpha\kappa\rho o\theta\upsilon\mu\iota\alpha$) is in Judaism a common characteristic of the behavior of God; here the word is used of Christ, who represents for the community the actuality of the divine action, and accordingly assumes to a great extent the designations of God's action (this process takes place before the designations of God's being are also transferred to Christ). Notice the twofold prepositional modification of "to believe," "to attain faith" ($\pi\iota\sigma\tau\epsilon\upsilon\epsilon\iota\nu$). The second ("for eternal life") is only loosely attached; such a construction is typical of the pattern of edifying discourse; "to believe" ($\pi\iota\sigma\tau\epsilon\upsilon\epsilon\iota\nu$) with "for" ($\epsilon\pi\iota$) and a following dative in the LXX designates the relationship to God. In the NT this con-

struction is found, except in this passage, only in quotations of Isa 28:17 (Rom 9:33; 10:11; 1 Petr 2:7). Jeremias assumes that the influence of this passage is also present in 1 Tim 1:16.[17]

■ **17** A solemn doxology rounds out the proem. It has its counterpart in 1 Tim 6:15f. Both formulas should be regarded as liturgical, as the Pastorals apparently quote formulaic liturgical material in other instances (1 Tim 2:5, 6; 5:21; 6:13–16; 2 Tim 1:9, 10; 2:8; 4:1). Since it is a question of formulaic language, it is difficult to define the meaning of "universe," "aeons," "ages" ($\alpha\iota\omega\nu\epsilon\varsigma$). "King of the ages" ($\beta\alpha\sigma\iota\lambda\epsilon\upsilon\varsigma\ \tau\omega\nu\ \alpha\iota\omega\nu\omega\nu$) is found in the hymn Tob 13:6, 10 and in the congregational prayer in *1 Clem.* 61.2 as a designation of God. Since this prayer contains much Jewish material, we may assume that we are dealing with a Jewish cultic formula.[18] In the magical papyri there occurs "King and Lord of the Universe" ($\alpha\iota\omega\nu\omega\nu\ \beta\alpha\sigma\iota\lambda\epsilon\upsilon\ \kappa\alpha\iota\ \kappa\upsilon\rho\iota\epsilon$)[19] and "God of the Universe" ($\alpha\iota\omega\nu\omega\nu\ \theta\epsilon o\varsigma$).[20] Cf. finally, Justin, *Apology* 1.41.2 (in a quotation): "to the Father of the Universe" ($\tau\omega\ \pi\alpha\tau\rho\iota\ \tau\omega\nu\ \alpha\iota\omega\nu\omega\nu$) and *Odes of Sol.* 7:13: "the perfection of the worlds and their father."[21] The cultic language of Greek–speaking Judaism, which was

14 Cf. the related passage *Barn.* 5.9: "[but when he chose] his own apostles . . . he chose those who were iniquitous above all sin" ($\tau o\upsilon\varsigma\ \iota\delta\iota o\upsilon\varsigma\ \alpha\pi o\sigma\tau o\lambda o\upsilon\varsigma$ . . . $\epsilon\xi\epsilon\lambda\epsilon\xi\alpha\tau o,\ o\nu\tau\alpha\varsigma\ \upsilon\pi\epsilon\rho\ \pi\alpha\sigma\alpha\nu\ \alpha\mu\alpha\rho\tau\iota\alpha\nu\ \alpha\nu o\mu\omega\tau\epsilon\rho o\upsilon\varsigma$).

15 Günther Klein, *Die zwölf Apostel* (Göttingen: Vandenhoeck & Ruprecht, 1961), 136.

16 Cf. Friedrich Leo, *Die griechisch–römische Biographie* (Leipzig: B. G. Teubner, 1901), pp. 2ff and Georgius Fraustadt, *Encomiorum in litteris Graecis usque ad Romanum aetatem historia*, Unpub. Diss. (Leipzig: 1909).

17 On the significance of this construction, cf. Bultmann, *Theology* 1, p. 91.

18 Cf. the form of address: "king of the world (age)" which is frequently found even today in Jewish prayers (מֶלֶךְ הָעוֹלָם, Jer 10:10 without the article); Tob 13:6, 10; and countless examples in the Jewish prayerbook, *Siddur Sephat Emeth*, tr. Simeon Singer (London: Eyre & Spottiswoode, ⁶1900), p. 4. Cf. also the prayer salutations in Josephus, *Ant.* 1.272: "O God, King of the All" ($\omega\ \theta\epsilon\epsilon\ \beta\alpha\sigma\iota\lambda\epsilon\upsilon\ \tau\omega\nu\ o\lambda\omega\nu$); cf. further "God of the ages" ($\theta\epsilon o\varsigma\ \tau\omega\nu\ \alpha\iota\omega\nu\omega\nu$, Sir 36:19) and "Lord of every age" ($\delta\epsilon\sigma\pi o\tau\alpha\ \pi\alpha\nu\tau o\varsigma\ \alpha\iota\omega\nu o\varsigma$, Josephus, *Ant.* 14.24). "Lord of the ages" (רִבּוֹן כָּל־הָעוֹלָמִים) is a Jewish prayer formula; see Berakoth 60b, where the parallel expression is "Lord of all the worlds [of creation]" (כָּל־

הַנְּשָׁמוֹת). On this see Adolf Schlatter, *Wie Sprach Josephus von Gott?* (Gütersloh: Bertelsmann, 1910), 9; idem, *Die Theologie des Judentums nach dem Bericht des Josephus* (Gütersloh: Bertelsmann, 1932), 26.

19 P. Leid. V, 7.36; Preis. *Zaub.* 2, Number XII, p. 75.

20 P. Par. 174.629; see Theodor Schermann, *Griechische Zauberpapyri und das Gemeinde– und Dankgebet im ersten Klemensbrief* (Leipzig: Hinrichs, 1909), 23.

21 Cf. Hermann Sasse, *TDNT* 1, p. 201 (especially 2a, excursus).

22 D* reads $\alpha\theta\alpha\nu\alpha\tau o\varsigma$ instead of $\alpha\phi\theta\alpha\rho\tau o\varsigma$; see 6:16; K P L add $\sigma o\phi o\varsigma$ after $\mu o\nu o\varsigma$, perhaps following Rom 16:27; see Lietzmann, *Römer, ad loc.*; and Gunnar Rudberg, "Parallela. 3. Vorsokratisches," *Con. Neot.* 7 (1942): 9–16. On "invisible" ($\alpha o\rho\alpha\tau o\varsigma$) cf. 1 Tim 6:16 and the commentaries on Rom 1:20; Col 1:16 and 1:18. Also Philo, *Abr.* 75f; *Vit. Mos.* 2.65; *De legibus alienis* 3.206; *Spec. leg.* 1.18.46; *Decal.* 60, 120; Josephus, *Bell.* 7. 345f. Cf. Erich Fascher, "Deus invisibilis," *Marburger Theologische Studien* 1 (1931): 41–77; Rudolf Bultmann, "Untersuchungen zum Johannesevangelium," *ZNW* 29 (1930): 169–92, reprinted in *Exegetica* (1967), 174ff; Wilhelm Michaelis, *TDNT* 5, pp. 368–70. On "Immortal" ($\alpha\phi\theta\alpha\rho\tau o\varsigma$) see Epicurus as quoted in Diogenes L. 10.123: "First believe that God is a living being, immortal and blessed, according to the notion of a god indicated by the common sense of mankind; and

doubtless of great importance for the beginnings of the entire Christian cultus, seems also to have exerted its influence on the language of the congregation presented in the Pastorals (see 1 Tim 2:10; 6:15f; and on 4:5). It is possible that even a portion of the treasure of typical Hellenistic formulas contained in the Pastorals came to the Christian congregations by way of Judaism. Thus

the very next formulaic expression is influenced by Greek thought: "the immortal, invisible, one God" (ἄφθαρτος ἀόρατος μόνος θεός).[22] The style of the passage makes it improbable that it was formulated in direct polemic against the cult of the emperor.[23]

---

so believing, thou shalt not affirm of him aught that is foreign to his immortality or that agrees not with blessedness, but shalt believe about him whatever may uphold his blessedness and his immortality." (πρῶτον μὲν τὸν θεὸν ζῷον ἄφθαρτον καὶ μακάριον νομίζων, ὡς ἡ κοινὴ τοῦ θεοῦ νόησις ὑπεγράφη, μηθὲν μήτε τῆς ἀφθαρσίας ἀλλότριον μήτε τῆς μακαριότητος ἀνοίκειον αὐτῷ πρόσαπτε. πᾶν δὲ τὸ φυλάττειν αὐτοῦ δυνάμενον τὴν μετὰ ἀφθαρ-

σίας μακαριότητα περὶ αὐτὸν δόξαζε). But cf. also Wisd Sol 12:1; Philo, *Vit. Mos.* 3.171 and Rom 1:23. On "one," "only" (μόνος), cf. Gerhard Delling, "ΜΟΝΟΣ ΘΕΟΣ," *ThLZ* 77 (1952): 469–76, where mention is made of the fixed cultic style which is found even in polytheism.

23 As Spicq, *ad. loc.*, argues. On the doxologies see L. G. Champion, *Benedictions and Doxologies in the Epistles of Paul*, Unpub. Diss. (Heidelberg: 1934).

1

Exhortation Regarding Heretics

18 **I transmit to you this instruction, Timothy my child, (in remembrance) of the words of the prophets, which were once given to you, 19/ so that (strengthened) by them you may fight the good fight in faith and with good conscience. 20/ Certain people have despised this and suffered shipwreck in the faith; among these belong Hymenaeus and Alexander, whom I have handed over to Satan, so that they may be delivered from their blasphemy through punishment.**

1:18–20 is important for the evaluation of the Pastorals' literary "pattern." Such summaries are found frequently in 1 Tim (see 3:14, 4:11; 5:21; 6:3), both to set off the paragraph and at the same time to connect the exhortations with the situation (cf. also 2 Tim 2:14 and Tit 2:15). In most of these passages the exhortation precedes a warning against false teachers. This warning is a negative counterpart of the warning which seems to belong to the schema. The (fictitious) situation of the epistle which is couched in personal terms and which assumes special importance in 2 Tim, is emphasized here for the first time: the reference to Timothy's calling. The analogous report in Acts 13:1–3 suggests that prophets participated in the installation of Timothy (see 1 Tim 4:14; 2 Tim 1:6). The names of the two apostates, however, belong perhaps to the real (and not the fictitious) situation of the author, who gives the lie to famous fathers of a heresy through the mouth of Paul.[1]

■ **18** With regard to the "instruction" ($\pi\alpha\rho\alpha\gamma\gamma\epsilon\lambda\iota\alpha$), Bernhard Weiss refers to the commandment in 1:3 and thus understands 1:18 as an admonition to carry out what was said there. But the author has dropped the subject of opposition to heresy already in v 9, and com-

pletely with v 12. Indeed even in 1:5 the same term ($\pi\alpha\rho\alpha\gamma\gamma\epsilon\lambda\iota\alpha$) is used to designate the right proclamation in general. So it would be better to take the words as referring to the "instruction," as it is handed over to Timothy, in what follows and in the epistle as a whole.[2] "I entrust" ($\pi\alpha\rho\alpha\tau\iota\theta\epsilon\mu\alpha\iota$) refers to the handing over of tradition.[3]

The Imagery of the Military Service of the Pious

This imagery was very common and widely used in antiquity.[4] In the immediate environment of primitive Christianity it is found in the texts of the Qumran sect. *The Scroll of the War of the Sons of Light against the Sons of Darkness* gives a detailed account.[5] In view of such evidence and considering the widespread usage of the imagery, it is not likely that the image arose spontaneously in primitive Christianity. To be sure, in the passage in 1 Tim the widespread mythical image of armor of faith does not occur. The expression "the good fight" is clearly a common one in the church and was understood not mythically but parenetically. The closest analogies to this usage are offered, not by the mysteries,[6]

---

1 (See below on 2 Tim 2:17 and 4:14, and the second excursus to 2 Tim 4:21.) These statements are also significant for the question of whether orthodoxy or heresy can claim historical priority (see the excursus to 1 Tim 4:14, section 2).

2 On "instruction" ($\pi\alpha\rho\alpha\gamma\gamma\epsilon\lambda\iota\alpha$), cf. $\pi\alpha\rho\alpha\gamma\gamma\epsilon\lambda\mu\alpha$ in Pseudo-Isocrates, *Ad Demonicum* 44 (cited below in Appendix 2); the analogy of 3:14 and 4:11 speaks against the dependency of "so that" ($\iota\nu\alpha$) upon "instruction" ($\pi\alpha\rho\alpha\gamma\gamma\epsilon\lambda\iota\alpha$, Chrysostom IX [Montfaucon, p. 575]).

3 See Heinrich Julius Holtzmann, *Lehrbuch der neutestamentlichen Theologie* 2 (Tübingen: J. C. B. Mohr

[Paul Siebeck], 2 1911), 317. See also the use of "deposit" ($\pi\alpha\rho\alpha\theta\eta\kappa\eta$) in 6:20. "To entrust," ($\pi\alpha\rho\alpha\tau\iota\theta\epsilon\nu\alpha\iota$) is equivalent to "to transmit" ($\pi\alpha\rho\alpha\delta\iota\delta\delta\nu\alpha\iota$) in *Herm.sim.* 9.10.6.

4 This is demonstrated by Dibelius–Greeven, *Epheser, Kolosser, Philemon*, excursus on Eph 6:10ff. The various materials from early Christian literature which pertain to this topic are collected in Adolf von Harnack, *Militia Christi* (Tübingen: J. C. B. Mohr [Paul Siebeck], 1905), pp. 93ff.

5 See Karl–Georg Kuhn, *TDNT* 5, pp. 298–302 (especially section 3c), and his article "Die in Palästina gefundenen hebräischen Texte," 192–211.

but by philosophical diatribe. In order to characterize the seriousness of the ethical task, the philosophers liked to compare life to military service.[7] The image of God as the commander–in–chief was quite frequently used.[8] Thus Epictetus can assume that the concept is familiar.[9] And it is precisely the widespread distribution of this concept in the diatribe which makes it probable that the early Christian use of the image is influenced by popular philosophy, at least in those passages where the image appears in an almost proverbial way (as here and in 1 Cor 9:7; 2 Tim 2:3f) or where it is argued in the style of the diatribe (as in *1 Clem.* 37). Images based on athletic competition form a group related to this one.[10]

■ **19** On "faith" ($\pi\acute{\iota}\sigma\tau\iota\varsigma$) and "conscience" ($\sigma\upsilon\nu\epsilon\acute{\iota}$-

$\delta\eta\sigma\iota\varsigma$), see 1:5 and the excursus *ad loc*. From "they have despised this" ($\mathring{\alpha}\pi\omega\sigma\acute{\alpha}\mu\epsilon\nu\sigma\iota$), it is clear that the opponents are being denounced not only as false teachers but also as persons with bad consciences (see 4:2). Of course the author states this without demonstrating it (see the excursus to 4:5). Again we are dealing with an early form of the heresy polemic, which is elaborated into a technique.[11] The image of shipwreck ($\mathring{\epsilon}\nu\alpha\upsilon\acute{\alpha}\gamma\eta\sigma\alpha\nu$) is found frequently in Greek philosophy.[12] It has already been shown above at 1:4ff that the author likes to characterize his opponents with words which are common in philosophy.

■ **20** Hymenaeus and Alexander are probably the same as those mentioned in 2 Tim 2:17 and perhaps 4:14 (see below p. 71 the excursus to 1 Tim 4:14, section 2d).

6   See Dibelius–Greeven, *Kolosser, Epheser, Philemon*, excursus on Eph 6:10ff.

7   See Plato, *Ap.* 28: "So I should have done a terrible thing, . . . if, when the commanders whom you chose to command me stationed me, . . . I remained where they stationed me, like anybody else, and ran the risk of death, but when the god gave me a station, . . . with orders to spend my life in philosophy and in examining myself and others, then I were to desert my post through fear of death or anything else whatsoever." ($\mathring{\epsilon}\gamma\grave{\omega}$ οὖν δεινὰ ἂν εἴην εἰργρασμένος . . ., εἰ ὅτε μέν με οἱ ἄρχοντες ἔταττον, οὓς ὑμεῖς εἵλεσθε ἄρχειν μου . . ., τότε μὲν οὗ ἐκεῖνοι ἔταττον ἔμενον ὥσπερ καὶ ἄλλος τις καὶ ἐκινδύνευον ἀποθανεῖν, τοῦ δὲ θεοῦ τάττοντος . . . φιλοσοφοῦντά με δεῖν ζῆν καὶ ἐξετάζοντα ἐμαυτὸν καὶ τοὺς ἄλλους, ἐνταῦθα δὲ φοβηθεὶς ἢ θάνατον ἢ ἄλλ' ὁτιοῦν πρᾶγμα λίποιμι τὴν τάξιν). See also Epictetus *Diss.* 3.24.34: "each man's life is a campaign, and a long and complicated one at that" (στρατεία τίς ἐστιν ὁ βίος ἑκάστου καὶ αὕτη μακρὰ καὶ ποικίλη). Cf. Johannes Leipoldt, "Das Bild vom Kriege in der griechischen Welt," *Gott und die Götter. Festgabe für Erich Fascher* (Berlin: Evangelische Verlagsanstalt, 1958), 16–30.

8   Especially in Epictetus; cf. also Sextus Emp., *Math.* 9.26; Philo, *On Providence* 2.102, J. B. Aucher, ed., *Philonis Iudaei, sermones tres hactenus inediti* (Venice: 1822), p. 112; this Latin translation of the Armenian text *Provid.* is also available in C. E. Richter, ed., *Philonis Judaei opera omnia* (Leipzig: E. B. Schwickert, 1828–30), vol. 8; and in the reprint of Richter in *Philonis Iudaei opera omnia* (Leipzig: Carolus Tauchnitius [Tauchnitz], 1851–53), vol. 8; Maxim. Tyr. 4.9; 13.3ff, and especially 10,9: "After the soul has been delivered from this world to that, . . . then it distinguishes and considers those very things which

are there, . . . accompanying the army of the gods, in which it has been given a position by the leader and general Zeus." (ἐπειδὰν δὲ ἀπαλλαγῇ ἡ ψυχὴ ἐνθένδε ἐκεῖσε . . . τότε διορᾷ καὶ λογίζεται τὰ ληθῆ αὐτά, . . . συμπεριπολοῦσα καὶ συντεταγμένη στρατιᾷ θεῶν ὑφ' ἡγεμόνι καὶ στρατηγῷ τῷ Διί); see Wilhelm Capelle, "Die Schrift von der Welt," *Neue Jahrbücher für das klassische Altertum* 15 (1905): 558, n. 6.

9   Epictetus, *Diss.* 3.23.31: "Is that what you used to hear when you sat at the feet of the philosophers? Is that what you learned? Do you not know that the business of life is a campaign?" (ταῦτα ἤκουες παρὰ τοῖς φιλοσόφοις, ταῦτ' ἐμάνθανες; οὐκ οἶσθ', ὅτι στρατεία τὸ χρῆμά ἐστιν).

10 Cf. Wendland, *Hellenistische Kultur*, 356f, n. 4.

11 See Bauer, *Orthodoxy and Heresy*, passim.

12 See Cebes, *Tabula* 24.2: "it is as though they were hard pressed, as though they lived wretchedly and as though they were shipwrecked in life" (ὡς κακῶς διατρίβουσι καὶ ἀθλίως ζῶσι καὶ ὡς ναυαγοῦσιν ἐν τῷ βίῳ) [Trans.]; Luc., *Somnium* 23: "But as for the others . . . you can see how sadly they come to grief when a Croesus with his wings clipped makes sport of the Persians by mounting the pyre, or a Dionysius, expelled from his tyrant's throne, turns up in Corinth as a schoolmaster, teaching children their a, b, c after holding sway so widely." (τῶν μέντοιγε ἄλλων . . . τὰ ναυάγια πάνυ αἰσχρὰ ἴδοις ἄν, ὅταν ὁ Κροῖσος περιτετιλμένος τὰ πτερὰ γέλωτα παρέχῃ Πέρσαις ἀναβαίνων ἐπὶ τὸ πῦρ ἢ Διονύσιος καταδύσης τῆς τυραννίδος ἐν Κορίνθῳ γραμματιστὴς βλέπεται μετὰ τηλικαύτην ἀρχὴν παιδία συλλαβίζειν διδάσκων); Galen, *Protreptikos* 2 (See Hermann Diels, *CMA* 1, p. 59): "When greater shipwrecks occur to many households, than to ships at sea" (μειζόνων ναυαγιῶν περὶ πολλοὺς

"I have handed over to Satan" ($\pi\alpha\rho\acute{\epsilon}\delta\omega\kappa\alpha\ \tau\hat{\omega}\ \sigma\alpha\tau\alpha\nu\hat{\alpha}$):
the author apparently knows 1 Cor 5:5, where Paul
uses the same expression to refer to the sinner's death.
The author of the Pastorals, however, does not intend
such an effect nor does he merely refer to the exclusion
from the congregation. That is unambiguously clear from
the following final clause. The purpose here is "educa-
tion through punishment" ($\pi\alpha\iota\delta\epsilon\acute{\upsilon}\epsilon\sigma\theta\alpha\iota$) which wants
to prevent further blasphemy (whether such blasphemy is
seen as false teaching or, possibly, in the mere fact of
opposition). On "education through punishment" see
1 Cor 11:32 and 2 Cor 6:9; clearly the author is thinking
more of punishment than education.[13] Since "Satan"
here can only refer to his function as the destroyer of the
body and of life, one has to think of sickness or the like.[14]

Of course, Paul himself could also have used the expression in this sense. But whoever accepts the inauthenticity
of the epistle will have the impression that the imitator
here presupposes, without further reflection on the
matter, that the apostle possesses magical powers. In this
case, one can, with Reitzenstein, compare this passage
with the description of the magician in Apuleius (*Apologia* 26): "(it is he) who, having commerce with the
immortal gods, has the power to do whatever he wishes
by the mysterious force of certain incantations" (qui
communione loquendi cum deis immortalibus ad omnia
quae velit incredibili quadam vi cantaminum polleat)
[Trans.].[15]

οἴκους γιγνομένων ἢ περὶ τὰ σκάφη κατὰ θάλασ-
σαν). Cf. Gustav Adolf Gerhard, *Phoinix von Kolophon* (Leipzig and Berlin: Teubner, 1909), pp. 98f;
Philo, *Mut. nom.* 215 and *Som.* 2.147.

13 Georg Bertram, *TDNT* 6, p. 624. But see also *1 Clem.*
56.16 and 57.1.

14 See Lietzmann–Kümmel, *Korinther*, excursus on 1
Cor 5:5 (also for additional literature); Richard
Wünsch, *Antike Fluchtafeln* (Bonn: Marcus & Weber,
[2]1912). On the function of Satan see Werner
Jentsch, *Urchristliches Erziehungsdenken* (Gütersloh:
Bertelsmann, 1951), 179; Rudolf Bohren, *Das Prob-
lem der Kirchenzucht im NT* (Zollikon and Zürich:
Evangelischer Verlag, 1952), 113ff. On Satan as

chastiser and/or tutor see the parallels in Brock–
Utne, " 'Der Feind.' Die alttestamentliche Satans-
gestalt im Lichte der sozialen Verhältnisse des nahen
Orients," *Klio* 28 (1935): 219–27; Rosa Schärf, *Satan
in the Old Testament*, tr. Hildegard Nagel (Evanston:
Northwestern University Press, 1967).

15 Cf. Richard Reitzenstein, *Die hellenistischen Mysterienreligionen* (Leipzig: Teubner, [3]1927; reprint 1956),
364.

2 On Prayers for All Men

1 First of all I exhort you to make petition,
prayer, intercession, and thanksgiving
for all men, 2/ for emperors and all
authorities, so that we may be able to
lead a quiet and peaceful life in all piety
and dignity. 3/ This is the way it should
be and is well–pleasing to God, our
Savior, 4/ who wants all men to be saved
and to come to the recognition of the
truth. 5/ For God is one, and there is one
mediator between God and men, the
man Christ Jesus, 6/ who gave himself
as a ransom for all, the testimony in
its (determined) time. 7/ I have been
appointed to be its preacher and apostle—I speak the truth and do not lie— as
teacher of the gentiles in faith and
truth.

2:1–3:13 contain the first part of the church order (see
the outline above). A summary of its content appears
in the conclusion of this section: "how one ought to con-
duct one's life in the household of God" ($\pi\hat{\omega}\varsigma$ δεῖ ἐν οἴκῳ
θεοῦ ἀναστρέφεσθαι 3:15). This makes clear why the
author clothes the instruction in the traditional schema
of regulations for the household, thereby transforming
this schema in a peculiar way.[1]

1:1–7 form the introduction to the list of regulations
for the household. These injunctions actually contain
more exhortation to those concerned than to the addressee of the epistle, Timothy. This is due to the literary
character of these epistles. The epistolary guise, according
to which all the "instructions" ($\pi\alpha\rho\alpha\gamma\gamma\epsilon\lambda\iota\alpha\iota$) are
presented as injunctions which Timothy is to carry out,
has a specific purpose. The preceding transitional passage, 1:18–20, already served this purpose, i.e. to give the
church order direct apostolic authority, which in turn
is sanctioned by the kerygmatic tradition.[2]

■ 1 We are dealing with instructions for the life of the
congregation; first of all, concerning prayer. Since it is
impossible that "for all men" (ὑπὲρ πάντων ἀνθρώπων)
belongs only with "thanksgiving" (εὐχαριστίας), it
must be connected with all four preceding nouns. The
request is, therefore, that petition and thanksgiving
be placed in a universal[3] perspective. The conception of
"thanksgiving for all men," which at first glance seems
strange, is explained if one recognizes that the prayer of
thanksgiving is the natural correlative to the prayer
of petition (see Phil 4:6). In the latter the prayer for "all
men" is a fixed topos (see below on 2:2). We can also
refer to the conception found in 1 Thess 3:9 and Col 1:12
that the prayer of thanksgiving—occasionally the cultic
prayer—is, as a matter of course, a work rendered to
God which increases God's "glory" (δόξα).[4] An example
of this usage in a specific case is offered in the *Shepherd
of Hermas*,[5] where it is assumed that the poor man is rich
in the power of prayer and uses this power for the benefit

1 See von Campenhausen, "Polykarp," p. 230.
2 Cf. the variant "exhort (imperative) therefore!"
($\pi\alpha\rho\alpha\kappa\alpha\lambda\epsilon\iota$ οὖν) D * G in 2:1.
3 See the justification for this view in 1 Tim 2:4 and
Ign. *Eph.* 10.1.
4 See G. H. Boobyer, *"Thanksgiving" and the "Glory
of God" in Paul*, Unpub. Diss. (Heidelberg: 1929),
where this conception is located in its history–of–
religions framework. On 1 Thess 3:9 and Col 1:12,
see Dibelius, *Thessalonicher, Philipper*; Dibelius–
Greeven, *Kolosser, Epheser, Philemon, ad loc.*; cf. also
Eduard Lohse, *Colossians and Philemon*, Hermeneia
(Philadelphia, Pa.: Fortress Press, 1971), *ad loc.*

5 *Herm. sim.* 2.6: "But the poor man, being helped by
the rich, makes intercession to God, giving him
thanks, for him who gave to him" (ὁ πένης δὲ ἐπι-
χορηγούμενος ὑπὸ τοῦ πλουσίου ἐντυγχάνει αὐτῷ
τῷ θεῷ εὐχαριστῶν ὑπὲρ τοῦ διδόντος αὐτῷ).

of the rich. The different terms for "prayer" do not invite a systematic differentiation,[6] nor do they offer a complete list—"supplication" (ἱκεσία), for example, is missing (see *1 Clem* 59.2). The word "intercession" (ἔντευξις), attested here,[7] is known to us from the papyri as a term for "application."[8] Thus, 2:1 introduces the prayer instruction with a sentence which sounds catechetical and which anticipates the essentials of the following commands.[9]

■ **2** "King" (βασιλεύς) was, in the East, the title of the Roman emperor.[10] It is tempting to take the plural "kings" (βασιλεῖς) as including the co-ruler, which would enable us to date the time of the composition of the epistle after 137 A.D.[11] But aside from the fact that chronological conclusions on the basis of an individual, and by no means certain phrase are generally dangerous, it must also be added that the relationship between the apologies and their addressees provide no satisfying parallels to our text. Rather, more general sentences must be referred to as parallels, such as "Pray also for kings and potentates and rulers" (orate etiam pro regibus et potestatibus et principibus, Pol. *Phil.* 12.3); "We recognize you as kings and rulers of men" (βασιλεῖς καὶ ἄρχ-

οντας ἀνθρώπων ὁμολογοῦντες, Justin, *Apol.* 1.17.3). In both cases the plural in question is explained by the parallelism with the following plural form and, above all, by the intention of formulating the phrase in its most general form. It derives, therefore, from the traditional character of the intercession for those in authority. "For the well–being of the Emperors" (*Pro salute imperatorum*) is a fixed formula for a sacrifice for the benefit of the rulers.[12] Spicq[13] refers not only to the emperor, but also to the petty kings of the East; the parallel, Pol. *Phil.* 12.3, speaks for this interpretation.[14] "To be in authority" (ἐν ὑπεροχῇ εἶναι or κεῖσθαι) in Hellenistic Greek designates a distinguished position.[15] The mention of those in authority in this passage seems to reflect the pattern of the regulations for the household. That there is such a connection seems to be supported by the proximate reference to "all men."[16] But this topos is not yet fixed as part of the early Christian rules for the household. Rom 13, like Pol. *Phil.* 12.3, which is structurally related to the Pastorals, introduces the topos outside this pattern. It is rather connected with the customary liturgical language of prayer (cf. *1 Clem.* 60f).

---

6   Such a differentiation is made by Origen, *Orationes* 14.2 (p. 331, Koetschau).

7   Also 4:5; *Herm. mand.* 5.1.6; 10.3.2f and 11.9.

8   Cf. Ludwig Mitteis and Ulrich Wilcken, *Grundzüge und Chrestomatie der Papyruskunde 2.1.1* (Leipzig: Teubner, 1912), 12ff; Richard Laqueur, *Quaestiones epigraph. et papyrol.*, Unpub. Diss. (Strassburg: 1904) 8ff; Ulrich Wilcken, "Bibliographie. Ein Authorenverzeichnis. S. 265," *Archiv für Papyrusforschung und verwandte Gebiete* 4 (1908): 224; Adolf Deissmann, *Bible Studies*, tr. A. Grieve (Edinburgh: T. & T. Clark, 1901), 121; Friedrich Preisigke, *Wörterbuch der griechischen Papyrusurkunden mit Einschluss der griechischen usw. . . . Ägypten* (Berlin: 1914–27), s.v.

9   Cf. *Herm. mand.* 1.1 and *vis.* 5.5 in relation to the following commandments.

10   Cf. *IG* 3.12.15, 17; *CIG* 2.2721.11; Josephus, *Bell.* 3.351; 4.596 and 598; many other examples are given in E. Magie, *De Romanorum iuris publici sacrique vocabulis sollemnibus in Graecum sermonem conversis* (Leipzig: Teubner, 1905), 62; in early Christianity cf. in addition to 1 Tim 2:2: 1 Petr 2:13, 17 (Rev 17:9); *1 Clem.* 37.3; Aristid., *Apol.* 1; Just., *Apol.* 1.14.4; Athenag., *Suppl.* 1.

11   Cf. Just., *Apol.* 1.14.4.: "I shall leave it to you, **as** powerful kings, to examine, whether in truth this is what we have been taught and teach" (ὑμέτερον

ἔστω ὡς δυνατῶν βασιλέων ἐξετάσαι εἰ ἀληθῶς ταῦτα δεδιδάγμεθα καὶ διδάσκομεν) [trans. by Ed.]; Athenag. *Suppl.* 2.1. Ferdinand Christian Baur, *Die sogenannten Pastoralbriefe*, pp. 126f had already proposed this argument for a late date.

12   Franz Dölger, *Antike und Christentum* (Münster i. W.: Aschendorff, 1932), pp. 117ff.

13   Spicq, *ad loc.*

14   On the position of the βασιλεύς as the essence of sovereignty see E. Bikermann, *Institutions des Seleucides* (Paris: Haut–Commissariat de la République Française en Syrie et au Liban, 1938), 5ff; Franz Cumont, *L'Égypte des Astrologues* (Brussels: Fondation égyptologique Reine Elisabeth, 1937), 25ff.

15   Cf. *Inscr. Perg.* 252.19f: "not less for the common people than for those in a distinguished position (τοὺς δη]μοτικοὺς μηδὲν ἧσσον τῶν | ἐν ὑπεροχῆι ὄντων); 2 Macc 3:11: "a man of very prominent position" (ἀνδρὸς ἐν ὑπεροχῆ κειμένου); *Ep. Ar.* 175: "envoys from kings or very important cities" (παρὰ βασιλέων ἢ πόλεων ἐν ὑπεροχαῖς) [trans. Charles, APOT].

16   Cf. Stob. *Ecl.* 4.27.23; Epict. *Diss.* 2.17.3 and Philo, *Poster. C.* 181.

17   See Eduard Meyer, *Die Entstehung des Judentums* (Halle: M. Niemeyer, 1896), 50ff; Wilhelm Rudolph, *Esra und Nehemiah*, HAT 1,20 (Tübingen:

Prayer for the Pagan Authority

Prayer for the pagan authority is first attested among the Jews in the decree of Darius preserved in the book of Ezra, if it is genuine.[17] Darius issued the following decree with regard to the Jewish temple and its priests (LXX 1 Esdras 6:9f): ". . . for sacrifices to the Lord, for bulls and rams and lambs, and likewise wheat and salt and wine and oil, regularly every year, without quibbling, for daily use as the priests in Jerusalem may indicate, in order that libations may be made to the Most High God for the king and his children, and prayers be offered for their life." (καὶ ὃ ἂν ὑστέρημα, καὶ υἱοὺς βοῶν καὶ κριῶν καὶ ἀμνοὺς εἰς ὁλοκαυτώσεις τῷ θεῷ τοῦ οὐρανοῦ, πυρούς, ἅλας, οἶνον, ἔλαιον, κατὰ τὸ ῥῆμα ἱερέων τῶν ἐν Ἱερουσαλήμ, ἔστω διδόμενον αὐτοῖς ἡμέραν ἐν ἡμέρᾳ, ὃ ἐὰν αἰτήσωσιν, ἵνα ὦσιν προσφέροντες εὐωδίας τῷ θεῷ τοῦ οὐρανοῦ, καὶ προσεύχωνται εἰς ζωὴν τοῦ βασιλέως καὶ τῶν υἱῶν αὐτοῦ). Bar 1:10ff claims—perhaps for reasons that reflect the interests of his own time—that the origin of this custom of offering sacrifices and prayers goes back to the time of the exile under Nebuchadnezzar (cf. also LXX Jer 36:7).

The offering for the pagan authority is mentioned further in *Ep. Ar.* 45; 1 Macc 7:33; Josephus, *Bell.* 2.197, 408ff; and Philo, *Leg. Gaj.* 157, 317. Philo mentions prayers in the synagogues and in the houses of prayer.[18] The special meaning of this custom, particularly among the Jews, is clear: it is the equivalent of the cult of the emperor and thus the most important sign of loyalty.

That the custom was continued in Christianity was not a matter of course, for precisely because of the imperial cult, the Christians were brought into a most severe conflict. Christianity had every reason to be hostile to the state, and the book of Revelation proves that such hostility was in fact present in certain circles. But the NT also testifies to the presence of loyalty to the state and its officials.[19] The thoughts which Paul expresses in Rom 13:1ff may have helped bring about this stance. But besides these, other considerations certainly existed: concern with missionary practice or apologetics, or the mere belief in authority. The widespread distribution of this complex of ideas marks the changeover from an eschatological world view to an ecclesiastical form of existence within an expanding world that provided more room for a Christian life. Thus the practice, as well as the thought, of the popular Jewish ideology of the state could be adopted. There are analogous phenomena in other cults; this is suggested by Apuleius, *Metamorphoses* 11.17: "(the *grammateus* in the temple ceremony of the Isis mysteries began to read out of a book), praying for good fortune for the great Prince, the Senate, to the noble order of Chivalry, and generally to all the Roman people" (principi magno senatuique et equiti totoque Romano populo). Yet the adoption of such prayers by the mystery cults might presuppose the evolution of the ideology of the state from the second century A.D. onward; see, however, *Inscr. Magn.* 98 (quoted by Norden, *Agnostos Theos, Untersuchungen zur Formengeschichte religiöser Rede* [Leipzig: Teubner 1913 = Darmstadt: ⁴1956], 151f, n. 4) from the second century B.C. The practice of the synagogues, at any rate, offered the historical point of

---

J. C. B. Mohr [Paul Siebeck], 1949), p. 59. On the Persian custom see Herodotus 1.132.2: "To pray for blessings for himself alone is not lawful for the sacrificer; rather he prays that it may be well with the king and all the Persians" (ἑωυτῷ μὲν δὴ τῷ θύοντι ἰδίῃ μούνῳ οὔ οἱ ἐγγίνεται ἀρᾶσθαι ἀγαθά, ὁ δὲ τοῖσι πᾶσι Πέρσῃσι κατεύχεται εὖ γίνεσθαι καὶ τῷ βασιλέϊ).

18   Philo, *Flacc.* 49: "and you do not understand that everywhere in the habitable world, the religious veneration of the Jews for the Augustan house has its basis, as all may see, in the meeting houses" (τοῖς πανταχόθι τῆς οἰκουμένης Ἰουδαίοις ὁρμητήρια τῆς εἰς τὸν Σεβαστὸν οἶκον ὁσιότητός εἰσιν αἱ προσευχαὶ ἐπιδήλως). Cf. *Pirke Aboth* 3.2: "R. Hanina, the deputy of the priests, said: Pray for the peace of the government (מלכות), for, except for the fear of that, we should have swallowed each other alive" [tr. R. Travers Herford, *Pirke Aboth* (New York: Schocken Books, 1962)]. Cf. further the inscription from Schedia, in Ditt. *Or.* II, p. 726: "The Jews pray for the king Ptolemy and for the queen Berenice, the sister and wife, and for the children" (ὑπὲρ βασιλέως Πτολεμαίου καὶ βασιλίσσης Βερενίκης ἀδελφῆς καὶ γυναικὸς καὶ τῶν τέκνων τὴν προσευχὴν οἱ Ἰουδαῖοι). See Emil Schürer, *A History of the Jewish People in the Time of Jesus Christ,* 1¹⁻² tr. John MacPherson, 2¹⁻³ tr. Sophia Taylor and Peter Christie (Edinburgh: T. & T. Clark, 1885–90), 1² pp. 76f; 2¹ pp. 360ff; 2³ pp. 301, 303.

19   In addition to 1 Tim 2:2; cf. Rom 13:1ff; 1 Petr 2:14, 17; Tit 3:1 and the description in the book of Acts of the position taken by the civil authorities toward early Christianity. (For other points of contact between the Pastoral Epistles and Acts, see below on 1 Tim 1:13; 6:11; 2 Tim 1:5; 4:17.)

connection with the Christian prayer.[20] The content of the prayer in question as used in Carthage is given by Tertullian, *Apology* 30: "we are constantly praying for all Emperors; our prayers are that their life be abundant, that the empire be secure, that their house be safe, that the armies be strong, the Senate faithful, the people reliable, the world peaceful, and whatever other prayers there be for a man and for the Emperor." (precantes sumus semper pro omnibus imperatoribus vitam illis prolixam, imperium securum, domum tutam, exercitus fortes, senatum fidelem, populum probum, orbem quietum, quaecumque hominis et Caesaris vota sunt) [Trans.].

Such a petition has been preserved verbatim for us in the prayer of the congregation in *1 Clem.* 61: "to our rulers and governors upon the earth. Thou, Master, hast given the power of sovereignty (to them) through thy excellent and inexpressible might, that they may know the glory and honour given to them by thee, and be subject to them, in nothing resisting thy will. And to them, Lord, grant health, peace, concord, firmness that they may administer the government which thou hast given them without offence . . . do thou, O Lord, direct their counsels according to that which is 'good and pleasing' before thee, that they may administer with piety in peace and gentleness the power given to them by thee,

and may find mercy in thine eyes." (τοῖς τε ἄρχουσι καὶ ἡγουμένοις ἡμῶν ἐπὶ τῆς γῆς σύ, δέσποτα, ἔδωκας τὴν ἐξουσίαν τῆς βασιλείας αὐτοῖς διὰ τοῦ μεγαλοπρεποῦς καὶ ἀνεκδιηγήτου κράτους σου, εἰς τὸ γινώσκοντας ἡμᾶς τὴν ὑπὸ σοῦ αὐτοῖς δεδομένην δόξαν καὶ τιμὴν ὑποτάσσεσθαι αὐτοῖς, μηδὲν ἐναντιουμένους τῷ θελήματί σου· οἷς δός, κύριε, ὑγίειαν, εἰρήνην, ὁμόνοιαν, εὐστάθειαν, εἰς τὸ διέπειν αὐτοὺς τὴν ὑπὸ σοῦ δεδομένην αὐτοῖς ἡγεμονίαν ἀπροσκόπως . . . σύ, κύριε, διεύθυνον τὴν βουλὴν αὐτῶν κατὰ τὸ καλὸν καὶ εὐάρεστον ἐνώπιόν σου, ὅπως διέποντες ἐν εἰρήνῃ καὶ πραΰτητι εὐσεβῶς τὴν ὑπὸ σοῦ αὐτοῖς δεδομένην ἐξουσίαν ἵλεώ σου τυγχάνωσιν). There is no inference that one is praying for the *conversion* of those in authority.[21] The prayer is rather for their prosperity, as in the Jewish models. The conclusion of the prayer in *1 Clem.* shows how the final clause in 1 Tim 2:2 ("so that we . . .") is to be understood.[22] This is clear regardless of the answer to the further question, whether the final clause still belongs to the petition,[23] or is already an injunction to the reader. Tit 2:11–14 does not enable us to come to a decision; Pol. *Phil.* 12.3 and the two passages just cited speak against the inclusion of the final clause in the petition. The ideal of a peaceful life expressed in this clause—Philo, *Vit. Mos.* 2.235 calls it the "quiet life of an ordinary citizen" (βίος ἀπράγμων καὶ ἰδιώτης) —is described in terms which, to be sure, stand out as

---

20 Prayers of this kind are mentioned in Pol. *Phil.* 12.3; Justin, *Apol.* 1.17.3; Theophilus, *Autol.* 1.11; Tertullian, *Apology* 30, 39 and elsewhere. Cf. W. Mangold, "De ecclesia primaeva pro Caesaribus ac magistratibus Romanis preces fundente," *Bonner Universitäts–Programm* (Bonn: 1881); Adolf von Harnack, *The Expansion of Christianity in the First Three Centuries*, tr. and ed. James Moffatt, vol. 1 (New York: G. P. Putnam's Sons, 1904), 321–24; Moffatt's translation was republished as *The Mission and Expansion of Christianity in the First Three Centuries* by Harper's in 1962; Rudolf Knopf, *Das nachapostolische Zeitalter* (Tübingen: J. C. B. Mohr [Paul Siebeck], 1905), 107f; *idem*, on *1 Clem.* 61 (see below, note 21); Ludwig Biehl, *Das liturgische Gebet für Kaiser und Reich* (Paderborn: Schöningh, 1937); Gerhard Kittel, *Christus und Imperator* (Stuttgart: Kohlhammer, 1939); Dibelius, "Rom und die Christen," *passim;* Otto Eck, *Urgemeinde und Imperium*, BFTh 42, 3 Gütersloh: Bertelsmann, 1940); Hans Werner Bartsch, *Die Anfänge urchristlicher Rechtsbildungen: Studien zu den Pastoralbriefen* (Hamburg: Herbert Reich, 1965), 34f.

21 Despite *1 Clem.* 59.4; nor can Ign. *Eph.* 10 be cited as contradictory evidence; with respect to *1 Clem.* 59.4, Bartsch is in disagreement; cf. *Anfänge*, p. 45 n. 27. But see Rudolf Knopf, *Die Lehre der Zwölf Apostel, die zwei Clemensbriefe*, HNT, Ergänzungsband 1 (Tübingen: J. C. B. Mohr [Paul Siebeck], 1920), on *1 Clem.* 59.4.

22 See Theodoret (III, 647, Schulze): "As they obtain peace, with them we also may obtain a share of quiet life" (ἐκείνων γὰρ πρυτανευόντων εἰρήνην, μεταλαγχάνομεν καὶ ἡμεῖς τῆς γαλήνης) [trans. by Ed.]; Athenag., *Suppl.* 37.1: "we, who pray . . . that your empire may receive prosperity and increase. . . . This is to our benefit too, that we should lead a quiet and a peaceful life." (εὐχόμεθα ἵνα . . . αὔξην δὲ καὶ ἐπίδοσιν καὶ ἡ ἀρχὴ ὑμῶν . . . λαμβάνῃ. τοῦτο δ' ἐστὶ καὶ πρὸς ἡμῶν, ὅπως ἤρεμον καὶ ἡσύχιον βίον διάγοιμεν) [Trans. by Joseph Hugh Crehan in *Ancient Christian Writers* 23 (Westminster, Md.: Newman Press, 1956), 78].

23 So Anton Fridrichsen, "Exegetisches zu den Paulusbriefen" in *Serta Rudbergiana*, edited by H. Holst and H. Mørland (Osloae: A. W. Brøgger, 1931), pp.

peculiar in the context of the NT, but which are frequently used in the environment of early Christianity.[24]

"Piety" (εὐσέβεια) and "dignity" (σεμνότης) are obviously intended to illustrate the ideal of good, honorable citizenship; the parallel term "dignity," (σεμνότης), makes it improbable that "piety" (εὐσέβεια) refers to one's behavior toward those in authority. Both expressions indicate the Hellenistic linguistic character of the Pastorals; "piety" (εὐσέβεια) in the NT is found only in writings with a markedly Hellenistic vocabulary, namely, besides the Pastorals, in Acts and 2 Petr. And of the 59 passages cited in the LXX concordance under εὐσέβεια (piety), 47 belong to the Fourth Book of the Maccabees! As seldom as this term occurs elsewhere in the Greek Bible, so frequently it appears in the inscriptions.[25] It designates not only the fulfillment of special cultic duties but also the general behavior which is pleasing to God. Thus in the honorary inscriptions "piety" is found along with "virtue" (ἀρετή), "righteousness" (δικαιοσύνη), "goodness" (καλοκἀγαθία), etc. in those schematic catalogues of virtues which were so popular. It is used in 1 Tim in the same sense.[26]

"Dignity" (σεμνότης) designates the reverence due to holy things (2 Macc 3:12 and *Ep. Ar.* 171) as well as external,[27] and internal[28] dignity. In 1 Tim 2:2, therefore, both nouns clearly refer to that behavior which is well–pleasing to God and men.[29]

The Ideal of Good Christian Citizenship

In this passage the ideal of Christian citizenship is depicted in characteristic and, as has been shown above, common words. It is an ideal to which the Pastorals refer again and again. This ideal of a peaceful life differs greatly from Paul's understanding of existence, which reflects the many conflicts of his life. To illustrate this difference, one need only compare this passage with the description which the apostle gives in 2 Cor 11:23–33 of his life's difficulties and dangers. Paul lives in the tension between this world and God's world. He joyfully affirmed (in 2 Cor 6:4–10) the suffering of this existence as part of citizenship in the other kingdom. The author of the Pastorals seeks to build the possibility of a life in this world, although on the basis of Christian principles. He wishes to become part of the world. Thus, for him, the peace of a secure life is a goal of the Christian. The *teaching* is "reasonable" (see the excursus to 1:10), enjoys general approval and can claim that it derives from tradition (2 Tim 2:2; 3:14–17; Tit 1:9). It consists in the "recognition of truth," (1 Tim 2:3, 4). He knows that piety is useful (1 Tim 4:8; 6:6). Teachers who arouse contention or are concerned with special personal accomplishments are for this very reason objects of suspicion (2 Tim 3:6 and 4:3), because they diverge from the commandment of sobriety.

24–9. Here he contends that the whole sentence is an ἔντευξις, which often expresses the idea that, if the ruler fulfills the petition, then the petitioner can live as he is expected to live.

24   See *CIG* III.5361.13f (Jewish inscription of Berenice): "In her conduct she displayed a quiet way of life" (ἔν τε τῆι ἀναστροφῆι ἡσύχιον ἦθος ἐνδεικνύμενος) [trans. by Ed.]; see also the addition to Esther 3:13 B 2, according to manuscript A: "in order to make my kingdom peaceable and open to travel" (τήν τε βασιλείαν ἤρεμον καὶ πορευτήν); Ditt. *Or.* II 519.9ff, which is a petition to the Emperor Philippus Arabs and his son (note that both are called "king" [βασιλεύς]): "in these times of your most blessed reign, the most pious and beneficent of all the kings anywhere, who lead a peaceful and quiet life" (πάντων ἐν τοῖς μακαριωτάτοις ὑμῶν καιροῖς, εὐσεβέσ[τατοι καὶ ἀλυ]πότατοι τῶν πώποτε βασιλέων, ἤρεμον καὶ γαληνὸν τὸν βίον δια[γόντων]) [Trans.]; see also Philo, *Conf. ling.* 43 "and live a life of calmness and fair weather" (εὔδιον καὶ γαληνὸν βίον ζῶσιν); *Rer. div. her.* 285: "having gained a calm, unclouded life" (γαληνὸν καὶ εὔδιον κτησά-

μενος βίον).

25   See for instance the index in Ditt. *Or.*

26   See also below on Tit 2:11–14 and compare the analogous use of "holiness" (ὁσιότης) in *1 Clem* 60.2.

27   E.g., the respect that is due to the beard according to Epict., *Diss.* 1.16.13.

28   With *Ep. Ar.* 5, cf. Ditt. *Syll.* II.807.11ff: "When he came into his homeland, he made his stay correspond to the dignity which was about his person in every respect." (παραγενόμενος | εἰς τὴν πατρίδα ἀνάλογον πεποίηται τὴν ἐπιδη|μίαν τῇ περὶ ἑαυτὸν ἐν πᾶσι σεμνότητι) [trans. by Ed.]; see also *Or.* II, 567.19.

29   Cf. *1 Clem* 62.1: "most helpful for a virtuous life to those who wish to guide their steps in piety and righteousness" (τοῖς θέλουσιν ἐνάρετον βίον εὐσεβῶς καὶ δικαίως διευθύνειν); Josephus, *Ant.* 15.375 (the Essene, Menaem, is speaking to Herod, as he prophesies to the latter that he will become ruler): "For the best attitude for you to take would be to love justice and piety toward God and mildness toward your citizens." (ἄριστος γὰρ ὁ τοιοῦτος λογισμός, εἰ καὶ δικαιοσύνην ἀγαπήσειας καὶ πρὸς τὸν θεὸν

Furthermore, the description of the *ideal of life* betrays (despite Tit 3:3, which probably reflects traditional ideas) nothing of the predicament from which, according to the genuine Pauline epistles, one is saved by faith. The description in 2 Tim of the preparedness for death is the only passage which goes beyond the realm of ideas that describe the normal, virtuous life of the good citizen. To be sure, this exception must not be overlooked in evaluating the meaning of "good citizenship." This ideal finds its limitation in the situation in which the Christian must bear witness.[30] Here, as in Luke–Acts, the ethics of good citizenship serve to regulate the time until the parousia, which is no longer felt to be imminent. The components of the regulation are: a good conscience, the idea that the Christian life aims at good works, faith and love, piety and dignity.[31] The Christian is supposed to grow into this life with the help of his education in grace (Tit 2:11) and the scriptures (2 Tim 3:16). Significant for this ideal of life is the relative frequency of the word "prudent" ($\sigma\acute{\omega}\phi\rho\omega\nu$) and its cognates: the group of words occurs nine times in the Pastorals, in the entire rest of the NT only six times (of these, two more passages must be omitted, since they refer to healed demoniacs). "Prudent" moderation also characterizes the attitude toward the *goods and necessities of life*: the asceticism of the Gnostics is rejected; all food should be enjoyed with thanksgiving (1 Tim 4:3ff). The Christian is warned against the intemperate use of wine (1 Tim 3:3, 8; Tit 1:7; 2:3), but moderate use is recommended (1 Tim 5:23). Youthful desires are to be shunned (2 Tim 2:22), but young women should marry (1 Tim 5:14; see also

1 Tim 3:2 and Tit 1:6). There is a warning against the dangers of riches; contentment is enjoined (1 Tim 6:6–10); but a certain amount of ownership of property in the congregation is taken for granted (1 Tim 6:17–19; see also 5:16).

The clearest sign of a Christianization of the world is seen in a developing family ethic, which goes substantially beyond traditional injunctions of rules for the household.[32] Already, a kind of religious family tradition appears (2 Tim 1:3, 5; 3:14f). From the example of Onesiphorus one learns that the piety of the father benefits the members of the family (2 Tim 1:16). Likewise, caring for aged members of the family is now emphasized as a specifically Christian duty (1 Tim 5:4, 8, 16). There is a similar emphasis on bringing up children so that they become faithful, obedient Christians (1 Tim 3:4, 12; 5:10 and Tit 1:6).[33] The duty of bearing children is given a Christian motivation (1 Tim 2:15 and 5:14), and is raised to equal standing beside the other duties of women: discipline, reserve, and obedience (1 Tim 2:9ff). Finally, the young women should be admonished by the older women to fulfill these duties (Tit 2:4f).

All this does not simply appear as a reproduction of popular ethics, but has been given new motivation by Christian ideas. Further, the fulfillment of these demands is urged for the church's sake. In no small degree the significance of the Pastoral Epistles rests on the fact that they are the only documents in the canon which enjoin such a structuring of life under the ideal of good Christian citizenship. For an historical understanding it is not enough simply to confront this ethical ideal with

---

$\epsilon\dot{\upsilon}\sigma\acute{\epsilon}\beta\epsilon\iota\alpha\nu$, $\dot{\epsilon}\pi\iota\epsilon\acute{\iota}\kappa\epsilon\iota\acute{\alpha}\nu$ $\tau\epsilon$ $\pi\rho\grave{o}s$ $\tau\upsilon\grave{s}$ $\pi o\lambda\acute{\iota}\tau\alpha s$). Spicq, *ad loc.*, attempts to interpret the term "piety" ($\epsilon\dot{\upsilon}\sigma\acute{\epsilon}\beta\epsilon\iota\alpha$) in closer association with the Roman concept of *pietas* and its political significance. See his excursus VI, pp. 125ff. On *pietas* see Theodor Ulrich, *Pietas (pius) als politischer Begriff im römischen Staate* (Breslau: M. & H. Marcus, 1930). Further literature can be found in Bauer, *s.v.*; and Friedrich Hauck, *TDNT* 5, p. 489–92. Werner Foerster, "Εὐσέβεια in den Pastoralbriefen," *NTS* 5 (1959): 213–18; *idem*, *TWNT* 7, pp. 175–84.

30 Cf. the political apologetics of Luke, who tirelessly assures the state of the Christian's loyalty, but who is acutely aware of the limits of such loyalty. See Hans Conzelmann, *The Theology of St. Luke*, tr. Geoffrey Buswell (London: Faber & Faber, 1965), 138ff.

31 Cf. the excursus on Good Conscience, pp. 18ff above; furthermore the commentary on 1 Tim 1:5;

2:10; 1:14; 2:2 and Tit 2:12.

32 See Dibelius–Greeven, *Kolosser, Epheser, Philemon*, excursus on Col 4:1; Lohse, *Colossians and Philemon*, on Col 4:1. Compare, on the other hand, the eschatological viewpoints which dominate these issues in Paul; see Werner Georg Kümmel, "Verlobung und Heirat bei Paulus," in *Neutestamentliche Studien für Bultmann*, ed. Walther Eltester (Berlin: Töpelmann, 1954), 275–95.

33 See the "education in Christ" ($\dot{\epsilon}\nu$ $X\rho\iota\sigma\tau\hat{\omega}$ $\pi\alpha\iota\delta\epsilon\acute{\iota}\alpha$) in *1 Clem* 21.8; cf. Werner Jentsch, *Urchristliches Erziehungsdenken*; and Georg Bertram, *TDNT* 5, pp. 596–625, esp. 619–25.

the ethics of Jesus or Paul. It is necessary to consider the changed situation of the church and to interpret the Pastorals, together with contemporary writings (Luke and the *Apostolic Fathers*), in the context of a changing conceptual structure—change had to follow the reorientation toward a longer duration of life in the world. If one keeps in mind the other alternative for dealing with this reorientation—i.e., the Gnostic alternative—one can understand this "Christian citizenship" as a genuine expression of an existence in the world based on faith, although doubtless the dialectic of the eschatological existence is no longer understood in its original keenness.

■ **3, 4** The extension of the intercessory prayer to refer to all people is based on the universal plan of God's (not Christ's) salvation. Cf. Epict., *Diss.* 3.24.2: "For God made all mankind to be happy, to be serene" (ὁ γὰρ θεὸς πάντας ἀνθρώπους ἐπὶ τὸ εὐδαιμονεῖν, ἐπὶ τὸ εὐσταθεῖν ἐποίησεν), and *Odes of Sol.* 9:13: "and wills that you be saved." "Savior" (σωτήρ) is used because of the following "to be saved" (σωθῆναι). This word has therefore its own force here and is not a mere title (see below the excursus to 2 Tim 1:10). "Recognition of truth" (ἐπίγνωσις ἀληθείας) in the Pastorals is a formula for Christianity, viz., conversion to the Christian faith. It is not explained nor more closely defined but rather presupposed as a phrase that has this explicit meaning. In Tit 1:1 it is thus parallel to and has the same weight as "faith," whereas in 2 Tim 2:25 and 3:7 it serves as a paraphrase for the state of salvation attained.[34] The origin of the expression is not to be sought in the terminology of mysticism, but rather in Hellenistic Judaism's rich store of Greek rational terminology, which now undergoes a characteristic transformation. Regard-

ing the content which these terms now describe, the supernatural element is strongly accentuated, but their usage is "rational," insofar as they are employed as criteria of knowledge in combatting misunderstanding and misuse. Since the "recognition of the truth" should be accessible to everyone, it is in precisely this connection that the mission of the Christian message is emphasized as applying to all men. It is not a question of "reconciliation of the All."[35] "Recognition" (ἐπίγνωσις) designates not only rational comprehension but also acknowledgement, just as "truth" (ἀλήθεια) is not merely a fact to be grasped theoretically, but also a state of affairs to be actualized. The phrase as a whole is a technical term for conversion.[36]

■ **5, 6** These verses are not easy to connect with what precedes. The contrast is not "*one* God and not *many*" (as in 1 Cor 8:6), but rather, looking back to "all men" (πάντες), "since there is *one* God, *all* shall be saved" (related to this are Rom 3:30 and Eph 4:6). However this connection seems secondary and the phrase is perhaps best explained by the assumption that the author concludes the thought with a solemn formula.[37] In that case, the words of this passage belong to the large number of "One God" (εἷς θεός) formulas.[38] If we are dealing with a quotation, it is to be explained first of all without reference to the context. These individual statements need not be seen as *ad hoc* creations in the interests of an anti-Gnostic polemic. With respect to its form, this is not a "credal formula" or "confession," but rather a liturgical piece, as style and content indicate. The extent of the quotation cannot be determined with certainty; does "the testimony . . ." (τὸ μαρτύριον κτλ.) still belong to the quotation or is it the elaboration of the writer?[39] The combination of statements about God (especially the predication "One God" [εἷς θεός]) and

---

34 On the meaning cf. Martin Dibelius, "Ἐπίγνωσις ἀληθείας" in *Botschaft und Geschichte. Gesammelte Aufsätze, 2: Zum Urchristentum und zur hellenistischen Religionsgeschichte,* in Verbindung mit Heinz Kraft, ed. Günther Bornkamm (Tübingen: J. C. B. Mohr [Paul Siebeck], 1956), 1–13; Rudolf Bultmann, *TDNT* 1, pp. 238–51, esp. 246, and pp. 703–13.

35 Against Wilhelm Michaelis, *Die Versöhnung des Alls* (Gümligen [Bern]: Siloah, 1950); cf. Johannes Schneider's review of this work in *ThLZ* 77 (1952): 158–61.

36 Heb 10:26; cf. also 2 John 1 and Philo, *Spec. leg.* 4.178: "by coming as a pilgrim to truth" (μεταβα-

στὰς εἰς ἀλήθειαν, referring to the conversion to Judaism).

37 See Eph 4:5, 6; cf. Norden, *Agnostos Theos,* 381.

38 See Dibelius–Greeven, *Kolosser, Epheser, Philemon* on Eph 4:5f; cf. Erik Peterson, ΕΙΣ ΘΕΟΣ (Göttingen: Vandenhoeck & Ruprecht, 1926), pp. 254ff. "One" (εἷς) is to be taken as a predicate, see Peterson, pp. 134 and 227ff; Albrecht Oepke, *TDNT* 4, p. 623.

39 See Easton, *ad loc.,* who assumes a formulated piece of tradition in five lines.

about Christ is old, although even in the earliest times it is not nearly so common as the Christological statements in just one part (see 1 Cor 8:6,[40] where Paul presupposes and comments upon a corresponding formula). For the further elaboration of the "first article," i.e., the part about God in these liturgical formulas, cf. 1 Tim 6:13.[41] The statement about Christ can refer to the person or to his work. In hymns and liturgical pieces the former appears to dominate. Both elements are then combined in such a way that the statement about the work is subordinated and taken as an interpretation of the statement about the person.[42] The classic example is the second article of the Apostolic Creed.[43] That the Savior is of divine essence is implied in the predication of his One-ness (εἷς). The term "mediator" (μεσίτης)

has, in addition to the legal, also cosmological and soteriological significance.[44] Although in this passage, in contrast to Heb 8:6, the διαθήκη is not mentioned, one must nevertheless presuppose the meaning "mediator of the covenant," as the context shows.[45] The mention of ἄνθρωπος in this connection raises the question whether the cosmological myth of the redeemer is in the background. In the Epistle to the Hebrews, this myth has been combined with the concepts of covenant and of sacrifice.[46] Admittedly, in 1 Tim 2 this context can at best be assumed by inference: only the idea of reconciliation is fully stated. Nor is there any reference to pre-existence.[47] The title "man" (ἄνθρωπος) is interpreted by the phrase which follows. In contrast to Phil 2:6ff, the work of salvation is not brought to completion by

---

40 Oscar Cullmann, *The Earliest Christian Confessions*, tr. from the French by J. K. S. Reid (London: Lutterworth Press, 1949); on the origin of the two-part formula see pp. 36f; cf. further Hans Lietzmann, "Symbolstudien, (Fortsetzung)," *ZNW* 22 (1923): 268ff, and Ernst von Dobschütz, "Zwei- und dreigliedrige Formeln," *JBL* 50 (1931): 117–47.

41 Lietzmann, "Symbolstudien," *ZNW* 21 (1922): 6ff.

42 Rudolf Bultmann, review of Oscar Cullmann, *Les premières confessions de foi chrétiennes* (French original of *The Earliest Christian Confessions*), *ThLZ* 74 (1949): 41.

43 On this see Ernst von Dobschütz, *Das Apostolicum in biblisch-theologischer Beleuchtung* (Giessen: Töpelmann, 1932), 45.

44 Cf. Philo, *Vit. Mos.* 2.166, concerning Moses, to whom God proclaimed on the mountain that the people were serving idols: "Struck with dismay, and compelled to believe the incredible tale, he yet took the part of mediator and reconciler and did not hurry away at once, but first made prayers and supplications, begging that their sins might be forgiven." (καταπλαγεὶς δὲ καὶ ἀναγκασθεὶς πιστεύειν ἀπίστοις πράξεσιν οἷα μεσίτης καὶ διαλλακτὴς οὐκ εὐθὺς ἀπεπήδησεν, ἀλλὰ πρότερον τὰς ὑπὲρ τοῦ ἔθνους ἱκεσίας καὶ λιτὰς ἐποιεῖτο συγγνῶναι τῶν ἡμαρτημένων δεόμενος). In what follows, Moses is called "protector and intercessor" (ὁ κηδεμὼν καὶ παραιτητής); cf. this with *Rer. div. her.* 206 (about Moses) " 'and I stood between the Lord and you' (Deut 5:5), that is neither uncreated as God, nor created as you, but midway between the two extremes, a surety to both sides." ("κἀγὼ εἱστήκειν ἀνὰ μέσον κυρίου καὶ ὑμῶν" [Deut 5:5] οὔτε ἀγένητος ὡς ὁ θεὸς ὢν οὔτε γενητὸς ὡς ὑμεῖς, ἀλλὰ μέσος τῶν ἄκρων, ἀμφοτέρους ὁμηρεύων). The same understanding can be applied to the much

discussed passage in Plutarch, *Isis et Osiris* 46 p. 269 E: "and for this reason the Persians call Mithra the mediatrix" (διὸ καὶ Μίθρην Πέρσαι τὸν μεσίτην ὀνομάζουσιν). With regard to this latter passage see Albrecht Oepke, *TDNT* 4, p. 606; on the concept in general, cf. *ibid.*, p. 598ff. See also Hans Lietzmann, *An die Galater*, HNT 10 (Tübingen: J. C. B. Mohr [Paul Siebeck], ³1932) on Gal 3:19, 20; Hans Windisch, *Der Hebräerbrief*, HNT 14 (Tübingen: J. C. B. Mohr [Paul Siebeck], ²1931), on Heb 8:6; Heinrich Schlier, *Der Brief an die Galater*, KEK 7 (Göttingen: Vandenhoeck & Ruprecht, ¹²1962), 151ff.

45 Cf. *Test. Dan.* 6.2: (concerning the angel who enters with his petition on behalf of Israel) "that this is a mediator between God and men" (ὅτι οὗτός ἐστι μεσίτης θεοῦ καὶ ἀνθρώπων).

46 See Ernst Käsemann, *Das wandernde Gottesvolk*, FRLANT 55 (Göttingen: Vandenhoeck & Ruprecht, ²1957); cf. in this connection *Odes of Sol.* 41.9ff: "For the Father of Truth remembered me;/He who possessed me from the beginning. . . . And His Word is with us in all our way, /The Savior, who makes alive and does not reject our souls: the man who was humbled,/ and was exalted by His own righteousness;/the Son of the Most High appeared /in the perfection of his Father. . . . The Messiah is truly one;/and He was known before the foundations of the world that He might save souls for ever by the truth of His name." Tr. James Rendel Harris and Alphonse Mingana, ed., *The Odes and Psalms of Solomon*, vol. 2 (Manchester: The University Press, 1920), p. 400. Cf. R. Abramowski, "Der Christus der Salomooden," *ZNW* 35 (1936): 44–69.

47 Especially Windisch, "Zur Christologie," doubts that the author had this in mind.

means of a cosmic descent understood as an act of obedience, but rather by means of the self–offering which is understood in the sense of the concept of "ransom."

■ **6** "Ransom" (ἀντίλυτρον), an intensive form of "price of release" (λυτρόν), is attested in *Orphica Lithica*.[48] This verse is hardly a quotation from Mk 10:45, but rather a Hellenistically colored variant of that word of Jesus.[49] If we are dealing with a formula, it is pointless to ask to whom, in the author's opinion, the ransom is to be paid. There is no indication that the background for this idea is the lawsuit of God with Satan.[50] "The testimony" (τὸ μαρτύριον) stands in apposition to "to hand over, to sacrifice oneself" (διδόναι) implied in "who gave himself" (ὁ δούς, see Rom 12:1).[51] "In its own (determined) times" (καιροῖς ἰδίοις) can refer to the process of nature,[52] but in the Pastoral Epistles (here as well as in 6:15 and Tit 1:3) it is a term referring to the history of salvation, a phrase which originally meant the time determined by God in the promises.

■ **7** A similar connection exists in Eph 3:7. There, as here, the mission to the pagans is rightly emphasized as Paul's true calling. Here this certainty is emphasized by a solemn assurance, which is unusual, because it seems superfluous to make such an assurance to Timothy. The passage is perhaps modeled after Rom 9:1. In any event the schema found in 1:15 is again present: the linking of the objective revelation with the person proclaiming it. The explicit mention of the application to the present through preaching is constitutive for the concept of revelation in the Pastorals, as is Ephesians' mention of the church in a comparable context.[53] Paul is also referred to as "herald" (κῆρυξ) in *1 Clem.* 5:6. It can mean simply "preacher," see 2 Petr 2:5. In the Greek societies the term was used to designate the functionary whose duty, at least in certain places, was to announce the honors which had been voted for someone.[54] It is more appropriate, however, to refer to the cultic functions of the herald which are also attested.[55]

48 *Orphica Lithica* 593 (p. 129, Abel). See also Bauer, *s.v.*

49 On the Hellenistic character see Joachim Jeremias, "Das Lösegeld für Viele (Mk 10:45)," *Judaica* 3 (1948): 249–64. On the concept as such, cf. the related passages Tit 2:14 and Mk 10:45, and see Vincent Taylor, *The Atonement in New Testament Teaching* (London: Epworth Press, ³1958), pp. 45ff.

50 Ragnar Asting, *Verkündigung*, 631ff; one should rather compare Rom 3:24ff. On the whole constellation of the concept of reconciliation, sacrifice, renewal of the covenant, see Ernst Käsemann, "Zum Verständnis von Römer 3:24–26," *ZNW* 43 (1950–51): 150–54; reprinted in Exegetische Versuche und Besinnungen 1 (Göttingen: Vandenhoeck & Ruprecht, 1960), 96–100.

51 Cf. Lietzmann, *Römer*, on Rom 12:1.

52 Cf. *1 Clem.* 20:4: "the earth teems according to his will at its proper seasons" (γῆ κυοφοροῦσα κατὰ τὸ θέλημα αὐτοῦ τοῖς ἰδίοις καιροῖς).

53 On this see Windisch, "Zur Christologie."

54 Cf. *CIG* II 2525[b] 31 (Rhodes), *IG* XII 1, 890.15 (Netteia); Philippe Le Bas, *Voyage archéologique en Grèce et en Asie Mineure* (Paris: P. Le Bas and W. H. Waddington, 1847ff), vol. II, explications, sect. VI, p. 203f, no. 341 a 3 (Tegea); and F. Poland, *Geschichte des griechischen Vereinswesen* (Leipzig: Teubner, 1909), 395.

55 See the attestations cited by Bauer and Gerhard Friedrich, *TDNT* 3, pp. 683–96, esp. pp. 689ff. The Cynic appears in Epict., *Diss.* 3.22.69 as ἄγγελος, κατάσκοπος and κῆρυξ τῶν θεῶν. *Corp. Herm.* 4:4 comes very near the NT usage. In *Gen. Rabba* 30 (18b) Noah, as the preacher of repentance, is called "herald."

2

On Prayer by Men and Women

8   As far as prayer is concerned, I wish that
men everywhere would raise holy hands,
without a thought of anger and strife.
9/ And the women should do likewise, in
modest deportment with chastity and
prudence, (and) should not decorate
themselves with braids and gold, (nor
with) pearls or expensive clothes,
10/ but rather with what is fitting for
women who profess the worship of
God: with good works. 11/ A woman
should learn by being silent (listening
and) subordinating herself; 12/ but I do
not allow a woman to teach nor to
have authority over a man, but rather
she should keep silent. 13/ For Adam
was created first and only then Eve.
14/ And Adam was not seduced, but
rather the woman succumbed to the seduction and fell into sin. 15/ But she
shall be saved through bearing children,
if they (all) remain in faith, love and
sanctification with dignity. 1a/ The
word stands firm.

The church order now details how men and women
should pray. It seems to stay with the theme which was
raised in 2:1. But in regard to the regulations for women,
it is questionable whether the words really refer to cultic
behavior. They rather comprise a general rule for women,
here applied to prayer (see below on 2:11f). The observation that the regulations are somewhat artificially
inserted into the pattern of rules for the household[1] points
in the same direction. After the general exhortation to
prayer, the quotation of the "faith" upon which prayer is
founded, and the reference to the apostle who is the

guarantor of the tradition, detailed instructions are given.
■ **8** On "I wish" ($\beta o \acute{u} \lambda o \mu a \iota$) see below on 5:14. "Holy
hands" ($\acute{o} \sigma \iota o \iota \ \chi \epsilon \hat{\iota} \rho \epsilon s$) in the Greek tragedians are
hands which are ritually pure.[2] Therefore in 1 Tim, the
stress lies not on this formulaic expression, but rather
on what follows.[3] On "without a thought of anger etc."
($\chi \omega \rho \grave{\iota} s \ \grave{o} \rho \gamma \hat{\eta} s \ \kappa \tau \lambda.$), cf. Phil 2:14. Cf. also the impressive representation of the raised hands on the pillar at
Rheneia, together with the prayer of revenge for the
Jewess, Heraclea, whose "innocent blood" ($\grave{a} \nu a \acute{\iota} \tau \iota o \nu$

---

1   See von Campenhausen, "Polykarp," p. 229f.
2   On $\acute{o} \sigma \iota o s$, "pure," see Erwin Rohde, *Psyche: The
    Cult of Souls and Belief in Immortality among the Greeks*
    (New York: Harcourt, Brace & Co., 1925), p. 233
    n. 18; Ulrich von Wilamowitz–Moellendorf, *Platon*
    (Berlin: Weidmannsche Buchhandlung, ²1920),
    vol. I, p. 61. Purity of the hands is also dealt with
    in the *Manual of Discipline* (1 QS IX, 15). This purity
    is also interpreted morally outside Christianity; see
    Seneca, *Naturales Quaestiones* 3 preface 14: "to raise
    pure hands to heaven" (*puras ad caelum manus tol-
    lere*). The expression seems to have been widely used
    in this sense; see the Heliodorus fragment in Galen,
    De antidotis 2.7 (vol. XIV, p. 145, Kühn): "But pure
    hands I raise into the bright air, and my mind is
    not at all defiled by any evil" ($\grave{a} \lambda \lambda$' $\acute{o} \sigma \acute{\iota} a s \ \mu \grave{\epsilon} \nu \ \chi \epsilon \hat{\iota}$-
    $\rho a s \ \grave{\epsilon} s \ \grave{\eta} \acute{\epsilon} \rho a \ \lambda a \mu \pi \rho \grave{o} \nu \ \grave{a} \acute{\epsilon} \iota \rho \omega \ \kappa a \grave{\iota} \ \kappa a \kappa \acute{\iota} \eta s \ \grave{a} \mu \acute{o} \lambda \upsilon \nu$-
    $\tau o \nu \ \acute{\epsilon} \chi \omega \ \kappa a \tau \grave{a} \ \pi \acute{a} \nu \tau a \ \lambda o \gamma \iota \sigma \mu \acute{o} \nu$) [trans. by Ed.];

and Josephus, *Bell.* 5.380: "uplifting pure hands"
($\kappa a \theta a \rho \grave{a} s \ \delta$' $\grave{a} \nu a \tau \epsilon \acute{\iota} \nu a s \ \tau \grave{a} s \ \chi \epsilon \hat{\iota} \rho a s$). On the latter
passage see Schlatter, *Theologie des Judentums*, p. 111.
See also *1 Clem.* 29.1: "Let us then approach him
in holiness of soul, raising pure and undefiled hands
to him" ($\pi \rho o \sigma \acute{\epsilon} \lambda \theta \omega \mu \epsilon \nu \ o \grave{u} \nu \ a \grave{u} \tau \hat{\omega} \ \grave{\epsilon} \nu \ \grave{o} \sigma \iota \acute{o} \tau \eta \tau \iota \ \psi \upsilon$-
$\chi \hat{\eta} s, \ \grave{a} \gamma \nu \grave{a} s \ \kappa a \grave{\iota} \ \grave{a} \mu \iota \acute{a} \nu \tau o \upsilon s \ \chi \epsilon \hat{\iota} \rho a s \ a \acute{\iota} \rho o \nu \tau \epsilon s \ \pi \rho \grave{o} s$
$a \grave{u} \tau \acute{o} \nu$). The point is especially clearly illustrated in
Athenag. *Suppl.* 13.2: "Whensoever we raise holy
hands to God . . . what further need have we of heca-
tombs?" ($\acute{o} \tau a \nu \ (o \grave{u} \nu) \ . . . \ \grave{\epsilon} \pi a \acute{\iota} \rho \omega \mu \epsilon \nu \ \grave{o} \sigma \acute{\iota} o \upsilon s \ \chi \epsilon \hat{\iota} \rho a s$
$a \grave{u} \tau \hat{\omega}, \ \pi o \acute{\iota} a s \ \acute{\epsilon} \tau \iota \ \chi \rho \epsilon \acute{\iota} a \nu \ \grave{\epsilon} \kappa a \tau \acute{o} \mu \beta \eta s \ \acute{\epsilon} \chi \epsilon \iota$) [Tr. J. H.
Crehan in *Ancient Christian Writers*, vol. 23, p. 44].
3   On gestures accompanying prayer, see Ludwig von
    Sybel, *Christliche Antike* (Marburg: Elwert, 1906),
    pp. 256, 258 with notes; G. Appel, *De Romanorum
    precationibus* (Giessen: A. Töpelmann, 1908–09), 194.
    Cf. also Tertullian, *Apology* 30: "Looking up to

αἷμα) was poured out.[4] By the words "without anger" (χωρὶς ὀργῆς) one is reminded of Mk 11:25 (Mt 6:14). An early Christian at prayer must have thought of such words of the Lord, as is shown by *Did.* 15.4: "But prayers . . . perform as you find it in the Gospel of our Lord" (τὰς δ' εὐχὰς ὑμῶν . . . οὕτως ποιήσατε ὡς ἔχετε ἐν τῷ εὐαγγελίῳ τοῦ κυρίου ἡμῶν). "Strife" (διαλογισμοῦ, ℵ[c] G 33 read the plural) can refer to thoughts that hinder prayer because they cast doubt upon the possibility that the request is answered (*Herm. mand.* 9.1f). Theodoret and Theodore of Mopsuestia accept this explanation. More recent scholars because of the sense of the word (διαλογισμός) and the parallel term "anger" (ὀργή), have been led to take it to mean "debate, strife."[5] For this use of the word, one is reminded of *Did.* 14.2f: "but let none who has a quarrel with his fellow join in your meeting until they be reconciled, that your sacrifice be not defiled. For this is that which was spoken by the Lord, 'In every place and time offer me a pure sacrifice. . . .'" (πᾶς δὲ ἔχων τὴν ἀμφιβολίαν μετὰ τοῦ ἑταίρου αὐτοῦ μὴ συνελθέτω ὑμῖν, ἕως οὗ διαλλαγῶσιν, ἵνα μὴ κοινωθῇ ἡ θυσία ὑμῶν, αὕτη γάρ ἐστιν ἡ ῥηθεῖσα ὑπὸ κυρίου. Ἐν παντὶ τόπῳ καὶ χρόνῳ προσφέρειν μοι θυσίαν καθαράν). This passage, together with the quotation from Mal 1:11 "Everywhere incense is offered to me and a pure offering" (ἐν παντὶ τόπῳ θυμίαμα προσάγεται τῷ ὀνόματί μου καὶ θυσία καθαρά),[6] explain the somewhat unmotivated phrase "everywhere" (ἐν παντὶ τόπῳ) in 1 Tim 2:8. One has to assume that this expression (like "pure hands") was taken into the Pastorals from an earlier instruction, and that Mal 1:11 was quoted there.[7]

■ 9 "Likewise the women" (ὡσαύτως) should be supplemented with "I wish them to pray" (προσεύχεσθαι βούλομαι), unless one combines it with "in modest deportment they should decorate themselves" (ἐν καταστολῇ κοσμίῳ . . . κοσμεῖν ἑαυτάς).[8] The rhetorical exchange of prepositions, "in" and "with" (ἐν-μετά, ἐν-διά) makes it difficult to decide.[9] It is probable that these regulations, here doubtless intended for the worship service, originally referred to the behavior of women in general. For the argument given in 2:13ff refers to the place of woman in creation, not to her behavior during the service. Also, the injunctions which immediately follow refer to the behavior of women in life in general. If we are dealing with traditional material, then the asyndetic position of the infinitive "decorate themselves" (κοσμεῖν ἑαυτάς) would be explained. "Deportment" (καταστολή) can refer sometimes to external appearance,[10] sometimes to character and disposition,[11] some

---

heaven the Christians—with hands outspread, because innocent" etc. (illuc [ad caelum] suspicientes Christiani manibus expansis, quia innocuis etc.); *1 Clem.* 2:3 "and with pious confidence you stretched out your hands to Almighty God" (μετ' εὐσεβοῦς πεποιθήσεως ἐξετείνετε τὰς χεῖρας ὑμῶν πρὸς τὸν παντοκράτορα θεόν).

4 Deissmann, *LAE*, 413ff.

5 Theodoret (III, 650, Schulze): "Without doubting. But believing that in all ways will you receive what you ask for" (ἀμφιβολίας χωρίς. πιστεύων ὅτι λήψῃ πάντως ὅπερ αἰτεῖς); and Theodore of Mopsuestia (II, p. 91, Swete): "with a believing heart, not in the least doubting that you will receive what you request" (fideli mente minime dubitantes illa accipere quae postulant) [trans. by Ed.] See also Bernhard Weiss, *Die Briefe Pauli an Timotheus und Titus*, KEK 11 (Göttingen: Vandenhoeck & Ruprecht, 1902); Walter Lock, *A Critical and Exegetical Commentary on the Pastoral Epistles*, ICC (Edinburgh and New York: T. & T. Clark, 1924); and Jeremias, *ad loc.*

6 This passage is also adduced by Theodoret (vol. III,

p. 649, Schulze).

7 Bartsch, *Anfänge*, 47ff. See the Introduction above, section 2, pp. 16f.

8 Gustav Wohlenberg, *Die Pastoralbriefe*, Zahn's Kommentar zum NT 13 (Leipzig: Deichert, [4]1923), *ad loc.*

9 Cf. Dibelius, *Thessalonicher, Philipper*, on 1 Thess 1:5.

10 Josephus, *Bell.* 2.126 (about the Essenes) "In their dress and deportment they resemble children under rigorous discipline" (καταστολὴ δὲ καὶ σχῆμα σώματος ὅμοιον τοῖς μετὰ φόβου παιδαγωγουμένοις παισίν). Cf. also Isa 61:3, and see Chrysostom commenting on this passage (XI, p. 590, Montfaucon): "What does he say about the deportment? This: clothing should be put on everywhere well and with modesty, not elaborately" (καταστολὴν τί φησι; τουτέστι. τὴν ἀμπεχόνην πάντοθεν περιεστάλθαι καλῶς, κοσμίως, μὴ περιέργως) [trans. by Ed.].

11 Epict., *Diss.* 2.10.15: ". . . self-respect and a dignified deportment and gentleness" (αἰδῶ καὶ καταστολὴν καὶ ἡμερότητα). *Inscr. Priene* 109.186f: "in mod

times to both.[12] Since "modest" (κοσμίως) is stressed in the honorary inscriptions precisely as a virtue of women, and since the language of the Pastorals shows a certain relationship with that of the inscriptions, the expression under discussion can hardly be restricted to clothing.[13] The reading "in modesty" (κοσμίως, ℵ^c D* G 33 Origen) in 1 Tim 2:9 is probably a modification occasioned by the frequent use of the adverb in such contexts. On the connection between "modesty" (κοσμιό-της) and "prudence" (σωφροσύνη), see below on 3:2. "Prudence" (σωφροσύνη) is also frequently mentioned as a womanly virtue, and in such contexts it has a special nuance: it is almost the equivalent of chastity. See Philo, *Spec. leg.* 1.102: "For a harlot is profane in body and soul, even if she has discarded her trade and assumed a decent and chaste demeanor, and he is forbidden even to approach her" (πόρνη μὲν γὰρ καὶ βεβήλῳ σῶμα καὶ ψυχὴν οὐδὲ προσελθεῖν ἐᾷ (scil. ὁ νομοθέτης τὸν ἱερέα), κἂν τὴν ἐργασίαν ἀποθεμένη σχῆμα κόσμιον καὶ σῶφρον ὑποδύηται). According to *Spec. leg.* 3.51, the harlot knows nothing about "modesty, chastity, and prudence" (κοσμιότης, αἰδώς, σωφροσύνη).[14] On the polemic against ornaments see 1 Petr 3:3 and especially *Ps. Clem. Hom.* 13.16: "The prudent woman adorns herself for the Son of God as her bridegroom, clothed with holy light as a beautiful mantle, dressed in chastity, wearing precious pearls, the prudent words, and she

appears in bright light, when her mind shines." (ἡ σώ-φρων γυνὴ ὡς νυμφίῳ τῷ υἱῷ τοῦ θεοῦ κοσμεῖται, ἐνδεδυμένη τὸ σεμνὸν φῶς . . . καλὰ φάρεα. ἠμφίε-σται τὴν αἰδώ, καὶ τιμίους μαργαρίτας περίκειται, τοὺς σωφρονίζοντας λόγους, λευκὴ δὲ τυγχάνει, ὅταν τὰς φρένας ᾖ λελαμπρυμένη) [trans. by Ed.].[15] The accent in the Pastorals lies not in the idea that women should (modestly!) adorn themselves, but rather that true ornamentation is not external at all. That Christian women are in a special sense "holy women" (ἱεραὶ γυναῖκες) is explicitly stated in the following verse.

■ **10** "To profess," "to confess" (ἐπαγγέλλεσθαι), is used as in Ign. *Eph.* 14.2: "No man who professes faith sins, nor does he hate who has obtained love." (οὐδεὶς πίστιν ἐπαγγελλόμενος ἁμαρτάνει, οὐδὲ ἀγάπην κεκτημένος μισεῖ), and further "they who profess to be of Christ" (οἱ ἐπαγγελλόμενοι Χριστοῦ εἶναι). See also Lucian, *Vit. auctio* 7: "What creed does he profess?" (τίνα τὴν ἄσκησιν ἐπαγγέλλεται;); it is clear that the object of the confession is implied in "religion," "worship of God" (θεοσέβεια). Since there is no mention of Christ, one can assume that the expression is a self–designation which was already common in Judaism, and compare it with a passage from Philo: "Who among those who profess piety deserve to be compared with these?" (οἷς τίνας συγκρίνειν ἄξιον τῶν ἐπαγγελλο-

---

esty and gracefulness" (τῆι δὲ καταστολῆι καὶ τῆι εὐσχημ[οσύνη]) [trans. by Ed.].

12 Epict., *Diss.* 2.21.11: "and now do you come to me with a solemn deportment, like a philosopher" (καὶ ἔρχῃ μοι καταστολὰς ποιήσας ὡς σοφός) [Loeb modified].

13 See *Inscr. Magn.* 162.6: "living in prudence and modesty" (ζήσαντα σωφρόνως καὶ κοσμίως); "Inschriften von Herakleia" in *Bulletin de correspondance hellénique*, 1898, p. 496, line 9: "The learned woman lived with modesty" (ἡ φιλόσοφος ζήσασα κοσ-μίως); cf. also Ditt. *Or.*, II, 474 A 5, and Philo, *Spec. leg.* 1.102 (see below). Material may be found in Gerhard Delling, *Die Stellung des Paulus zu Frau und Ehe* (Stuttgart: Kohlhammer, 1931), 131, and Bartsch, *Anfänge*, 60ff; J. J. B. Mulder, *Quaestiones nonnullae ad Athenensium matrimonia vitamque coniuga-lem pertinentes*, Unpub. Diss. (Utrecht: 1920).

14 In Josephus, *Ant.* 18.66ff the "prudence" (σωφρο-νεῖν, σωφροσύνη) of a certain Pauline is extolled, a woman whose chastity is being emphasized; cf. Sextus 235 (ed. Henry Chadwick, TS, N. S. 5, 1959): "It is prudence (=chastity) which should be con-

sidered the adornment of a believing woman" (πιστῆ γυναικὶ κόσμος σωφροσύνη νομιζέσθω) [trans. by Ed.]. Musonius also seems to assume that "pru-dence" is a virtue of woman: "To be prudent (chaste) is praiseworthy in a woman, and it is equally praiseworthy in a man" (σωφρονεῖν μὲν αὖ καλὸν τὴν γυναῖκα, καλὸν δ᾽ ὁμοίως καὶ τὸν ἄνδρα, Mu-son. p. 14, 12ff, Hense) [trans. by Ed.]. Cf. the burial column of Seratus cited in Dibelius, *Thessalonicher, Philipper*, on 1 Thess 1:8; *Inscr. Magn.* 162.6 (see above n. 13); see also Tit 2:4.

15 Cf. the regulations concerning clothing in the great mystery inscriptions of Andania (Ditt. *Syll.* II 736, 15ff., esp. 22f.), where it is said about the "holy women" (ἱεραὶ γυναῖκες): "She must not wear any gold ornament, nor put on rouge, nor white paint, nor a wreath, nor braid her hair; nor put on shoes; but she should only wear clothes of felt or skins of sacrificed animals" (μὴ ἐχέτω δὲ μηδεμία χρυσία μηδὲ φῦκος μηδὲ ψιμίθιον μηδὲ ἀνάδεμα μηδὲ τὰς τρίχας ἀνπεπλεγμένας μηδὲ ὑποδήματα εἰ μὴ πίλινα ἢ δερμάτινα ἱερόθυτα) [trans. by Ed.]. See also the material provided by Karl Weidinger,

μένων εὐσέβειαν; *Vit. cont.* 3).[16] Even the parallel to
1 Tim 2:10, 1 Petr 3:3ff (both passages probably derive
from the same list of rules for the household), contains
a reminiscence of the "holy women" (ἅγιαι γυναῖκες)
of the OT.

The true ornamentation consists in "good works." It is
striking that again and again they are mentioned in
the Pastoral Epistles as a sign of genuine Christianity,
whereas the genuine Pauline epistles use only the singular, and consequently understand the expression in a
different way (however, see Eph 2:10 and Heb 10:24).
The influence of Jewish parenesis may be operative here;
but its terms would not have been appropriated if the
rational conception of Christianity, with its goal of a
Christianized life, had not favored their adoption (cf.
above, the second excursus to 2:2, pp. 39ff).

■ **11, 12** The context lets this injunction to silence appear as a commandment relating to the worship service.[17]
The parallelism of vss 11 and 12 is helpful in explanation: "subordination" (ὑποταγή) means that women
should subordinate themselves to what the men in the
congregation teach; "to be domineering" (αὐθεντεῖν)
would be the opposite, and would mean in this context
that they should not "interrupt" men who speak in
church. But it is questionable whether the phrases were
originally intended as such an injunction for the worship service.[18] Accordingly one must ask whether the

verb in question did not originally have a more general
meaning.[19] We now know of a passage from the first
century B.C. which speaks of "self–assured, firm conduct"
(κἀμοῦ αὐθεντηκότος πρὸς αὐτόν).[20]

The relationship of 1 Tim 2:11–12 to 1 Cor 14:34f
will be evaluated in different ways, depending on whether
one takes the passage in 1 Cor 14 as an interpolation.[21]
As for "to keep silent" (εἶναι ἐν ἡσυχίᾳ) one must
supply an "I wish" (βούλομαι) from the preceding "I
do not allow" (οὐκ ἐπιτρέπω). On the thought, cf. a
fragment from the comedian, Philemon: "It is a good
wife's duty, O Nikostrate, to be devoted to her husband,
but in subordination; a wife who prevails is a great evil."
(ἀγαθῆς γυναικός ἐστιν, ὦ Νικοστράτη, μὴ κρεῖττον᾿
εἶναι τἀνδρὸς ἀλλ᾿ ὑπήκοον. γυνὴ δὲ νικῶσ᾿ ἄνδρα
κακόν ἐστιν μέγα).[22] In 1 Tim, to be sure, the commandment was taken over from Jewish parenesis, as is
shown by what follows.

■ **13–15** Since the following proof is for the author
clearly a matter of course and unimpeachable,[23] he can
content himself with allusions such as "salvation shall
come to her by bearing children" (σωθήσεται διὰ τῆς
τεκνογονίας). If this is taken into consideration, the
hypothesis becomes credible that in using the phrase
"succumbed to the seduction" (ἐξαπατηθεῖσα), the

Die Haustafeln (Leipzig: J. C. Hinrichs, 1928), pp.
65, and 67, and in Hans Windisch, *Die katholischen
Briefe*, HNT 15, rev. Herbert Preisker (Tübingen:
J. C. B. Mohr [Paul Siebeck] ³1951), on 1 Petr 3:3.

16 There is some question about the authenticity of the
passage. On θεοσέβεια see the seat–inscription in
the theater at Miletus: "Place of the Jews who are
also called God–fearing" (τόπος Εἰουδέων τῶν καὶ
θεοσεβίον) (Deissmann, *LAE*, 451f). On this passage see Schürer, *A History of the Jewish People*, 2²
p. 314 n. 291.

17 B. Weiss, *ad loc.*, Heinrich Julius Holtzmann, *Die
Pastoralbriefe kritisch und exegetisch bearbeitet* (Leipzig:
Wilhelm Engelmann, 1880), Jeremias, *ad loc.* agree
on this point, as do Theodore (II, 94, Swete) and
Theodoret (III, 650, Schulze), all of whom appeal
to 1 Cor 7:16.

18 See above the introductory remark on 2:8–15; 2:9
and the Introduction, section 2 (p. 44 and pp. 6f).

19 That it did is confirmed by the lexicographer, Moe-
ris (p. 54, Pierson) who points out that the word is
the equivalent of an Attic word meaning "to have
one's own jurisdiction" αὐτοδίκην (αὐτοδικεῖν)

᾿Αττικῶς, αὐθέντην (αὐθεντεῖν) ῾Ελληνικῶς.

20 *BGU* IV 1208.37f (from 27–26 B.C.). The word appears also in two other passages, but has there a technical business sense *BGU* I 103.3, 5 (6th or 7th cent.
A.D.), and *P. Masp.* II 67, 151.174 (6th cent. A.D.).

21 See Lietzmann–Kümmel, *Korinther, ad loc.* Cf. also
Hans Windisch, "Sinn und Geltung des apostolischen *Mulier taceat in ecclesia* (Die Frau schweige in
der Gemeinde)," *Christliche Welt*, 1930, col. 411–25
[continued under the title: "Noch einmal: *Mulier
taceat in ecclesia*; Ein Wort zur Abwehr und zur Klärung," *ibid.*, Col. 837–40]; see also Martin Dibelius,
"Von Stellung und Dienst der Frau im Neuen Testament," *Die Theologin* (1942): 33ff.

22 Philemon No. 132 (vol. 2, p. 519, Kock) [trans. by
Ed.].

23 Sir 25:24: "The beginning of sin was by the woman,
and through her we all die" (ἀπὸ γυναικὸς ἀρχὴ
ἁμαρτίας καὶ δι᾿ αὐτὴν ἀποθνήσκομεν πάντες);
cf. also 1 Cor 11:8f and Lietzmann–Kümmel, *Korinther, ad loc.*

author was referring to sexual seduction.[24] The Jewish tradition, according to which the serpent indulged in unchaste practices with Eve, is already mentioned in 2 Cor 11:3.[25] This assertion becomes even more convincing when we notice that any "being deceived" ($\dot\alpha\pi\alpha\tau\hat\alpha$-$\sigma\theta\alpha\iota$) is categorically denied with respect to Adam. Furthermore, after such an interpretation of "succumbed to seduction" ($\dot\epsilon\xi\alpha\pi\alpha\tau\eta\theta\epsilon\hat\iota\sigma\alpha$), the mention of the feminine calling to motherhood (naturally influenced by Gen 3:16) receives a more comprehensive significance: "where someone sins, through that he is saved" (quo quis peccat, eo salvatur). The Jewish parenesis (a fixed list of "rules for the household"?) which was the model for all this, probably expressed these ideas even more clearly. Since the word "sin," "transgression" ($\pi\alpha\rho\dot\alpha\beta\alpha\sigma\iota s$) has been mentioned, the question of salvation from divine wrath becomes an urgent one. The answer is: "salvation shall come to her by child-bearing" ($\sigma\omega\theta\dot\eta\sigma\epsilon\tau\alpha\iota$ $\delta\iota\dot\alpha$ $\tau\hat\eta s$ $\tau\epsilon\kappa\nu o\gamma o\nu\dot\iota\alpha s$). The words do not refer to Eve,[26] nor to all women, but only to Christian women, as the qualifying clause shows (on "faith" and "love" see above on 1:14). If we compare Tit 2:4, we cannot exclude the possibility that the author here also has the education of children in mind; cf. b Ber. 17a: "How do women attain merit? By letting their children be instructed in the house of learning." But the subject of the verb "to remain" ($\mu\epsilon\dot\iota\nu\omega\sigma\iota\nu$) is problematic in any case. According to E. G. Gulin,[27] what we have here is a reference to the atoning power of the birth pangs. But it is not the suffering which is emphasized, but the giving birth itself. It may be that the same ideas about the Christianization of

the natural order, its healing through faith viz. worship, are present here as well as in 1 Tim 3:4, 12; 5:10, 14.[28]

Instructions for Women

In these instructions for women, rules for the worship service and injunctions for daily life seem to stand side by side. This results from the fact that the church order has been expanded with general parenetic material (derived from rules for the household). The motivation and objectives of this extensive treatment of the questions relating to women are to be sought in the situation of the congregations which the author has in mind. The commandment to silence during the assembly of the congregation was explained by Theodoret (III, 650, Schulze) this way: "Since women too have the benefit of the prophetic gift, it was necessary that he give instructions also about that." ($\dot\epsilon\pi\epsilon\iota\delta\dot\eta$ $\kappa\alpha\dot\iota$ $\gamma\upsilon\nu\alpha\hat\iota\kappa\epsilon s$ $\pi\rho o\phi\eta\tau\iota\kappa\hat\eta s$ $\dot\alpha\pi\dot\eta\lambda\alpha\upsilon\sigma\alpha\nu$ $\chi\dot\alpha\rho\iota\tau os$, $\dot\alpha\nu\alpha\gamma\kappa\alpha\dot\iota\omega s$ $\kappa\alpha\dot\iota$ $\pi\epsilon\rho\dot\iota$ $\tau o\dot\upsilon\tau o\upsilon$ $\nu o\mu o\theta\epsilon\tau\epsilon\hat\iota$) [trans. by Ed.]. That within the scope of Paul's mission it was possible for women to teach is shown by Acts 18:26. In Gnostic circles individual virgins had privileged positions. 2 Tim 3:6 shows that women played some kind of role among the opponents of the Pastoral Epistles. The *Acts of Paul* also provide material on this question. To be sure, their relationship to the Pastorals is a matter of controversy.[29] But it seems likely that they point to movements similar to those which must be presupposed for the context of our author, and especially of his opponents. The position which Thekla assumes in the *Acts of Paul*[30] as teacher and preacher is very relevant to this context.[31] But Gnostic or semi-

---

24 See Martin Dibelius, *Die Geisterwelt im Glauben des Paulus* (Göttingen: Vandenhoeck and Ruprecht, 1909), 177ff.

25 In addition to the texts given in Lietzmann–Kümmel, *Korinther*, on 2 Cor 11:3; cf. *Gen. Rabba* 18 on Gen 2:23; *Protevangelium Jacobi* 13.1.

26 Not to speak of referring it to Mary; see John A. Cramer, *Catene in Sancti Pauli: Epistulas ad Timotheum, Titum, Philemona et ad Hebraeos*, Catenae Graecorum Patrum in Novum Testamentum 7 (Oxford: Clarendon Press, 1843), 7, 22: "through her giving birth, according to the flesh, to Christ" ($\delta\iota\dot\alpha$ $\tau o\hat\upsilon$ $\dot\epsilon\xi$ $\alpha\dot\upsilon\tau\hat\eta s$ $\kappa\alpha\tau\dot\alpha$ $\sigma\dot\alpha\rho\kappa\alpha$ $\tau\iota\kappa\tau o\mu\dot\epsilon\nu o\upsilon$ $X\rho\iota\sigma\tau o\hat\upsilon$).

27 "Die Freiheit in der Verkündigung des Paulus," *ZSTh* 18 (1941): 478. On the whole passage cf. also Robert Falconer, "1 Timothy 2:14–15, Interpretative Notes," *JBL* 60 (1949): 375–79.

28 On the style of the list, cf. Plutarch, *Tranq. An.* 468 B:

"For abuse and rage on their part, envy and malevolence and jealousy, coupled with ill–will, are the bane of those who are subject to these faults." ($\beta\lambda\alpha\sigma\phi\eta\mu\dot\iota\alpha\iota$ $\gamma\dot\alpha\rho$ $\kappa\alpha\dot\iota$ $\dot o\rho\gamma\alpha\dot\iota$ $\kappa\alpha\dot\iota$ $\phi\theta\dot o\nu o\iota$ $\kappa\alpha\dot\iota$ $\kappa\alpha\kappa o\dot\eta$-$\theta\epsilon\iota\alpha\iota$ $\kappa\alpha\dot\iota$ $\zeta\eta\lambda o\tau\upsilon\pi\dot\iota\alpha\iota$ $\mu\epsilon\tau\dot\alpha$ $\delta\upsilon\sigma\mu\epsilon\nu\epsilon\dot\iota\alpha s$ $\alpha\dot\upsilon\tau\hat\omega\nu$ $\mu\dot\epsilon\nu$ $\epsilon\dot\iota\sigma\iota$ $\tau\hat\omega\nu$ $\dot\epsilon\chi\dot o\nu\tau\omega\nu$ $\kappa\hat\eta\rho\epsilon s$).

29 See Adolf von Harnack, *Geschichte der altchristlichen Literatur*, vol. 2: *Die Chronologie* (Leipzig: Hinrichs, ²1958), 498f; Carl Schlau, *Die Acten des Paulus und der Thekla* (Leipzig: Hinrichs, 1877), 79ff; Wendland, *Hellenistische Kultur*, 337f.

30 *Act. Pl.* 37, 39, 41, 43, (Lipsius–Bonnet, 1, pp. 263ff; see also pp. 269, 271 according to manuscript Gr).

31 Leopold Zscharnack, *Der Dienst der Frau im Neuen Testament* (Göttingen: Vandenhoeck & Ruprecht, 1902), 53ff.

Gnostic ideas could also provide the background for the positive mention of "childbearing" (τεκνογονία) in 1 Tim. In the *Gospel of the Egyptians*,[32] the Lord answers the question: "How long will men continue to die?" (μέχρι τίνος οἱ ἄνθρωποι ἀποθανοῦνται;) by saying "As long as women give birth" (Μέχρις ἂν τίκτωσιν αἱ γυναῖκες). Cf. Irenaeus, *Adv. haer.* 1.24.2, on the Gnostics (Saturninus): "He says that marriage and procreation are from Satan" (nubere autem et generare a Satana dicunt esse); Tertullian, *Praescr. haer.* 33 speaks in a similar way of Marcion and Apelles. And among the few characteristics of his opponents which our author is able to name is "they forbid marriage" (κωλυόντων γαμεῖν, 1 Tim 4:3). In this respect, in other instances, the author of the Pastoral Epistles has advocated the position of preserving the natural order (cf., above all, Tit 2:3ff). This view, incidentally, is also stressed in *Corp. Herm.* 2.17 (p. 39, Nock) with reference to the father: "For the procreation of children is held by wise men to be the most important and the holiest function in life; and the man who leaves life without a child is regarded as the most unfortunate and miserable of men." (διὸ καὶ μεγίστη ἐν τῷ βίῳ σπουδὴ καὶ εὐσεβεστάτη τοῖς εὖ φρονοῦσίν ἐστιν ἡ παιδοποιία. καὶ μέγιστον ἀτύχημα καὶ ἀσέβημά ἐστιν, ἄτεκνόν τινα ἐξ ἀνθρώπων ἀπαλλαγῆναι) [Trans.]. That the author of the Pastorals advocated this "reasonable teaching" and the sound ethics of good citizenship can be regarded as his greatest contribution historically. We can appreciate this precisely if we see in him, not Paul, but a man of the second generation who had to withstand the mighty assault of syncretistic and ascetic tendencies and movements.[33]

---

32 The passage is quoted in Clem. Alex., *Strom.* 3.9.64 (KlT 8², p. 12, No. 1).

33 On the whole problem see Zscharnack, *Der Dienst der Frau*; Delling, *Die Stellung des Paulus zu Frau und Ehe*; Albrecht Oepke, *TDNT* 1, pp. 776–89; Irene M. Robbins, "St. Paul and the Ministry of Women," *ExpT* 46 (1934–35): 185–88.

3

Conduct of Bishops

1b Whoever strives for the office of bishop,
desires to take upon himself a good
work. 2/ For the bishop should be without reproach, the husband of one wife,
sober, prudent, moderate, hospitable,
skillful in teaching, 3/ not given to wine
nor brawling, but kind, peaceable,
and not covetous, 4/ one who governs
his own house well and keeps his children in respectful obedience—5/ for
whoever does not know how to govern
his own house, how can he take care
of the church of God?—6/ nor should
he be newly baptized, lest he become
puffed up and fall into the condemnation of the devil. 7/ He should also
have a good reputation among those
outside (of the congregation), so that he
may not fall into the devil's snare, (if)
something reproachful is said about him.

3:1–13. The following statements regarding bishops and deacons confront the interpreter not only with historical problems (see the excursus to 3:7 below pp. 54ff), but also with exegetical ones. The most important of these are: why are "bishops" (ἐπίσκοποι) and "deacons" (διάκονοι) described in very similar ways? In the cata-logue of their duties, why are particular requirements for office not specified, but instead qualities which for the most part are presupposed for every Christian? (On this question see the following excursus.) Doubtless the existence of the episcopate and the diaconate is presup-posed. According to the *fictitious* situation, Timothy is not supposed to appoint bishops and deacons, but rather to see to it that these functionaries comply with the ethical demands laid upon them. The real interest of the author, however, is directed not to instructing the disciple of the apostle, but rather to the ethical admonition of the bishops and those who are to become bishops.[1] And there are clearly many of these (see 3:1). As a link with what follows, therefore, it might be well to add: "to be sure it is 'good work' (καλὸν ἔργον), but precisely for this reason examine yourselves, viz. let yourselves be examined (3:10)." It follows that the author did not find it necessary to describe the duties of the functionaries.[2] He could restrict his instructions to an exhortation to office holders in the form of a schematic catalogue of virtues.

Teachings About Duties

Teachings regarding duties, as we find them in early Christianity (here, in Tit 1:5ff and in Pol. *Phil.* 5:2),[3] are also known in the Hellenistic world. It corresponds to the relation between "panegyric" (ἔπαινος) and parene-sis (mentioned above, p. 30, on 1:16) which is illustrated in descriptions of heroes, colored by the language of moral philosophy. Aristotle writes: "The panegyric and the counsels have the same form" (ἔχει δὲ κοινὸν εἶδος ὁ ἔπαινος καὶ αἱ συμβουλαί, *Rhet.* p. 1367 b 36) [trans. by Ed.]. Compare, say, Xenophon, *Ag.* 11, with Pseudo–Isocrates, *Ad Demonicum*; or see how the requirements which Socrates (in Xenophon) asks of the military commander are fulfilled in the representation of the idealized Cyrus in Xenophon's *Cyropaedia*.[4] So it could happen that in the biographies, "virtues" (ἀρεταί) of the heroes are mentioned which do not derive from observation of their activity, but are mentioned because the description of that activity was made to fit a fixed schema. Perhaps the most striking example of this phe-nomenon is provided by the imperial biographies of Suetonius.[5] Conversely, this technique of biography could be applied to the teaching of duties. As an example, read the passage given in Appendix 3 from the *Strategikos* by the tactician, Onosander (see below p. 158). In this list, which is strikingly similar to the list in 1 Tim 3:2ff,

---

1   See above on 2:1, p. 35, and the Introduction sec-
     tion 2, pp. 5ff.

2   The case is slightly different in Tit 1:5ff, see below
     pp. 132f.

3   Cf. the outline given below p. 133, on Tit 1:7.

4   Socrates is quoted in Xenophon's *Commentaries* 3.1–5;
     cf. Xenophon, *Cyrop.* 1.6.26.

5   Friedrich Leo, *Die griechisch–römische Biographie*

we find scarcely one virtue which would be especially appropriate to a military commander. No doubt, we have a fixed pattern which is only applied to military leadership by means of the explanatory notes. The instruction of a future physician in Libanius[6] contains, in addition to pieces of advice for the physician, also general schematic instruction: "practice kindness, cultivate love" ($\chi\rho\eta\sigma\tau\acute{o}\tau\eta\tau\alpha$ $\ddot{\alpha}\sigma\kappa\epsilon\iota$, $\phi\iota\lambda\alpha\nu\theta\rho\omega\pi\acute{\iota}\alpha\nu$ $\mu\epsilon\lambda\acute{\epsilon}\tau\alpha$); see also the quotation below, p. 72. An interesting connection between professional qualities and generally human attributes is found in Lucian, *De saltatione* 81.[7]

Such a schema clearly underlies the teaching of duties in 1 Tim 3. This explains why so little is mentioned which would especially characterize a bishop or deacon. For this reason the specifically Christian element is missing. The popularization of such schematic doctrines of virtue was furthered not only by the philosophical definitions (e.g., the Platonic "$O\rho o\iota$, the Aristotelian divisions and the like), but above all by the honorary inscriptions. By listing the virtues of the person being honored, their intention was to inspire posterity to similar accomplishment.[8] The relationship between the honorary inscriptions and moral philosophy (see also below, pp. 72f on 1 Tim 5:1)—which is very important precisely for the everyday ethics of early Christianity—[9] has not as yet been thoroughly explored.

It is very probable that Judaism also inherited something from the ancient popular morality depicted here. To be sure, the list pattern does not seem to have been adopted in Rabbinic literature. But perhaps we can find its echo in the list given in the Babylonian Talmud[10] attributed to Rabhs (3rd cent.)—a passage which, in its lack of context or connection, is reminiscent of 1 Tim 3: "The forty–two lettered Name is entrusted only to him who is pious, meek, middle–aged, free from bad

temper, sober, and not insistent on his rights" [Trans. Epstein]. It has not yet been clarified how extensively Hellenistic literature and thought influenced the parenesis of the sect of Qumran at the Dead Sea.[11]

■ **1** Even ancient exegetes did not agree whether the formula $\pi\iota\sigma\tau\grave{o}s$ $\acute{o}$ $\lambda\acute{o}\gamma os$ should be taken with what goes before (Chrysostom XI, p. 596, Montfaucon) or what follows (Theodore of Mopsuestia II, p. 97, Swete). If one sees in the words a quotation formula (see above pp. 28ff, the excursus to 1:15), it is only possible to connect the words with what follows; the result would then fit very well with the presuppositions of the chapter sketched above. Cf. Theodoret (III, p. 651, Schulze): "He teaches not to strive for honor but for virtue; not to long for reputation, but to seek the work of (real) value." ($\delta\iota\delta\acute{a}\sigma\kappa\epsilon\iota$ $\mu\grave{\eta}$ $\tau\iota\mu\hat{\eta}s$ $\dot{a}\lambda\lambda$' $\dot{a}\rho\epsilon\tau\hat{\eta}s$ $\acute{o}\rho\acute{\epsilon}\gamma\epsilon\sigma\theta\alpha\iota$. $\mu\grave{\eta}$ $\tau\grave{\eta}\nu$ $\dot{a}\xi\acute{\iota}a\nu$ $\pi o\theta\epsilon\hat{\iota}\nu$, $\dot{a}\lambda\lambda\grave{a}$ $\tau\hat{\eta}s$ $\dot{a}\xi\acute{\iota}as$ $\tau\grave{o}$ $\ddot{\epsilon}\rho\gamma o\nu$ $\dot{\epsilon}\pi\iota\zeta\eta\tau\epsilon\hat{\iota}\nu$) [Trans.]. The words "Whoever strives for the office of bishop" ($\epsilon\ddot{\iota}$ $\tau\iota s$ $\dot{\epsilon}\pi\iota\sigma\kappa o\pi\hat{\eta}s$ $\dot{o}\rho\acute{\epsilon}\gamma\epsilon\tau a\iota$ $\kappa\tau\lambda$.) then would be derived from a common saying, which, to be sure, Pseudo–Paul sanctions, but against which he asserts the ethical prerequisites of the episcopate. This understanding also underlies the variant reading "it is a human word" ($\dot{a}\nu\theta\rho\acute{\omega}\pi\iota\nu os$ $\acute{o}$ $\lambda\acute{o}\gamma os$). Its originator wishes to stress what he clearly felt to be a discrepancy between 3:1 and 3:2 and, therefore, designated the saying in 3:1 as a human saying.[12] If one takes the formula as an affirmation and relates it to the preceding verse, 2:15, the new beginning in 3:16 admittedly creates a rough effect. It can be explained by the sententious character of 3:1b, which is obvious, no matter how one interprets the formula. It is good literary style to introduce the parenesis with the mention of something that is well–known. "Episcopate" ($\dot{\epsilon}\pi\iota\sigma\kappa o\pi\acute{\eta}$) here refers to the office of

(Leipzig: Teubner, 1901), takes this occurrence as his starting point.

6 Libanius, *Progymnasmata* in *Loci communes* 3.7 (7th ed., p. 184f, Förster), cited below p. 72 on 1 Tim 5:1, 2.
7 Quoted below, pp. 160f in Appendix 4.
8 Cf. *Inscr. Priene* 108.311ff; 109.233ff (cit. above on 1:15, p. 29).
9 Deissmann, *LAE*, 308ff, explicitly refers to this relationship.
10 *Talmud Kidduschin* 71a.
11 Cf., e.g. the list in 1 QS 4! The literature on the subject, teachings about duties, has been gathered by

B. S. Easton, "New Testament Ethical Lists," *JBL* 51 (1932): 1ff; see also Vögtle, *Tugend– und Lasterkataloge* (bibliography), where an extensive amount of material is presented and organized according to types (portraits of rulers, teachings as to professional duties, praise and fault–finding in oratory).
12 Among other scholars, Dibelius (2d German ed. of this commentary), Jeremias, and Spicq, *ad loc.*, connect this phrase with what follows; Schlatter, *ad loc.*, and Bover, " 'Fidelis sermo,' " 74–79, relate it to what has gone before. On the synthesis of the formula's use as a formula of quotation and affirmation, see George William Knight, *The Faithful Say-*

the "bishop" (ἐπίσκοπος), as "for" (οὖν) in v 2 shows.[13]

■ **2, 3** "Without reproach" (ἀνεπίλημπτος)[14] is found in the NT only in this epistle, but it is common in the higher Koine.[15] With regard to "the husband of one wife" (μιᾶς γυναικὸς ἄνδρα, see v 12), the question has long since been raised (as it has with regard to Tit 1:6 and 1 Tim 5:9) whether unchastity, viz. polygamy, or a second marriage, is excluded.[16] The arguments for the latter assumption are: 1. that the prohibition of unchastity among Christians is a matter of course—but this depiction of the bishop is not specifically Christian (see above); and Rabbinic Judaism still knows of polygamy, at least in theory.[17] 2. In the regulation regarding widows in 5:9, the words would have to refer to the prohibition of a second marriage—but even in that passage such an interpretation is improbable (see below p. 75). 3. If the author only wished to offer a warning against unchastity, why did he not forbid "fornication" (πορνεία) directly? In answer to these questions, it would be possible to appeal to the (probably non–Christian) tradition which influenced the author. But above all one would have to consider that, in view of his opponents (see 1 Tim 4:3) and in view of the explicit high evaluation which he places upon the natural order, the author wished to commend marriage to the "bishop" (ἐπίσκοπος).[18] But since nothing is said about a second marriage, the following statement by Theodore of

Mopsuestia could apply: "He who marries one wife, lives with her prudently, keeps to her, and directs to her the desire of nature" (ὃς ἀγαγόμενος γυναῖκα σωφρόνως ἐβίω μετὰ ταύτης, προσέχων αὐτῇ καὶ μέχρις αὐτῆς ὁρίζων τῆς φύσεως τὴν ὄρεξιν, II, 103, Swete) [trans. by Ed.]. On the other hand, according to the funerary inscriptions, special esteem is accorded the person who was married only once (especially in contrast to a multiplicity of marriages as the result of separation).[19] Thus some scholars find here the prohibition of remarriage for persons who are separated.[20] In either case we are not dealing with a special instruction for bishops.

The next virtue also belongs among those which are a "matter of course" for everyone: "sober" (νηφάλιος) is found in this form of the Greek word in the NT only in the Pastoral Epistles.[21] To be sure, a widespread interpretation, one which takes into consideration both the use of "to be sober" (νήφειν) in Paul and also the following "not given to wine" (μὴ πάροινον), understands "sober" (νηφάλιος) in a figurative sense. But if one considers the literary character of such lists and includes by analogy the catalogue of vices in one's considerations,[22] one will find it possible that the word "sober" (νηφάλιος) is used in its literal sense together with "not given to wine" (μὴ πάροινος). Such lists are often quite plentiful and profuse in their enumeration

---

ings in the Pastoral Letters (Kampen: Kok, 1968).

13   On the word ἐπίσκοπος see Knopf, Lehre der Zwölf Apostel, Clemensbriefe, on 1 Clem 44.1; as well as Preisigke, s.v.; Bauer, s.v. See also U. Holzmeister, "Si quis episcopatum desiderat, bonum opus desiderat," Biblica 12 (1931): 41–69; Ceslaus Spicq, "Si quis episcopatum desiderat," RSPT 29 (1940): 316–25, and excursus no. III in his commentary (p. 84). On the episcopacy itself, see also von Campenhausen, Ecclesiastical Authority, p. 112.

14   On the μ before ππ see Ludwig Radermacher, Neutestamentliche Grammatik, HNT 1, 1 (Tübingen: J. C. B. Mohr [Paul Siebeck], ²1925), 40.

15   Cf. also the text given in Appendix 4, see below pp. 160f.

16   Cf. the extensive presentation in Theodore of Mopsuestia (II, 99ff, Swete).

17   See the documentation in Billerbeck, ad loc.

18   It is different in the case of the Apostolic Church Order: "It is good to be without a wife, otherwise one should have only one wife" (καλὸν μὲν εἶναι ἀγύναιος, εἰ δὲ μή, ἀπὸ μιᾶς γυναικός) [trans. by Ed.]; cf. the second excursus to 2:2 (see above pp. 39f) and the

excursus to 2:15 (see above pp. 48f).

19   Especially with regard to the Jewish inscriptions see Jean–Baptiste Frey, "La signification des termes μόνανδρος et univira," RechSR 20 (1930): 48–60; idem, CII (vol. I: Rome, 1936), e.g., Nos. 81, 392, 541.

20   E.g., Albrecht Oepke, TDNT, 1, pp. 776ff; Jeremias, ad loc.; cf. Cuthbert Lattey, "Unius uxoris vir (Tit. 1, 6)," Verbum Domini 28 (1950): 288–90; Wilhelm A. Schulze, "Ein Bischof sei eines Weibes Mann . . ." KD 4 (1958): 287–300; B. Kötting, "Bigamus," RAC 3 (1957), 1016–24.

21   But see Philo, Sobr. 2; Vit. Mos. 1.187; Josephus, Ant. 3.279; cf. the use of νήπτης in the list in Onosander (Appendix 3 below pp. 153f).

22   See Lietzmann, Römer, excursus to Rom 1:31, and the material in Vögtle, Tugend– und Lasterkataloge, passim.

of virtues, without any very systematic delineation of the concepts. Cf. also the parallel instructions in 3:11 and 3:8. Whereas in the former the requirement is given by the term "sober" (νηφαλίους), the latter uses instead "not given to much wine" (μὴ οἴνῳ πολλῷ προσέχοντας). A specifically cultic character of the requirement is not implied.[23]

The coupling of "prudent" (σώφρων) and "modest" (κόσμιος) is very common.[24] On "hospitality" (φιλοξενία) in primitive Christianity see (in addition to 1 Tim 5:10) also Rom 12:13; Heb 13:2; 1 Petr 4:9; 3 Jn 5ff; *1 Clem* 1.2 and chs. 10–12, and the characteristic combination "bishops and hospitable men" (ἐπίσκοποι καὶ φιλόξενοι) in *Herm. sim.* 9.27.2. "Skillful in teaching" (διδακτικός) does not prove that the bishop had already assumed, as his regular duty, the office of teaching (but see below the following excursus, section 1), but only that some capability in this regard was desired. The term "skillful in teaching" (διδακτικός) is found in Philo (*Congr.* 35; *Praem. Poen.* 27), but both times it is used to designate Abraham's διδακτικὴ ἀρετή, i.e., virtue attained by means of teaching. In 1 Tim it stands as one virtue among others, as it does in 2 Tim 2:24.

■ **4, 5** Cf. Pol. *Phil.* 11.2: "For how may he who cannot attain self-control in these matters enjoin it on another?" (qui autem non potest se in his gubernare, quomodo alii pronunciat hoc?). Greek parenesis provides a precedent for drawing conclusions from a person's private life about his qualifications for office. See Isocrates, *Ad Nicoclem* 19 (the text is not quite certain): "Manage the city as you would your ancestral estate: in the matter of its

appointments, splendidly and royally, in the matter of its revenues, strictly, in order that you may possess the good opinion of your people" (οἴκει τὴν πόλιν ὁμοίως ὥσπερ τὸν πατρῷον οἶκον ταῖς μὲν κατασκευαῖς λαμπρῶς καὶ βασιλικῶς, ταῖς δὲ πράξεσιν ἀκριβῶς, ἵν' εὐδοκιμῇς ἅμα καὶ διαρκῇς); Pseudo–Isocrates, *Ad Demonicum* 35: "Whenever you purpose to consult with any one about your affairs, first observe how he has managed his own; for he who has shown poor judgment in conducting his own business will never give wise counsel about the business of others." (ὅταν ὑπὲρ σεαυτοῦ μέλλῃ τινι συμβούλῳ χρῆσθαι, σκόπει πρῶτον πῶς τὰ ἑαυτοῦ διῴκησεν. ὁ γὰρ κακῶς διανοηθεὶς περὶ τῶν οἰκείων οὐδέποτε καλῶς βουλεύσεται περὶ τῶν ἀλλοτρίων).[25] As in Tit 1:6 the existence of the Christian family is presupposed.

■ **6, 7** These mention specifically episcopal characteristics, and therefore have probably been added to the traditional schema. They express the experience of the Christian communities who, e.g., feel that the approval of those outside the congregation is desirable.[26] The term "newly baptized" (νεόφυτος) in non–Christian literature has so far been attested only in its literal meaning, "newly planted."[27] Even those who hold that the Pastorals are genuine would not, precisely because of this requirement, date them too early in Paul's life. For in the first years of the mission this commandment could not have been carried out. It is clear what the author fears with respect to a newly baptized person becoming bishop: "If he had been elevated for this purpose, namely, to teach others, should he be puffed up at this ordina-

---

23 Here I disagree with Otto Bauernfeind, *TDNT* 4, pp. 936–41.
24 Plato, *Gorg.* 508a; Lucian, *Bis accusatus* 17; *Inscr. Magn.* 162.6 (cited above p. 46 on 1 Tim 2:9).
25 Cf. also Euphronius, *Fragments* 4 (3d ed., p. 320, Kock): "He who cannot manage his own life, how can he help another person?" (ὁ γὰρ τὸν ἴδιον οἰκονομῶν κακῶς βίον, πῶς οὕτως ἂν σώσειε τῶν ἔξω τινά;) [trans. by Ed.]; Plutarch, *Lycurg.* 19 (52A): "to one who demanded the establishment of democracy in the city: 'Go thou,' said he, 'and first establish democracy in thy household'" (πρὸς τὸν ἀξιοῦντα ποιεῖν δημοκρατίαν ἐν τῇ πόλει. σὺ γάρ, ἔφη, πρῶτος ἐν τῇ οἰκίᾳ σου ποίησον δημοκρατίαν). Further information is found in Helge Almqvist, *Plutarch und das Neue Testament; ein Beitrag zum Corpus Hellenisticum Novi Testamenti* (Uppsala: Appelberg, 1946), 125. On the term "to govern," "to take

care of" (προΐστασθαι) see Dibelius, *Thessalonicher, Philipper*, on 1 Thess 5:12.
26 Cf. the requirements in 1 Thess 4:12; 1 Cor 10:32; Col 4:5; and the way in which these demands are taken into account, both here and in 1 Tim 5:14; 6:1; Tit 2:5, 8, 10; 1 Petr 2:12, 15; 3:1, 16; Ign. *Eph.* 10.1.
27 The word is attested in the LXX; in Pollux 1.231 (p. 72, Bethe), according to whose testimony the word is found in Aristophanes; see *Fragments* 828 (1st ed., p. 581, Kock); in the papyri (*BGU* II, 563, I 9.14.16; II 6.12; 565.11; 566.3) see Deissmann, *Bible Studies*, 220f; Joachim Jeremias, *Infant Baptism in the First Four Centuries*, tr. David Cairns (Philadelphia, Pa.: Westminster Press, 1961), 33.

tion, he will have no understanding of the great things" (si productus fuerit ad hoc ut alios ipse doceat, ab ipsa ordinatione elatus magna desipiet) [trans. by Ed.].[28]

Noteworthy in what follows is the double mention of the "devil" (διάβολος, see Eph 4:27). V 6 cannot refer to a "slanderous person," for the following verse would then add nothing new. Therefore here (and naturally also in v 7) the meaning "devil" is to be assumed. A reference to a human slanderer is also excluded by 2 Tim 2:25f. Therefore we must take "condemnation of the devil" (κρίμα τοῦ διαβόλου) as referring either to the judgment which Satan, whose office it is to accuse or to tempt,[29] speaks over the fallen neophyte, or to the judgment under which the devil himself once came.[30] But perhaps we have no right to make the alternatives so distinct, since obviously one cannot differentiate clearly between "condemnation" (κρίμα) and "snare of the devil" (παγὶς τοῦ διαβόλου). 1 Tim 6:9 shows that the term "the snare" or "the devil's snare," could occur in edifying language without having a very exact sense. The mythological sense had long since faded.[31] "Fall into a snare" (ἐμπίπτειν εἰς παγίδα) is a common expression (Pr 12:13; Sir 9:3; Tob 14:10f). The *Manual of Discipline* shows how widely it was disseminated. During the initiation the priest and the Levites say: "Cursed be he when he passes, together with the idols of his heart, who enters into this covenant putting before himself the snares (מכשול) that cause him to fall into iniquity and to turn away from God. . . . the snare that causes him to stumble into sin! May he place his lot among the eternally damned" (1 QS II, 11f, 17) [trans. adapted from Dupont–Sommer, *Essene Writings*, p. 75]. Cf. also the *Damascus Document*: "These are Belial's three nets (מצודות) . . . the first is lust, the second is riches, (and) the third is defilement of the Sanctuary." (CD IV, 15.17f).

The Position of the Bishop in the Pastoral Epistles

The evidence pertaining to the meaning of "bishop" (ἐπίσκοπος) has been collected by Dibelius and supplemented by Lietzmann.[32] On the basis of this evidence it becomes clear that "bishop" was admittedly the title of an office in the pagan world; the word was nevertheless not used to designate one and the same office in all instances. The mere title therefore tells us nothing in itself about the "bishop" in the Pastorals. The historical problems with which the passage under discussion confronts the exegete may be summarized in two questions: 1. What are the duties of the "bishop"? 2. What is the relationship between the designations "bishop" (ἐπίσκοπος) and "elder," "presbyter" (πρεσβύτερος)?

1. It is often assumed (even in the 2d German ed. of the present work) that the function of the "bishops" in the earliest times was primarily economic, having to do with the care of the poor and perhaps also with the cult and the correspondence of the congregation. The arguments for this assumption are as follows: a) it was precisely within this circle of duties that the free activity of the charismatic gifts had to yield to the orderly efficiency of chosen functionaries (cf. the account in Acts 6). b) The parallelism of the "bishops" (ἐπίσκοποι) and the "deacons" (διάκονοι)—the latter doubtless had their duties in these areas—[33] makes it possible that the bishops were economic functionaries of the congregation. c) In the Greek associations the title "bishop" was also used to refer to the financial officers; see the inscription[34] according to which the bishops Dion and Maleiptos are requested to invest the money collected, at interest. Note also that Symmachus[35] calls the financial officers (τοπάρχαι), who are mentioned in Gen 41:34 (LXX), "bishops" (ἐπίσκοποι). For this reason Hatch stresses the technical

---

28 Theodore of Mopsuestia (II, p. 113, Swete).
29 See Dibelius, *Geisterwelt*, 38.
30 Theodore of Mopsuestia (II, p. 113, Swete): "But if he vainly pride himself because of the aspect of teacher that has been laid upon him, he will seem in no way to differ from the devil, who, appointed a servant of God, strove to understand on his own what things are great, usurping for himself both the name and the office of God" (vane vero extollens se propter inpositam magisterii speciem, nihil differre videbitur diabolo, qui minister Dei creatus quae magna de se sapere est adnisus, Dei sibi adsciscens et nomen et honorem) [trans. by Ed.].

31 With regard to the mythological sense, see Isidor Scheftelowitz, *Das Schlingen– und Netzmotiv im Glauben und Brauch der Völker* (Giessen: A. Töpelmann, 1912), 11.
32 Dibelius, *Thessalonicher, Philipper*, excursus on Phil 1:1; Hans Lietzmann, "Zur altchristlichen Verfassungsgeschichte," *ZWTh* 55 (1914): 97–153.
33 This is shown both here and Phil 1:1; see also Rom 12:7 and Lietzmann–Kümmel, *Korinther*, on 1 Cor 16:15. We might also perhaps include the mention of both in the preface to Phil (with regard to sending money); see Dibelius, *Thessalonicher, Philipper*, on Phil 1:1. Finally, cf. the description in *Herm. sim.*

character of the "episcopal office," in contrast to the charismatic and patriarchal offices, and illustrates this with examples from the Greek societies.[36] The question is, however, how much we can infer from the economic functions, which were doubtless present, as to the concept and the development of the Christian episcopate as von Campenhausen has argued.[37] He does not deny the economic duties, but the essence of the episcopal office is not determined by these duties. Rather a sharp distinction is made between two basic forms of early Christian church constitution: the Pauline episcopal–diaconate constitution and the non–Pauline presbyterial constitution. The consolidation took place in three types: Rome—First Epistle of Clement; Syria—Ignatius of Antioch; Asia Minor—Pastoral Epistles.

To what extent, therefore, does the office of the bishop imply a position of authority according to the Pastorals? The solution of the problem is made more difficult by the fact that the character of the episcopacy in 1 Tim 3 and Tit is not described but taken for granted, furthermore by the fact that the verbs in question can vary in meaning between "undertake responsibility for welfare" and "hold the chief office, the office of the director." In the case of the verb "to govern" ($\pi\rho o\ddot{\iota}\sigma\tau\alpha\sigma\theta\alpha\iota$), this double meaning is attested in 1 Thess 5:12 (cf. the verb $\pi\rho o\sigma\tau\alpha\tau\epsilon\hat{\iota}\nu$); "to take care" ($\dot{\epsilon}\pi\iota\mu\epsilon\lambda\epsilon\hat{\iota}\sigma\theta\alpha\iota$) could mean "to hold the office of a caretaker" ($\dot{\epsilon}\pi\iota$-$\mu\epsilon\lambda\eta\tau\dot{\eta}s$)."[38] Despite the uncertainty in our understanding, the text of the Pastoral Epistles, nevertheless, allows one to assume a certain *authority of the bishop*. For only on the premise of such a position of authority is it possible to explain the role accorded the bishop in Tit 1 in combatting heresy. That the episcopal office was accorded a high significance can also be inferred from the fact that such a detailed list of virtues was associated

with it (1 Tim 3 and Tit 1). The man described here—albeit in the usual moralizing way—is no welfare agent or treasurer, but a significant representative of the congregation, even to the outside world (see 1 Tim 3:7).

If the later position of the monarchical bishop rests upon the multiplicity of economic, authoritative, and pastoral functions, the third group, especially the cultic duties, is less prominent in the Pastorals. The "pastoral" teaching activity is clearly desired in Tit 1:9 and also recommended in 1 Tim 3:2. But since, according to 1 Tim 2:2, the teaching office is still carried on charismatically, teaching cannot be presupposed as a *special* function of the bishop.[39]

What we find here is apparently a stage of development which is also visible in *Did.* 15.1: "Appoint therefore for yourselves bishops and deacons, worthy of the Lord . . . for they also minister to you the ministry of the prophets and teachers" ($\chi\epsilon\iota\rho o\tau o\nu\dot{\eta}\sigma\alpha\tau\epsilon$ $o\dot{\upsilon}\nu$ $\dot{\epsilon}\alpha\upsilon\tauo\hat{\iota}s$ $\dot{\epsilon}\pi\iota\sigma\kappa\dot{o}\pi o\upsilon s$ $\kappa\alpha\dot{\iota}$ $\delta\iota\alpha\kappa\dot{o}\nu o\upsilon s$ $\dot{\alpha}\xi\dot{\iota}o\upsilon s$ $\tauo\hat{\upsilon}$ $\kappa\upsilon\rho\dot{\iota}o\upsilon$ . . . $\dot{\upsilon}\mu\hat{\iota}\nu$ $\gamma\dot{\alpha}\rho$ $\lambda\epsilon\iota\tauo\upsilon\rho\gamma o\hat{\upsilon}\sigma\iota$ $\kappa\alpha\dot{\iota}$ $\alpha\dot{\upsilon}\tauo\dot{\iota}$ $\tau\dot{\eta}\nu$ $\lambda\epsilon\iota\tauo\upsilon\rho\gamma\dot{\iota}\alpha\nu$ $\tau\hat{\omega}\nu$ $\pi\rho o\phi\eta\tau\hat{\omega}\nu$ $\kappa\alpha\dot{\iota}$ $\delta\iota\delta\alpha\sigma\kappa\dot{\alpha}\lambda\omega\nu$). According to this, to be sure, the bishops do teach, but "prophets" and "teachers" still engage in this activity; cf. also Eph. 4:11 where the individual congregation has its "pastors" ($\pi o\iota\mu\dot{\epsilon}\nu\epsilon s$), but also—apparently in addition to these—its "teachers" ($\delta\iota\delta\dot{\alpha}\sigma\kappa\alpha\lambda o\iota$).

2. The relation between "bishop" ($\dot{\epsilon}\pi\dot{\iota}\sigma\kappa o\pi os$) and "presbyter" ($\pi\rho\epsilon\sigma\beta\dot{\upsilon}\tau\epsilon\rho os$) in the Pastoral Epistles seems all the more problematic, since the questions relating to the Pastorals' unity and purpose are connected with this problem. From the present text of the Pastorals the following observations can be made: a) mention is made, on the one hand, of "presbyters" (1 Tim 5:1, 17; Tit 1:5) and, on the other hand, of "bishops" and "deacons" (1 Tim 3:1ff; Tit 1:7ff). But where the author

---

9.27.2: "and the bishops ever ceaselessly shelter the destitute and the widows by their ministration" ($o\dot{\iota}$ $\delta\dot{\epsilon}$ $\dot{\epsilon}\pi\dot{\iota}\sigma\kappa o\pi o\iota$ $\pi\dot{\alpha}\nu\tauo\tau\epsilon$ $\tauo\dot{\upsilon}s$ $\dot{\upsilon}\sigma\tau\epsilon\rho\eta\mu\dot{\epsilon}\nuo\upsilon s$ $\kappa\alpha\dot{\iota}$ $\tau\dot{\alpha}s$ $\chi\dot{\eta}\rho\alpha s$ $\tau\hat{\eta}$ $\delta\iota\alpha\kappa o\nu\dot{\iota}\alpha$ $\dot{\epsilon}\alpha\upsilon\tau\hat{\omega}\nu$ $\dot{\alpha}\delta\iota\alpha\lambda\epsilon\dot{\iota}\pi\tau\omega s$ $\dot{\epsilon}\sigma\kappa\dot{\epsilon}\pi\alpha\sigma\alpha\nu$).

34 *IG* 12.3.329; it is quoted in Dibelius, *Thessalonicher, Philipper*, in the excursus on Phil 1.1, and in Lietzmann–Kümmel, *Korinther*, Appendix 6.

35 Cited in Origen, *Hexapla* (I, 59, Field).

36 Edwin Hatch, *The Organization of the Early Christian Churches* (London and New York: Longmans, Green & Co., ⁴1892).

37 Cf. the wide-ranging fundamental criticism of the

Hatch–Harnack position by von Campenhausen, *Ecclesiastical Authority*, esp. pp. 65ff, 73f, 81f, and 85.

38 The "caretaker" ($\dot{\epsilon}\pi\iota\mu\epsilon\lambda\eta\tau\dot{\eta}s$) is the equivalent of the "bishop" ($\dot{\epsilon}\pi\dot{\iota}\sigma\kappa o\pi os$) in the Greek societies, as Hatch, *Organization*, demonstrates.

39 This is true despite the strong emphasis upon the bishop's task of supervising the teachers. See von Campenhausen, *Ecclesiastical Authority*, 109f.

speaks of the latter he does not speak of the former, and conversely; there is no mention of a structure of the congregation in three hierarchically arranged offices.[40]
b) It seems at first that "presbyter" and "bishop" may refer to the same function; for 1 Tim 5:17 attributes the function "to govern" the church ($\pi\rho\sigma\sigma\tau\hat{\eta}\nu\alpha\iota$) to the presbyter, whereas 1 Tim 3:5 ascribes the same function to the bishop; and "bishop" in Tit 1:7 is clearly connected to the mention of the "presbyters" in Tit 1:5. But one important fact speaks against this conclusion; namely, "bishop" ($\dot{\epsilon}\pi\dot{\iota}\sigma\kappa\sigma\pi\sigma s$) is always used in the singular.

There are two ways of resolving these contradictions: The first is to see in the "bishop" ($\dot{\epsilon}\pi\dot{\iota}\sigma\kappa\sigma\pi\sigma s$) of the Pastoral Epistles the monarchical bishop of later times. In that case, however, since there is no further mention of the monarchical episcopate in the Pastorals, one must assume that the passages in question (i.e., 1 Tim 3:1–13 and Tit 1:7–9) are later interpolations. Such hypotheses are more acceptable in principle for congregational regulations like the Pastoral Epistles, which could be varied according to the changing needs of the times, than for actual letters. Moreover the assumption of an interpolation is not unfounded here, because 1 Tim 3:14f logically continues the last verse before such an assumed interpolation (2:15), and Tit 1:10 would follow well upon 1:6. On the other hand, the literary type of this parenesis and the use of traditional material make it easy to see literary seams where none exist, or where a form–critical explanation is appropriate. Thus we are left with the second option for resolving the contradiction, which is to explain the passages about the bishop as parts of the original text of the Pastorals, and to take the singular generically.[41] One will then assume that the "bishops" were members of the presbytery, whether or not they were "elders" in their own right. That is, they either came from the college of the "presbyters" ($\pi\rho\epsilon\sigma$–$\beta\dot{\upsilon}\tau\epsilon\rho\sigma\iota$); see below pp. 77f the excursus to 1 Tim 5:17, or, in case they did not already belong, they became members of the presbytery after their appointment as bishops.

Analogies for such a combination of administrative and patriarchal organization are known from the culture of that time. In civic assemblies of the Roman world the government officials had *ex officio* votes, even the chairmanship, but only during their years of office.[42] In Egypt the terms "president of the assembly" ($\dot{\alpha}\rho\chi\iota\sigma\upsilon\nu\dot{\alpha}\gamma\omega$–$\gamma\sigma s$)[43] and "leader" ($\pi\rho\sigma\sigma\tau\dot{\alpha}\tau\eta s$) were occasionally used to refer to the same person.[44] The "priests" (sacerdotes) of Mithra were chosen, in part, from the circle of the "fathers" (patres).[45]

Provided there is a similar situation in the Pastorals, we would have to understand the "presiding presbyters" ($\pi\rho\sigma\epsilon\sigma\tau\hat{\omega}\tau\epsilon s$ $\pi\rho\epsilon\sigma\beta\dot{\upsilon}\tau\epsilon\rho\sigma\iota$) in 1 Tim 5:17 as $\pi\rho\epsilon\sigma\beta\dot{\upsilon}$–$\tau\epsilon\rho\sigma\iota$ $\dot{\epsilon}\pi\iota\sigma\kappa\sigma\pi\sigma\hat{\upsilon}\nu\tau\epsilon s$; that is, presbyters who, in addition to the patriarchal position which they hold, also exercise the administrative function of the "bishop" ($\dot{\epsilon}\pi\dot{\iota}\sigma\kappa\sigma\pi\sigma s$). Tit 1:5, 7 would then mean that every presbyter must also be qualified to take over the "office of the bishop" ($\dot{\epsilon}\pi\iota\sigma\kappa\sigma\pi\dot{\eta}$). Perhaps there was only one from the circle of presbyters who was to become bishop. This would explain the use of the word "bishop" in the singular. The strange interchange of "presbyter" and "bishop" in Tit 1:5, 7 could then be explained by the thesis that Tit 1:7ff (like 1 Tim 3:2ff) came from a traditional regulation which only spoke of "the bishop." At any rate, there could also have been, in addition to the "presiding presbyters" ($\pi\rho\epsilon\sigma\beta\dot{\upsilon}\tau\epsilon\rho\sigma\iota$ $\pi\rho\sigma\epsilon\sigma\tau\hat{\omega}\tau\epsilon s$), other presbyters who never became bishops. The relations among the various types of office may not have been uniform from one congregation to another.

That the expressions are used side by side in the same sense seems to be demonstrated, if not by Tit 1:5, 7, at least by Acts 20:17, 28, as well as by *1 Clem.* 42.4 and 44:1 in comparison with 44.5 and 47.6. In any event, the identification of the two offices was one which gradually developed,[46] not one which existed from the beginning.

In all this, it must not be forgotten that the church or-

---

40 Von Campenhausen, *Ecclesiastical Authority*, 120f.
41 Cf. the singular "presbyter" ($\pi\rho\epsilon\sigma\beta\dot{\upsilon}\tau\epsilon\rho\sigma s$) in 1 Tim 5:1, where plurals also follow.
42 See Hatch, *Organization*, pp. 86f, n. 13.
43 The word is understood in a patriarchal sense, even in the sense of the "founder of the society," see Franz Poland, *Geschichte des Griechischen Vereinswesens* (Leipzig: Teubner, 1909), 357.
44 Cf. the inscription found in the *Archiv für Papyrus-*

forschung 2 (1902): 430, No. 5 (?) and 429, No. 2: "Synhistor, who founded the assembly and was its leader" ($\Sigma\upsilon\nu\dot{\iota}\sigma\tau\omega\rho$ $\sigma\upsilon\nu\alpha\gamma[\omega\gamma\dot{\eta}\sigma\alpha s]$ $\kappa\alpha\dot{\iota}$ $\pi\rho\sigma\sigma\tau\alpha$–$\tau\dot{\eta}\sigma\alpha s$) [trans. by Ed.].
45 F. Cumont, "Mithras," in W. H. Roscher, ed., *Ausführliches Lexikon der griechisch-römischen Mythologie* (Leipzig: B. G. Teubner, 1884–1937), vol. II, col. 3028–71.
46 Cf. also Clem. Alex., *Quis div. salv.* 42, where the

der of the Pastorals actually implies a monarchical head in the position of the addressee, a position which as an "office" is just as much a fiction as the instructions for this office given in the epistles. Are they historical to the extent that the disciple of the apostle in fact inherited a certain rank? Note how Theodore of Mopsuestia (II, p. 121, Swete) tries to reconstruct the situation: "Those who had the authority to ordain, who are now called bishops, did not belong to a single congregation, but had authority over a whole province, and were called apostles" (οἱ δὴ τὴν τοῦ χειροτονεῖν ἐξουσίαν ἔχοντες, οἱ νῦν ὀνομαζόμενοι ἐπίσκοποι, οὐ μιᾶς ἐκκλησίας γινόμενοι ἀλλ᾽ ἐπαρχίας ὅλης ἐφεστῶτες, τῇ τῶν ἀποστόλων ἐκαλοῦντο προσηγορίᾳ) [trans. by Ed.]. To be sure, as far as the Pastoral Epistles are concerned, the disciple of the apostle is not primarily the representative of a type of office, but rather the guarantor of the genuine tradition. Thus his position cannot at all be defined in terms of ecclesiastical organisation (e.g., as something like the position of a metropolitan). Although the tradition is strongly emphasized, there is no concept of succession, no extension of the position of the addressee into the present.[47]

---

same person is referred to as "bishop," "presbyter," and "elder" (ἐπίσκοπος, πρεσβύτερος, and πρεσβύτης).

47 On the whole question, aside from commentaries and general works on primitive Christianity, see Olof Linton, *Das Problem der Urkirche in der neueren Forschung* (Uppsala: Lundequist, 1932); Holtzmann, *Die Pastoralbriefe*, 190ff; Ernst Kühl, *Die Gemeindeordnung in den Pastoralbriefen* (Berlin: Besser'sche Buchhandlung, 1885); Adolf von Harnack, *The Constitution and Law of the Church in the First Two Centuries*, tr. F. L. Pogson, ed. H. D. A. Major (New York: G. P. Putnam's Sons, 1910); Burnett Hillman Streeter, *The Primitive Church* (New York: Macmillan Co., 1929); Heinz Wolfgang Beyer, *TDNT*, 2, pp. 608–20; *idem* and Heinz Karpp, "Bischof," *RAC* II (1954), col. 394–407; Karl Ludwig Schmidt, "Le ministère et les ministères dans l'Église du Nouveau Testament," *RHPR* 17 (1937): 313–36; Arthur Cayley Headlam and Friedrich Gerke in Roderic Dunkerley and A. C. Headlam, ed., *The Ministry and the Sacraments* (New York: Macmillan, 1937), 326ff; E. J. Palmer, *ibid.*, 768ff; Eduard Schweizer, *Church Order in the New Testament* (Naperville, Ill.: Alec R. Allenson, 1961); Richard Loewe, *Ordnung in der Kirche im Lichte des Titus* (Gütersloh: Der Rufer, 1947); Philippe–Henri Menoud, *L'Église et les ministères selon le NT* (Paris: Delachaux & Niestle, 1949); Joseph Brosch, *Charismen und Ämter in der Urkirche* (Bonn: Hanstein, 1951); von Campenhausen, *Ecclesiastical Authority*; on the connection between the episcopal office and the *mebaqqer* of the Damascus sect cf., in addition to CD 13.7–11, now also 1 QS VI, 11f. Joachim Jeremias argues that there is a connection: *Jerusalem in the Time of Jesus*, tr. F. H. and C. H. Cave (Philadelphia, Pa.: Fortress Press, 1969), 261f, and in his commentary *ad loc.* The following scholars are against any connection: K. G. Goetz in *ZNW* 30 (1931): 89ff; cf. Beyer, *TDNT* 2, pp. 618f; Alfred Adam, "Die Entstehung des Bischofsamtes," *Wort und Dienst* NF 5 (1957): 104ff. On the tendency in Catholic scholarship to identify bishops and presbyters, cf. U. Holzmeister, "Si quis episcopatum desiderat"; this position is modified in Spicq, pp. 91ff.

3

On Conduct of Deacons

8   Likewise the deacons should be honorable,
     not double–tongued, 9/ not given to
     immoderate enjoyment of wine, not
     greedy, (people) who cherish the
     mystery of faith with a pure conscience.
     10/ They should first be tested, then
     they should execute their duty, if they
     are irreproachable. 11/ The women
     likewise should be honorable, not slan-
     derous, sober, reliable in everything.
     12/ The deacons should be the husband
     of one wife and govern their children
     and their homes well. 13/ For those who
     perform their service well obtain for
     themselves a good position and real
     cheerfulness in Jesus Christ.

On deacons; this too is a traditional list of duties (see above pp. 50f, the excursus to 1 Tim 3:1–13). It is only in v 9 that peculiarly Christian conditions relating specifically to this office are named.

■ **8** "Likewise" (ὡσαύτως) is used to introduce a new list; this is typical of the style of parenesis; cf. v 11 and the corresponding ὁμοίως in 1 Petr 3:1, 7.

■ **9** If one compares the use of "mystery" (μυστήριον) in 1 Cor 2:7; 4:1; 13:2; 14:2; 15:51; Col 1:26f; 2:2; 4:3, one notices divergence of usage in 1 Tim 3:9. But one must also note that, already at an earlier time, in the Epistle to the Ephesians, "mystery" (μυστήριον) and other expressions of this type are used to refer to the fundamental realities of the gospel and of the life of the congregation.[1] Moreover in the Pastorals still other sublime and weighty words have become formulas for ordinary Christian community life.[2] Here one finds the solution to the riddle of the formulaic use of such terms in the language of the congregation.[3] Indeed, "mystery of faith" (μυστήριον τῆς πίστεως) is almost the equivalent of the simple expression "faith" (πίστις). Despite the elaborate term, the sentence does not emphasize that the deacons are of the Christian faith, but that they are

Christians of good conscience (see above pp. 18ff, the excursus to 1:5).

■ **10** is rightly understood, not as a specific examination, but as a more general evaluation. This is indicated above in the qualifications for the bishop in vss 6, 7, and here by means of the word "irreproachable" (ἀνέγκλητοι).

■ **11** The question whether the reference here is to deaconesses,[4] or to the wives of deacons[5] can hardly be answered with certainty. If the entire passage, including 3:12, 13, is taken as a list of duties for deacons, then v 11 refers perhaps to the wives. But one could also hold that the author is speaking of the deaconesses before he mentions (in v 12) those duties which apply only to male deacons. The uncertainty of the interpretation is perhaps connected with the fact that the author did not sufficiently modify the traditional list of duties, so that the application to Christian circumstances did not become completely clear.[6]

■ **12** See above at 3:2–5.

■ **13** "Position" (βαθμός) is used in the sense of "degree" or "rank."[7] Also the stage in which one has obtained "gnosis" can be designated in this way and even

---

1   Cf. Dibelius–Greeven, *Kolosser, Epheser, Philemon*, excursus on Eph 4:16; Lohse, *Colossians, Philemon*, on Col 1:26.
2   See above p. 41 on 1 Tim 2:4.
3   "Like a phrase that has been snatched up," Friedrich Schleiermacher, *Sendschreiben*, 101.
4   As Theodoret, Theodore of Mopsuestia, Holtzmann, Wohlenberg, Lock, and Spicq, *ad loc.*, hold.

5   As Ambrosiaster, B. Weiss, von Soden, and Easton, *ad loc.*, believe.
6   See above pp. 50f, the excursus to 3:1–13; Karl Weidinger, *Die Haustafeln: Ein Stück urchristlicher Paränese*, Untersuchungen zum Neuen Testament 14 (Leipzig: Hinrichs, 1928), pp. 69f.
7   See *IG*, II 243.16 on the rank of the office; *P. Masp.* 67.169.10 on the degree of relationship.

one stage in the journey of the soul into heaven.[8] The meaning of the word in each instance can only be defined according to the context. The parallel "true cheerfulness" ($\pi o\lambda\lambda\grave{\eta}\nu$ $\pi a\rho\rho\eta\sigma\acute{\iota}a\nu$) would point to a rank in the kingdom of heaven, rather than to a promotion to the rank of bishop.[9] However, in that case the term "position" ($\beta a\theta\mu\acute{o}s$) would perhaps appear at the end of the sentence. For this reason the simplest explanation is to understand only the second promise ("real cheerfulness") in a religious sense, and the first ("good position") as referring to reputation within the congregation.[10] Perhaps the author was trying to emphasize something that would form a contrast to service.[11]

---

8 On the former see Clem. Alex., *Strom.* (II, 45.4, Stählin); on the latter, *Corp. Herm.* 13.9.

9 Theodore of Mopsuestia and Theodoret, *ad loc.*

10 The latter meaning is similar to the meaning of "to win glory" ($\kappa\lambda\acute{e}os$ $\pi\epsilon\rho\iota\pi o\iota\epsilon\hat{\iota}\sigma\theta a\iota$) in *1 Clem.* 54.3 and of "honor" ($\tau\iota\mu\grave{\eta}\nu$) in *Herm. mand.* 4.4.2.

11 Cf. Mark 10:43 and parallels, which is also cited in the section dealing with deacons in *Didasc.* 16 (p. 86, Flemming). On "cheerfulness" ($\pi a\rho\rho\eta\sigma\acute{\iota}a$) see Erik Peterson, "Zur Bedeutungsgeschichte von $\pi a\rho\rho\eta\sigma\acute{\iota}a$" in *Reinhold–Seeberg–Festschrift* I: *Zur Theorie des Christentums*, ed. Wilhelm Koepp (Leipzig: A. Deichertsche Verlagsbuchhandlung, 1929), 283–97.

3

Word Concerning the Church

14 (All) this I am writing to you in the hope of
coming to you soon; 15/ but in case I
am delayed, you should (at least) know
how one ought to conduct one's life
in the household of God; that is the
church of the living God, the support
and fortress of the truth. 16/ And most
certainly great is the mystery of (our)
religion:
   "(who) was revealed in the flesh—
   vindicated in the spirit
   made manifest to the angelic powers—
   preached among the nations
   believed in the world—
   lifted up in glory."

This is a transitional passage. It does not intend primarily
to picture the situation of the writing of this epistle out
of a romantic biographical interest in the apostle's person.
Rather, the aim of the passage is to present the concept
of tradition. In 1 Tim 1:15 the apostle functioned as a
model for conversion. In 1:18–20 he authorized the
controversy over the true teaching; in 2:7 he appeared
as guarantor of the tradition; here his "testament"
(4:1ff) is introduced, i.e. the church is prepared for the
post–apostolic period. The basis for this testament is a
liturgical piece, which thus appears as apostolic tradition.[1]

■ **14** "Soon" ($\tau\acute{\alpha}\chi\iota o\nu$) is a colloquial term.[2]

■ **15** On "household of God" ($o\mathring{i}\kappa o s \ \theta\epsilon o\hat{v}$), Adolf
Wilhelm[3] has demonstrated that "house" ($o\mathring{i}\kappa o s$), instead of referring to the meeting place, can also be used
to refer to the assembly itself, and hence to a religious
community.[4] But for the meaning of the term, the NT
parallels point to another context; namely that of fixed

liturgical language, possibly of a Hellenistic–Jewish
Christian type: "house of God" is the community as it is
gathered together.[5] There is no development of the
symbolism of "building" (despite the second half of the
verse). On the contrary, one can understand in retrospect
why the author impressed upon his church order a certain pattern of rules for the household. Above all, the
statement about the "church of God" ($\mathring{\epsilon}\kappa\kappa\lambda\eta\sigma\acute{\iota}\alpha \ \theta\epsilon o\hat{v}$)
has a liturgical ring which is obvious in the phrase
"living God" and in the motif of the church's foundation.[6] The image in v 15a is not carried further in 15b,
but rather replaced by a new one. It is clear that common
expressions are being used. "Support" ($\sigma\tau\hat{v}\lambda o s$), usually
meaning "pillar," has in Sir 36:29 (26)[7] the more general
meaning "foundation," which is to be accepted here
because of the parallel "fortress" ($\mathring{\epsilon}\delta\rho\alpha\acute{\iota}\omega\mu\alpha$). On
"fortress of truth" ($\mathring{\epsilon}\delta\rho\alpha\acute{\iota}\omega\mu\alpha \ \tau\hat{\eta}s \ \mathring{\alpha}\lambda\eta\theta\epsilon\acute{\iota}\alpha s$), cf. 1 QS V,
5f: ". . . in order to lay a foundation of truth for Israel,
for the Community of the everlasting covenant; that

---

1   On the artificiality of the situation see above p. 3,
    the excursus to 1:3 and the Introduction (above
    pp. 15f).

2   See Walter Bauer, *Das Johannesevangelium erklärt*,
    HNT 6 (Tübingen: J. C. B. Mohr [Paul Siebeck],
    ³1933), on John 13:27; F. Blass and A. Debrunner,
    *A Greek Grammar of the New Testament and other Early
    Christian Literature*, tr. and rev. Robert W. Funk
    (Chicago: University of Chicago Press, 1961), 244,
    1.

3   *Beiträge zur griechischen Inschriftenkunde* (Wien: A.
    Holder, 1909).

4   *Inscr. Magn.* 94.5ff: "because of his virtue and the
    goodwill which he continuously displays toward the
    holy community and the public" ($\mathring{\alpha}\rho\epsilon\tau\hat{\eta}s \ \mathring{\epsilon}\nu\epsilon\kappa\epsilon\nu \ \kappa\alpha\mathring{\iota}$
    $\epsilon\mathring{v}\nuo\acute{\iota}\alpha s \ [\mathring{\eta}\nu \ \mathring{\epsilon}\chi]\omega\nu \ \delta\iota\alpha\tau\epsilon\lambda\epsilon\hat{\iota} \ \epsilon\mathring{\iota}s \ \tau\epsilon \ \tau\grave{o}\nu \ o\mathring{\iota}\kappa o\nu \ \tau\grave{o}\nu$
    $\mathring{\iota}\epsilon\rho\grave{o}\nu \ \kappa\alpha\mathring{\iota} \ \tau\grave{o}[\nu \ \delta\hat{\eta}\mu o\nu]$) [trans. by Ed.]. Further illus-
    trations in Wilhelm, *Beiträge* (see the preceding foot-

note).

5   Cf. 1 Petr 4:17 (compare with 2:5); Heb 3:6; Ernst
    Käsemann, *Das wandernde Gottesvolk*, 109.

6   Cf. below, p. 112, on 2 Tim 2:19 where similar dic-
    tion occurs. On the imagery of building see Dibe-
    lius–Greeven, *Kolosser, Epheser, Philemon*, on Eph
    2:20; Philipp Vielhauer, *Oikodome* (Karlsruhe–
    Durlach: G. Tron, 1940); J. Pfammatter, "Die
    Kirche als Bau," *Analecta Gregoriana* 110 (1960):
    124ff.

7   It is used in parallelism with "support" ($\beta o\eta\theta\acute{o}s$);
    cf. Gal 2:9 and *1 Clem* 5.2; cf. also Heinrich Schlier,
    Christus und die Kirche im Epheserbrief, Beiträge zur
    historischen Theologie (Tübingen: J. C. B. Mohr
    [Paul Siebeck], 1930), 6, 30, 50f, 72.

they may atone for all who are volunteers for the holiness of Aaron and for the House of truth in Israel." [Trans. Dupont–Sommer, *Essene Writings*, p. 83].[8] From the liturgy it becomes understandable that the celebration not only takes place in the church, but that the church itself is also being praised.[9] This change is inaugurated by the concept that the tradition is expressed and exercised in the liturgy. This context is important in any consideration of the "moralism" of the Pastoral Epistles. What follows, with its characteristic use of the word "mystery" ($\mu\nu\sigma\tau\acute{\eta}\rho\iota o\nu$),[10] also corresponds to this concept.

■ **16** "Mystery of religion" ($\mu\nu\sigma\tau\acute{\eta}\rho\iota o\nu$ $\tau\hat{\eta}s$ $\epsilon\dot{\nu}\sigma\epsilon\beta\epsilon\acute{\iota}as$) is practically synonymous with "mystery of faith" ($\mu\nu\sigma\tau\acute{\eta}\rho\iota o\nu$ $\tau\hat{\eta}s$ $\pi\acute{\iota}\sigma\tau\epsilon\omega s$) in 3:9, see above. The term here designates the core of the message of salvation, as it is outlined in the following poetic quotation. "Mystery" ($\mu\nu\sigma\tau\acute{\eta}\rho\iota o\nu$) refers to the hidden occurrence as well as to its proclamation.[11] It therefore appears in the context of the epiphany Christology (hidden from of old—now revealed, viz. proclaimed).[12] The rationalistic character of the teaching, which was noted above in the discussion of 1 Tim 2:4, and the prominent occurrence of the "mystery" correspond to one another. That the words are to be regarded as a quotation is indicated by the division into three rhythmically equal couplets; by the content, which goes far beyond the immediate context; and by the introduction with "most certainly" ($\dot{o}\mu o\lambda o\gamma o\nu\mu\acute{\epsilon}\nu\omega s$).[13] It is, in fact, only a fragment that is quoted here.[14] To take one or several of the verbs as the main clause would destroy the parallelism. That the fragment was taken

from a hymn, and not, e.g., from a confessional formula,[15] is indicated by the comprehensive content and the hymnodic style, which can be compared with *Odes of Sol.* 19.10ff: "10 And she brought forth a man, by (God's) will: (Or, of her own will) and she brought (him) forth with demonstration and acquired (him) with great dignity; *11* and loved (him) in majesty." ($\dot{\omega}s$ $\ddot{a}\nu\theta\rho\omega\pi o\nu$ $\ddot{\epsilon}\tau\epsilon\kappa\epsilon\nu$ $\dot{\epsilon}\kappa o\hat{\nu}\sigma a$ $\kappa a\grave{\iota}$ $\dot{\epsilon}\gamma\acute{\epsilon}\nu\nu\eta\sigma\epsilon\nu$ $\dot{\epsilon}\nu$ $\pi\rho o\theta\nu\mu\acute{\iota}a$ $\kappa a\grave{\iota}$ $\dot{\epsilon}\kappa\tau\acute{\eta}$-$\sigma a\tau o$ $\dot{\epsilon}\nu$ $\delta\nu\nu\acute{a}\mu\epsilon\iota$ $\pi o\lambda\lambda\hat{\eta}$ $\kappa a\grave{\iota}$ $\dot{\eta}\gamma\acute{a}\pi\eta\sigma\epsilon\nu$ $\dot{\epsilon}\nu$ $\pi\rho o\nu o\acute{\iota}a$ $\kappa a\grave{\iota}$ $\dot{\epsilon}\phi\acute{\nu}\lambda a\xi\epsilon\nu$ $\dot{\epsilon}\nu$ $\dot{\epsilon}\pi\iota\epsilon\iota\kappa\epsilon\acute{\iota}a$ $\kappa a\grave{\iota}$ $\pi a\rho\acute{\epsilon}\sigma\tau\eta\sigma\epsilon\nu$ $\dot{\epsilon}\nu$ $\mu\epsilon\gamma a\lambda\epsilon\iota\acute{o}$-$\tau\eta\tau\iota$).[16] On the basis of this poetic style with its parallelism, we are also able to explain the otherwise puzzling passive form "believed" ($\dot{\epsilon}\pi\iota\sigma\tau\epsilon\acute{\nu}\theta\eta$). *Dg.* 11.3 seems to be influenced by the passage under discussion or by the hymn cited here: "that He might be manifested to the world; and He, being despised by the people [of the Jews], was, when preached by the apostles, believed on by the Gentiles." ($\ddot{\iota}\nu a$ $\kappa\acute{o}\sigma\mu\omega$ $\phi a\nu\hat{\eta}$, $\ddot{o}s$ $\dot{\nu}\pi\grave{o}$ $\lambda a o\hat{\nu}$ $\dot{a}\tau\iota$-$\mu a\sigma\theta\epsilon\acute{\iota}s$, $\delta\iota\grave{a}$ $\dot{a}\pi o\sigma\tau\acute{o}\lambda\omega\nu$ $\kappa\eta\rho\nu\chi\theta\epsilon\acute{\iota}s$, $\dot{\nu}\pi\grave{o}$ $\dot{\epsilon}\theta\nu\hat{\omega}\nu$ $\dot{\epsilon}\pi\iota$-$\sigma\tau\epsilon\acute{\nu}\theta\eta$) [Trans. from Alexander Roberts and James Donaldson ed., *Ante-Nicene Christian Library*, vol. 1 (Edinburgh: T. & T. Clark, 1867–72)].

The content of the fragment in its present form must not be understood as a chronological list of "the facts of salvation." In that case "lifted up" ($\dot{a}\nu\epsilon\lambda\acute{\eta}\mu\phi\theta\eta$) would have to come before "preached" ($\dot{\epsilon}\kappa\eta\rho\acute{\nu}\chi\theta\eta$) and "believed" ($\dot{\epsilon}\pi\iota\sigma\tau\epsilon\acute{\nu}\theta\eta$). Rather, the contrasts "flesh–

---

8   See also CD III, 19; on the significance of this latter passage see Nauck, *Die Herkunft*, p. 28.

9   There is a similar combination of motifs in Heb; cf. Käsemann, *Das wandernde Gottesvolk, passim.*

10 At the same time, there is a reminder of the mystery of the confession; cf. Günther Bornkamm, "Homologia," in *Geschichte und Glaube 1*, Gesammelte Aufsätze 3 (München: Chr. Kaiser, 1968), 140–56.

11 Günther Bornkamm, *TDNT* 4, p. 820ff.

12 Cf. Rom 16:25f; Col 1:26; Eph 1:9 and 3:9f.

13 D* reads "we confess that" ($\dot{o}\mu o\lambda o\gamma o\hat{\nu}\mu\epsilon\nu$ $\dot{\omega}s$). On $\dot{o}\mu o\lambda o\gamma o\nu\mu\acute{\epsilon}\nu\omega s$ see Josephus, *Ant.* 1.180; 2.229. This passage has been pointed out by Alfred Seeberg, *Der Katechismus der Urchristenheit* (Leipzig: A. Deichert, ²1913; reprint 1966), 113, n. 2. On the Stoic usage cf. Bornkamm, "Homologia," 151ff; see, e.g. Epict., *Diss.* 3.1.5. On the connection with a relative particle and on the style of the fragment, cf.

Norden, *Agnostos Theos*, 254ff.

14 The variant reading "God" ($\theta\epsilon\acute{o}s$, P Ψ $\mathfrak{M}$ pl) instead of "who" ($\ddot{o}s$), is intended to establish it as an independent piece. The reading "that" ($\ddot{o}$, D* 061 lat) tries to establish a connection to what has gone before.

15 Joseph Kroll, "Die christliche Hymnodik" in the *Verzeichnis der Vorlesungen an der Akademie zu Braunsberg Sommer 1921–Sommer 1925* (Königsberg and Braunsberg: Bender's Buchhandlung, 1921), 16, tries to make the case for a confessional formula, as does Walter Bauer, *Der Wortgottesdienst der ältesten Christen* (Tübingen: J. C. B. Mohr [Paul Siebeck], 1930), 59.

16 [Trans. by Harris–Mingana, *The Odes and Psalms of Solomon.*] The Greek text is that of the retroversion by Hugo Gressmann in his review of J. Laboust and P. Batiffol's *Les Odes de Salomon*, *ZDMG* 65 (1911): 852.

spirit" ($\sigma \acute{\alpha} \rho \xi – \pi \nu \epsilon \hat{\upsilon} \mu \alpha$), "world–glory" ($\kappa \acute{o} \sigma \mu o \varsigma – \delta \acute{o} \xi \alpha$)[17] demonstrate clearly that the corresponding "angelic powers–nations" ($\ddot{\alpha} \gamma \gamma \epsilon \lambda o \iota – \ddot{\epsilon} \theta \nu \eta$) is intended to represent the same contrast between the heavenly and the earthly world: angels–man (the latter here designated by the missionary term "nations," "pagans" [$\ddot{\epsilon} \theta \nu \eta$]).

The two problematic expressions "vindicated in the spirit" ($\dot{\epsilon} \delta \iota \kappa \alpha \iota \acute{\omega} \theta \eta \; \dot{\epsilon} \nu \; \pi \nu \epsilon \acute{\upsilon} \mu \alpha \tau \iota$) and "made manifest to angelic powers" ($\ddot{\omega} \phi \theta \eta \; \dot{\alpha} \gamma \gamma \acute{\epsilon} \lambda o \iota \varsigma$) must be interpreted on this basis. The first of these expressions is clearly a paraphrase for the exaltation into the sphere of the "spirit" ($\pi \nu \epsilon \hat{\upsilon} \mu \alpha$), as is indicated in a very similar manner in Rom 1:4.[18] The correspondence "in the flesh–in the spirit" excludes the possibility of understanding "in" ($\dot{\epsilon} \nu$) in an instrumental sense ("through"). The phrases speak about realms of being. That the process is designated by "vindicated" ($\delta \iota \kappa \alpha \iota o \hat{\upsilon} \sigma \theta \alpha \iota$) shows a use of the word which in no way corresponds to the usual usage in Paul. A parallel is Ign. *Phld.* 8.2: "I want to be vindicated in your prayer" ($\theta \acute{\epsilon} \lambda \omega \; \dot{\epsilon} \nu \; \tau \hat{\eta} \; \pi \rho o \sigma \epsilon \upsilon \chi \hat{\eta} \; \dot{\upsilon} \mu \hat{\omega} \nu \; \delta \iota \kappa \alpha \iota \omega \theta \hat{\eta} \nu \alpha \iota$) [trans. by Ed.] where the last word has approximately the meaning of "to attain to God" ($\theta \epsilon o \hat{\upsilon} \; \dot{\epsilon} \pi \iota \tau \upsilon \chi \epsilon \hat{\iota} \nu$).[19] Therefore, "vindicated" or "justified" ($\delta \iota \kappa \alpha \iota o \hat{\upsilon} \sigma \theta \alpha \iota$) does not refer to the forgiveness of sins, but rather to the entrance into the divine realm, the realm of "righteousness" ($\delta \iota \kappa \alpha \iota o \sigma \acute{\upsilon} \nu \eta$). In this sense the word is also found in the mystery of rebirth

in the *Corp. Herm.* 13.9: "See how it punished injustice without a trial. We have been justified [exalted], O my child, now that injustice is no longer there" ($\chi \omega \rho \grave{\iota} \varsigma \; \gamma \grave{\alpha} \rho \; \kappa \rho \acute{\iota} \sigma \epsilon \omega \varsigma \; \dot{\iota} \delta \grave{\epsilon} \; \pi \hat{\omega} \varsigma \; \tau \grave{\eta} \nu \; \dot{\alpha} \delta \iota \kappa \acute{\iota} \alpha \nu \; \dot{\epsilon} \xi \acute{\eta} \lambda \alpha \sigma \epsilon \nu. \; \dot{\epsilon} \delta \iota \kappa \alpha \iota \acute{\omega} \theta \eta \mu \epsilon \nu, \; \hat{\omega} \; \tau \acute{\epsilon} \kappa \nu o \nu, \; \dot{\alpha} \delta \iota \kappa \acute{\iota} \alpha \varsigma \; \dot{\alpha} \pi o \acute{\upsilon} \sigma \eta \varsigma$) [Trans.].[20]

It is then no longer surprising that the victory of the redeemer is also designated by "vindicated," or "justified." In this usage it occurs in the *Odes of Sol.* 31.5: "And his face was justified;/For thus His Holy Father had given to Him."[21] Therefore "vindicated" refers to the exaltation of Jesus.[22] The exaltation was frequently represented as the triumph over the world of the spirits.[23]

That triumph is expressed in the next statement "made manifest to angelic powers." Cf. *Asc. Isa.* 11.23: "and he was in the firmament, but he had not changed to their form; and all the angels of the firmament and the Satan saw him, and they worshipped him;" cf. 11.25, 26.[24] That this conception of the epiphany before semi–divine beings for the purpose of exaltation is found in the thought of other religions is shown by Virgil, *Ecloge* 4.15f: "(he) shall see heroes mingled with gods, and shall himself be seen of them" (divisque videbit/permixtos heroas et ipse videbitur illis).[25] Such passages as Eph 2:6f; 3:9ff, show how well established this formal presentation of the exalted person was in the nexus of motifs surrounding cosmic exaltation. One also finds here an elaborate epiphany schema (see above) together with the desig-

---

17 $\delta \acute{o} \xi \alpha$ refers here to the heavenly "glory" (כבוד) and thus has almost a special meaning.

18 It is further described in Phil 2:9ff and Col 2:15; cf. A. Klöpper, "Zur Christologie der Pastoralbriefe (1 Tim 3,16)," *ZWTh* 45 (1902): 347–61; Lohse, *Colossians, Philemon,* on Col 2:15.

19 Heinrich Schlier, *Religionsgeschichtliche Untersuchungen zu den Ignatiusbriefen,* BZNW 8 (Giessen: Töpelmann, 1929), 171.

20 On this passage see Reitzenstein, *Mysterienreligionen,* 257f.

21 [Trans. Harris–Mingana]. See also *Odes of Sol.* 17.2, 25.12 and 29.5, referring to the redeemer or the redeemed; cf. Rudolf Bultmann "Die Bedeutung der neuerschlossenen mandäischen und manichäischen Quellen für das Verständnis des Johannesevangeliums," *ZNW* 24 (1925): 128ff (reprinted in *Exegetica,* ed. by Erich Dinkler [Tübingen: J. C. B. Mohr (Paul Siebeck), 1967], 55ff); cf. also Rudolf Bultmann, *The Gospel of John,* tr. G. R. Beasley-Murray (Oxford: Blackwell, 1971), on John 16:8.

22 Possibly, this can also be compared with the greeting to Horus at his entrance into the heavenly hall in

the "Great Hymn" to Osiris: "O brave one, O justified one!" See Eduard Norden, *Die Geburt des Kindes* (Leipzig: Teubner, 1924; reprint 1958), 124.

23 Cf. Dibelius, *Thessalonicher, Philipper,* on Phil 2:9f; Dibelius–Greeven, *Kolosser, Epheser, Philemon,* and Lohse, *Colossians, Philemon,* on Col 2:15. Somewhat different is the explanation in Eduard Schweizer, *Erniedrigung und Erhöhung bei Jesus und seinen Nachfolgern* (Zürich: Zwingli–Verlag, 1955), p. 64, n. 273 (only partially tr. in *Lordship and Discipleship,* p. 65, n. 2).

24 Trans. by J. Flemming and H. Duensing, in Edgar Hennecke, *New Testament Apocrypha* 3d ed. Wilhelm Schneemelcher, tr. R. McL. Wilson (Philadelphia, Pa.: Westminster Press, 1965), p. 662; see also Dibelius, *Geisterwelt,* 178ff.

25 On this passage see Norden, *Geburt des Kindes,* 127f. Further, cf. J. A. Festugière, ed., *Hermes Trismegiste*[3] (Paris: l'Association Guillaume Budé, 1953), pp. 137ff; Schweizer, *Erniedrigung und Erhöhung,* p. 64, n. 274.

nation of the church as bearer of the announcement (cf. also Heb 1). In contrast to Phil 2:6ff, it is not the death which is marked as the turning point, nor is the contrast between humiliation and exaltation accentuated. The juxtapositions seem rather to emphasize the universality of this event throughout all (cosmic) regions. But the contrast between the world above and the world below is not further elaborated. The epiphany appears as a unified process, although it is divided into stages which begin with birth.[26] This is also the case in the related passage, Ign. *Eph.* 19 (hence the uncertainty as to whether the signs of the incarnation or of the ascension are of primary importance). The use of the aorist passive for the description of this event is also characteristic of this hymnic style, in this case used without any change (cf. on the other hand the change of subject between Phil 2:8 and 9!).

Some questions are still left open: Is the preexistence of the redeemer presupposed? This concept does not neces-sarily belong to the epiphany schema as an essential element, but is by nature easily combined with it.[27] How should the outline of the fragment be understood? Jeremias, *ad loc.*, explains the whole passage as a hymn that describes the ascension to the throne. Thus he arrives at a unified conception, even structurally: 1. exaltation 2. presentation 3. enthronement, each before the earthly and the heavenly world (in chiastic structure).[28] At any rate, proclamation and faith itself are included in the salvation event (cf. Tit 1:3f and Ign. *Eph.* 19.1: "mysteries of a 'cry'" [$\mu\nu\sigma\tau\acute{\eta}\rho\iota\alpha$ "$\kappa\rho\alpha\nu\gamma\hat{\eta}s$"]).[29] Note the combination of the two in Ignatius and in the *Odes of Sol.* (e.g., 41.10ff, cit. above at 1 Tim 2:5).[30]

---

26 Albert Descamps, *Les justes et la justice dans les évangiles et le christianisme primitif* (Louvain: Gembloux, 1950), 87, and Schweizer, *Erniedrigung und Erhöhung*, 63ff.

27 On this question see Windisch, "Zur Christologie," 222.

28 Yet cf. the analysis by Schweizer, *Erniedrigung und Erhöhung*, 65, n. 280.

29 On the relation between the Christological statement and its soteriological application, see Abramowski, "Der Christus der Salomooden," 44ff.

30 On the poetic verse used here, cf. Karl Heinrich Rengstorf, *Die Auferstehung Jesu* (Witten, Ruhr: Luther–Verlag, ⁴1960), 125ff; Eduard Schweizer, "New Testament Creeds Compared," *Neotestamentica* (Zürich: Zwingli Verlag, 1963), 122ff.

4

Concerning the False Teaching

1 **The spirit says explicitly that in future times people will fall away from faith, will adhere to spirits of error and demonic teachings, 2/ based on deceitful preaching by liars, who carry a brand on their consciences; 3/ they forbid marriage and (demand) abstinence from foods, which God created to be received with thanksgiving by all those who have come to the faith and to the recognition of the truth. 4/ For everything that God created is good and none (of it) is to be rejected which is received with thanksgiving; 5/ for it is made holy through God's word and prayer.**

This is the only part of the epistle which deals systematically with the false teaching. It is true that formally vss 1–5 do not make the assertion that the error which was prophesied has now begun (in this respect it is different from 2 Tim 3:1, 6). It only makes the demand upon Timothy to continue the appropriation of the prophecy. But the very fact that the mention of the false teaching is directly continued by its refutation (4:3–5) shows that the author regards it as a present danger. If one believes that the epistle is not genuine and sees the epistolary form as secondary, one understands why the polemic against the heretics appears in the future tense: Paul only warned Timothy that such people would come—those who come later, who actually experience them (i.e., the author's actual readers) should admit that they were warned. With respect to the motifs of a "farewell address" found in this section, see below at 2 Tim 3:1ff.

"Explicitly" ($\dot{\rho}\eta\tau\hat{\omega}s$) is found in prophecies, see Justin, *Apol.* 1.35.10; 63.10. What is meant is the "prophetic spirit" ($\pi\nu\varepsilon\hat{\upsilon}\mu\alpha\ \pi\rho\phi\eta\tau\iota\kappa\acute{o}\nu$, see *ibid.* 1.63.10), which had prophesied the coming apostasy, e.g., in an apocalypse.[1] On the appearance of transgressors "at the end of days" cf. 1 QpHab II, 5f.[2] The choice of the expression "future times" ($\H{\upsilon}\sigma\tau\varepsilon\rho o\iota\ \kappa\alpha\iota\rho o\acute{\iota}$), not "last days" ($\H{\varepsilon}\sigma\chi\alpha-\tau\alpha\iota\ \H{\eta}\mu\acute{\varepsilon}\rho\alpha\iota$) is perhaps conditioned by the artificial futuristic nature of the passage (see above). The author

brands the error as demonic; Paul also saw behind the activity of his opponents in Corinth the work of Satan.[3]

The author accuses his opponents of concealing secret sins behind their teaching (see the excursus below on 1 Tim 4:5, section 3b). Since we are dealing with a topos of heresy polemic, one must be cautious in drawing historical conclusions.[4]

■ **3–5** The question as to why in these verses the prohibition of food only, and not of marriage, is contested, can best be answered from the context. The author argues in terms of the theme of "bodily training" ($\sigma\omega\mu\alpha-\tau\iota\kappa\grave{\eta}\ \gamma\upsilon\mu\nu\alpha\sigma\acute{\iota}\alpha$). There can be no question in light of 1 Tim as to the author's positive position with regard to marriage. Perhaps he is conscious of being closer to the historical Paul on the question of food than on marriage (see Col 2:21ff in comparison with 1 Cor 7:1, 7). In Col 2:22f the rejection of asceticism with regard to food is based upon purely rational grounds. In 1 Tim there is also a cultic motif involved: "those who have come to the faith and to the recognition of truth" ($\pi\iota\sigma\tau o\grave{\iota}\ \kappa\alpha\grave{\iota}\ \H{\varepsilon}\pi\varepsilon-\gamma\nu\omega\kappa\acute{o}\tau\varepsilon s\ \tau\grave{\eta}\nu\ \mathring{\alpha}\lambda\acute{\eta}\theta\varepsilon\iota\alpha\nu$)—a self-designation of the Christians, (see 1 Tim 2:4 and Tit 1:1)—accept food with thanksgiving[5] and thereby make it holy. Also in 1 Cor 10:30 the prayer of thanksgiving is woven into the train of thought in a similar manner. Thus "word of God" ($\lambda\acute{o}\gamma os\ \theta\varepsilon o\hat{\upsilon}$) is best understood as referring to table prayers using Biblical expressions. The cultic language of

---

1   See Dibelius, *Thessalonicher, Philipper,* on 2 Thess 2:3.

2   The text is translated in Dupont–Sommer, *Essene Writings,* p. 259. See Karl Elliger, *Studien zum Habakuk–Kommentar vom Toten Meer,* BHT 15 (Tübingen: J. C. B. Mohr [Paul Siebeck], 1953), pp. 168, 278f.

3   See 2 Cor 4:4; 11:3, 13f and Dibelius, *Geisterwelt,* 48ff and 63ff.

4   On the zeugma (ellipsis), in which "demand" ($\kappa\varepsilon-$ $\lambda\varepsilon\upsilon\acute{o}\nu\tau\omega\nu$) must be supplied to "abstinence"—literally "to abstain" ($\mathring{\alpha}\pi\acute{\varepsilon}\chi\varepsilon\sigma\theta\alpha\iota$), see Blass–Debrunner, 479.2. On the issue see the excursus below on 1 Tim 4:5.

5   "Thanksgiving" ($\varepsilon\mathring{\upsilon}\chi\alpha\rho\iota\sigma\tau\acute{\iota}\alpha$) in vss 3, 4 is equivalent to "prayer" ($\H{\varepsilon}\nu\tau\varepsilon\upsilon\xi\iota s$) in v 5.

Judaism seems to play a great role, precisely in the Christianity attested by the Pastoral Epistles (see above at 1:17). Others interpret "the word of God" as the divine word of creation.[6]

The "False Teachers" of the Pastoral Epistles

The passages in the Pastorals devoted to the controversy with false teachers are as follows: 1 Tim 4:1–10; 2 Tim 3:1–9; Tit 1:10–16; 1 Tim 1:3–11; 6:3–5, 20f; 2 Tim 2:14, 23; 3:13; 4:3, 4; Tit 3:9–11; in addition to these are a few personal remarks in 1 Tim 1:19, 20; 2 Tim 1:15 and 2:16–18. If all these sections are interpreted as referring to the same heresy, and a distinction is made only between the seducers and the seduced, a comparatively clear picture can be obtained. This interpretation is especially justified if one doubts the epistolary nature of the Pastorals, and assumes that all polemical statements of the three "epistles" actually refer to the same heretical movement. If on the other hand, an actual epistolary situation is presupposed, it is of course necessary to assume that certain definite allusions are comprehensible only to the addressees, and that every such allusion refers to a special case of which we have no knowledge.[7]

1. If, however, one holds firmly to the unity of the depiction of the heretics, the following characteristic features emerge: a) the prohibition of marriage— in the passage under discussion, and indirectly attested by the positive stress upon marriage in 1 Tim 2:15; 5:14; Tit 2:4. Such continence—practiced in many religions for the most diverse motives—was especially congenial for a man

of the Hellenistic age on antimaterialistic grounds. It is, therefore, no wonder that we meet the prohibition of marriage in connection with Gnostic and semi–Gnostic ideas. (Attestations for this view are given above, pp. 48f, in the excursus to 2:15). Evidence can be found, above all, in certain of the apocryphal Acts of the Apostles. In the *Acts of Paul* 5 (Lipsius–Bonnet, 1, p. 238) Paul preaches the "word of God concerning continence and resurrection" (λόγος θεοῦ περὶ ἐγκρατείας καὶ ἀναστάσεως). In ch. 11 (*ibid.*, p. 243) he urges the young men and women not to marry (cf. also ch. 12 and see below section 1c). That the preaching of the false teachers concerns itself to a great extent with women seems to be proved by 2 Tim 3:6f in conjunction with 1 Tim 5:13.[8]

b) Abstinence from foods is attested here directly; in 1 Tim 5:23 and Tit 1:15, indirectly. It derives partly from the same motivations as the sexual asceticism, and partly from traditional ritual (Judaism!) and other customs.[9] This kind of continence can assume very diverse forms: fasting,[10] viz. taking very little food,[11] abstention from wine (on the basis 1 Tim 5:23 this is to be assumed for the ascetics mentioned in the Pastorals), and vegetarianism.[12] Most of the attestations are derived from the same sources mentioned above, section a. Incidentally, asceticism with regard to food is also a characteristic of the Colossian syncretism (of a Judaizing Gnosticism!).[13]

c) Enthusiasm, together with a spiritualizing of the hope of resurrection, is also directly attested in 2 Tim 2:18 (see below *ad loc.*). Also, the fact that the opponents

---

6   On the connection between eucharist and thanksgiving for the gifts of the creator, cf. *Did.* 10; see also Martin Dibelius, "Die Mahlgebete der Didache," *ZNW* 37 (1938): 32–41.

7   See Michaelis, *Echtheitsfrage*, who distinguishes between the pagan agitators opposed in 1 Tim 4 and insincere Christian missionaries in 2 Tim 3.

8   See Wendland, *Hellenistische Kultur*, 237; Knopf, *Das nachapostolische Zeitalter*, 410f; Ernst von Dobschütz, *Die urchristlichen Gemeinden* (Leipzig: Hinrichs, 1902), 181ff; Hans von Campenhausen, "Early Christian Asceticism" in *Tradition and Life in the Church: Essays and Lectures in Church History*, tr. A. V. Littledale (Philadelphia, Pa.: Fortress Press, 1968), 90–122.

9   P. R. Arbesmann, *Das Fasten bei den Griechen und Römern* (Giessen: Töpelmann, 1929), 19ff.

10   *Act. Pl.* 23 (Lipsius–Bonnet, 1, p. 251); *Act. Thom.* 5

(Lipsius–Bonnet, 3, p. 106).

11   *Act. Thom.* 20 (Lipsius-Bonnet, 3, p. 131): one date every Sunday.

12   In regard to the last two, see Rom 14:1ff and Lietzmann, *Römer*, excursus on Rom 14:1ff; compare also the correction of the gospel tradition in the *Gospel of the Ebionites*; see Hennecke–Schneemelcher 1, pp. 155f.

13   Günther Bornkamm, "Häresie des Kolosserbriefes," 139ff; Lohse, *Colossians and Philemon*, on Col 2:21ff; Dibelius–Greeven, *Kolosser, Epheser, Philemon*, excursus on Col 2:23; Knopf, *Das nachapostolische Zeitalter*, 410ff; von Dobschütz, *Die urchristlichen Gemeinden*, 274ff.

are called "sorcerers" (γόητες) and their teaching "false gnosis" (2 Tim 3:13 and 1 Tim 6:20) is relevant here, in addition perhaps to what is said about myths and genealogies and about the "racking of one's brain" (ζητήσεις 1 Tim 1:4; 4:7; 6:4; 2 Tim 4:4). All this would mean that these spiritualists were proud of their relations to the heavenly world; but their self–assurance was scandalous. One can see polemic against such enthusiasm also in the emphasis upon "reasonable teaching" as well as upon the order of nature and that of the congregation, including the offices and the "scriptures" (2 Tim 3:15). Tendencies toward emancipation could be connected with such a spiritualized understanding of Christianity and with the high regard for virginity (see above section a). These tendencies can be assumed on the basis of 1 Tim 2:11ff. The *Acts of Paul* offer noteworthy parallels both to the emancipation (see above p. 48, the excursus to 2:15) and to spiritualizing tendencies. In the present Greek text of these Acts, Paul connects resurrection with chastity, while his false friends Demas and Hermogenes,[14] say that the resurrection has already occurred in our children.[15] In the Latin fragment from Brescia, the latter reference is missing and Paul's only *magica ars* is described as "we will not rise into the life of the resurrection unless we lead a pure life" (in resurrectionem vitae non resurgemus nisi castam duxerimus vitam) [Trans.].[16] It is clear that the image of Paul is dominated by semi–Gnostic tendencies in the *Acts of Paul*, and by anti–Gnostic tendencies in the Pastoral Epistles.

2. A combination at that particular period in history of the three components outlined above, possibly originating in Asia Minor, and containing clearly Judaizing components must always be attributed to a kind of Gnosticism (see 1 Tim 6:20). However, it is impossible to identify the particular heresy attacked here with one of the Gnostic sects known to us. For one thing, the style of polemic of the author does not premit a more precise definition. As is shown in the commentary, the author frequently uses the same weapons with which the philosophers attacked the sophists.[17] It is questionable whether certain other passages may be justifiably interpreted as heresy polemics. Thus, for example, it is very doubtful whether one can draw conclusions about the Christological errors of heretics from formulations like 1 Tim 2:5f and 3:16. We are, after all, dealing with traditional christological formulations. What is characteristic is precisely the general way in which the confession as such is used.

There are two possible ways of explaining why the author's polemic did not designate a particular group more clearly. The first is to deal with the problem historically: the author already "confronts a colorful repertory of disagreeable phenomena."[18] The second is to seek a literary solution: The author attempts to characterize his opponents as broadly as possible, in order to create an apologetic *vademecum* for all sorts of anti–Gnostic conflicts. If one accepts the literary characterization of the Pastoral Epistles given in the Introduction of this commentary, one will take the latter option. The forms which the polemic takes correspond to a concept of heresy just being developed.[19]

3a) The position of the false teachers with regard to Judaism and the Law is uncertain. A connection between the heretical movement attacked here and Judaism seems to be indicated especially by Tit 1:10, 14, as well as by the fact that a syncretistic "Judaism" is also attested in Colossae, Magnesia and Philadelphia.[20] Admittedly the passages in Ignatius (*Mag.* 8–11; *Phld.* 5–8) are controversial. Ultimately, any asceticism relating to food

---

14   On Demas see 2 Tim 4:10; on Hermogenes, 2 Tim 1:15.

15   *Act. Pl.* 12, 14 (Lipsius–Bonnet, 1, pp. 244f.); but cf. below p. 112 on 2 Tim 2:18.

16   The fragment from Brescia can be found in Oskar von Gebhardt, *Die lateinischen Übersetzungen der Acta Pauli et Theclae*, TU 22, 2 (Leipzig: Hinrichs, 1902), p. 134; with regard to this fragment see P. Corssen, "Die Urgestalt der Paulusakten," *ZNW* 4 (1903): 41.

17   See above pp. 20f on 1 Tim 1:6; and cf. 1 Tim 1:4; 4:7f; 6:3f; 2 Tim 2:23; 3:13; 4:3f; Tit 3:9.

18   Von Harnack, *Chronologie*, 481.

19   See Bauer, *Orthodoxy and Heresy*, *passim*.

20   On Colossae see Dibelius–Greeven, *Kolosser, Epheser, Philemon*; Lohse, *Colossians and Philemon*, on Col 2:16ff; and Bornkamm, "Häresie des Kolosserbriefes." On Magnesia and Philadelphia, see Ign. *Mag.* 8–11 and *Phld.* 5–9.

or any special sanctification of a day could be called "Judaism" by the Christians. The connection of the Gnostics of the Pastorals with Judaism cannot, therefore, be asserted without qualifications, but it is highly probable.

b) The question of libertinism is vigorously contested. The catalogues of vices,[21] which are products of a literary convention, of course prove nothing in this connection. 1 Tim 1:8 and 2 Tim 3:6 do not prove antinomianism. So there remain only the charges of demonic teachings (1 Tim 4:9; 2 Tim 2:26), bad conscience (1 Tim 1:19; Tit 1:16), evil (1 Tim 6:5; 2 Tim 3:13), defilement (Tit 1:15) and greed (1 Tim 6:5; Tit 1:11). However, even the spirited polemicist Paul, in accusing his opponents, derived his reproaches clearly and demonstra-

bly either from their position regarding his own gospel, or from their particular type of piety. But in the Pastoral Epistles, there is no such derivation; no grounds are given for the accusation of bad conscience. Therefore, one should not infer from the Pastoral Epistles that the opponents were men of bad faith, or masquerading sinners. There are indications[22] that the Gnostics tended to preach asceticism to women who had been sinners. Regarding these accusations, one must always bear in mind that ethical reproaches belong to the style of polemic.[23]

---

21 See 1 Tim 1:9f (and pp. 22f above on this passage); 6:4f; 2 Tim 3:2ff (except 3:5, see below, p. 116).

22 Such an indication is found, namely, in 2 Tim 3:6, see p. 116 below.

23 On polemical style, see Bauer, *Orthodoxy and Heresy*, *passim*. On the whole issue see Wilhelm Mangold, *Die Irrlehrer der Pastoralbriefe* (Frankfurt: Völcker, 1856); Adolf Hilgenfeld, "Die Hirtenbriefe des Paulus neu untersucht," *ZWTh* 40 (1897): 1–86; Lütgert, *Irrlehrer*; Michaelis, *Echtheitsfrage*, 102ff.

4

Instructions for Timothy

6 If you instruct the brothers in this way,
you will be a true servant of Christ
Jesus, (one) who is being reared by the
words of faith and of the good teaching
of which you have become a follower.
7/ But reject godless old wives' tales.
Continue to train yourself in piety.
8/ For bodily training is of little benefit,
but piety brings the greatest possible
benefits, for it promises life now and in
eternity. 9/ The word stands and is
worthy of all recognition; 10/ for that is
the goal of our toil and labor; because
we have placed our hope in the living
God, the Savior of all men, especially of
those who believe.

■ **6** The transitional passage which begins here (see 3:14; 1:18; 5:21) deals with the way Timothy should conduct himself. On "to be reared by" (ἐντρέφεσθαι) with the dative, see Epict., *Diss.* 4.4.48: "reared by these arguments" (τούτοις τοῖς διαλογισμοῖς ἐντρεφόμενος) and Josephus, *Bell.* 6.102: "You, a Jew, who has been reared by the law" (σὺ ὁ Ἰουδαῖος ὁ τοῖς νόμοις ἐντραφείς). "The good teaching" (καλὴ διδασκαλία) is here equivalent to "the sound teaching" (ὑγιαίνουσα διδασκαλία) of 1 Tim 1:10. "To follow," "to be a follower" (παρακολουθεῖν) is used to designate the intellectual grasp of the teaching and is an important term in Epictetus.[1]

■ **7** On "myths" (μύθους) see above on 1:4. "Of old women" (γραώδεις): the image is found not infrequently in philosophical polemic.[2] Likewise "to train" (γυμνάζειν) is used even in earlier parenesis to refer to the soul; e.g., in Isocrates and Pseudo–Isocrates.[3]

■ **8, 9** The formula in v 9 can be a sign of a quotation, see above on 1 Tim 1:15. The first phrase of v 8, indeed, sounds almost like an aphorism. But the author might have intended the formula in v 9 to refer to v 10, a phrase from Col 1:29, which has already become traditional for him (see below). The aphorism in v 8 is possibly meant as a polemic against Gnostic asceticism (provided that this first clause is not simply adduced for the sake of the second, but see above on 4:3–5). But it was doubtless originally directed against the physical training (ἄσκησις) of athletes. In contrast to this, intellectual activity was recommended as especially "useful," perhaps originally philosophy. In its place, Jews or Christians who used the motif may have substituted piety with its corresponding promise. Philosophers would use "it promises" (ἐπαγγελίαν ἔχειν) with reference to what proceeds from virtue, viz. philosophy.[4]

■ **10** "For that is the goal" (εἰς τοῦτο) is perhaps best taken as a reference to the content of v 8, to the "goal" (τέλος) of Christian "training" (γυμνασία); for after

---

1   See Epict., *Diss.* 1.7.33: "to fail to follow an argument, or demonstration, or sophism" (μὴ παρακολουθεῖν λόγῳ μηδ' ἀποδείξει μηδὲ σοφίσματι); cf. 2.24.19.

2   See Epict., *Diss.* 2.16.39: "lamentations of old women" (γραῶν ἀποκλαύματα) [Loeb modified] and Strabo 1.2.3: "declare that poetry is an old wives' tale" (τὴν ποιητικὴν γραώδη μυθολογίαν ἀποφαίνων) [trans. by Ed.]; and Lucian, *Philopseudes* 9: "your stories still remain old wives' fables" (ἔτι σοι γραῶν μῦθοι τὰ λεγόμενά ἐστιν).

3   See Isocrates *Ad Nicoclem* 11: "Therefore, no athlete is so called upon to train his body as a king to train

his soul" (ὥστ' οὐδενὶ τῶν ἀσκητῶν οὕτω προσήκει τὸ σῶμα γυμνάζειν ὡς τοῖς βασιλεῦσι τὴν ψυχὴν τὴν ἑαυτῶν); Pseudo–Isocrates, *Ad Demonicum* 21: "Train yourself in self–imposed toils, that you may be able to endure those which others impose upon you" (γύμναζε σεαυτὸν πόνοις ἑκουσίοις, ὅπως ἂν δύνῃ καὶ τοὺς ἀκουσίους ὑπομένειν). Cf. also Epict. *Diss.* 2.18.27 and 3.3.14.

4   Cf. Epict., *Diss.* 1.4.3 and 4.8.6. On the Cynic–Stoic aversion to athletes see Eduard Norden, "In Varronis saturas Menippeas observationes selectae," *Jahrbücher für Classische Philologie*, Supplementband 18 (1892): 299f; Paul Wendland, *Philo und die ky–*

all "to train" ($\gamma \nu \mu \nu \acute{\alpha} \zeta \epsilon \iota \nu$) of v 7 is resumed by "our toil" ($\kappa o \pi \iota \hat{\omega} \mu \epsilon \nu$). The last clause is then introduced by "because" ($\ddot{o} \tau \iota$). The first clause reproduces Col 1:29 (see above on 1:1). But the tone is different. In the Epistle to the Colossians, "for this toil . . ." refers to the character of the Pauline mission; here the "training" ($\gamma \nu \mu \nu \alpha \sigma \acute{\iota} \alpha$) of piety is intended, in which both Paul and Timothy participate. On "savior" ($\sigma \omega \tau \acute{\eta} \rho$) see below (pp. 100ff), the excursus to 2 Tim 1:10. Here the word seems to have an especially pregnant meaning, in which the divine predicate "the Living One" ($\zeta \hat{\omega} \nu$) is under-stood in a causative way: "it is the living God who makes the promise of life ($\dot{\epsilon} \pi \alpha \gamma \gamma \epsilon \lambda \acute{\iota} \alpha \zeta \omega \hat{\eta} s$) come true." The juxtaposition of "all men" and "those who believe" is indicative for the position of a later generation. For Paul all men are, theoretically, capable of becoming believers. The Pastorals are reconciled to the fact that the faithful represent only a portion of humanity. Thus the church is not just a preliminary form of the kingdom of God but already its substitute.

---

nisch–stoische Diatribe in Paul Wendland and Otto Kern, Beiträge zur Geschichte der griechischen Philosophie und Religion (Berlin: Reimer, 1895), 43f; Johannes Geffken, Kynica und Verwandtes (Heidelberg: Carl Winter, 1909), 22; Dibelius, "Rom und die Christen," 195f; and the excursus in Spicq, 151ff (who directs attention to the Jewish passages like 1 Macc 1:14; 2 Macc 4:9f; Josephus, Ant. 15.267ff).

4

Timothy as Example

11 Thus you should preach and teach. 12/ Let
no one be contemptuous of your youth;
rather, become an example to those
who believe, in word and in conduct, in
love, faith, and purity. 13/ Until I come
(again), continue the reading aloud
(of the scriptures), the exhortation, the
teaching. 14/ Use the gift of grace that
is in you, which was imparted to you
through the word of the prophet, when
the elders laid (their) hands upon you.
15/ Practice this, occupy yourself with
these things, in order that your progress
may be visible to everyone. 16/ Take
pains with yourself and with the teaching, hold on to these things! If you do
that, you will save yourself as well as
your hearers.

5

1 Do not rebuke an older man, but admonish
him as (one would) a father, 2/ younger
men as brothers, older women as
mothers, younger women as sisters, in
all propriety.

In 4:11, the exhortation to the leader of the congregation, which was begun in 4:6, is continued. The problem
here is the youth of the addressee (cf. Ign. *Mag.* 3.1).
That this problem is raised does not argue against authenticity, for the historic Timothy need not have been born
before 30 A.D. If the epistle is held to be inauthentic
on other grounds, one will interpret this passage as a
general word to youthful officeholders in the congregation; for example, those who carry out the functions
named in v 13.[1]

■ **12** On "example" (τύπος), cf. the inscription of
Antiochus I of Commagene: "I have set forth clearly an
example of that religious observance, which a holy man
gives the gods and his ancestors, for my children and
grandchildren, both in these ways and in many other
ways, and I trust that they have a fine example to imi-
tate" (τύπον δὲ εὐ|σεβείας, ἣν θεοῖς καὶ προγόνοις |
εἰσφέρειν ὅσιον, ἐγὼ παισὶν || ἐκγόνοις τε ἐμοῖς
ἐμφανῆ <ι> | καὶ δι' ἑτέρων πολλῶν καὶ | διὰ τούτων

ἐκτέθεικα, νομί|ζω τε αὐτοὺς καλὸν ὑπόδειγμα |
μιμήσασθαι, Ditt. *Or.* I, 383.212ff) [trans. by Ed.]. The
style of this inscription (triads) betrays its edifying
character, which is quite distinct from the paradoxical
way in which Paul uses the concept "example."

■ **14** This is a significant reference to Timothy's dignity.
Ordination has the status of a sacramental act, in which
not only the apostolic tradition, but also the grace of
the office is transferred.[2]

The Laying on of Hands

1. The passage 4:14, together with 5:22 and 2 Tim 1:6, is
evidence for the laying on of hands in primitive Christianity. Here, as elsewhere, the hand serves as the means
of transferring power, be it upon the sick for healing,[3]
upon the young, the weak, or the religiously impure for
the purpose of blessing (Mk 10:13ff), or upon those
who did not have the Spirit for transmitting the Spirit.[4]
1 Tim 4:14 and 2 Tim 1:6 surely belong to the last named

---

1   On the connection between the public reading of
scriptures and preaching, see Knopf, *Lehre der Zwölf
Apostel, Clemensbriefe,* on *2 Clem.* 19.1.

2   See von Campenhausen, *Ecclesiastical Authority,* 115f;
Joachim Jeremias, "ΠΡΕΣΒΥΤΕΡΙΟΝ ausser-
christlich bezeugt," *ZNW* 48 (1957): 127–32.

3   See Otto Weinreich, *Antike Heilungswunder* (Giessen:
Töpelmann, 1909), 1ff. In this case, was the refer-

ence originally to the hand of a god?

4   Laying on of hands, not connected with baptism, occurs in Acts 8:17; during baptism: Acts 19:6 and
Heb 6:2; at an installation: Acts 6:6 and 13:3; and
later, at the ceremony where penitents and heretics
were received back into the church (the practice is
illustrated by *Didasc.* 7 [p. 28, Flemming]).

group. Timothy had been consecrated to his office,[5] which gives him authority over several congregations, by the laying on of hands.[6] It is characteristic of the relation between the pneumatic and legal elements in the concept of office that, according to 1 Tim 1:18 and to this passage, it is a pronouncement of a prophet which designates the future bearers of the spirit.[7] One can conceive of the event by analogy with Acts 13:2, 3. There are difficulties in interpreting the laying on of hands in 1 Tim 5:22 (see below), since the context excludes neither a reference to ordination nor the readmission of sinners.[8]

2. The passages relating to the laying on of hands are sometimes used to decide the question of the Pastorals' order of composition. The following points are relevant to such an investigation: a) the epistolary situation of the Pastorals. Yet this is significant only if we assume authenticity. In that case the problem largely resolves itself after we come to a decision about the situation of 2 Tim.[9]

b) The attitude toward the opponents. The heretics mentioned in 2 Tim (2:17) are to be treated gently (2:24ff). According to the Epistle to Titus (1:13 and 3:10), the opponents should be briefly refuted. But according to 1 Tim (1:19f), those who in 2 Tim 2:17 and 4:14 are merely threatened have already been "handed over to Satan." From this observation one has occasionally deduced the sequence: 2 Tim, Tit, 1 Tim (but cf. section d below).

c) In 1 Tim 4:14, the laying on of hands is based on the authority of the assembled presbyters (the $\pi\rho\epsilon\sigma\beta\nu\tau\acute{\epsilon}$-$\rho\iota\rho\nu$, see the epistles of Ignatius); in 2 Tim 1:6, on that of the apostle. Schwartz[10] regards the former as relatively

historical, the latter as an adjustment to the "apostolic tradition." Since he considers the rise of church law an indication of priority, he arrives at the sequence: 1 Tim, Tit, 2 Tim.

d) The divergence in the question of the laying on of hands is perhaps most easily explained from the character of the letters: congregational regulations in 1 Tim and Tit, a "testament" of the apostle in 2 Tim. If church regulations are recognized as the core of 1 Tim and Tit (see the Introduction), then 2 Tim may have been designed to provide for these regulations (which were supposed to appear under the name of Paul) a personal, historical background. 2 Tim also serves to represent the ecclesiastical authority of Paul (1 Tim and Tit) at the same time as an ethical authority. In this way the typical functions of the apostle in post–apostolic times are brought together. For this reason 2 Tim contains so many personal references, such as the emphasis upon Paul's suffering (see below on 2 Tim 1:8). Other elements of this function of 2 Tim are: the provision of a supplementary background for 1 Tim 1:20 in 2 Tim 2:17 and possibly 4:14; the careful distinction between present and future;[11] and finally, the close connection of the "ordination" of Timothy with Paul (2 Tim 1:6). Since, throughout the three epistles, the participation of the presbytery in the ordination is not explicitly excluded, one need not infer from the divergence between 1 Tim 4:14 and 2 Tim 1:6 that two different authors existed. No conclusions can be drawn as to the sequence of the letters except to say that they imply a unified, consistent conception.

---

5   On the historicity of this office see above, pp. 55f, the excursus to 1 Tim 3:7, section 2.

6   On the variations between the epistles see below. On the relation between the Christian and Jewish rites of ordination see Eduard Lohse (see below).

7   This applies no matter whether $\pi\rho\sigma\phi\eta\tau\epsilon\acute{\iota}\alpha s$ in 4:14 is taken as an accusative plural ("as a result of," "because of,") or as a genitive singular; cf. Theodore of Mopsuestia (II, p. 149, Swete) who uses the singular expression "through prophesy" (*per prophetiam*). In any case one need not distinguish between the two passages; cf. Johannes Behm, *Die Handauflegung im Urchristentum* (Leipzig: A. Deichert, 1911), pp. 47f, who tries to differentiate between them by arguing that in the former passage the prophecy occurred before the laying on of hands, while in the latter it was simultaneous with it.

8   On the entire question see Behm, *Handauflegung*,

(which contains abundant history–of–religions material), and Eduard Lohse, *Die Ordination im Spätjudentum und im Neuen Testament* (Berlin: Evangelische Verlagsanstalt, 1951); Georg Strecker, *Das Judenchristentum in den Pseudoklementinen*, TU 70 (Berlin: Akademieverlag, 1958), 97–116 (Exkurs: Die Ordination in den Pseudoklementinen).

9   But cf. Bruston, "De la date," 272ff. Bruston dates 2 Tim during the time of Paul's first imprisonment and 1 Tim during one of the following years.

10 Eduard Schwartz, "Über die pseudapostolischen Kirchenordnungen," *Schriften der wissenschaftlichen Gesellschaft Strassburg* 6 (1910): 1.

11 2 Tim 3:1ff. The false teaching is still in the process of formation.

■ **15** "This" (ταῦτα) is clearly connected with the exhortation in vss 13–14, which is to be taken as a whole: Do your duty and make use of your gift. "These things" (ἐν τούτοις) means: "in this kind of activity."[12] Such an accumulation of imperatives, with general references to the preceding exhortations, is also found in Pseudo–Pythagoras.[13] "Progress" (προκοπή) is of great importance in Stoicism, but cf. also Sir 51:17 and 2 Macc 8:8. The formula "that you may be visible to everyone" (ἵνα φανερὸν πᾶσιν ᾖ . . .) is found frequently in the honorary inscriptions.[14]

■ **16** The first imperative of the verse suggests that "to these things" (αὐτοῖς) refers to "this" (ταῦτα) and "these things" (τούτοις) in v 15. Promises given to teachers (or missionary preachers), and at the same time to the disciples, are also common elsewhere.[15]

■ **5:1–2** These verses are often taken with what follows, and placed under the heading: Timothy's behavior toward certain classes of people in the congregation. In fact, the regulation regarding widows would, from a formal standpoint, be linked quite well with these exhortations. On the other hand, the regulations in 5:3ff have been formed into an independent church order, whereas in 5:1f we are dealing with a different type of exhortation which belongs to a pattern of popular moral philosophy.[16] The proof of the dissemination of such expressions throughout the culture is again supplied by the inscriptions (see also the excursus to 3:1). The following passages may serve as examples: *Inscr. Priene*, (1st cent. B.C.) 117.55f: "continually honoring older men as parents, peers as brothers, and younger men as sons"

([ἀεί π]οτε μὲν πρεσβυτέ[ρους τιμῶν ὡς γονεῖ]ς, τοὺς δὲ καθήλικας ὡς ἀδελφούς, τοὺς δὲ [νεωτέρους ὡς παῖδας]) [Trans. by Ed.]; B. Latyschev, ed., *IPE* 1.22.28ff (cf. Deissmann, *LAE*, 309f): "bearing himself to his equals in age as a brother, to his elders as a son, to children as a father" (τοῖς μὲν ἡλικιώταις προσφερόμενος ὡς ἀδελφός, τοῖς δὲ πρεσβυτέροις ὡς υἱός, ‖ τοῖς δὲ παισὶν ὡς πατήρ). Cf. also Iambl., *Vit. Pyth.* 8.40: "to exercise on the one hand, good will toward fathers through the orderly behavior toward elders, and, on the other hand, (to practice) fellowship with brothers through benevolence towards others" (μελετᾶν ἐν μὲν τῇ πρὸς τοὺς πρεσβυτέρους εὐκοσμίᾳ τὴν πρὸς πατέρας εὔνοιαν, ἐν δὲ τῇ πρὸς ἄλλους φιλανθρωπίᾳ τὴν πρὸς τοὺς ἀδελφοὺς κοινωνίαν) [trans. by Ed.]; Libanius, *Progymnasmata* 7, (p. 185.3, Förster) (in an instruction to the would–be physician): "consider yourself a brother of your peers, a child of your elders and a father to those younger" (τῶν μὲν ἡλικιωτῶν νόμιζε σεαυτὸν ἀδελφόν, τῶν δὲ πρεσβυτέρων παῖδα, τῶν δὲ νεωτέρων πατέρα) [trans. by Ed.]. It is clear from these parallels that "elder" (πρεσβύτερος, see below, pp. 77f, the excursus to 5:17) does not refer to an office, but rather to "any elderly person" (περὶ παντὸς γεγηρακότος).[17]

---

12 As in Xenophon, *Hist. Graec.* 4.8.7; see also Bauer, s.v. εἰμί, section 4.

13 Pseudo–Pythagoras, *Carmen aureum* 45f: "Gain these by toil; practice these diligently; you must love these, they will set you on the track of divine virtue" (ταῦτα πόνει, ταῦτ' ἐκμελέτα. τούτων χρὴ ἐρᾶν σε, | ταῦτά σε τῆς θείης ἀρετῆς εἰς ἴχνια θήσει) [trans. by Ed.].

14 Jean Rouffiac, *Recherches sur les caractères du Grec dans le NT* (Paris: École Pratique des Hautes Études, 1911), 53.

15 Cf. Jas 5:20; *2 Clem.* 15.1 and 19.1: "that you may save both yourselves and him who is the reader among you" (ἵνα καὶ ἑαυτοὺς σώσητε καὶ τὸν ἀναγινώσκοντα ἐν ὑμῖν).

16 Cf. Plato, *Resp.* 5.463c: "for no matter whom he meets, he will feel that he is meeting a brother, a sister, a father, a mother, a son, a daughter, or the offspring or forebears of these" (παντὶ γὰρ ᾧ ἂν ἐντυγχάνῃ τις, ἢ ὡς ἀδελφῷ ἢ ὡς ἀδελφῇ ἢ ὡς πατρὶ ἢ ὡς μητρὶ ἢ υἱεῖ ἢ θυγατρὶ ἢ τούτων ἐκγόνοις ἢ προγόνοις νομιεῖ ἐντυγχάνειν).

17 J. A. Cramer, *Catene*, 7, p. 37.

5 On Widows

3 Honor widows, if they are true widows!
4/ If a widow has children or grandchildren, they should first learn to show
piety toward their own family and to
show gratitude to their forebears. This
is well–pleasing before God. 5/ The
one who is a true widow and solitary,
however, has placed her hope in God and
remains in prayer and supplication day
and night. 6/ The one who lives voluptuously is dead while she lives. 7/ Give
this instruction so that their conduct
may be beyond reproach. 8/ But if someone does not provide for his own people,
not even for his own family, he has
denied the faith and has become worse
than an unbeliever.

9 She alone may be enrolled as a widow,
who is not younger than sixty, who was
the wife of one man, 10/ who is well
attested in good works, inasmuch as she
has raised children, practiced hospitality, washed the feet of the saints, and,
in general devoted herself to every good
work. 11/ Reject younger widows.
Because when sensuous impulses lead
them away from Christ, they want to
marry 12/ and thus are under the verdict
that they have broken their first faith.
13/ At the same time, they also learn
idleness, when they run from house to
house—not only idleness, but they also
become gossips and busybodies; then
they say what is not proper. 14/ Thus, I
wish that the younger ones should
marry, bear children, manage their
households, and do not give the adversary an opportunity for slander, 15/ because
some have already turned away and
followed Satan. 16/If a faithful woman
has widows, she should provide for
them; the congregation should not be
burdened, so that it can provide for the
true widows.

The regulations concerning widows include a regulation about those widows who are to be regarded as "true widows" (ὄντως χῆραι, see v 9), who serve the congregation (v 10) and who are supported by it (v 16). "Honor" (τίμα) in v 3 probably does not yet refer to the support by the congregation. Other scholars[1] divide the passage into two parts, referring 5:3–8 to the care of widows in general, and 5:9ff to the conduct of widows in the congregation. But the section is unitary, and a parenesis on the conduct of widows is unknown in the non–Christian lists of duties.[2] Again we are dealing with a section which intersperses a general teaching about duties with instructions for specific classes within the congregation. Formal discrepancies result from such a procedure. The

---

1   E.g., B. Weiss, Jeremias, J. E. Belser, *Die Briefe des Apostel Paulus an Timotheus und Titus übersetzt und er- klärt* (Freiburg i. B.: Herder, 1907), *ad loc.*

2   See Weidinger, *Die Haustafeln,* 71.

"true widow" (ὄντως χῆρα) of 5:3, 5 is probably the same as the "widow" (χῆρα) of vss 9ff. The passage under discussion is, together with three other passages,[3] the earliest attestation to a special class of widows. The origin of this class should probably be dated during the period of the consolidation of the churches in the world. This passage attests to the fact that special duties and rights were given those in the class of widows. But it also shows that not every widow could qualify as a "widow" in the technical sense. This passage illustrates the development of the technical use of the term, a process which led to the definition of the office "widows of the congregation," but which at the same time allowed the continued use of the word as a designation for anyone who had been widowed. The situation is very similar to that of "elder" (πρεσβύτερος, see below pp. 77f, the excursus to 5:17).[4]

■ 3, 4 The author takes pains to eliminate from the number of true widows, all superfluous and unreliable persons (cf. also vss 11ff and 16).

The first of these are the widows with families (v 4). The regulation with regard to them is hard to interpret because of the change of subject.[5] The old interpretation, which supplies "the widows" as the subject of the clause "they shall learn," is made impossible by the term "to show piety" (εὐσεβεῖν), which is a variant of the word "to honor" (τιμᾶν),[6] and by the term "forebears" (προγόνοις). Therefore, the "members of the family" must be seen as the subject of "they shall learn." The change of the subject can be explained as a brachylogy. One could paraphrase the passage this way: "If a widow has a family, then she has no need of such honors by the church (see v 3). Rather, before the relatives devote themselves to other works of love, they should first of all "show piety toward their own family, etc." (τὸν ἴδιον οἶκον εὐσεβεῖν κτλ.). This viewpoint is also consistent with the canon enunciated below in 3:5. "Gratitude" (ἀμοιβή) is common in inscriptions about "gratitude of the fatherland" and the like.[7] Edifying language is used in the endorsement of 4b (cf. 2:3), as well as in the following description of the behavior of the "true widows."[8]

■ 5 On "day and night" (νυκτὸς καὶ ἡμέρας), cf. 1 Thess 3:10; on the expression "to place one's hope in God," see 1 Tim 4:10; 6:17.[9]

■ 6 As the second category, "the one who lives voluptuously" (σπαταλῶσα)[10] is excluded from the number of "real widows." This is not intended as an actual instruction, but rather more as an admonition, as v 7 shows.[11]

■ 7 On "beyond reproach" (ἀνεπίλημπτος) see above on 3:2.

■ 8 furnishes a supplement to v 4. Once again responsibility is placed upon family members for providing for their own widows (v 16 makes the same point). Here the religious motif is stressed. "To deny the faith" (τὴν πίστιν ἤρνηται)[12] means not apostasy, but practical disavowal. The unity of belief and action is presupposed. (This presupposition illuminates the style of the heresy polemic: dogmatic and moral reproaches are combined.) The passage shows how community duties are increasingly felt to be specifically Christian. In this way a Christian

3   These are Ign. *Sm.* 13.1; Ign. *Pol.* 4.1; Pol. *Phil.* 4.3.
4   On the whole question see Zscharnack, *Der Dienst der Frau*, 100ff.
5   Johannes Müller–Bardoff, "Zur Exegese von I. Timotheus 5, 3–16," in *Gott und die Götter, Festgabe für E. Fascher* (Berlin: Evangelische Verlagsanstalt, 1958), 113–33. See also Wohlenberg, *ad loc.*
6   Cf. Belser, *ad loc.*
7   Cf. *Inscr. Priene* 119.27; 113.120; 112,17; *IG* XIV, 744.5; 748.14. The verb ἀμείβεσθαι is also a term for "honoring" someone. Günther Gerlach, *Griechische Ehreninschriften* (Halle: Niemeyer, 1908), 50.
8   Bartsch, *Anfänge*, 125f.
9   See also Rudolf Bultmann, *TDNT* 2, p. 532f.
10 Is there perhaps an intentional rhyme with "ζῶσα" (living)? On the word see Windisch–Preisker, *Katholische Briefe*, on Jas 5:5.
11 On the usage, cf. Philo, *Fug.* 55: "some people are

dead while living, and some alive while dead" (ζῶντες ἔνιοι τεθνήκασι καὶ τεθνηκότες ζῶσιν); on the thought, cf. Rev 3:1; see also Sextus 7 b (ed. Henry Chadwick, *TS*, N. S. 5, 1959): "The faithless in faith is a dead man in a living body" (ἄπιστος ἐν πίστει νεκρὸς ἄνθρωπος ἐν σώματι ζῶντι) [trans. by Ed.]; *ibid.* 175: "Dead before God are those through whom the name of God is blasphemed" (νεκροὶ παρὰ θεῷ δι᾽ οὓς τὸ ὄνομα τοῦ θεοῦ λοιδορεῖται) [trans. by Ed.].
12 On this expression, cf. Anton Fridrichsen, "Einige sprachliche und stilistische Beobachtungen," *Con. Neot.* 2 (1936): 8–13; and *ibid.*, 6 (1942): 94ff.

family ethic is formed, which goes essentially beyond the traditional "rules for the household" (see above, pp. 39ff, the second excursus to 2:2).[13]

■ **9** "To enroll" (καταλέγειν) is the technical term for the registration, e.g., of levied troops.[14] Tertullian, *Ad uxorem* 1.7, seems to translate ecclesiastically: adlegere in ordinem ("to accept into the clergy"). "The wife of *one* man" (ἑνὸς ἀνδρὸς γυνή) see above at 3:2, especially if one takes 5:3–16 as a unity. There is no reason whatever to infer a prohibition of a second marriage here. Naturally, in every case the requirement "if she is solitary" (μεμονωμένη 5:5), must be fulfilled, i.e. the woman must be without a family. The interpretation of this passage by Theodore of Mopsuestia is thus correct: "If she has lived in chastity with her husband, no matter whether she has had only one, or whether she was married a second time" (si pudice cum suo vixerit viro, sive unum tantum habuerit, sive et secundo fuerit nupta).[15]

■ **10** On the works which widows are expected to perform, cf. 2:10 and *Herm. vis.* 2.4.3: "and Grapte shall exhort the widows and orphans" (Γραπτὴ δὲ νουθετήσει τὰς χήρας καὶ τοὺς ὀρφανούς). But above all, cf. the description of the Christian work of love in Lucian, *De morte Peregrini* 12: "and from the very break of day aged widows and orphan children could be seen waiting near the prison" (καὶ ἕωθεν μὲν εὐθὺς ἦν ὁρᾶν παρὰ τῷ δεσμωτηρίῳ [where Peregrinus, who has converted to Christianity, lies captured] περιμένοντα γρᾴδια, χήρας τινὰς καὶ παιδία ὀρφανά); cf. ch. 13 where the Christians are described as: "to succour and defend and encourage the hero" (βοηθήσοντες καὶ ξυναγορεύσοντες καὶ παραμυθησόμενοι τὸν ἄνδρα). "To raise children" (τεκνοτροφεῖν) is here, as in Epict., *Diss.* 1.23.3, not to be limited to the provision of food. If one takes the section as a unity (see above on 5:3ff), one will,

because of 5:4, not think of the children of widows but rather, say, of orphans (see the passages from Hermas and Lucian cited above). On foot washing see Jn 13:4.[16] It is mentioned here as an example of Christian humility and hospitality. This attitude, not each and every work of love, is the prerequisite for service as a widow.

■ **11, 12** "Faith" (τὴν πίστιν) here refers to an agreement.[17] On antiquity's admiration for young, chaste widows see Delling, and cf. Plutarch and Josephus.[18]

■ **13** The continuation of the sentence "not only idleness etc." (οὐ μόνον δὲ ἀργαί κτλ.) shows that in the first half of the clause "idleness" (ἀργαί) is the main concern. "They learn" (μανθάνουσιν) must, therefore, be connected with "idleness," and any attempt to connect it with "they run from house to house" (περιερχόμεναι) or with "what is not proper" (τὰ μὴ δέοντα) is just as much ruled out as it would be to take "they learn," by analogy with 2 Tim 2:7, in an absolute sense. It also eliminates the conjectural reading "they are hidden" (λανθάνουσι). It is therefore to be supplemented with "to be" (εἶναι),[19] i.e. they learn to be idle, viz. "idleness." "To run from house to house" (περιέρχεσθαι τὰς οἰκίας) refers to pastoral house calls. The context clearly indicates that such calls were among widows' duties, and it is precisely in this connection that a danger might arise for the younger ones. On "busybody" (περίεργος) see Acts 19:19 and 2 Thess 3:11.[20]

■ **14** "I wish" (βούλομαι) is used in legislative regulations.[21] The resolute formulation witnesses to the high value placed upon morality and order in the Pastoral Epistles. The ideal of Christian citizenship of the Pastorals (see above pp. 39ff, the excursus to 2:2) is shown in an ordinance based upon the founding of families. Paul's attitude (as expressed in 1 Cor 7:1, 7f, 29ff) is completely different. His point of view is eschatologically deter-

---

13 On the term οἱ ἴδιοι, see Bauer, *Johannesevangelium*, on Jn 1:11.
14 Examples are to be found in Liddell–Scott, *s.v.* But in Plato, *Leg.* 743e. it is used with a double accusative, meaning "to regard as."
15 Theodore of Mopsuestia (II, p. 161, Swete); cf. also Theodoret (III, p. 664, Schulze). A different interpretation is given by Delling, *Stellung des Paulus zu Frau und Ehe*, 136f. See also Livy 10.23.9: service at the altar of Pudicitia was permitted only to matrons who had been wedded to one man alone.
16 Cf. Bauer, *Johannesevangelium*, on Jn 13:4; on ἁγίων πόδας see Blass–Debrunner 295.3.
17 Cf. Cramer, *Catene* 7, p. 40: "faith; he calls it an agreement" (τὴν πίστιν· συνθήκην λέγει).
18 Delling, *Stellung des Paulus zu Frau und Ehe*, 134; Plutarch, *Aemilius Paulus* 2 (p. 749 D); Josephus, *Ant.* 18.66.
19 See the translation, and Blass–Debrunner, 416.2.
20 Cf. Dibelius, *Thessalonicher, Philipper*, on 2 Thess 3:11.
21 *P. Lond.* III 904.30, p. 125; Josephus, *Ant.* 12.150; see 1 Tim 2:8.

mined; here the world is expected to endure, and taking root in it is desirable. "The adversary" (ἀντικείμενος) is probably the one who casts blame, i.e., the opponent.[22]

■ **15, 16** On "to turn away" (ἐκτρέπεσθαι), see 1:6. It is hard to say whether the sin is unchastity or false teaching, and it is equally hard to determine whether here, and in the preceding verses, the author is still thinking about widows. If he is, and if the somewhat better attested reading of v 16, "if a faithful, i.e. widow" (εἴ τις πιστή, ℵ A C 33), is correct, then the case described is that of a widow, otherwise qualified for congregational service, who was herself in the business of caring for widows. She should continue her work. But if "a faithful one" (πιστή) refers to Christian women in general, or if the reading "of a faithful man or woman" (εἴ τις πιστὸς ἢ πιστή D 𝔐 sy Ambst) is accepted, then the principle already mentioned in vss 4 and 8 is here emphasized once more.

---

22 See above on 3:6, 7; but cf. *1 Clem.* 51.1 and *Mart. Pol.* 17.1: Satan.

5 On Presbyters

17 The presbyters who govern well as presiding officers should be deemed worthy of a double compensation, especially those who are engaged in speaking and teaching. 18/ For the scripture says: "You shall not muzzle an ox when it is treading out the grain," and "the worker is worthy of his wages." 19/ Do not accept a complaint against a presbyter, unless on the basis of the witness of two or three persons. 20/ If any (of them) sin, convict them in the presence of all (presbyters), so that the others too may have fear.

Presbyter

The problem of the word "presbyter" ($\pi\rho\epsilon\sigma\beta\acute{u}\tau\epsilon\rho os$) in the Pastoral Epistles lies in the ambiguous character of the word, which is sometimes a reference to age, sometimes a title. The use of "presbyter" as a title among the Jews of the Diaspora is not attested until quite late in inscriptions and imperial decrees.[1] On the other hand, the LXX translation of the Hebrew title "elders" (זְקֵנִים) with "presbyters" ($\pi\rho\epsilon\sigma\beta\acute{u}\tau\epsilon\rho o\iota$) seems to indicate that for the Judaism of the LXX the "elders" stood at the head of the congregations.[2]

The non–Jewish texts attesting to the titular usage of "presbyter" cannot be regarded as more than analogies to the Jewish and Christian use of the word. We can distinguish between two groups:

1. Associations of seniors, i.e. associations of older people in contrast to the associations of the "youths" ($\nu\acute{e}o\iota$).[3] In addition to the more common designations "the aged" ($\gamma\epsilon\rho\alpha\iota o\acute{\iota}$) and "the senators" ($\gamma\epsilon\rho o\upsilon\sigma\iota\alpha\sigma\tau\alpha\acute{\iota}$), they are also called "the seniors," "the elders" ($\pi\rho\epsilon\sigma\beta\acute{u}\tau\epsilon\rho o\iota$).[4] It is questionable whether titles such as "the synod of the senior receivers" ($\sigma\acute{u}\nu o\delta os\ \tau\hat{\omega}\nu\ \acute{e}\nu$ Ἀλεξανδρείαι $\pi\rho\epsilon\sigma\beta\upsilon\tau\acute{e}\rho\omega\nu\ \acute{e}\gamma\delta o\chi\acute{e}\omega\nu$),[5] or "the senior craftsmen" ($\tau\acute{e}\kappa\tau o\nu\epsilon s\ \pi\rho\epsilon\sigma\beta\acute{u}\tau\epsilon\rho o\iota$)[6] or "the senior minstrels" ($\acute{u}\mu\nu\omega\delta o\grave{\iota}\ \pi\rho\epsilon\sigma\beta\acute{u}\tau\epsilon\rho o\iota$)[7] belong to this group. It is not clear whether older members of the profession in question formed such clubs,[8] or whether the names of the clubs were intended to show that such associations were older than their more recent competitors.[9] The former interpretation seems to be corroborated by the analogous terminology of the inscription from Hypaepa:[10] "of the younger Jews" (Ἰουδαίων $\nu\epsilon\omega\tau\acute{e}\rho\omega\nu$); this probably designates younger Jews and not the younger of two Jewish congregations.[11]

2. At least in Egypt, "presbyters" ($\pi\rho\epsilon\sigma\beta\acute{u}\tau\epsilon\rho o\iota$) referred to committees and councils of different kinds.[12] Regional managers are called "elders" ($\pi\rho\epsilon\sigma\beta\acute{u}\tau\epsilon\rho o\iota$)

---

1 See Schürer, *A History of the Jewish People* 2² p. 249. For a more complete treatment, see *idem, Geschichte des jüdischen Volkes* 3, pp. 89 ff; *Monumenta Asiae Minoris Antiqua* 3 (1931), Nos. 344, 447; cf. *ZNW* 31 (1932): 313f; *CJJ*, p. LXXVI and Nos. 581, 590, 595 and *passim*.

2 Cf. also the synagogue inscription from Jerusalem, *Suppl. Epigr. Graec.* 7, 170.9 (see Deissmann, *LAE*, 439ff). Note too that the "elders" ($\pi\rho\epsilon\sigma\beta\acute{u}\tau\epsilon\rho o\iota$) were members of the Sanhedrin according to the Gospels, and see Lietzmann, "Verfassungsgeschichte," 123f.

3 The abundant literature is listed in Schürer, *Geschichte des jüdischen Volkes*, vol. 3, p. 91, n. 57.

4 Attestations, mainly from Asia Minor and its insular territory, are found in Poland, *Griechisches Vereinswesen*, 98ff.

5 Ditt. *Or.* I, 140.7ff.

6 The phrase is found in an Alexandrian inscription, see Erich Ziebarth, *Das griechische Vereinswesen* (Leipzig: Teubner, 1896), 213.

7 The phrase is found in an inscription from Radanovo; Ziebarth, *Das griechische Vereinswesen*, 90.

8 Max L. Strack, "Die Müllerinnung in Alexandrien," *ZNW* 4 (1903): 232.

9 Ziebarth, *Das griechische Vereinswesen*, 30, 90, 213; Poland, *Griechisches Vereinswesen*, 171f, note.

10 Salomon Reinach, "Les Juifs d'Hypaepa," *Revue des études juives* 10 (1885): 74–8.

11 On the "presbyters" ($\pi\rho\epsilon\sigma\beta\acute{u}\tau\epsilon\rho o\iota$) of the Hypsistarian congregations in the Crimea, cf. Lietzmann, "Verfassungsgeschichte:" 118ff.

12 For instance, there were "the elders of the millers" (or bakers) ($\pi\rho\epsilon\sigma\beta\acute{u}\tau\epsilon\rho o\iota\ \tau\hat{\omega}\nu\ \acute{o}\lambda\upsilon\rho o\kappa\acute{o}\pi\omega\nu$); see Max L. Strack, "Referate und Besprechungen. Inschriften aus ptolemäischer Zeit. II," *Archiv für Papy-*

in the emancipation petition[12a] which was submitted to the "elders and tax-officials of the village of Apias" (πρεσβυτέροις καὶ πράκτορσι κώμης Ἀπιάδος). Especially important for the Pastoral Epistles is the occurrence of the title of "elder" in the "Priesthood of the Great God Soknopaios": "The five elder priests" (τῶν ε̄ πρεσβυτέρων ἱερέων) BGU 1, 16.5f and 387.7.[13]

The early Christian usage of this term for a more or less patriarchal committee is therefore not surprising.[14] From the Pastorals the following information may be obtained concerning the presbyters: they form a council (1 Tim 4:14) and lay hands upon the man who is set apart by the word of the prophet (1 Tim 1:18 and 4:14). The fact that they are presbyters does not imply that they are already "presiding officers" (προεστῶτες) or "engaged in speaking" (κοπιῶντες ἐν λόγῳ), (1 Tim 5:17). Certain requirements are made of them, requirements which are also made of the "bishop" (ἐπίσκοπος, Tit 1:5, 7; cf. above pp. 54ff, the excursus to 3:7). The evidence taken as a whole makes it impossible to see in the term "presbyter" only a designation of age.[15] It is characteristic of the Pastorals that physical state and status within the congregation stand side by side. Cf. also

the evidence in related writings, above all in the First Epistle of Clement.[16]

■ **17** The phrase "double compensation" (διπλῆς τιμῆς) applied to "the presiding presbyters" (προεστῶτες πρεσβύτεροι) implies that two functions or honorary positions were given to the same person. The patriarchal character of the congregation's leadership is not thereby excluded. One can hardly interpret the expression "govern well as presiding officers" (οἱ καλῶς προεστῶτες πρεσβύτεροι) as referring only to a special quality of their service, a quality which was supposed to be honored doubly. Rather it is the expression of approval of their additional service.[17] A financial compensation is certainly intended here,[18] one which is meant to be just twice that of other presbyters.[19] The next verse makes the connection with material reimbursement unmistakably clear.[20] Teaching is regarded as a voluntary service.

■ **18** The use of the technical term for "Holy Scripture" (γραφή) is noteworthy; while the first saying comes from the OT (Deut 25:4; cf. 1 Cor 9:9), the second is known to us from Lk 10:7 as a saying of Jesus. This saying

---

rusforschung und verwandte Gebiete 2 (1902): 544, and idem, "Müllerinnung," 230, where there is a list of the earlier attestations. Note also the frequent occurrence of "the elders of the farmers" (πρεσβύτεροι τῶν γεωργῶν) in the P. Tebt. I, 13.5; 40.17f; 43.8; 50.20; P. Lond. II, 255.7, p. 117; BGU I, 6ff; and Deissmann, Bible Studies, 154–57 and 233ff.

12a Cf. Veröffentlichungen aus den badischen Papyrus–Sammlungen, 2.33.1.

13 See H. Hauschildt, "πρεσβύτεροι in Ägypten im I–III Jahrhundert n. Chr.," ZNW 4 (1903): 235–42. On p. 239 of this article it is demonstrated that these "elders" were sometimes not old at all, and that the usage was thus only titular.

14 See Acts 11:30; 14:23; ch. 15 passim; 20:17; 21:18; 1 Petr 5:1; Jas 5:14.

15 Thus Jeremias, ad loc.

16 Von Campenhausen, Ecclesiastical Authority, 84ff; on the entire question see Wilhelm Michaelis, Das Ältestenamt (Bern: Haller, 1953), and Günther Bornkamm, TDNT 6, pp. 651–80.

17 Günther Bornkamm, TDNT 6, p. 666f.

18 Michaelis, Echtheitsfrage, believes that "double compensation" (διπλῆς τιμῆς) only refers to the honor, since according to 3:4, 12, the officers of the community for the most part kept their regular occupations and, hence, had no need of financial compensation.

19 Cf. Bartsch, Anfänge, 93ff. Lock, ad loc., substantiates this with his reference to Did. 13 (support of the prophets) and Const. Ap. 2.28 (double compensation for deacons and presbyters).

20 Cf. the statutes of the "worshippers of Diana and Antinous" (cultores Dianae et Antinoi) CIL 14.2112 (reprinted as Appendix 2 in Lietzmann–Kümmel, Korinther): according to No. 11, "double shares of all allotments" (ex omnibus divisionibus partes dupl[as]) [trans. by Ed.].

21 Michaelis, Echtheitsfrage, 62, would exclude the saying as a gloss.

22 Another opinion is that this refers to the congregation in general; see J. Hoh, Die kirchliche Buße im zweiten Jahrhundert (Breslau: Müller & Seiffert, 1932), p. 79; Bernhard Poschmann, Paenitentia secunda (Bonn: Hanstein, 1940), p. 103; von Campenhausen, Ecclesiastical Authority. 146ff. On the significance of Dt 19:15, see Hendrick van Vliet, No Single Testimony: A Study on the Adoption of the Law of Deut. 19:15 Par. into the New Testament (Utrecht: Kremink en Zoon, 1958).

could be a quotation either from Lk or from one of his sources as "Holy Scripture" (which would indicate a late date for the Pastoral Epistles). The saying in question could also be of earlier origin, stemming from an "holy" apocryphon (i.e. of the OT). Lk 10:7 almost gives the impression that Jesus is appealing to a recognized saying from Scripture, i.e. that such a saying is ascribed to him.

Finally, "Holy Scripture" could simply refer to the first saying, with which the second is only loosely connected. In light of this possibility, it is unnecessary to exclude the verse as a gloss, even though it designates a saying of Jesus as a portion of Scripture.[21]

■ **19, 20** belong together; the "others," "all" (λοιποί), then, are the rest of the presbyters.[22]

5

Exhortation to Timothy

21   I adjure you before God and Christ Jesus
and the chosen angels: observe this
without prejudice and do nothing according to partiality. 22 / Do not be
hasty in the laying on of hands and do
not have any part in the sins of others.
23 / Keep yourself pure. Do not drink
water only, but take some wine because
of your stomach and your frequent ill
health. 24 / Some peoples' sins are evident, since they go before them into the
judgment, but the sins of others follow
after them. 25 / Likewise, good works
are also evident, and those which are
not, cannot (ultimately) remain hidden.

■ **21, 22**   The context is problematic. If both verses belong to v 20, then "this" (ταῦτα) refers to the instructions given in 19f, and v 22 probably has to do with the
ordination of presbyters. "To have part in the sins of
others" (κοινωνεῖν ἁμαρτίαις ἀλλοτρίαις) would
then refer to the possibility that Timothy had unknow-
ingly made a sinner a presbyter. If, on the other hand,
v 22 is unconnected with what has gone before, then
the reference is to the readmission of sinners or heretics.
The reference to "sins of others" is thus most easily
explained. Since a transitional passage clearly begins
with 5:21 (see above on 4:6), a closer connection with
what has gone before is improbable. Therefore, it seems
more likely that the verse should be interpreted as a
reference to the reconciliation of those who have fallen
from faith.[1] Moreover, v 21 need not be limited to behavior toward presbyters.[2] "Partiality" (πρόσκλισις)
means taking sides, perhaps in the sense of favoritism
(as in *1 Clem.* 21.7 and 47.3, 4). But there is also a neutral

usage "without human partisanship" (δίχα προσκλί-
σεως ἀνθρωπίνης in *1 Clem.* 50.2). "Prejudice" (πρό-
κριμα)[3] can refer to favorable or unfavorable judgment.
The triad God, Christ, angels arose originally perhaps
from an eschatological conception. Christ comes from
the father with the angels (cf. the change which Mk 8:38
has undergone in Lk 9:26). Here the formula is perhaps
already a liturgical one (see above at 1:17). On the
expression "chosen angels" see *Odes of Sol.* 4.8: "for thy seal
is known: . . . and the elect archangels are clad with it."

On v 22, see above pp. 70ff, excursus on 1 Tim 4:14.[4]

■ **23**   is a qualification of "pure" (ἁγνόν), which clearly
assumes that the fictional or real addressee has a tendency to abstinence. The author says this "not in order to
encourage luxury" (οὐ πρὸς τρυφήν).[5] If one places
the epistle at the time of the incipient Gnostic contro-
versies, one will, however, see in the admonition not an
advice concerning diet, but an anti–Gnostic motif: the
author wishes to keep his people from resembling in any

---

1   Cf. P. Galtier, "La réconciliation des pécheurs dans
la première Épître à Timothée," *RechSR* 39 (1951):
317–20.

2   Cf. the oath of Aurelius of Utica at the synod of
Carthage, Sept. 1, 256: "Though the apostle says
we must not share the sins of others, what is a man
doing, who has a share with heretics without the
baptism of the church, except sharing the sins of
others?" (cum dicat apostolus non communican-
dum peccatis alienis, quid aliud quam peccatis alienis, communicat, qui haereticis sine ecclesiae bap-
tismo communicat?) [trans. by Ed.]; cf. Hermann
von Soden "Sententiae LXXXVII episcoporum.

Das Protokoll der Synode von Karthago am 1. Sep-
tember 256," NGG 1909, p. 266.

3   See Bauer, *s.v.*

4   Cf. also on this verse Nikolaus Adler, "Die Handauflegung im NT bereits ein Bussritus? Zur Auslegung
von I Tim. 5, 22," *Neutestamentliche Aufsätze: Festschrift für Josef Schmid*, ed. Joseph Blinzler, Otto
Kuss und Franz Mussner (Regensburg: F. Pustet,
1963), 1–6.

5   The phrase is from Chrysostom (XI, p. 691, Montfaucon). The admonition thus expresses the same
thought as Pseudo–Pythagoras, *Carmen aureum* 32f:
"There is no need to be indifferent to the health of

way the false teachers mentioned in 4:3. "To drink water only" (ὑδροποτεῖν) among Jews as well as Greeks belongs to the pious life, the life full of renunciation.[6]

■ **24, 25** Here too the relation to the context is uncertain. In this transitional parenetic passage, which does not seem to contain a systematic development of thought (see 4:11–16), it is best to regard vss 23, 24, and 25 as supplements to "keep yourself pure" (σεαυτὸν ἁγνὸν τήρει). We are therefore dealing in vss 24–25 neither with warnings addressed specifically to presbyters, nor with reflections about the drinking of wine. The "judgment"

(κρίσις) is the divine judgment. On "they go before them" (προάγουσαι), cf. Isa 58:8: "Your righteousness goes out before you" (προπορεύσεται ἔμπροσθέν σου ἡ δικαιοσύνη σου); *Barn.* 4.12: "If he be good, his righteousness will go before him" (ἐὰν ᾖ ἀγαθός, ἡ δικαιοσύνη αὐτοῦ προηγήσεται αὐτοῦ) [trans. by Ed.].

---

the body, but rather one should observe moderation in drink, food and exercise" (οὐδ' ὑγιείης τῆς περὶ σῶμ' ἀμέλειαν ἔχειν χρή· ἀλλὰ ποτοῦ τε μέτρον καὶ σίτου γυμνασίων τε ποιεῖσθαι) [Trans.].

6   See Dan 1:12; *Pirke Aboth* 6.4; Epict., *Diss.* 3.13.21.

6

On Slaves

1 All those who are slaves under the yoke must count their masters worthy of all respect, so that the name of God and the teaching are not blasphemed. 2/ But those who have masters who are believers should not think lightly of them because they are brothers, but should serve (them) all the more eagerly, because they are believers and beloved (by God), who devote themselves to good works.

■ **1, 2a** is a regulation concerning slaves. It is a piece of early Christian parenesis, the counterparts of which are found in the "rules for the household."[1] The verses form therefore a kind of continuation of the ordinances for presbyters in 5:17ff. "Their (own)" (ἴδιος) is used here in a weakened sense.[2] On the final clause ("so that . . ."), see Isa 52:5; Rom 2:24, and above on 1 Tim 3:7. Both dependent clauses in v 2 ("because . . ." [ὅτι]) are paraphrases of the description of the masters (δεσπόται) as Christians. It would not suit the context to relate them to the slaves. "Good works" (εὐεργεσία) designates, then, a typically Christian virtue, and "beloved" (ἀγαπητοί) must somehow be connected with the Christianity of the masters. The slaves who must be admonished to serve cannot, in the same injunction, be expected to act out of love for the masters. Therefore one has to supply "by God" (θεοῦ) to "beloved," as in Rom 11:28 and Ign. *Phld.* 9.2. "Beloved" (ἀγαπητός), like "those who love God [or: him]" (ἀγαπῶντες τὸν θεόν [αὐτόν]), could have been first a Jewish, then a Christian title; cf. *Odes of Sol.* 8:23: "as beloved in the Beloved." On "to devote oneself to . . ." (ἀντιλαμβάνεσθαι) see Ditt. *Or.* I, 51.9f: "he devoted himself to each individually and to all as a group" (καὶ κατ᾽ ἰδίαν ἑκάστου καὶ κατὰ κοινὸν πάντων ἀντιλαμβάνεται) [trans. by Ed.]; especially 339.32f: "he devoted himself well and eagerly to the other elegant activity that went on in the gymnasium" (τῆς τε ἄλλης εὐσχημοσύνης τῆς κατὰ τὸ γυμνάσιον ἀντελάβετο καλῶς καὶ φιλοτίμως) [trans. by Ed.].

---

1   See Col 3:22ff; Eph 6:5ff; 1 Petr 2:18ff. (*Did.* 4.11); cf. also Tit 2:9f. On these passages see above pp. 5ff (the Introduction, section 2); furthermore Dibelius–Greeven, *Kolosser, Epheser, Philemon*, excursus on Col 4:1; Lohse, *Colossians*, on Col 4:1ff; Weidinger, *Die Haustafeln*, 72ff; Bartsch, *Anfänge*, 144ff.

2   See Deissmann, *Bible Studies*, 123f; James Hope Moulton, *A Grammar of the New Testament Greek 1: Prolegomena* (London: The Epworth Press, ⁴1952), 87–90.

6 Warning Against False Doctrine

2b This is the way you should teach and preach. 3/ But if someone spreads false teachings and does not adhere to the sound words of our Lord Jesus Christ and to the teaching which is in accordance with (right) religion, 4/ then he is a pompous (person) who does not understand anything, but is diseased with racking of the brain and disputes about words. 5/ Out of these comes jealousy, quarreling, slandering, false suspicions—(anyway) quarrelsome disputes by people who have a corrupted mind, who have been deprived of the truth, and who think that religion is a profit–making business.

2b–16 is a concluding exhortation to Timothy (see above on 1 Tim 1:18–20). It can be divided into three parts: the refutation of heretics (6:3–5), a sequence of sayings which are attached to the catchwords "business" (πo-$\rho \iota \sigma \mu \acute{o} s$) and "religion" ($\epsilon \dot{v} \sigma \acute{\epsilon} \beta \epsilon \iota a$) (6:6–10), and a concluding parenesis to Timothy (6:11–16).

■ **3–5** resumes the thought and the words of 1 Tim 1:3ff; cf. "to spread false teachings" ($\dot{\epsilon} \tau \epsilon \rho o \delta \iota \delta a \sigma \kappa a \lambda \epsilon \hat{\iota} \nu$), "not understanding anything" ($\mu \eta \delta \dot{\epsilon} \nu \dot{\epsilon} \pi \iota \sigma \tau \acute{a} \mu \epsilon \nu o s$, cf. 1:7 $\mu \grave{\eta} \nu o o \hat{v} \nu \tau \epsilon s$). On "to adhere to" ($\pi \rho o \sigma \acute{\epsilon} \rho$-$\chi \epsilon \sigma \theta a \iota$), cf. Epict. *Diss.* 4.11.24: "to adhere to philosophy."[1] If the expression "sound words" ($\dot{v} \gamma \iota a \acute{\iota} \nu o \nu \tau \epsilon s$ $\lambda \acute{o} \gamma o \iota$) is meant as a designation of the Gospel, then the phrase "of our Lord Jesus Christ" ($\tau o \hat{v} \kappa v \rho \acute{\iota} o v \dot{\eta} \mu \hat{\omega} \nu$ $\dot{\text{I}} \eta \sigma o \hat{v} X \rho \iota \sigma \tau o \hat{v}$) does not characterize these "words" as sayings of Jesus—a meaning which we would associate with the term "words of the Lord." Rather, the expression is analogous to "word of the Lord" ($\lambda \acute{o} \gamma o s \tau o \hat{v}$ $\kappa v \rho \acute{\iota} o v$, 1 Thess 1:8).[2] On "racking of the brain" ($\zeta \eta \tau \acute{\eta}$-$\sigma \epsilon \iota s$) and "disputes about words" ($\lambda o \gamma o \mu a \chi \acute{\iota} a \iota$) see 1 Tim 1:4. Just as in the latter passage, the opponents are here criticized with expressions coined in part by popular philosophy, but such terms do not yield any factual in-

formation about them. On the catalogue of vices see above p. 67, the excursus to 1 Tim 4:5 (3b). "Quarrelsome disputes" ($\delta \iota a \pi a \rho a \tau \rho \iota \beta a \acute{\iota}$ or, as certain minuscules read, $\pi a \rho a \delta \iota a \tau \rho \iota \beta a \acute{\iota}$) is an augmented form of the term "rubbing against each other," "friction" ($\pi a \rho a$-$\tau \rho \iota \beta \acute{\eta}$), viz. the term "disputation," "diatribe" ($\delta \iota a$-$\tau \rho \iota \beta \acute{\eta}$).[3] The accusation that the opponents think only of business and profits is also derived from the arsenal of polemic drawn upon by the wandering philosophers.[4] What actually occasioned this attack upon the "false teachers," is impossible to say with certainty. Quite probably their zealous propaganda (see 2 Tim 3:6) gained them a following and an income (see also Tit 1:11). The inference of bad behavior from false teaching, viz. lack of understanding, is quite characteristic of polemical style. The false teachers are painted in colors which the Jews used to mirror the gentiles, as this depiction in turn had assimilated motifs from the moral teachings of popular philosophy.[5] Even the abrupt introduction of the heretics shows this characteristic tendency.

---

1 The reading "he (does not) follow" ($\pi \rho o \sigma \acute{\epsilon} \chi \epsilon \tau a \iota$, ℵ* 1912 lat) derives from 1 Tim 1:4.
2 See Dibelius, *Thessalonicher, Philipper* on 1 Thess 1:8. Cf. also "the manners of the Lord" ($\tau \rho \acute{o} \pi o \iota \kappa v \rho \acute{\iota} o v$) *Did.* 11:8.
3 Chrysostom's explanation of this passage is much too learned (XI, p. 648, Montfaucon). He is reminded of "(mangy) sheep, (which) as they rub themselves against each other, fill also the healthy ones with disease" ($\pi \rho \acute{o} \beta a \tau a \pi a \rho a \tau \rho \iota \beta \acute{o} \mu \epsilon \nu a \nu \acute{o}$-$\sigma o v \kappa a \grave{\iota} \tau \grave{a} \dot{v} \gamma \iota a \acute{\iota} \nu o \nu \tau a \dot{\epsilon} \mu \pi \acute{\iota} \pi \lambda \eta \sigma \iota \nu$) [trans. by Ed.].
4 For the evidence see Dibelius, *Thessalonicher, Philipper*, on 1 Thess 2:5f.
5 See Vögtle, *Tugend– und Lasterkataloge.*

6

Warning Against Avarice

6 (And indeed) religion is of great profit if it is coupled with self–sufficiency. 7/ After all, we brought nothing into the world with us, as also we can take nothing with us out (of this world). 8/ If we have food and clothing, then we will be content. 9/ But those who want to become rich, fall into temptation and snares and many foolish and harmful desires, which cause men to sink into destruction and ruin. 10/ For the love of money is the root of all evil; inflamed by such desire some have gone astray from the faith, and have pierced themselves with many pains.

This is a warning against greed which is only superficially connected with the polemic against heresy in 6:3–5. It is apparently an exhortation of (Jewish–)Hellenistic origin, as is shown by the lack of any specifically Christian motivation. The absence of a strict connection between the sayings, which are simply placed in a series, is also significant. The viewpoint of the source is that of a naive eudaemonism, such as was prevalent in popular philosophy and in the teaching of "wisdom." This naive perspective stands in some tension with the last verse of the preceding section (6:5b).

■ **6** The term "profit" (πορισμός) is used here in the same way as in 4:8. Of course, religion is of some benefit, naturally so to those who are religious. The view that the "religion" (εὐσέβεια) of man is "profitable" (πορι-στική) for God is categorically denied by Philo (*Det. pot. ins.* 55). But it is not exactly religion of which the author speaks, but rather "self–sufficiency" (αὐτάρκεια), the favorite virtue of the Stoics and Cynics. See the apothegm in Stobaeus, *Ecl.* 3 (p. 265.13, Hense): "Self–sufficiency is nature's wealth" (αὐτάρκεια γὰρ φύσεώς ἐστι πλοῦτος) [trans. by Ed.], and the saying of Epictetus (quoted by Stobaeus, who ascribes it to Epictetus'

Gnomology) which says that "The art of living well . . . is contingent upon self–control, self–sufficiency, orderliness, propriety, and thrift" (τὸ καλῶς ζῆν . . . ἐκ σωφρο-σύνης καὶ αὐταρκείας καὶ εὐταξίας καὶ κοσμιότητος καὶ εὐτελείας παραγίνεται) [trans. by Ed.].[6]

■ **7** On the relation of v 7 to what has gone before, compare the first similitude in the Shepherd of Hermas, which is full of ideas taken from popular philosophy;[7] cf. especially *Herm. sim.* 1.6: "Take heed, then, make no further preparations for yourself beyond a sufficient competence for yourself, as though you were living in a foreign country, and be ready in order that, whenever the master of this city wishes to expel you for resisting his law, you may go from his city, and depart to your own city" (βλέπε οὖν σύ· ὡς ἐπὶ ξένης κατοικῶν μηδὲν πλέον ἑτοίμαζε σεαυτῷ εἰ μὴ τὴν αὐτάρκειαν τὴν ἀρκετήν σοι καὶ ἕτοιμος γίνου, ἵνα ὅταν θέλῃ ὁ δε-σπότης τῆς πόλεως ταύτης ἐκβαλεῖν σε ἀντιταξάμε-νον τῷ νόμῳ αὐτοῦ, ἐξέλθῃς ἐκ τῆς πόλεως αὐτοῦ καὶ ἀπέλθῃς ἐν τῇ πόλει σου).[8] The thought expressed in this verse occurs only late in Greek literature, though

---

6   See further "Being content with the present state of affairs" (ἀρκεῖσθαι τοῖς παροῦσιν) Teles (ed. Hense, pp. 11.5; 38.10f;41.12f); Pseudo–Phocylides 5f; Dio Chrys. *Or.* 30.33. Examples of the contrast between "self–sufficiency" (αὐτάρκεια) and "love of money" (φιλαργυρία) are found in Gerhard, *Phoinix*, pp. 57ff; see also the use of "things sufficient in themselves" (τὰ αὐτάρκη) in Philo, *Leg. all.* 3.165;

and "I am contented" (ἀπαρκεῦμαι) in *Veröf-fentlichungen aus der Heidelberger Papyrus–Sammlung* IV, 1:310.46 (ed. G. A. Gerhard); see on the latter passage, as well as on the theme itself, Gerhard, *Phoinix*, 61; also Windisch, *Hebräerbrief*, on Heb 13:5.

7   On the theme see Paul Wendland, "Philo und die kynisch–stoische Diatribe," 59f.

8   Cf. the parallels which are quoted in Martin Dibe-

perhaps as traditional material.[9] But it is also found in Jewish literature,[10] and in Hellenistic Jewish writings.[11] Naturally there are also parallels outside the circle of Jewish and Greco–Roman literature.[12] Since the thought is so widely attested, the passage Pol. *Phil.* 4.1[13] cannot be regarded as conclusive proof for the dependency of Polycarp upon the Pastoral Epistles (see also below on 1 Tim 6:10).[14]

■ **8** The reference to food and clothing reflects the spirit of Stoicism.[15] But, on the Cynics, see Diogenes Laertius 6.105: "It pleased them also to live simply, (taking) just sufficient food and using a single worn garment." (ἀρέσκει δὲ αὐτοῖς καὶ λιτῶς βιοῦν, αὐτάρκεσι χρωμένοις σιτίοις καὶ τρίβωσι μόνοις) [trans. by Ed.]; see also 10.131. In this context the second term (σκεπά-

σματα) refers naturally to clothing first of all; still, the idea of housing ("roofing") may be included in the word used.[16] Whether the future tense serves to make a statement ("we shall be content") or to exhort ("we should, or will be content") cannot be determined, since in such a loosely connected list of sayings the context does not offer any firm proof.

■ **9** "To sink" (βυθίζω) is used in a figurative sense.[17]

■ **10** The first part of the verse is a maxim which occurs frequently elsewhere; cf. Stobaeus, *Ecl.* 3 (p. 417, Hense): "Bion the Sophist used to say that love of money is the mother–city of all evil." (Βίων ὁ σοφιστὴς τὴν φιλαργυρίαν μητρόπολιν ἔλεγε πάσης κακίας εἶναι) [trans. by Ed.].[18] The obvious disparity between the first and second halves of the verse may be another proof of

---

lius, *Der Hirt des Hermas*, HNT, Ergänzungsband 4 (Tübingen: J. C. B. Mohr [Paul Siebeck], 1923), on *Herm. sim.* 1.1.

9 See the *Anthologia Palatina* 10:58: "Naked I came onto the earth, naked I go beneath the earth; and why should I vainly toil, since I see that the end is nakedness" (γῆς ἐπέβην γυμνός, γυμνὸς ὑπὸ γαῖαν ἄπειμι. καὶ τί μάτην μοχθῶ γυμνὸν ὁρῶν τὸ τέλος) [trans. by Ed.].

10 See Job 1:21: "Naked I came forth from my mother's belly, and naked shall I return there" (γυμνὸς ἐξῆλθον ἐκ κοιλίας μητρός μου, γυμνὸς καὶ ἀπελεύσομαι ἐκεῖ); cf. Eccl 5:14.

11 See Wisd Sol 7.6: "There is one entrance into life and a like exit for all men" (μία δὲ πάντων εἴσοδος εἰς τὸν βίον ἔξοδός τε ἴση). Above all see Philo, *Spec. leg.* 1.294f: "how ought you to treat other men . . . you who brought nothing into the world, not even yourself? For naked you came into the world, worthy sir, and naked will you again depart" (σὲ τί ποιεῖν ἁρμόττει πρὸς ἀνθρώπους . . . τὸν μηδὲν εἰς τὸν κόσμον ἀλλὰ μηδὲ σαυτὸν εἰσενηνοχότα; γυμνὸς μὲν γάρ, θαυμάσιε, ἦλθες, γυμνὸς δὲ πάλιν ἄπεις). Cf. also Seneca, *Epistulae morales* 102.25: "Nature strips you as bare at your departure as at your entrance. You may take away no more than you brought in" (excutit redeuntem natura sicut intrantem. non licet plus efferre quam intuleris).

12 See Hans Schmidt and Paul Kahle, *Volkserzählungen aus Palästina* (Göttingen: Vandenhoeck & Ruprecht, 1918), 17, n. 3; or the conclusion of the Egyptian song of the harpist in Hugo Gressmann, *Altorientalische Texte und Bilder zum Alten Testamente* (Tübingen: J. C. B. Mohr [Paul Siebeck], 1909), 29. A secondary expression of the thought is found in *bYoma* 86[b]: "naked did man come into the world, naked he leaves it" ("naked" here means "without sin").

13 Pol. *Phil.* 4.1: "Knowing therefore that 'we brought nothing into the world and we can take nothing out of it'" (εἰδότες οὖν ὅτι οὐδὲν εἰσενέγκαμεν εἰς τὸν κόσμον, ἀλλ' οὐδὲ ἐξενεγκεῖν τι ἔχομεν . . .).

14 The linking of both clauses in this verse by means of ὅτι (translated above by "as") is quite peculiar. For this reading (ℵ * A G) is to be retained, since the other readings can best be explained on its basis: "it is true that" (ἀληθὲς ὅτι, D * Ambst) and "it is clear that" (δῆλον ὅτι, 𝔐 sy). The ὅτι could have resulted from dittography of κοσμ ο ν (as Hort suggests). Otherwise, it must be taken as a conjunction without a strictly causal force.

15 One can find the evidence most easily by reading the sections in which Musonius treats of "food" (περὶ τροφῆς) and "shelter" (περὶ σκέπης), pp. 94–109, ed. Hense.

16 See Musonius (p. 107, Hense): "But since we make ourselves also houses with a view to covering, I say that also these must be made with a view to what is absolutely necessary for our needs." (ἐπεὶ δὲ σκέπης ἕνεκα καὶ τὰς οἰκίας ποιούμεθα, φημὶ καὶ ταύτας δεῖν ποιεῖσθαι πρὸς τὸ τῆς χρείας ἀναγκαῖον). On the treatment of the theme in the diatribe see Wendland, "Philo und die kynisch–stoische Diatribe," 15ff.

17 An analogous usage is found in Alciphro 1.16.1 (p. 19, Schepers): "The sober element in me is continually sinking under the weight of passion" (τὸ νῆφον ἐν ἐμοὶ συνεχῶς ὑπὸ τοῦ πάθους βυθίζεται); *Ditt. Syll.* 2.730.7: "the city brought to the point of sinking by continual wars" (συνεχέσι πολέμοις καταβυθισθ[ε]ί[σαν τὴν πόλιν]) [both passages trans. by Ed.].

18 Cf. Diogenes Laertius 6.50: "He called love of money the mother–city of all evils" (τὴν φιλαργυρίαν εἶπε μητρόπολιν πάντων τῶν κακῶν). Diod. S. (Library

the fact that the author is using a traditional concept. "The love of money" is itself a desire (ὄρεξις). Thus some interpreters refer the relative pronoun (translated above "by such") to the "money" (ἀργύριον) in the composite noun "love of money" (φιλαργυρία): "in the desire of which (i.e. of the money)."[19]

---

of History 21.1) makes a similar statement concerning "greed" (πλεονεξία). See further, *De Gnomologio Vaticano inedito* 265 (ed. Sternbach, *Wiener Studien* 10 [1888]: 231): "Democritus used to call love of money the mother–city of all evil" (Δημόκριτος τὴν φιλαργυρίαν ἔλεγε μητρόπολιν πάσης κακίας); Apollodorus Comicus, *Philadelph. Fragmenta* 4, (III, 280, Kock): "But you have named what is pretty much the chief of all evils: they are all included in love of money." (ἀλλὰ σχεδόν τι τὸ κεφάλαιον τῶν κακῶν εἴρηκας· ἐν φιλαργυρίᾳ γὰρ πάντ᾽ ἔνι); Pseudo–Phocylides 42: "Love of money is the mother of all wickedness" (ἡ φιλοχρημοσύνη μήτηρ κακότητος ἁπάσης). Cf. also Philo,

Spec. leg. 4.65; *Sib.* 8.17 [all Trans. in this note by Ed.].

19 Pol. *Phil.* 4.1 quotes the same common maxim: "But the beginning of all evils is the love of money" (ἀρχὴ δὲ πάντων χαλεπῶν φιλαργυρία). In view of the frequent use of the phrase elsewhere, its occurrence in Polycarp is even less valuable than the parallel to 1 Tim 4:7 (see above) for the proof that Polycarp was directly dependent upon the Pastoral Epistles. On the other hand, this parallel can point to a relationship in the tradition used by both authors; cf. also von Campenhausen, "Polykarp," 229.

6   The Battle of Faith

11 But you, man of God, flee from (all) this!
Pursue uprightness, piety, faith, love,
patience, gentleness. 12/ Fight the good
fight of faith, take hold of eternal life!
To this you have been called, this you
professed in the good confession of
faith before many witnesses. 13/ I command you in the presence of God,
who gives life to everything, and of
Jesus Christ, who testified to the good
confession before Pontius Pilate, 14/ to
keep (this) commandment unblemished
and undamaged until the appearance
of our Lord Jesus Christ, 15/ which the
blessed, the one ruler will show to us in
its own time—the king of kings, the
lord of lords, 16/ the only immortal one,
who lives in inaccessible light, whom
no man has seen nor is able to see; to
him be honor and eternal power! Amen.

It is difficult to determine the position of these verses in
relation to their context. To be sure, there is a formal
connection reminiscent of the schema of the teaching of
the "two ways."[1] But as a whole, the section appears to be
an intrusion between vss 10 and 17.[2] Are these verses,
as a whole, a unit that was inserted here? If so, their
source might have been a baptismal address[3] or a parenesis at an ordination.[4] If one accepts the latter hypothesis, he must assume that the ordination address (to
which the author of the epistle obviously refers) contained, in any case, elements of baptismal parenesis.

■ **11** clearly points to such elements of baptismal parenesis. See, for instance, the contrast between what is
to be avoided and what is to be accepted (cf. the list with
specifically Christian virtues), or the call to battle connected with the image of eternal life. Thus the ambiguity
of the expression "man of God" (ἄνθρωπος θεοῦ) can
be explained. In this context it refers to Timothy in particular, not to the Christian in general. This seems to be
a secondary application. The expression no doubt comes
from a Semitic background; more precisely, from the
OT (1 Kings 2:27; Deut 33:1; Ps 89:1). But the parallel
in 2 Tim 3:17 shows that the author did not have in

mind the image of the "man of God" which the OT
suggests. In Philo, *Gig.* 61, there is already a mystical
shading of this image: "But the men of God are priests and
prophets who have refused to accept membership in the
commonwealth of the world and to become citizens
therein, but have risen wholly above the sphere of sense-
perception and have been translated into the world of
the intelligible and dwell there, registered as freemen of
the commonwealth of Ideas which are imperishable
and incorporeal" (θεοῦ δὲ ἄνθρωποι ἱερεῖς καὶ προ-
φῆται, οἵτινες οὐκ ἠξίωσαν πολιτείας τῆς παρὰ τῷ
κόσμῳ τυχεῖν καὶ κοσμοπολῖται γενέσθαι, τὸ δὲ
αἰσθητὸν πᾶν ὑπερκύψαντες εἰς τὸν νοητὸν κόσμον
μετανέστησαν κἀκεῖθι ᾤκησαν ἐγγραφέντες ἀφθάρ-
των [καὶ] ἀσωμάτων ἰδεῶν πολιτείᾳ). In *Corp. Herm.*
1.32 and 13.20, the reborn person is called "your man"
(ὁ σὸς ἄνθρωπος). The closest parallel is offered by
Ep. Ar. 140: "Hence the leading Egyptian priests . . . call
us (the Jews!) 'men of God,' a title which does not belong
to the rest of men, save to such as worship the true God"
(ὅθεν Αἰγυπτίων οἱ καθηγεμόνες ἱερεῖς . . . ἀνθρώπους θεοῦ ὀνομάζουσιν ἡμᾶς, ὃ τοῖς λοιποῖς οὐ πρόσε-
στιν, εἰ μή τις σέβεται τὸν κατ' ἀλήθειαν θεόν)

---

1   Upon the presentation of the vices (see the catalogue
    in 1 Tim 6:4), and of their consequences and causes,
    follows the summons to walk on the right path. Cf.
    Herm. mand. 6.1.2 and 11.1.17.

2   Or, as Jeremias, *ad loc.*, argues, vss 17–19 seem to
    be a supplement.

3   Windisch, "Zur Christologie," p. 219.

4   With regard to this suggestion see Ernst Käsemann,

[trans. by Ed.]. Cf. also Sextus 1–3 (ed. Henry Chadwick, TS, N.S. 5, 1959): "The faithful man is an elect man. The elect man is a man of God. The man of God is worthy of God" (Πιστὸς ἄνθρωπος ἐκλεκτός ἐστιν ἄνθρωπος. ἐκλεκτὸς ἄνθρωπος ἄνθρωπός ἐστι θεοῦ. θεοῦ ἄνθρωπος ὁ ἄξιος θεοῦ) [trans. by Ed.]; cf. Ps. Clem. Recg. 8.5.4. The term, therefore, refers to any Christian, specifically to him who has been baptized; i.e., one who has been endowed with the spirit of God, and who henceforth "serves" God. This does not exclude the possibility that the author refers particularly to Timothy, the prototype of a "man of God" since he is the leader of the congregation.

"Uprightness," "righteousness" (δικαιοσύνη) appears as one virtue among others; cf. Chrysostom (XI p. 693, Montfaucon) who writes, in commenting on 2 Tim 2:22: "Virtue in general, he calls 'righteousness': godliness of life, 'faith, love, meekness' " (δικαιοσύνην τὴν καθόλου ἀρετὴν λέγει, τὴν ἐν τῷ βίῳ εὐσέβειαν, πίστιν, ἀγάπην, πραότητα) [trans. by Ed.]. Tit 3:5ff shows that the Pastorals did not forget Paul's concept of "righteousness" (δικαιοσύνη). But in the understanding of "righteousness," which means "the right behavior," "upright conduct" (cf. 2 Tim 2:22 and 3:16), the Pastoral Epistles agree with Acts.[5]

■ 12[6] "Confession" (ὁμολογία) refers to baptism or "ordination"; see 1 Tim 1:18; 4:14; 2 Tim 1:6; 2:2.[7] The reference to the "calling" seems to indicate that the former is meant. But the mention of many witnesses reminds some scholars of 2 Tim 2:2, which speaks of installation in an office.[8]

■ 13 The words from "in the presence of" (ἐνώπιον) to "Pilate" (Πιλάτου) probably come from a credal formula. They are not prompted by the context, at least not in their present form (even if they came to the author of the Pastoral Epistles as a part of their present context; see above). With their direct naming of Pilate, they are reminiscent of kerygmatic formulations[9] as well as of the ancient Roman Symbol itself. Influences of liturgical language can be observed throughout the Pastoral Epistles (see above on 1 Tim 1:17). On the basis of this passage (as on the basis of 2 Tim 4:1 and 1 Cor 8:6), one can reconstruct an ancient confessional formula in two parts.[10]

But it is precisely in such an understanding of the passage that the meaning of "who testified" (μαρτυρήσας) becomes problematic. The question must be raised whether a confession by word or by deed is meant. This question has consequences for the discussion of the title "martyr."[11] In this connection one must also ask how the parallel between Timothy and Christ is to be understood, and whether on the basis of such a parallel, the "confession" (ὁμολογία) of Timothy is to be interpreted as a confession of faith before public authorities.[12] But in no case is there any emphasis upon a confrontation with the Roman empire.[13] The questions raised can be answered by means of the following hypotheses: the traditional kerygmatic statement originally said only that Jesus "testified" before Pilate, but it did not speak about the "confession" (ὁμολογία). Thus it did not refer to Jesus' behavior, but rather to his fate.

"Das Formular einer neutestamentlichen Ordinationsparänese," NT Studien für Bultmann, 261–68.

5 See Acts 10:35; 13:10; 24:25; so also 1 Clem. 5.7. Cf. also Pseudo–Pythagoras, Carmen aureum 13: "Then practice uprightness, both in deed and in word" (εἶτα δικαιοσύνην ἄσκει ἔργῳ τε λόγῳ τε) [trans. by Ed.].

6 On the image of the fight, see Wendland, Hellenistische Kultur, 357.

7 See Käsemann, "Formular."

8 On the question of the formulation of this creed see Seeberg, Katechismus, 143, 172 and 186; Otto Michel, TDNT 5, pp. 207–12.

9 See Acts 3:13; 4:27; 13:28; Ign. Mag. 11.1; 9.1; Sm. 1.2.

10 See von Harnack, Chronologie, 525; Lietzmann, "Symbolstudien" (2), 269. Cf. also the quite different, essentially Christological, reconstruction by

Reinhold Seeberg, "Zur Geschichte der Entstehung des apostolischen Symbols," ZKG 3 (1921): 2. On the formula "God who gives life to everything," cf. Joseph and Aseneth 8.10 (ed. Marc Philonenko): ". . . who has given life to everything, and has called (everything) out of darkness into light" (. . . ζωοποιήσας τὰ πάντα καὶ καλέσας ἀπὸ τοῦ σκότους εἰς τὸ φῶς) [trans. by Ed.]; cf. ibid. 8.2.

11 See Hans von Campenhausen, Die Idee des Martyriums in der Alten Kirche (Göttingen: Vandenhoeck & Ruprecht, 1936), pp. 50f; Strathmann, TDNT 4, pp. 504–08, and the bibliography in Bauer, s.v., μάρτυς and μαρτυρέω.

12 Cf. G. Baldensperger, " 'Il a rendu témoignage devant Ponce Pilate,' " RHPR 2 (1922): 1ff, 95ff; Maurice Goguel, Jesus the Nazarene. Myth or History? tr. Frederick Stephas (London: T. Fisher Unwin, 1926), p. 178; Cullmann, Confessions, pp. 20ff;

All analogies corroborate this.[14] On "to testify," "to be a witness" (μαρτυρεῖν) in this sense, cf. *1 Clem.* 5.4: "Peter who . . . suffered . . . many trials, and having thus given his testimony etc." 5.7: Paul "gave his testimony before the rulers" ([Πέτρος] πλείονας ὑπήνεγκε πό-νους . . . οὕτω μαρτυρήσας κτλ., and 5.7 Παῦλος . . . μαρτυρήσας ἐπὶ τῶν ἡγουμένων). For the sake of the parallel with Timothy's confession, the author added the word "the good confession" (τὴν καλὴν ὁμολογίαν) in the quotation of the kerygmatic formula in v 13. But this addition gave the formula a reference to the verbal confession, and the meaning of "to testify" (μαρτυρεῖν) became ambiguous, which has often been noticed. The tendency to employ Christological statements in a secondary, paradigmatic way is present in 1 Petr (2:21; 3:18).[15]

■ **14** "Commandment" (ἐντολή) has been taken to refer to v 11[16] or even to the decalogue.[17] Neither interpretation is in any way indicated. This word must therefore be taken as designating everything entrusted to Timothy, by analogy with "deposit" (παραθήκη) in 1 Tim 6:20.

"Unblemished" (ἄσπιλον) and "undamaged" (ἀνε-πίλημπτον) need in no way be considered personal qualities, as in 1 Tim 3:2 (see above, p. 52). Cf. also the use of "unblemished" (ἄσπιλος) in Jas 1:27; 1 Petr 1:19; 2 Petr 3:14.[18] Compare to this the use of ἄσπιλος in the *Anthologia Palatina* (6.252.3) concerning an apple, and *IG* II (vol. 4, 1054 c. 4) concerning stones: "in good condition, white, without blemish" (ὑγιεῖς λευκοὺς ἀσπί-λους). In 1 Tim 6:14, it seems to mean something like "uninjured," "unhurt," or the like. On "undamaged" (ἀνεπίλημπτος), cf. the Jewish emancipation document from Panticapaeum: "According to my vow not liable to be damaged or to be troubled by any heir of mine"

(κατὰ εὐχή[ν] μου ἀνεπίλημπτον καὶ ἀπα[ρ]ενόχλη-τον ἀπὸ παντὸς κληρονόμου), *IPE* II 52, 8ff [trans. by Ed.]. Therefore, the words "unblemished" and "undamaged" could well be applied to "the commandment" (ἐντολήν) rather than to Timothy.

The use of the same term "appearance" (ἐπιφάνεια see below pp. 102f, the excursus to 2 Tim 1:10) for both the past and future appearances of the Lord gives an intimation of the schema of the two advents which is just being developed (similarly in the Lucan writings), although it is not yet conceptually elaborated to its full extent. Here, as in Luke, one finds the characteristic emphasis upon God's authority to establish the appointed time (cf. 1 Tim 2:6 and Tit 1:3). In this way the eschatological expectation, as well as the present understanding of salvation (and here especially the establishment of a basis for the parenesis), have become independent of the *imminent* expectation of the parousia.

■ **15** "Blessed" (μακάριος) is used to refer to God (see above on 1 Tim 1:11). On "ruler" (δυνάστης) see 2 Macc 12:15 and Sir 46:5. The designation of God as the "one" or "only" (μόνος) is common in such formulas.[19] "King of kings, lord of lords" (βασιλεὺς τῶν βασιλέων καὶ κύριος τῶν κυρίων) are titles of God which were already current in Judaism. It is obvious that they had already become part of the cultic language of Christianity by the time of the Pastoral Epistles. These liturgical designations belong to the same history–of–religions context reflected in 1 Tim 1:17 and 2:10. The particular designation here seems to have been formed in contrast to the titles of oriental kings.[20] This title also appears as a designation of God outside the Jewish

against this view see Rudolf Bultmann, review of Cullmann's *Les premières confessions*, p. 40, and Windisch, "Zur Christologie," 219 (according to Windisch, the parallelism lies only in the content of the testimony: that Jesus is the Christ—Matt 27:11).

13 Against Cullmann, *Confessions*, pp. 20ff; Spicq, *ad loc.*
14 See Lietzmann, "Symbolstudien" (2), *passim.*
15 See Windisch–Preisker, *Katholische Briefe*, on 1 Petr 2:21.
16 B. Weiss, *ad loc.*
17 Baldensperger, " 'Il a rendu témoignage.' "
18 Cf. B. Weiss and von Soden, *ad loc.*

19 See above on 1 Tim 1:17; cf. Rev 15:4; Philo, *Abr.* 202 (cited above at 1:11).
20 Cf. 2 Macc 13:4; 3 Macc 5:35 with Ez 26:7; Dan 2:37; 2 Ezra 7:12. Cf. further Philo, *Cher.* 99; *Spec. leg.* 1.18; and the synagogal designation "King of the kings of kings" (מֶלֶךְ מַלְכֵי הַמְּלָכִים) in *Sanh.* 4.5, and "king of kings" (מֶלֶךְ מְלָכִים) in the song of the prayer leader, Mose ben Samuel. This song is found in Leopold Zunz, *Die Synagogale Poesie des Mittelalters* (Berlin: Springer, 1855), 247, mentioned by Hermann Strack. See also Adolf Schlatter, *Das Alte Testament in der johanneischen Apokalypse* (Gütersloh: C. Bertelsmann, 1912), 34.

world.[21] The ongoing opposition to the glorification of kings and emperors again and again lent new pathos to the Jewish and Christian formulations of titles for God.[22]

Notice how strongly the antithetical character of the title was felt by the Scilitan martyrs; cf. Acts of the Scilitan Martyrs 3 and 6: against the statement of the Roman proconsul "we take oaths by the genius of our lord, the emperor" (iuramus per genium domni nostri imperatoris), one of the Christians states: "I acknowledge as my lord the king of kings and emperor of all nations" (cognosco domnum meum, regem regum et imperatorem omnium gentium) [trans. by Ed.].[23]

■ 16 On "the only immortal one" (μόνος ἔχων ἀθανασίαν) see above on 1 Tim 1:17.[24] This title and the one following have a parallel in the concept of God of the Kerygma Petri.[25] The rich variety of titles results from the combination of Jewish and Hellenistic material. This indicates that the process took place in the Hellenistic synagogues. "Light" (φῶς) in Hellenistic, as well as in Christian literature, is used, in general, to designate the *essence* of God or Christ[26] and that which is the inheritance of Christians.[27] Here, however, it refers to the *place* where God *lives*.[28]

21 Dio Chrysostom 2.75. A survey of the occurrence of the title as a designation of oriental rulers is given by Friedrich Bilabel and Adolf Grohmann, *Geschichte Vorderasiens und Ägyptens* (Heidelberg: Carl Winter Verlag, 1927), 207–14.

22 Cf. Rev 17:14 and 19:16. On the problem see Deissmann, *LAE*, 356, 362f.

23 Text according to Gustav Krüger, *Ausgewählte Märtyrerakten*, SAQ 3 (Tübingen: J. C. B. Mohr [Paul Siebeck], ⁴1965), 23; cf. Joseph Armitage Robinson, *The Passion of S. Perpetua with an Appendix on the Scilitan Martyrdom*, TS 1, 2 (Cambridge: The University Press, 1891), 112f.

24 Cf. also Theodor Schermann, *Griechische Zauberpapyri und das Gemeinde– und Dankgebet im ersten Klemensbrief* (Leipzig: Hinrichs, 1909), p. 18, n. to line 4.

25 Cited in Clem. Alex., *Strom.* 6.5.39; text in Erich Klostermann, *Apocrypha* 1, KlT 3 (Berlin: DeGruyter, 1933) p. 13 (fr. 2); ET in Hennecke–Schneemelcher 2, p. 99; cf. further Dibelius, *Hirt des Hermas*, on *Herm. mand.* 1.

26 The idea is expressed as "unapproachable light" (ἀπρόσιτον φῶς) in Clem. Alex., *Exc. Theod.* 12.3.

27 See Col 1:12. The phrase *lumen inaccessibile* is found in the *Acts of Peter* 20 (Lipsius–Bonnet, 1, p. 66).

28 Cf., e.g., the description given in 1 Enoch 14.15ff. On the motif "whom no man has seen," see Bultmann, "Untersuchungen zum Johannesevangelium," *Exegetica; Aufsätze zur Erforschung des Neuen Testaments* (Tübingen: J. C. B. Mohr [Paul Siebeck], 1967), 124ff.

6   Rules for the Wealthy

17 Command those who are rich in this world
not to be proud, nor to place their hope
in the uncertainty of riches, but in God
who grants us everything richly for
enjoyment. 18/ They should do good, be
rich in good works, generous and
ready to share; 19/ they should lay up
a good foundation for the future that
they may obtain eternal life.

This passage presents an admonition which is directed to rich people. It could refer to 1 Tim 6:9f, but it appears to be just as much out of context as the ordinance for slaves in 1 Tim 6:1. It cannot be convincingly demonstrated that these clauses are interpolations.[29] It is characteristic of parenetic texts that certain passages seem out of context. Since this passage is clearly parenetic, and since parenetical passages are scattered throughout 1 Tim, one should not be surprised to find such a lack of logical coherence here. As far as the content is concerned, one should not overlook the fact that the judgment concerning the rich is not nearly as sharp as in Jas 1:10, 11; 5:1ff; further, it avoids any ideology of poverty (one may compare Lk 12:21).

■ **17, 18** The stress upon "uncertainty" ($\dot{\alpha}\delta\eta\lambda\delta\tau\eta s$) as

the object of hope is an intended paradox. Notice also the wordplay with the terms "riches," "rich," "richly" ($\pi\lambda o\hat{v}\tau os$, $\pi\lambda o\upsilon\tau\epsilon\hat{\iota}\nu$, $\pi\lambda o\upsilon\sigma\iota\omega s$) in different meanings. "For enjoyment" ($\epsilon\dot{\iota}s$ or $\pi\rho\dot{o}s$ $\dot{\alpha}\pi\dot{o}\lambda\alpha\upsilon\sigma\iota\nu$) is a Hellenistic expression.[30]

■ **19** On the figurative meaning of "foundation" ($\theta\epsilon$-$\mu\dot{\epsilon}\lambda\iota o\nu$ [-os]), see Philo, *Sacr. AC.* 81: "The bad man's foundation is vice and passion" ($\theta\epsilon\mu\dot{\epsilon}\lambda\iota os$ $\gamma\dot{\alpha}\rho$ $\tau\hat{\omega}$ $\phi\alpha\dot{\upsilon}\lambda\omega$ $\kappa\alpha\kappa\dot{\iota}\alpha$ $\kappa\alpha\dot{\iota}$ $\pi\dot{\alpha}\theta os$) [Loeb modified]. Thus the word seems to have taken on a meaning approaching the ambiguous word "funds."

---

29 This has been argued by von Harnack, *Chronologie* 1, p. 482.
30 See Nägeli, *Wortschatz*, 30, and cf. *IG* XII, vol. III, 326.12; *1 Clem.* 20.10; *Did.* 10.3 (in a prayer).

6   Warning Against False "Gnosis"

20   O Timothy, guard the deposit (which has been entrusted to you), turn away from godless chatter and the contradictions of the false "knowledge," 21/ which some have professed and have fallen away from faith.
        The grace be with you.

■ **20** "Deposit" (παραθήκη), here as in 2 Tim 1:12, 14, designates what the individual Christian, as a Christian, has received. The use of this term in 2 Tim 1:12 speaks against its complete identification with the related term "tradition" (παράδοσις).[31] The word, which is equivalent to the Attic term for a deposit of money or property (παρακαταθήκη), designates a "deposit,"[32] but is also used, already in earlier literature, in a figurative sense. For example, it can refer to "words" (ἔπεα) in Herodotus 9.45; cf. especially Pseudo–Isocrates, *Ad Demonicum* 22: "Guard more faithfully the secret which is confided to you than the money which is deposited in your care" (μᾶλλον τήρει τὰς τῶν λόγων ἢ τὰς τῶν χρημάτων παρακαταθήκας) [Loeb modified]; Philo, *Det. pot. ins.* 65: "(to do this is to commit) a fair deposit of knowledge (to a trustworthy guardian)" (ἐπιστήμης καλὴν παρακαταθήκην). The author has characteristically used the word in a special sense to designate the apostolic traditions which "Timothy" has received in order to transmit them.[33] The content of the "deposit" can be naturally derived from the epistle. On "chatter" (κενοφωνία), cf. Epict., *Diss.* 2.17.8: "Or were we sounding for the mere chatter" (κενῶς τὰς φωνὰς ταύτας ἀπη-

χοῦμεν) [Loeb modified].

"Contradictions" (ἀντιθέσεις), together with "endless talk" (ἀπεραντολογία) (see 1:4), are two things which the rhetorician in Lucian's *Dialogi Mortuorum* (10.10) wants to take with him in Charon's ferry.

Even if "contradictions" (ἀντιθέσεις) is not used in the rhetorical, technical sense, this passage supports the observation which was made above on 1 Tim 1:6; namely, that the opponents in the Pastoral Epistles are often attacked with weapons which were used in the non–Christian world against false rhetoricians and philosophers. It is not necessary to connect this reference to "contradictions" or "antitheses" (ἀντιθέσεις) with the work of the same name by Marcion. The fact that later Marcionites accepted the Pastoral Epistles[34] also speaks against such an assumption. "Knowledge" (γνῶσις) is used here in the technical sense as the self–designation of the false teachers. The question as to what kind of Gnosis is represented by these people is not answered by this designation. But it certainly was a particular teaching which could be differentiated from that of the church.

■ **21** demonstrates this by the word "to profess" (ἐπαγ-

---

31   This was argued by Seeberg, *Katechismus*, 108ff. But see Hans von Campenhausen, "Lehrreihen und Bischofsreihen im zweiten Jahrhundert" in *In memoriam Ernst Lohmeyer*, ed. Werner Schmauch (Stuttgart: Evangelisches Verlagswerk, 1951), 244ff. Von Campenhausen assumes that the word "tradition" (παράδοσις) had become an object of suspicion because of its use in Gnosticism. It is avoided by the Pastoral Epistles and replaced by the juridical term "deposit" (παραθήκη), which stresses the idea of inviolability, not that of the chain of transmission. This fits well with the fact that the Pastoral Epistles stress the tradition but do not emphasize the concept of succession.

32   On the Attic term, see Nägeli, *Wortschatz*, 27. On the use of the word, see the papyri, e.g., *P. Oxy.* VII, 1039.12f: "According to the law of deposits" (κατὰ τὸν τῶν παρ(α)θηκῶ[ν νόμον]) [trans. by Ed.], and

many others.

33   On the concept, see Ceslaus Spicq, "St. Paul et la loi des dépôts," *RB* 40 (1931): 481–502; and Spicq, *ad loc.* Spicq derives this term from the Roman legal regulations regarding deposits; J. Ranft ("Depositum," *RAC* 3 [1957]: 781) assumes that the term must be understood on the basis of Rabbinic and Hellenistic–Roman literature in general.

34   See von Harnack, *Marcion*, 150f (but cf. von Campenhausen, "Polykarp," 204). A reference to Marcion has been assumed by Bauer, *Rechtgläubigkeit*, p. 229; see also von Campenhausen, "Polykarp," 204ff. On the other hand, Oscar Cullmann, *Le Problème littéraire et historique du Roman Pseudo–Clémentin* (Paris: Félix Alcan, 1930), p. 246, connects this term with the Jewish–Christian concept of syzygies.

γέλλεσθαι), which, as in 1 Tim 2:10, designates allegiance to a particular group or school. The plural "with you" (ὑμῶν) reflects the acknowledgement that a writing with this particular content is directed to a wider circle, despite the address.[35]

---

35   The singular "with thee" (μετὰ σοῦ) in D 𝕽 vg sy is an understandable correction.

Second Epistle to Timothy

Outline

Salutation 1:1, 2

Proem: thankful remembrance of the Christian tradition, in which Paul and Timothy stand by extraction and upbringing, as well as of the significance of the apostolic suffering, 1:3–14. Apostasy or authentication of the individual Christian, 1:15–18.

Exhortation to suffering, introduced by the request to transmit the tradition, 2:1–13. Exhortation to personal authentication in view of the heretics, 2:14–26. The sinners of the last days, 3:1–5, have appeared in the heretics, 3:6–9.

Summary exhortation referring to the idea of suffering, the danger of heretics and the security of the tradition, 3:10–4:8.

Personal conclusion: description of Paul's situation, 4:9–12, instructions 4:13–15, some information 4:16–18, greetings 4:19–21, valediction 4:22.

1
Salutation; Christian Tradition and Apostolic Suffering

1 Paul, apostle of Christ Jesus through the will of God, (entrusted) with the promise of life in Christ Jesus, 2/ to Timothy, his beloved child: grace, mercy and peace from God the father and Christ Jesus our Lord.

3/ I must (always) thank God, whom I serve, as my ancestors did, with a pure conscience, when I remember you constantly, day and night, in my prayers. 4/ I long to see you and I recall your tears, in order to be filled with joy. 5/ For in my mind is the sincere faith, that (lives) in you, as it lived first in your grandmother, Lois, and in your mother, Eunice, (and now)— of this I am sure—also in you. 6/ Therefore I remind you: rekindle the gift of God, which is in you through the laying on of my hands. 7/ For it was not a spirit of fear that God gave us, but rather of strength and love and prudence. 8/ Thus do not be ashamed of the witness about our Lord, nor of me, his prisoner, but join with me in the sufferings of the gospel in the power of God, 9/ who saved us and called us with a holy calling, not according to our works, but according to his own design and grace; it was granted unto us before time began, 10/ but now it has been revealed through the appearance of our savior Christ Jesus, who dethroned death and brought immortal life to light through the gospel, 11/ for which I have been appointed herald, apostle, and teacher. 12/ For this reason I (must) also suffer this, but I am not ashamed, because I know who it is in whom I have placed my trust, and I am convinced that he has power to guard the deposit entrusted to me until that day! 13/ Take as an example of sound preaching what you have heard from me (and thus remain) in faith and love, as they are (contained) in Christ Jesus. 14/ Guard the wonderful deposit (that was) entrusted (to you) through the holy spirit that dwells in us.

■ **1, 2** On "promise of life" (ἐπαγγελίαν ζωῆς), cf. 1 Tim 4:8. As the "promise of life" is the mark of piety in the latter passage, so it appears here as characteristic of the apostleship of Paul who is entrusted with it. Cf. Theodoret's explanation (III, p. 676, Schulze): "So that I proclaim the promised eternal life to men" (ὥστε με τὴν ἐπαγγελθεῖσαν αἰώνιον ζωὴν τοῖς ἀνθρώποις κηρύξαι) [trans. by Ed.]. On v 2 see above pp. 13ff, on 1 Tim 1:2.

The proem of the "epistle" is in the epistolary style of thanksgiving and of the assurance of intercession.[1] Such a proem does not appear in the other Pastoral Epistles, and even here it is formed with "I must thank" ($\chi \acute{\alpha} \rho \iota \nu$ $\check{\epsilon} \chi \epsilon \iota \nu$), not with "I give thanks" ($\epsilon \grave{\upsilon} \chi \alpha \rho \iota \sigma \tau \epsilon \hat{\iota} \nu$). It is, therefore, at least not a slavish imitation of the Pauline epistles which are known to us. But taken as a whole, 1:3–5 is perhaps reminiscent of the proem in Rom 1:8–11. The content is made up of expositions on the Christian tradition of faith, in which the apostle and the disciple stand by extraction and education (see 1:3, 5, 6, 13). In this way a traditional motif is stressed (see 3:14ff) that well suits the Pastorals' concept of Christian citizenship.[2] But it is foreign to the most primitive stage of Christianity.

The Second Epistle to Timothy bases the exhortation to suffer for the faith upon the bond between teacher and disciple. This exhortation recurs throughout the epistle (1:8, 12; 2:3–13; 3:10–12; 4:5–8). This complex of ideas in 2 Tim presents a problem. The advocate of authenticity will resolve it by reference to the historical situation of Paul. But then he must leave unresolved the even greater problem of such an early date for the Pastoral Epistles' concept of Christian citizenship. If the inauthenticity of the epistles is assumed, the situation of the readers must be reconstructed. They too know persecutions (see below on 2 Tim 3:12), and in their tribulations they look to the apostle, who becomes a model of suffering for his disciple as well as for the reader. Thus, in addition to the tradition of the apostle as teacher (2 Tim 2:2), the Pastoral Epistles also proclaim an image of the apostle, valid for all times, as the prototype of life, especially of suffering.

■ **3** The phrase "as my ancestors did" ($\grave{\alpha} \pi \grave{o}$ $\pi \rho o \gamma \acute{o} \nu \omega \nu$) is a reference to the virtue of the forebears. It appears frequently in inscriptions.[3]

■ **4** The paradoxical coupling of mourning and joy is an attempt to recapture Paul's feelings as they are expressed in Phil 2:17 and, above all, in 2 Cor 7:8f. But the change from one to the other is more abrupt here than it is in Paul.

■ **5** The mention of the mother and grandmother[4] of Timothy has its counterpart in the reference to the "ancestors" of Paul in 2 Tim 1:3. This reference to forebears does not include a theory of a history of salvation to explain the relationship between Israel and the church. What dominates is rather the concept of a religious upbringing. Furthermore, the virtue of reverence, which the Pastorals also stress in other connections (1 Tim 5:4), can also have meaning in the religious area. There is no indication that it is limited to persons of Jewish extraction, as on the other hand, there is no mention whether Lois was a Christian (cf. Acts 16:1). In contrast to the Pastorals, Luke understands the reference to the "fathers" in terms of a history of salvation (Acts 23:1; 24:14f; 26:6, 22f). In the Pastorals, as well as in Luke, mention is made of the good conscience (Acts 23:1; 24:16; see above pp. 18ff, the excursus to 1 Tim 1:5.)

■ **6** On the laying on of hands see above pp. 70f, the excursus to 1 Tim 4:14. In 2 Tim 1:6, the author refers to the participation of the apostle, not, as in 1 Tim 4:14, to that of the presbytery. This is in line with the concept of tradition of 2 Tim, which is understood in terms of personal relation, as was pointed out above in the introduction to this passage. The preposition "through" ($\delta \iota \acute{\alpha}$) must not be accorded too much importance. The grace is not yet understood as an habitual disposition transferred from person to person.

■ **7** On the basis of v 6, Belser interprets "spirit" ($\pi \nu \epsilon \hat{\upsilon} \mu \alpha$) here as referring to the grace of the profession.[5] But the connection between the two verses can be explained in a different way:[6] because the spirit of Christ is not a spirit of fear, therefore the Christian should use his "gift" ($\chi \acute{\alpha} \rho \iota \sigma \mu \alpha$) bravely. If the verse is interpreted thus, its relation to Rom 8:15 should not be considered merely accidental. Rather, one must assume that the author intended to support the concept of tradition expressed in v 6 with a genuine Pauline thought. To the charismatic

---

1 See Dibelius, *Thessalonicher, Philipper*, excursus to 1 Thess 1:2; Paul Schubert, *Form und Function of the Pauline Thanksgivings*, BZNW 20 (Berlin: Töpelmann, 1939).

2 See above pp. 39ff, the second excursus to 1 Tim 2:2. On the presuppositions of this traditional motif, cf. below on 2 Tim 1:5.

3 See, e.g., Ditt. *Or.* II, 485.3; 504.14; 529.1; 771.8;

Inscr. Magn. 163.2; *Inscr. Priene* 102.5; 107.10; 108.19; furthermore, cf. below on v 5.

4 On "grandmother" ($\mu \acute{\alpha} \mu \mu \eta$), see Ditt. *Syll.* II, 844 B5.

5 Belser, *ad loc.*; see also Chrysostom (XI, p. 661, Montfaucon).

6 See B. Weiss, *ad loc.*

virtues of strength and love, which are effected by the spirit, "prudence" (σωφρονισμός) is added as a third virtue. On the use of this word–stem in the Pastorals, see above p. 40, the second excursus to 1 Tim 2:2; cf. also Cramer, *Catene* 7, ". . . he refers either to the soundness of the mind or the soul (cf. above pp. 24f, the excursus on 1 Tim 1:10), or (speaks) so that we become prudent, and thus make further progress" (ἤτοι τὴν ὑγίειαν τῆς διανοίας ἢ τῆς ψυχῆς ἢ ὥστε σωφρονίζεσθαι ἡμᾶς καὶ τὰ περιττὰ προκόπτειν) [trans. by Ed.].

■ **8** On the situation, see below pp. 126f, the excursus on 4:21. Here too the echo of the Epistle to the Romans (1:16) is probably intentional. The exhortation to suffering which follows gives, to be sure, a special meaning to the term "witness" (μαρτύριον). One is reminded of the absolute use of the word "to witness" (μαρτυρεῖν) in *1 Clem.* 5.4 and 7 (see above at 1 Tim 6:13). One is led to ask whether the understanding "witness through deed" is not also intended here (see above, the introduction to 1:3–14). On "join in suffering" (συγκακοπάθησον), see Chrysostom (XI, p. 666, Montfaucon): "(He says this) not as if the Gospel were suffering, but by way of arousing his disciple to suffer (with him) on behalf of the Gospel" (οὐχ ὡς τοῦ εὐαγγελίου κακοπαθοῦντος, ἀλλὰ τὸν μαθητὴν διεγείρων ὑπὲρ τοῦ εὐαγγελίου πάσχειν) [trans. by Ed.].

■ **9, 10** are apparently formulated in a kerygmatic style, for they contain elements which are unnecessary to the context, and they exhibit the characteristics of formulaic participial predication.[7] They also reproduce a well–known schema of early Christian preaching, which contrasts the "now" of the revelation of salvation with the "then," when salvation was still hidden.[8] One could debate the question how firmly fixed these sentences were, and whether they are simply stylized or whether they are a quotation. One can observe again the Christology of epiphany characteristic of passages coined for liturgical purposes, with its "realized eschatology" (C. H. Dodd) that appears in the Pauline school (see above on 1 Tim 3:16).[9] Characteristic of such an eschatology is the extension of the statement about the objective past occurrence of the salvation event into the present proclamation, which thereby explicitly becomes part of the salvation event. Salvation is made a present reality in the liturgical recitation and preaching. Furthermore, the firm connection with Paul (not the "apostle" in general),[10] as bearer of the proclamation, is a typical feature of such statements. This connection is made from the standpoint of the receiver, not from the perspective of the apostle who offers the proclamation. "To save" (σῴζειν) and "to call" (καλεῖν) are perhaps introduced in this order because the event of salvation and its mediation in the proclamation form the entirety of the salvation occurrence "for us" (*ad nos*). "Holy calling" (κλῆσις ἁγία): if one observes how Paul uses the expressions "to call in" (καλεῖν ἐν) and "to call into" (καλεῖν εἰς) as synonymous,[11] one will also interpret the "holy calling" by this analogy. "He called us in holiness" (ἐκάλεσεν ἐν ἁγιασμῷ) in 1 Thess 4:7 means: "He called us to be holy." See Cramer, *Catene*, 7, p. 59: "i.e., he made them holy, who were sinners and enemies" (τουτέστιν, ἁγίους εἰργάσατο, ἁμαρτωλοὺς ὄντας καὶ ἐχθρούς) [trans. by Ed.]. Only in this passage and in Tit 3:5 do the Pastoral Epistles take a position with regard to righteousness by works; elsewhere they simply enjoin a new Christian righteousness (see 1 Tim 6:11 and 2 Tim 2:22). Since here, as in Tit 3:5, kerygmatic formulations are reproduced or even quoted, these clauses must be seen as traditional Pauline teachings which have been adopted.

■ **10** The use of the terms "savior" (σωτήρ) and "epiphany," "appearance" (ἐπιφάνεια) is particularly characteristic of the language of the Pastorals. It is clear that the author found both terms (and a connection between them) already firmly established, but also that he used them in a unique configuration (cf. the prescripts of 1 Tim and Tit).

---

7 See Norden, *Agnostos Theos*, 201ff and 381.
8 See Eph 3:4f; 3:9–11; Rom 16:25f; 1 Petr 1:2; see also below on Tit 1:2. On the "schema of revelation" see Dahl, "Formgeschichtliche Beobachtungen," 3ff; Ceslaus Spicq, *Agape in the New Testament*, tr. Marie Aquinas McNamara and Mary Honoria Richter, vol. 3 (St. Louis: Herder, 1966), 15ff; Dieter Lührmann, *Das Offenbarungsverständnis bei Paulus und in den paulinischen Gemeinden*, WMANT 16 (Neukirchen–Vluyn: Neukirchen, 1965), 124–33.
9 On the question whether personal preexistence is to be assumed, see Windisch, "Zur Christologie," 224f.
10 Cf. Windisch, "Zur Christologie," 224f.
11 Cf. Lietzmann–Kümmel, *Korinther*, on 1 Cor 7:15.

"Savior" in the Pastoral Epistles

The term "Savior" (σωτήρ) in early Christian literature has many shades of meaning. Since the word is doubtless used in a technical sense in certain expressions, it is necessary to investigate not only the word's meaning, but also the associations it evokes. We must also distinguish between passages in which the sense requires the word "savior" (see below on 1, 2b, 3b), and those in which the use of the term is technical, i.e. in which the meaning is a special one which cannot be etymologically derived from the verb "to save" (see below on 4, 5).

1. The first attestation for the word "savior" (σωτήρ) in early Christianity is from Paul in Phil. 3:20. There the context clearly indicates an eschatological reference. In contrast to "those who think earthly things" (τὰ ἐπίγεια φρονοῦντες), the Christians are citizens of heaven. In support of this, a clause is added which can be interpreted differently depending on where the emphasis is placed: either, they wait for *their* "savior" (in contrast to other saviors) from heaven; in this case "savior" would be a Hellenistic term designating gods or princes (see below). Or it is *from heaven* that they also expect the "savior" on the last day; in this case "savior" would stand for the participle: "he who will save us." Since nothing is said in the context about the "saviors" of other people,[12] and furthermore, since Paul is clearly using a common expression that also appears in 1 Thess 1:10 with the participle of the verb "to save," the latter explanation must be adopted. "Savior" in this case has no technical Hellenistic meaning.[13]

2. a) With this we must compare the position of the LXX. There "savior" is used of men: it refers to the judges in Judg 3:9, 15; Neh 19:27; in a more general sense it refers to the helper in battle (Judg 12:3).[14] This usage does not come from a specifically religious terminology and is necessitated by the Hebrew original. It is difficult to say whether the use of the word in the LXX is influenced by the Greek usage, where "savior" can be an honorary title of worthy men; see Xenophon, *Ag.* 11.13.[15]

b) In several passages "savior" (σωτήρ) is equivalent to "he who saves" (σώζων) or "he who delivers" (ῥυόμενος), as can be seen from the context.[16]

c) Among the many other passages, those which show the formulaic use of "God and Savior" (θεὸς καὶ [or ὁ] σωτήρ) in the Prophets and Psalms may be noted as a special group. However, since the expression is necessitated by the Hebrew original, and since conceptions already listed under b) are present, Hellenistic influence may not be presupposed under any circumstances. The same point may also apply to the remaining LXX passages with two exceptions.

d) Est 15:2 D, 2,[17] which reads "invoking the all-seeing God and Savior" (ἐπικαλεσαμένη τὸν πάντων ἐπόπτην θεὸν καὶ σωτῆρα), can, because of the term "all-seeing" (ἐπόπτης),[18] be regarded as Hellenistic. The same applies to Bar (LXX) 4:22: "mercy will come . . . from your eternal savior" (ἐλεημοσύνη ἥξει . . . παρὰ τοῦ αἰωνίου σωτῆρος ὑμῶν), where at least the use of "eternal" (αἰώνιος) as a designation of the divine sphere points to Hellenistic influence.[19] In view of what

---

12 On the term "citizenship," "commonwealth" (πολίτευμα), see Dibelius, *Thessalonicher, Philipper,* on Phil 3:20.

13 A different view is held by Adolf von Harnack, "Der Heiland," *Reden und Aufsätze* (Giessen: Töpelmann, 1904), 310; Hans Lietzmann, *Der Weltheiland* (Bonn: Marcus & Weber, 1909), 56; and Ernst Lohmeyer, *Christuskult und Kaiserkult* (Tübingen: J. C. B. Mohr [Paul Siebeck], 1919), 27f.

14 Manuscript A reads the participial form "he who saves" (σώζων).

15 See Günther Gerlach, *Griechische Ehreninschriften* (Halle: Niemeyer, 1908), p. 60.

16 Note the parallelism with "he who made him" (ποιήσας) in Deut 32:15, or with "helper" (βοηθός) in Jdth 9:11, or with other, similar terms. Note the connection with "he saved" (ἔσωσεν) in 1 Chr 16:35 S*, the antithesis to "you have rejected"

(ἐξουθενήκατε) in 1 Kings 10:19, and the connection with "to save" (σώζειν) and "he who delivers" (ῥυόμενος) in Wisd Sol 16:7f.

17 This verse is 5:1a in Rahlfs' LXX edition, verse 15:2 in the OT Apocrypha "Additions to Esther" (*RSV*).

18 On the use of "all-seeing" (ἐπόπτης), see 2 Macc 3:39; 7:35; 3 Macc 2:21; *Ep. Ar.* 16; Epict., *Diss.* 3.11.6.

19 "Eternal" (αἰώνιος) is equivalent to "immortal" (ἀθάνατος); see BMI, p. 894.1, reprinted in Wendland, *Hellenistische Kultur,* p. 410. An opposing view is given by Karl Prümm, "Herrscherkult und Neues Testament," *Biblica* 9 (1928): 138.

20 Ludwig Köhler, "Christus im Alten und im Neuen Testament," *ThZ* 9 (1953): 242f.

21 Cf., for example, Ps Sol 3:6; 8:33; 16:4; 17. Further information can be found in Wilhelm Bousset, *Die*

follows we must note that "savior" ($\sigma\omega\tau\eta\rho$) does not appear in the Greek OT as the equivalent of the Hebrew word "redeemer" (גּוֹאֵל).[20]

3. a) The conception of the savior in Judaism raises a problem which cannot be completely resolved with the means available to us. We may assume from the LXX, that "savior" ($\sigma\omega\tau\eta\rho$) was a designation for God in Hellenistic Judaism. We can conclude indirectly from a number of passages that God was called "savior" also in Semitic circles.[21] It is difficult to answer the question as to whether "savior" was already a designation for the Messiah in pre-Christian times. 1 En 48:7, as also the *Prayer of the Eighteen Petitions* in the Babylonian recension,[22] and a number of later midrashim[23] speak of the coming "redeemer" (גּוֹאֵל).[24] But even if earlier and less doubtful attestations for "redeemer" as a designation of the Messiah were available, the problem of the origin of the term would not be resolved. Was the Messiah understood as avenger, and thus received the title "redeemer" (גּוֹאֵל)? Or does the influence of oriental–Hellenistic expectations of the redeemer come into play here?[25]

b) A connection between Hellenistic and Jewish terminology is perhaps present in Philo: *Spec. leg.* 1.209 sounds Hellenistic since "savior and benefactor" ($\sigma\omega\tau\eta\rho$ $\tau\epsilon$ $\kappa\alpha\iota$ $\epsilon\upsilon\epsilon\rho\gamma\epsilon\tau\eta\varsigma$) is found beside "maker and begetter of the universe" ($\pi\omega\iota\eta\tau\eta\varsigma$ $\kappa\alpha\iota$ $\gamma\epsilon\nu\nu\eta\tau\eta\varsigma$ $\tau\omega\nu$ $\delta\lambda\omega\nu$).[26] Since the usage of the Pastoral Epistles, like that of the prayer in *1 Clem.* 59ff, is influenced by Hellenistic–Jewish formulas, the formulaic designation of God as "savior" in 1 Tim 1:1; Tit 1:3; 2:10; 3:4 (but see below under 5),

Jude 25 and *1 Clem.* 59.3[27] may be traced back to the formulaic usage of Hellenistic Judaism. 1 Tim 2:3 is somewhat more pointed, for here we have the corresponding verb "to be saved" ($\sigma\omega\theta\eta\nu\alpha\iota$, see above, section 2b). On the other hand, Lk 1:47 belongs to the group discussed in section 2c.

The technical designation of Christ as "savior," however, cannot have its origin in a Jewish designation for the messiah. In that case the title would not be absent in the earliest strata of Christian literature, and it would be hard to explain why it only makes its appearance in the Christian Hellenistic literature: the Pastorals, Luke–Acts, the Johannine writings, the Second Epistle of Peter, and the letters of Ignatius of Antioch. Even if a Jewish context is occasionally suggested,[28] it is necessary to assume that non-Jewish influences have been predominant. There are two primary Hellenistic, i.e., oriental–Greek, conceptual contexts to be considered.

4. "Savior" designates not only "saving" deities in general, like Asclepius and the Dioscuri, but in the mystery religions it designates the god who gives new life to the mystic by effecting his rebirth.[29] The word takes on this meaning for the first time during the Hellenistic period, and not without the influence of the general

Religion des Judentums im späthellenistischen Zeitalter, ed. Hugo Gressmann (Tübingen: J. C. B. Mohr [Paul Siebeck], ⁴1966) p. 362 n. 2.

22   For the text of this prayer, see Oskar Holtzmann's edition of the Mishnah, 1, 1, p. 13.

23   Billerbeck 1, p. 69.

24   It is very questionable whether "he who saves" ($\sigma\omega\zeta\omega\nu$) in *Test. L.* 2:11 belongs to the original Jewish text.

25   Cf. Lietzmann, *Der Weltheiland*; Wilhelm Bousset, *Kyrios Christos*, tr. John E. Steeby (Nashville, Tenn. and New York: Abingdon, 1970); Norden, *Geburt des Kindes, passim*. On the discrepancy between the Jewish title "redeemer" and the Christian title "savior," see Willy Staerk, *Soter*, 1 (Gütersloh: Bertelsmann, 1933), p. 133. On the entire history of religions problem see *ibid.* 1 (1933) and 2 (1938).

26   Cf. also *Sobr.* 55: "For while the words 'Lord and

God' proclaim Him master and benefactor of the world which is open to our senses, to that goodness which our minds perceive He is saviour and benefactor only, not master or lord. For wisdom is rather God's friend than His servant" ($\tau\omega\hat{\upsilon}$ $\mu\epsilon\nu$ $\gamma\alpha\rho$ $\alpha\iota\sigma\theta\eta\tau\omega\hat{\upsilon}$ $\kappa\omega\sigma\mu\omega\upsilon$ $\delta\epsilon\sigma\pi\omega\tau\eta\varsigma$ $\kappa\alpha\iota$ $\epsilon\upsilon\epsilon\rho\gamma\epsilon\tau\eta\varsigma$ $\alpha\nu\epsilon\iota\rho\eta\tau\alpha\iota$ $\delta\iota\alpha$ $\tau\omega\hat{\upsilon}$ $\kappa\upsilon\rho\iota\omicron\varsigma$ $\kappa\alpha\iota$ $\theta\epsilon\omicron\varsigma$, $\tau\omega\hat{\upsilon}$ $\delta\epsilon$ $\nu\omega\eta\tau\omega\hat{\upsilon}$ $\alpha\gamma\alpha\theta\omega\hat{\upsilon}$ $\sigma\omega\tau\eta\rho$ $\kappa\alpha\iota$ $\epsilon\upsilon\epsilon\rho\gamma\epsilon\tau\eta\varsigma$ $\alpha\upsilon\tau\omicron$ $\mu\omega\nu\omicron\nu$, $\omicron\upsilon\chi\iota$ $\delta\epsilon\sigma\pi\omega\tau\eta\varsigma$ η $\kappa\upsilon\rho\iota\omicron\varsigma$. $\phi\iota\lambda\omicron\nu$ $\gamma\alpha\rho$ $\tau\omicron$ $\sigma\omega\phi\omicron\nu$ $\theta\epsilon\omega\hat{\omega}$ $\mu\hat{\alpha}\lambda\lambda\omicron\nu$ η $\delta\omega\hat{\upsilon}\lambda\omicron\nu$). In *Migr. Abr.* 124, it is significant that God is called "savior" ($\sigma\omega\tau\eta\rho$) as giver of the "most all-healing remedy" ($\pi\alpha\nu\alpha\kappa\epsilon\sigma\tau\alpha\tau\omicron\nu$ $\phi\alpha\rho\mu\alpha\kappa\omicron\nu$). "The Father and Saviour in pity (gave)" ($\omicron$ $\pi\alpha\tau\eta\rho$ $\kappa\alpha\iota$ $\sigma\omega\tau\eta\rho$ $\eta\lambda\epsilon\eta\sigma\epsilon$) in *Praem. poen.* 39, suggests a more general meaning for the term (see above, section 2c).

27   *1 Clem.* 59.3 quotes Jdth 9:11 verbatim.

28   Lk 2:11; Acts 13:23; perhaps also 5:31.

29   See Reitzenstein, *Mysterienreligionen*, p. 39.

oriental conception of redemption,[30] which also exerted an influence upon the cult of the ruler (see below, section 5). The predications of Isis and Sarapis as "bringers of salvation" are probably best understood in the sense of such a granting of life.[31] One should neither isolate nor overestimate these texts.[32] It may be asserted, however, that the use of the title "savior," especially in the case of deities coming from the East, does suggest the power to endow with divine life. Philo provides passages attesting to this meaning, passages which diverge widely from those cited above, section 3b; cf. *Leg. all.* 3.27: "What soul, then, was it that succeeded in hiding away wickedness and removing it from sight, but the soul to which God manifested Himself, and which He deemed worthy of His secret mysteries?" (τίνι οὖν ψυχῇ ἀποκρύπτειν καὶ ἀφανίζειν κακίαν ἐγένετο, εἰ μὴ ᾗ ὁ θεὸς ἐνεφανίσθη, ἣν καὶ τῶν ἀπορρήτων μυστηρίων ἠξίωσε;). After the quotation of Gen 18:17 follows: "It is meet, O Saviour, that thou displayest Thine own works to the soul that longs for all beauteous things, and that Thou hast concealed from it none of Thy works" (εὖ, σῶτερ, ὅτι τὰ σεαυτοῦ ἔργα ἐπιδείκνυσαι τῇ ποθούσῃ τὰ καλὰ ψυχῇ καὶ οὐδὲν αὐτὴν τῶν σῶν ἔργων ἐπικέκρυψαι);[33] and *Conf. ling.* 93: "Which of the wisely–minded, when he sees the tasks which many men endure (and the extravagance of the zeal which they commonly put forth to win money or glory or the enjoyment which pleasures give), would not in the exceeding bitterness of his heart cry aloud to God the only Savior to lighten their tasks and provide a price of the soul's salvation to redeem it into liberty?" (τίς δ' οὐκ ἂν

τῶν εὖ φρονούντων τὰ τῶν πολλῶν ἀνθρώπων ἰδὼν ἔργα ... σφόδρα κατηφήσαι καὶ πρὸς τὸν μόνον σωτῆρα θεὸν ἐκβοῆσαι, ἵνα τὰ μὲν ἐπικουφίσῃ, λύτρα δὲ καὶ σῶστρα καταθεὶς τῆς ψυχῆς εἰς ἐλευθερίαν αὐτὴν ἐξέληται;). 1 Tim 4:10 also belongs here, if the assumption made above, *ad loc.*, is correct, that God is conceived as the fulfiller of the "promise of life" (ἐπαγγελία ζωῆς). Likewise in Acts 5:31 the parallel term "leader" (ἀρχηγός, see also Acts 3:15) can mean "founder of a new life"; cf. *2 Clem.* 20.5: "the savior and initiator of immortality" (τὸν σωτῆρα καὶ ἀρχηγὸν τῆς ἀφθαρσίας), and perhaps even Eph 5:23. The idea under discussion is very clearly stated in *Dg.* 9.6: "Having convinced us then of the inability of our nature to attain life in time past, and now having shown the Saviour who is able to save, even where it was impossible" (ἐλέγξας οὖν ἐν μὲν τῷ πρόσθεν χρόνῳ τὸ ἀδύνατον τῆς ἡμετέρας φύσεως εἰς τὸ τυχεῖν ζωῆς, νῦν δὲ τὸν σωτῆρα δείξας δυνατὸν σώζειν καὶ τὰ ἀδύνατα); and *Odes of Sol.* 41.12: "the Savior, who makes alive . . . our souls." Perhaps this meaning of the term also explains the preference of both Gnostic[34] and anti–Gnostic[35] writers for the designation of Jesus as the "savior."

5. "God, the Savior" (θεὸς σωτήρ) became a technical term, not only in the language of the mystery religions, but also in the cult of the ruler. Paul Wendland[36] has shown how the tendency to make certain human beings into demigods was active in the religion of Hellenism and was intensified in the apotheosis of the living ruler. This cult of the ruler was given new life and strength around the beginning of the Christian era

---

30 On this conception, see Staerk, *Soter, passim.*

31 See Friedrich Preisigke, *Sammelbuch griechischer Urkunden aus Ägypten,* 2 vol. (Strasbourg: 1915 and 1922; rev. ed. 1927–50), No. 169: "To Serapis Osiris, the greatest savior" (Σαράπιδι Ὀσείριδι μεγίστωι σωτῆρι, Ptolemaic age); *ibid.* No. 596 (deals with Serapis); No. 597: "To Serapis and Isis, saviors" (Σαράπιδι καὶ Ἴσιδι Σωτῆρσιν, 3rd cent. B. C.); *CIG* 4930ᵇ "The greatest goddess, the mighty savior Isis" (τὴν μεγίστην θεὰν κυρίαν σώτειραν Ἶσιν); Aelius Aristides, *In Sarapin* 20 (II, p. 358, Keil): "God, protector and savior of man, all–sufficient." (κηδεμόνα καὶ σωτῆρα ἀνθρώπων αὐτάρκη θεόν); *ibid.,* 25 (p. 360): "himself savior and conductor of souls" (σωτὴρ αὐτὸς καὶ ψυχοπομπός) [trans. by Ed.].

32 See Franz Dölger, *Ichthys,* 1 (Freiburg i. B.: Herder, 1910), 406–22; and E. B. Allo, "Les dieux sauveurs

du paganisme greco–romain," *RSPT* 15 (1926): 5–34. The latter author argues onesidedly against the overvaluation of the concept of salvation in connection with such gods, as does H. Haerens, "ΣΩΤΗΡ et ΣΩΤΗΡΙΑ," *Studia Hellenistica* 5 (1948): 57–68.

33 On this passage see Oskar Holtzmann, "Zwei Stellen zum Gottesbegriff des Philo," *ZNW* 13 (1912): 270f.

34 See Irenaeus writing on the Valentinians, *Adv. haer.* 1.2.6.

35 See Georg Wobbermin, *Religionsgeschichtliche Studien zur Frage der Beeinflussung des Urchristentums durch das antike Mysterienwesen* (Berlin: E. Ebering, 1896), 105ff.

36 "Soter: Eine religionsgeschichtliche Untersuchung," *ZNW* 5 (1904): 335–53; cf. *idem, Hellenistische Kultur,* 123ff. Further bibliography is given

through the mood of the Empire, which after many years of disorder was finally pacified under Augustus' rule and which celebrated the emperor as a being who was, in a special sense, its "savior."[37] Examples are provided in the inscriptions cited by Wendland.[38] One ancient example is the inscription to honor "Ptolemy, the Savior and God" (Πτολεμαίου τοῦ σωτῆρος καὶ θεοῦ, 3rd cent. B.C.).[39]

The religious meaning of this term is about as follows: one sees in the man so designated a revelation of the divinity, in his works divine blessings, in his government a time of salvation. Thus, what is historical is raised to the level of the metaphysical; the history of the ruler becomes a history of salvation. For the understanding of the term "savior" in the NT, one may refer to the ruler cult whenever the context speaks about the dawn of a new world epoch, especially when the terminology used in such contexts is similar to that of the emperor cult. This is especially true in 2 Tim 1:10, which describes the emergence of the new age with the "appearance" (ἐπιφάνεια) of the Savior (to be sure, the giving of life is then mentioned).[40] This interpretation also applies to 2:10 (ἐπιφάνεια, see below); Tit 3:6 (see the terms in 3:4, where "savior" is used to refer to God); 2 Petr 1:11 ("everlasting kingdom" [αἰώνιος βασιλεία]), and perhaps also in Ign. Phld. 9.2 ("advent" [παρουσία]). The formula "Savior of the world" (σωτὴρ τοῦ κόσμου, Jn 4:42; 1 Jn 4:14) belongs here because of its universalism, if for no other reason.[41] In the early Christian use of the term, it is still questionable whether the Christians simply adopted the "pagan" word, or whether its usage

was meant as an antithesis to the usage of the cult of the ruler. In documents written during the time of explicit opposition to Rome, the latter assumption is probable (see above on 1 Tim 6:15). Yet this does not apply to all passages. After all, even in the cult of the ruler, many terms used were designations for divine figures which were only secondarily applied to the emperor. The use of "savior" in Christianity can, accordingly, be traced back just as easily to a naive borrowing as to a polemical intention. The fact that the earliest usage is not polemically determined, and a glance at the way Philo uses the term, seem to substantiate the former assumption. Hellenistic Judaism may have been an intermediary.

6. It therefore seems impossible to find only one derivation for the Christian title "savior." Nor are we limited to the three possibilities discussed: Jewish predicate, giver of life, or ruler of the time of salvation. In the first place, the Hellenistic usage of the term is much more varied. The epithet "savior" was given not only to figures who were seen primarily as gods of salvation, such as Asclepius, but to many other gods as well.[42] Moreover, in some passages the Christian usage is formulaic and hence cannot be explained with any precision (Tit 1:4; 2 Petr 1:1; 2:20; 3:2, 18; Ign. Eph. 1.1; Mg. pref.; Phld. 9.2; Sm. 7.1). Thus the title, which gradually became current even in narrative materials as a substitute for "Jesus,"[43] did not essentially modify the christological frame of reference. Christians who later called Jesus "savior," such as Ignatius, simply wanted to attest to his divinity.[44]

---

in the latter work.

37 See Wendland, *Hellenistische Kultur*, 142ff; Lietzmann, *Der Weltheiland, passim*; Lohmeyer, *Christuskult und Kaiserkult, passim*; Eduard Meyer, *Ursprung und Anfänge des Christentums* 3 (Stuttgart: Cotta, Nachfolger, 1923), 390ff; Julius Kaerst, *Geschichte des Hellenismus* (Leipzig: Teubner, ²1926), 309ff; Heinrich Linssen, "Entwicklung und Verbreitung einer liturgischen Formelgruppe," *Jahrbuch für Liturgiewissenschaft* 8 (1928): 1–75; Karl Prümm, *Der christliche Glaube und die altheidnische Welt* (Leipzig: Hegner, 1935), 195ff; the material on σωτήρ can be found in Wendland, "Soter;" David Magie, *De Romanorum iuris publici sacrique vocabulis sollemnibus in Graecum sermonem conversis* (Leipzig: Teubner, 1905); Wilhelm Weber, *Untersuchungen zur Geschichte des Kaisers Hadrianus* (Leipzig: Teubner, 1907), 225ff; Walter Otto, "Augustus Soter," *Hermes* 45 (1910): 448ff.

38 Wendland, *Hellenistische Kultur*, 406ff.

39 The inscription is found in *BMI* IV, 1, 906.2f.

40 This would belong to the pattern described above in section 4. See also the criticism by Windisch, "Zur Christologie," p. 213, and Karl Prümm's skeptical attitude in "Der Herrscherkult im Neuen Testament," *Biblica* 9 (1928): 3ff, 129ff.

41 Cf. Bauer, *Johannesevangelium*, on Jn 4:42.

42 See Dölger, *Ichthys*, I, 420ff. See also a usage inspired by Stoicism, mentioned in Haerens, "ΣΩΤΗΡ et ΣΩΤΗΡΙΑ," 57ff.

43 *P. Oxy.* VIII 1081 a, 5.

44 See Dölger, *Ichthys* I, p. 422. On the entire issue see F. Dornseiff, "Soter," in Pauly–Wissowa, III A¹ (1929), 1211–21. Franz Joseph Dölger, *Antike und Christentum* 6, 4 (Münster: Aschendorff, 1950), 241–72.

"Epiphany" in the Pastoral Epistles

"Epiphany," "appearance" (ἐπιφάνεια) in 2 Tim 1:10 is intimately related to the term "savior" (σωτήρ). Strictly speaking, the religious term "epiphany" means the appearance of a divinity that is otherwise hidden, manifested as a *deus praesens* either in a vision, by a healing or some other helping action, or by any manifestation of power. In any of these instances, the emphasis is not on revelations in myth, but rather on events in history and in the present. The god is thus "such as he appears and is shown forth by his deeds" (οἶος ἐκ τῶν ἔργων ἐπιφαίνεται καὶ δείκνυται).[45] The term "epiphany" (ἐπιφάνεια) is also applied to entire incidents related in legendary form, which focus upon an appearance and action of the divinity. Thus the narrative portion of the temple chronicle of Lindos is entitled "Epiphanies" (ἐπιφάνειαι), while the revelations taken as a whole are designated by the singular "Epiphany" (ἐπιφάνεια).[46] The LXX passages 2 Kings 7:23; 2 Macc 3:24; 5:5; 12:22; 14:15;[47] 3 Macc 2:9; 5:8; 5:51 belong in this context. The passages from 2 Macc are especially instructive, for they show that it is completely irrelevant to the use of the term, in what manner one becomes certain of the presence of the god (*deus praesens*).[48] Thus "appearance" in 2 Macc 3:24 designates the miraculous appearance of the rider before Heliodorus, while the clause, "upholds his own heritage by manifesting himself" (μετ᾽ ἐπιφανείας ἀντιλαμβάνεσθαι), in 2 Macc 14:15 simply means "to extend help in a visible (in any way apprehensible) form."

In the cult the epiphany is celebrated as the birth-festival of the god, as the feast of his accession to power, as the festival of an individual miracle,[49] or, finally, as the festival of his return from a foreign country.[50] This "visitation" (ἐπιδημία) corresponds, in the Christian context, to the eschatological coming, to the parousia, which is designated as "epiphany" (ἐπιφάνεια) in several passages.[51] However, according to the usage of the word elsewhere, it is not surprising that the Christians came to apply the term "epiphany," and later the word "parousia,"[52] also to the earthly "appearance" of Jesus, namely his birth.[53] Even the life of Jesus is seen as the breaking in of the time of salvation and the proclamation of God on earth. This interpretation of Jesus' earthly work is based on the same patterns of thought which the Hellenistic cult of the ruler applied to the rule of the god–king. In fact, the word "epiphany" (ἐπιφάνεια) appears together with cognates in this context as well; cf. Caesar's title, "God manifest, descendent of Ares and Aphrodite, common savior of human life" (τὸν ἀπὸ Ἄρεως καὶ Ἀφροδε[ί]της θεὸν ἐπιφανῆ καὶ κοινὸν τοῦ ἀνθρωπίνου βίου σωτῆρα.)[54]

Passages like these show how the delay of the parousia caused no disappointment. The consciousness of the presence of the gifts of salvation dominates. The whole sequence of concepts with its terminology (examined in the excursus) is intended to transfer to Christ's *first* epiphany all those effects which were originally expected

---

45 Aelius Aristides, *In Sarapin* 15 (II, p. 357, Keil); cf., e.g., the manifestation of Zeus Tropaios and of Sabazios in Pergamon (*Inscr. Perg.* I, 247; II, 4.248, 52), of Artemis in Ephesus (Ditt. *Syll.* II, 867.35), Magnesia (*Inscr. Magn.* 16–87, *passim*, cf. Index), and Knidos (see Rudolf Herzog, "Vorläufiger Bericht über die koische Expedition im Jahre 1904," *Jahrbuch des deutschen archäologischen Instituts* 20 [1905], Beiblatt 11, pp. 1–15); cf. "the appearances of the Virgin" (τὰ[ς ἐπιφαν]είας τῆς Παρθένου) *IPE* I, 184. Cf. A. Wilhelm in: *Archäologische–epigraphische Mitteilungen aus Österreich* 20 (1897): 87, and Michael Rostovtzeff, "Ἐπιφάνειαι," *Klio* 16 (1920): 204.

46 KlT 131, p. 34 D 1, and p. 4 A 3.

47 15:27 in the codex Venetus.

48 Cf. the similarly lax, yet just as technical usage of "he appeared" (ὤφθη) in the LXX.

49 Cf. the relation of the Christian festival of the Epiph-

any to Lk 2 or Matt 2, to the baptism of Jesus, or to the miracle in Cana.

50 The attestations are found in F. Pfister, "Epiphanie" in Pauly–Wissowa, Suppl. IV (1924): 277ff (see below).

51 2 Thess 2:8; 1 Tim 6:14; 2 Tim 4:1, 8; *2 Clem* 12.1; 17.4 (cf. Acts 2:20).

52 See Dibelius, *Thessalonicher, Philipper*, the excursus to 1 Thess 2:10.

53 See 2 Tim 1:10; Just. *Apol.* 1.14.3; 40.1; cf. the use of "he appeared" (ἐπεφάνη) in Tit 2:11; 3:4.

54 Ditt. *Syll.* II, 760.6ff. Cf. further *Inscr. Magn.* 157. c 6; 256.14; W. R. Paton and E. L. Hicks, ed., *The Inscriptions of Cos* (Oxford: Clarendon Press, 1891), 391.4; Weber, *Hadrianus*, p. 196. Also W. M. Ramsey, "The Greek of the Early Church and the Pagan Ritual," *ExpT* 10 (1899): 208; Thieme, *Inschriften von Magnesia*, 34ff; Deissmann, *LAE*, 373f. On the

from the glorious epiphany in the last days.[55] The words regarding the death already point in this direction (cf. 1 Cor 15:26).[56] "To bring to light" ($\phi\omega\tau\iota\zeta\epsilon\iota\nu$) is less fraught with meaning here than in 1 Cor 4:5, where "darkness" ($\sigma\kappa\acute{o}\tau os$) appears in the context as a contrast. To bring to light is not used as a technical term of mysticism in either case.[57] Rather, we find here liturgical language of revelation.[58]

■ 11 The mention of the gospel forms a connecting link to the "personal" conclusion of the kerygmatic exposition (see above on 1 Tim 1:11). This transitional passage again applies the kerygma to the present and binds together the two functions of the apostle, that of the guarantor of the teaching and that of the prototype for suffering (see the introduction above to 2 Tim 1:3–14). On "herald" ($\kappa\hat{\eta}\rho\upsilon\xi$) see above on 1 Tim 2:7.

■ 12 The exemplary character of the apostle is emphasized in such a way that the admonitions to Timothy become statements about Paul: that he is not ashamed (see 1:8, 14; also 1:16), and that the "deposit" ($\pi\alpha\rho\alpha\theta\dot{\eta}\kappa\eta$) is being preserved (see 1:14; cf. 1 Tim 6:20). The general use of this term in the Pastorals (see also v 14), the eschatological orientation ("until that day" [$\epsilon\dot{\iota}s$ $\dot{\epsilon}\kappa\epsilon\dot{\iota}\nu\eta\nu$ $\tau\dot{\eta}\nu$ $\dot{\eta}\mu\dot{\epsilon}\rho\alpha\nu$]), the link with v 13—[59] all these things require that we understand "deposit" ($\pi\alpha\rho\alpha\theta\dot{\eta}\kappa\eta$) as "faith" entrusted to the church in the form of the tradition; cf. v 14.[60] Paul and the tradition are essential components of the event of salvation. Note the change from "my" to the "good" tradition, and see above on 1 Tim 1:12.

■ 13 On "sound preaching" ($\dot{\upsilon}\gamma\iota\alpha\dot{\iota}\nu\text{o}\nu\tau\epsilon s$ $\lambda\acute{o}\gamma\text{o}\iota$), see the excursus to 1 Tim 1:10 (above pp. 24f). "Example" ($\dot{\upsilon}\pi\text{o}\tau\acute{\upsilon}\pi\omega\sigma\iota\nu$) (see above on 1 Tim 1:16) is perhaps to be taken as predicate object (see the translation); then we would have to supply as the object "the words, which you have heard from me" ($\tau\text{o}\dot{\upsilon}s$ $\lambda\acute{o}\gamma\text{o}\upsilon s$ [$\text{o}\ddot{\upsilon}s$ $\pi\alpha\rho$' $\dot{\epsilon}\mu\text{o}\hat{\upsilon}$ $\ddot{\eta}\kappa\text{o}\upsilon\sigma\alpha s$]). On "in faith and love" ($\dot{\epsilon}\nu$ $\pi\dot{\iota}\sigma\tau\epsilon\iota$ $\kappa\alpha\dot{\iota}$ $\dot{\alpha}\gamma\dot{\alpha}\pi\eta$), see above on 1 Tim 1:14. Such expressions, which seem to be formulaic, are often found at the end of clauses. Hence the phrase "in faith and love" is not to be connected with v 14,[61] but with v 13, specifically with the main verb, because they characterize the religious status of the Christian.

■ 14 On "deposit" ($\pi\alpha\rho\alpha\theta\dot{\eta}\kappa\eta$), see above, v 12.[62]

---

entire issue see Odo Casel, "Die Epiphanie im Lichte der Religionsgeschichte," *Benediktinische Monatsschrift* 4 (1922): 13ff; F. Pfister, "Epiphanie" in Pauly–Wissowa, Suppl. IV (1924): 277ff; Prümm, "Herrscherkult," 3ff, 129ff, and 289ff. According to the last article cited, the word belongs rather to the courtly style than to the sacral; W. Grossow, "Epiphania in de pastorale brieven," *Nederlandse katholieke stemmen* 49 (1953): 353ff; Elpidius Pax, ΕΠΙΦΑΝΕΙΑ (München: Zink, 1955).

55 Indeed, in the Pastoral Epistles, "epiphany" is used in two ways, referring to the past as well as to the future appearance of Christ, whereas the formula quoted in v 10 knows only of the first epiphany (cf. the analogous Christology in 1 Tim 3:16).

56 This shift can already be observed in the writings of Paul; cf. Dibelius, *Geisterwelt*, 199ff; 206.

57 See Reitzenstein, *Mysterienreligionen*, Index, *s.v.* $\phi\omega\tau\dot{\iota}\zeta\epsilon\iota\nu$.

58 There is also a purely figurative use of the term; see Epict., *Diss.* I.4.31: "but to him who found the truth, and brought it to light" ($\tau\hat{\omega}$ $\delta\dot{\epsilon}$ $\tau\dot{\eta}\nu$ $\dot{\alpha}\lambda\dot{\eta}\theta\epsilon\iota\alpha\nu$ $\epsilon\dot{\upsilon}\rho\acute{o}\nu\tau\iota$ $\kappa\alpha\dot{\iota}$ $\phi\omega\tau\dot{\iota}\sigma\alpha\nu\tau\iota$).

59 The phrase "sound preaching" ($\dot{\upsilon}\gamma\iota\alpha\dot{\iota}\nu\text{o}\nu\tau\epsilon s$ $\lambda\acute{o}\gamma\text{o}\iota$) in v 13 refers back to "deposit" ($\pi\alpha\rho\alpha\theta\dot{\eta}\kappa\eta$) in v 12.

60 In v 14 it becomes clear that "deposit" ($\pi\alpha\rho\alpha\theta\dot{\eta}\kappa\eta$) does not mean the inner equipment of the missionary (this disagrees with the 2d German ed. of the present commentary). The latter is described instead by the concept of the spirit.

61 B. Weiss, *ad loc.*, connects them with v 14.

62 On the link between tradition and spirit, see Maurice Goguel, *The Birth of Christianity*, tr. H. C. Snape (London: George Allen & Unwin, 1953), 355.

1

Apostasy or Authentication

15 This you know, that all those in Asia
have turned away from me, including
Phygelus and Hermogenes. 16/ But may
the Lord give (his) mercy to the family of
Onesiphorus, for he has often refreshed
me and was not ashamed of my chains,
17/ but rather, when he came to Rome,
he diligently sought and found me:
18/ may the Lord (now also) grant that
he find mercy with the Lord on that
day. And you know best what his
service has accomplished in Ephesus.

The personal references (see 1 Tim 1:19f) are intimately connected with the preceding section. "He was not ashamed" (οὐκ ἐπαισχύνθη) is reminiscent of v 8. Onesiphorus is set up as a good example for Timothy; the case of Phygelus and Hermogenes is described as a warning; and Timothy is requested to come to Paul (see 2 Tim 4:9). This connection is worthy of notice with respect to the problem of the personal references (see below pp. 127f, the second excursus to 2 Tim 4:21).

■ **15** The phrase "all have turned away from me" (ἀπεστράφησάν με πάντες) cannot be understood to imply apostasy from the gospel, because of the comparatively mild terminology and because of the word "all" (πάντες). The phrase probably refers to an event like that described in 2 Tim 4:10f. According to the Acts of Paul, the Demas mentioned there is joined with the Hermogenes referred to here (*Act. Pl.* 12, Lipsius–Bonnet 1, p. 244).

■ **16, 17** On Onesiphorus, see the Acts of Paul (*Act. Pl.* 2f, Lipsius–Bonnet 1, pp. 236ff). On the basis of 2 Tim 1:18 and the mention of Onesiphorus's family, excluding the master of the house (here and in 2 Tim 4:19), scholars have occasionally concluded that Onesiphorus

was already dead at the (alleged) time of the writing of the epistle. Thus v 18 becomes, for the Roman Catholic interpretation, a proof–text for the intercession for the dead. But nothing of the sort is implied.[1] For the impartial reader the phrase "when he came to Rome" (γενόμενος ἐν Ῥώμῃ) can only be interpreted in this way: "Onesiphorus came to Rome, sought me and found me there." One can escape this interpretation if one translates these words as "when he regained his strength" (reading ῥώμῃ = "strength" instead of "Rome"). But since nothing was said before about a sickness, such a hint is improbable, especially in a pseudonymous epistle. Paul is therefore seen as being in Rome, and, more precisely, as experiencing his first and only imprisonment (see below pp. 126f, the first excursus to 4:21).

■ **18** In "to find" (εὑρεῖν) is there a reference to "he found" (εὗρεν) in v 17? Is the roughness of the formulation (with the double "Lord" [κύριος]) to be explained by postulating the combination of two formulaic expressions?[2] "You know best" (βέλτιον) is to be taken as an elative (see the translation) or, if translated as "better," supplied with "than I know."

---

1 Jeremias, Easton, *ad loc.*, disagree.
2 See Jeremias and Easton, *ad loc.*, on these questions.

2

Exhortation to Suffering

1 But you, my child, be strong in the grace
(as it is) in Christ Jesus, 2/ and that
which you have heard from me before
many witnesses, entrust to reliable
people who, in turn, are capable of
teaching others. 3/ As a good soldier of
Christ Jesus accept your share in
suffering. 4/ No one who goes forth
into the battlefield becomes entangled
with business affairs: (he only wishes)
to please his commander. 5/ Also, if
someone competes in an athletic
contest, he does not receive the wreath
unless he competes according to the
rules. 6/ The farmer who has done the
work should be the first to enjoy the
fruits. 7/ Consider what I say—the Lord
will give you understanding in all things.
8/ Remember Jesus Christ, raised from
the dead, from the seed of David,
(thus he is proclaimed) in my gospel.
9/ In this (proclamation) I suffer hard-
ship, even bonds like a criminal, but the
word of God is not fettered. 10/ Therefore I endure everything for the sake
of those who are chosen, so that they
too may obtain salvation in Christ Jesus
and eternal glory.
11/ The word stands firm:
"For if we died with him, we shall also
live with him,
if we endure, we shall also rule with
him,
if we deny, he will also deny us,
if we are unfaithful, he remains
faithful,
because he cannot deny himself."

After "Paul" has introduced himself as an example in the first section, the next section of 2 Tim presents the actual parenesis (extending to 2 Tim 4:8). It is a summary statement of the several regulations upon which the central sections of 1 Tim were based. The parenesis of 2 Tim has the character of a testament.[1]

■ **1, 2** The introduction comprises an exhortation of fundamental importance to the understanding of the "epistle." Timothy himself must become strong (see Paul in 1 Tim 1:12), and he must begin to pass on the tradition which he has received from Paul. The passage is significant, together with *1 Clem.* 42:1–4, for the concept of the apostolic tradition in early Christianity (see also on Tit 1:9 below). Here one can see early, as is the case with the regulations in 1 Tim, that the author is less interested in the fictional addressee of the epistle than in the members of the congregation who are to be instructed by him. His concern is to extend the line of tradition into his own times. The personal parenesis of the epistle, therefore, is significant because it goes beyond Timothy and applies to later generations of Christian readers. In contrast to *1 Clem.*, the concept of tradition is not sup-

---

1   On this point see Johannes Munck, "Discours
    d'adieu dans le Nouveau Testament et dans la lit-
    térature biblique" in *Aux sources de la tradition chré-*
    tienne (Neuchatel and Paris: Delachaux & Niestle,
    S.A., 1950), 155–70. See also below, on 2 Tim 3:1ff.

plemented by a concept of succession. Nor do the Pastorals develop a general concept of the apostle. They are oriented only to Paul.

"Before many witnesses" ($\delta\iota\grave{\alpha}$ $\pi o\lambda\lambda\tilde{\omega}\nu$ $\mu\alpha\rho\tau\acute{\nu}\rho\omega\nu$): the solemnity involved in the appeal to many witnesses makes it improbable that "you have heard" ($\mathring{\eta}\kappa o\nu\sigma\alpha\varsigma$) refers only to the missionary preaching and teaching, whose content was to be verified "through" many persons. The reference must be to baptism, or rather to "ordination," which provided the occasion on which the "deposit" ($\pi\alpha\rho\alpha\theta\acute{\eta}\kappa\eta$) was transmitted to Timothy. Then "through" ($\delta\iota\acute{\alpha}$), here translated as "before," designates the circumstances. Since, according to this passage, Timothy is supposed to transmit the "deposit" ($\pi\alpha\rho\alpha\theta\acute{\eta}\kappa\eta$) to the future leaders of the congregation— not to all Christians—it is the "Great Catechism," not the "Small Catechism,"[2] which is at issue. Therefore, the act alluded to here is the appointment of Timothy to his office. "What you have heard" ($\mathring{\alpha}$ $\mathring{\eta}\kappa o\nu\sigma\alpha\varsigma$) refers to a formulated summary of the teaching, cf. 1 Cor 15:3ff; Rom 6:17.[3]

■ **3–7** The first part of the parenesis is permeated with the thought of suffering and of Paul as the prototype of suffering (see above on 1:3–14).[4] The first exhortation is further substantiated by three metaphorical sayings, which doubtless come from the tradition. The first of these is connected to the key word "soldier" ($\sigma\tau\rho\alpha\tau\iota\acute{\omega}\tau\eta\varsigma$). It is not explicitly stated how these metaphors are to be applied; the reader is left to find out for himself (see 2:7). All three images are also common in the diatribe.[5] The idea that "he who has done the work" ($\kappa o\pi\iota\tilde{\omega}\nu$) is entitled to a share in the fruits is also found in Deut 20:6 and Pr 27:18. As proof for this idea Paul uses three similar images in 1 Cor 9:7. But in 2 Tim 2, no interest is shown in the concept of a reward that is simply presupposed.

Rather the emphasis rests upon the one "who has done the work" ($\kappa o\pi\iota\tilde{\omega}\nu\tau\alpha$), which corresponds to "compete according to the rules" ($\nu o\mu\acute{\iota}\mu\omega\varsigma$ $\mathring{\alpha}\theta\lambda\epsilon\tilde{\iota}\nu$) and to the renunciation of interest in "business affairs" in the preceding verses. Only thus can one understand the meaning common to all three examples: hard work brings its reward. Although the author may have patterned the passage after 1 Cor 9:7, he has given the idea a completely different emphasis. To be sure, this emphasis is to be gathered from the composition and combination of the three examples rather than from the wording of the phrases. That characteristic perhaps results from the fact that the author has appropriated well–known parables without reformulating them for their new context.[6]

■ **8** is apparently a kerygmatic formulation.[7] The source is probably a two–part formula of the same type as Rom 1:3f. It implies no preexistence, but rather distinguishes between the earthly status of the son of David and the stage of exaltation (in Rom 1:3f this is designated as sonship) after the raising from the dead (not "resurrection"). The Pastoral Epistles work with conflicting Christological materials. The development of a reflection about the Son of David appears in Ignatius.[8] "My gospel" ($\tau\grave{o}$ $\epsilon\mathring{\nu}\alpha\gamma\gamma\acute{\epsilon}\lambda\iota\acute{o}\nu$ $\mu o\nu$) is also found in Rom 2:16 and 16:25. The latter passage is not Pauline, and the former has been suspected of being a gloss.[9] Again the confession is immediately connected with the person of Paul, as is also what follows.

■ **9** See above, on 2 Tim 1:8. "In this" ($\mathring{\epsilon}\nu$ $\mathring{\omega}$) refers to the "gospel" ($\epsilon\mathring{\nu}\alpha\gamma\gamma\acute{\epsilon}\lambda\iota o\nu$), represented in the following clause by "the word of God" ($\mathring{o}$ $\lambda\acute{o}\gamma o\varsigma$ $\tau o\tilde{\nu}$ $\theta\epsilon o\tilde{\nu}$). On "even bonds" ($\mu\acute{\epsilon}\chi\rho\iota$ $\delta\epsilon\sigma\mu\tilde{\omega}\nu$), cf. Phil 2:8. A kind of personification of the "word" is also found in 2 Thess 3:1.[10]

■ **10** The preceding verse had already shifted from the

---

2   The reference is to the analogous distinction between Martin Luther's Small and Great Catechism [Ed.].

3   See Seeberg, *Katechismus*, 143, 172 and 186; Norden, *Agnostos Theos*, 269ff.

4   On "soldier" ($\sigma\tau\rho\alpha\tau\iota\acute{\omega}\tau\eta\varsigma$), see the excursus above, pp. 32f on 1 Tim 1:18; furthermore Dibelius–Greeven, *Kolosser, Epheser, Philemon*, the excursus on Eph 6:10.

5   On "soldier" ($\sigma\tau\rho\alpha\tau\iota\acute{\omega}\tau\eta\varsigma$) see the excursus mentioned, n. 4 above. On "athlete" ($\mathring{\alpha}\theta\lambda\eta\tau\acute{\eta}\varsigma$) see Wendland, *Hellenistische Kultur*, 357. On "farmer" ($\gamma\epsilon\omega\rho\gamma\acute{o}\varsigma$), see Epictetus (ed. Schenkl, Index).

6   See also below on 2:20. On the differences in the

tenses of "to compete" ($\mathring{\alpha}\theta\lambda\epsilon\tilde{\iota}\nu$) in v 5, see Radermacher, *Grammatik*, 178.

7   See 2 Tim 1:9f; 1 Tim 6:13. Cf. Seeberg, *Katechismus*, 173; Norden, *Agnostos Theos*, 381.

8   Ign. *Tr.* 9; *Sm.* 1.1. Cf. Lietzmann, "Symbolstudien" (2), pp. 264ff; Cullmann, *Confessions*, 50.

9   See Rudolf Bultmann, "Glossen im Römerbrief," *ThLZ* 72 (1947): 201; reprinted in *idem, Exegetica* (Tübingen: J. C. B. Mohr [Paul Siebeck], 1967), 283.

10   See Asting, *Verkündigung*, 187.

theme of the kerygma to the concept of suffering. Here the suffering of the apostle is evaluated in terms of its significance for the history of salvation. In this context one is tempted to refer to the concept of the suffering of Christ in the apostle;[11] but nothing of the sort is implied in 2 Tim 2. Thus the final clause must refer to the mission.

■ **11–13** The author concludes this section with a quotation of unknown origin, in the style of a hymn, confirming the promise of salvation made in v 10. On the introductory formula see above, pp. 28f, the excursus to 1 Tim 1:15. A close parallel is found in Pol. *Phil.* 5.2: "even as he promised us to raise us from the dead, and that if we are worthy citizens of his community, 'we shall also reign with him,' if we but have faith" (καθὼς ὑπέσχετο ἡμῖν ἐγεῖραι ἡμᾶς ἐκ νεκρῶν, καὶ ὅτι, ἐὰν πολιτευσώμεθα ἀξίως αὐτοῦ, καὶ συμβασιλεύσομεν αὐτῷ, εἴγε πιστεύομεν). This passage is not necessarily based on 2 Tim 2:11ff, but both could rely upon a common source (especially if the Pastorals and Pol. *Phil.* originated in the same area, as von Campenhausen believes). Pol. *Phil.* conceived of "word" (λόγος) as a saying of the Lord. Actually, he may have been influenced by the statement of Paul in Rom 6:8, because, in contrast to other quotations in this epistle, here life is understood strictly in reference to the future—a fact which is significant in view of 2 Tim 2:18.

The first two couplets of the quotation entirely agree with one another, from the standpoint of both form and content (except for the change in tense in the first clause). The third is different in content, but contains, like the first, two parts that are parallel to one another.[12] The fourth, in three parts, rounds out the whole very impressively. But it stands in contrast to all three preceding couplets because of its paradox. The idea of v 13 does not belong in the context of 2 Tim 2; this too proves that it is a quotation. On "to deny" (ἀρνεῖσθαι), cf. the translation: "if we fail, he fails us."[13] "He remains faithful" (πιστὸς μένει) cannot refer to God's insistence upon formal recompense; such an interpretation contradicts the usage of the terms. Rather it is the thought of God's faithfulness to the covenant (cf. Rom 3:2f). On the coexistence of formal retaliation and its suppression, cf. also the *Manual of Discipline* from Qumran (1 QS XI, 11f): "And I, if I stagger, God's mercies are my salvation forever; if I stumble because of the sin of the flesh, my justification is in the righteousness of God which existed forever" [Trans. Dupont–Sommer, *Essene Writings*, p. 102].

---

11 See Dibelius–Greeven, *Kolosser, Epheser, Philemon,* the excursus to Col 1:24; Lohse, *Colossians and Philemon,* on Col 1:24.

12 Is there dependence on Matt 10:33? See Günther Bornkamm, "Das Wort Jesu vom Bekennen," *Monatsschrift für Pastoraltheologie* 34 (1938): 108–18.

13 "Wenn wir versagen, gibt er uns Absage," Anton Fridrichsen, "Einige sprachliche und stilistische Beobachtungen," *Con. Neot.* 2 (1936): 8–13, and 6 (1942): 96.

2 Personal Authentication in View of Heretics

14 You must remind (the people) of this and
adjure (them) in the face of God not
to bring ruin upon their hearers through
disputes about words (which are) useful
for nothing. 15/ Make every effort to
present yourself before God as proven,
as a worker who need not be ashamed,
who teaches the word of truth rightly.
16/ But flee from godless chatter;
because (throughout) they will make
more and more progress into godlessness, 17/ and their teaching will feed
upon (them) like gangrene. Among them
are Hymenaeus and Philetus, 18/ who
have missed the mark with regard to
truth, for they say that the resurrection
has already happened, and (thus) they
destroy the faith of some people. 19/ But
the firm foundation of God stands and
it bears this seal: "The Lord knows
his own," and "Whoever names the
name of the Lord, stay away from injustice!" 20/ In a large house there are
not only vessels of gold and silver, but
also of wood and clay, and some are
(designated) for honorable (use), some
for disreputable (use). 21/ If a man
cleanse himself of these things, then he
will be a vessel (that is destined) for
honor, sanctified, useful to the master,
prepared for every good work. 22/ Flee
the desires of youth, but pursue uprightness, faith, love, peace, together
with (all) those who call upon the Lord
with a pure heart. 23/ Reject foolish and
uninstructed speculations, since you
know that they will (only) create
quarrels. 24/ But a servant of the Lord
should not quarrel; rather he should
be gentle toward everyone, skillful in
teaching, without resentment; 25/ he
should instruct his opponents in gentleness, that God might perhaps grant
them repentance for the recognition of
truth, 26/ and that they might escape
from the snare of the devil, since they
have been captured by him to do his will.

The second part of the parenesis is formulated with a view to the heretics (see 3:1ff). It begins with a summary reference to the preceding exhortations (see above on 1 Tim 1:18–20).

■ **14** This is difficult to interpret because of the lack of any connecting or contrasting particle in the clauses introduced by the Greek particle ἐπί (translated with "upon" and "for"). If "useful for nothing" (ἐπ' οὐδὲν χρήσιμον) is not to be deleted as a gloss, it must be in apposition to the preceding infinitive, literally, "to dispute about words" (λογομαχεῖν); in this interpretation, "for nothing" (ἐπ' οὐδέν) is seen as dependent on "useful" (χρήσιμον). If the reading "do not dispute about words" (μὴ λογομάχει)[1] is adopted, a rather clumsy asyndeton results, since only one of the two clauses in question can be dependent upon this main verb. If the reading "[not] to dispute . . ." ($\lambda o\gamma o\mu\alpha\chi\epsilon\hat{\iota}\nu$) is adopted, then "ruin upon the hearers" completes the thought of this infinitive, and the particle introducing this clause ($\epsilon\pi\iota$) refers to the accompanying condition, as in Rom 8:20. In this case also, the meaning "to bring ruin" for the Greek words $\epsilon\pi\iota\ \kappa\alpha\tau\alpha\sigma\tau\rho o\phi\hat{\eta}$ fits;[2] cf. *Herm. mand.* 5.2.1 and 6.2.4, in which "to ruin" ($\kappa\alpha\tau\alpha$-$\sigma\tau\rho\epsilon\phi\epsilon\iota\nu$) is used to refer to the effect of wrath.

■ **15** The best medicine against the disease of "disputes about words"[3] is Timothy's good conduct itself. "Who need not be ashamed" ($\alpha\nu\epsilon\pi\alpha\iota\sigma\chi\upsilon\nu\tau o\varsigma$) is used in the same sense as in 2 Tim 1:8.[4] "Worker" ($\epsilon\rho\gamma\alpha\tau\eta\varsigma$) is used in 2 Cor 11:13 and Phil 3:2 to refer to the activity of the missionary; here it refers to the work of the leader of mission congregations. The Greek term translated with "teach rightly" ($\delta\rho\theta o\tau o\mu\epsilon\hat{\iota}\nu$) has not been adequately explained so far. It seems—in view of its occurrence in Pr 3:6 and 11:5, where it is connected with "ways" ($\delta\delta o\iota$) in a figurative sense—to presuppose the meaning "to clear a way" ($\tau\epsilon\mu\nu\epsilon\iota\nu\ \delta\delta\delta\nu$); cf. Plato, *Leg.* 810: "to proceed along the way of legislation which has been cleared by our present discourse" ($\tau\eta\nu\ \nu\hat{\upsilon}\nu\ \epsilon\kappa\ \tau\hat{\omega}\nu\ \pi\alpha$-$\rho\delta\nu\tau\omega\nu\ \lambda\delta\gamma\omega\nu\ \tau\epsilon\tau\mu\eta\mu\epsilon\nu\eta\nu\ \delta\delta\delta\nu\ \tau\hat{\eta}\varsigma\ \nu o\mu o\theta\epsilon\sigma\iota\alpha\varsigma\ \pi o$-$\rho\epsilon\upsilon\epsilon\sigma\theta\alpha\iota$) [Loeb modified]. But in a compound with "right" ($\delta\rho\theta o$-), the verb "to cut" ($\tau\epsilon\mu\nu\epsilon\iota\nu$) could be

weakened to the same extent as in the compound with "new" ($\kappa\alpha\iota\nu o$-).[5] Here too the stress is on "right" ($\delta\rho\theta o$-) and not on the verbal meaning "to cut" (see the translation). On the formation of the word, cf. "to walk rightly" ($\delta\rho\theta o\pi o\delta o\hat{\upsilon}\sigma\iota\nu$) in Gal 2:14; or is this an idiom?[6] "The word of truth" ($\lambda\delta\gamma o\varsigma\ \tau\hat{\eta}\varsigma\ \alpha\lambda\eta\theta\epsilon\iota\alpha\varsigma$) is here, as in Eph 1:13, equivalent to the gospel.[7]

■ **16** On "chatter" ($\kappa\epsilon\nu o\phi\omega\nu\iota\alpha\iota$), see above on 1 Tim 6:20. The subject of "they will make progress" ($\pi\rho o\kappa\delta$-$\psi o\upsilon\sigma\iota\nu$) which is used ironically, is, as the context shows, "people who engage in chatter" ($\kappa\epsilon\nu o\phi\omega\nu o\hat{\upsilon}\nu\tau\epsilon\varsigma$). Their talk leads further into godlessness.

■ **17** The image of gangrene ($\gamma\alpha\gamma\gamma\rho\alpha\iota\nu\alpha$) is also found in Plutarch.[8] The image may therefore be a common one, and need not be derived from an [alleged] medical counselor of the author.[9] "To feed (upon)," "graze" ($\nu o\mu\eta\nu\ \epsilon\chi\epsilon\iota$) is consistent with the image.[10] It thus refers to the spread of the sickness—here, the spread of the godless teaching—perhaps among the congregations (but see 2 Tim 3:9). Therefore one might better think of it as the spread of godlessness in human souls; thus, in the sense of 2 Tim 3:13. Hymenaeus is probably the same person as the one mentioned in 1 Tim 1:20; here he has obviously not yet been "handed over to Satan." In deciding the question of priority, this state of affairs can be interpreted in different ways (see above p. 71, the excursus to 1 Tim 4:14, section 2).

---

1 This is the reading of A C* lat.

2 Wohlenberg, *ad loc.*, interprets it differently as "subjugation."

3 That is, of heretical preachers; cf. 2 Tim 2:23; 1 Tim 1:4; 6:4; Tit 3:9.

4 The word is also used in Josephus, *Ant.* 18.243; the adverb in Agapetus, *De officio boni principis* 57 (p. 174, Groebel), and Hippolytus, *Philos.* 1 (p. 3.14, Wendland).

5 Cf. Lucian, *Phalaris* 2.9: "Therefore we ought not to make any innovation in the present case" ($\delta\epsilon\hat{\iota}\ \tau o\iota\nu\upsilon\nu\ \mu\eta\delta'\ \epsilon\nu\ \tau\hat{\omega}\ \pi\alpha\rho\delta\nu\tau\iota\ \kappa\alpha\iota\nu o\tau o\mu\epsilon\hat{\iota}\nu\ \mu\eta\delta\epsilon\nu$), where it means "to make an innovation"; cf. also Tatian, *Or. Graec.* 35.2: "Tatian . . . renews the teachings of the barbarians" ($T\alpha\tau\iota\alpha\nu\delta\varsigma\ ...\ \kappa\alpha\iota\nu o$-$\tau o\mu\epsilon\hat{\iota}\ \tau\grave{\alpha}\ \beta\alpha\rho\beta\alpha\rho\omega\nu\ \delta\delta\gamma\mu\alpha\tau\alpha$) [trans. by Ed.].

6 Cf. *b. Ber.* 61a (with רבנן חנו): "the kidneys prompt, the heart discerns, the tongue shapes (the words), the mouth articulates" (נמר פה מחתך לשון).

7 See Dibelius–Greeven, *Kolosser, Epheser, Philemon*; Lohse, *Colossians, Philemon*, on Col 1:6.

8 Plut., *Adulat.* 24 (p. 65 D) says of Alexander, whose band of flatterers spreads slander against his best friends: "In fact it was by such scars, or rather such gangrenes and cancers, that Alexander was consumed so that he destroyed Callisthenes etc." ($\tau\alpha\acute{\upsilon}$-$\tau\alpha\iota\varsigma\ \mu\epsilon\nu\tau o\iota\ \tau\alpha\hat{\iota}\varsigma\ o\upsilon\lambda\alpha\hat{\iota}\varsigma,\ \mu\hat{\alpha}\lambda\lambda o\nu\ \delta\grave{\epsilon}\ \gamma\alpha\gamma\gamma\rho\alpha\iota\nu\alpha\iota\varsigma\ \kappa\alpha\grave{\iota}\ \kappa\alpha\kappa\rho\iota\nu\omega\mu\alpha\sigma\iota\ \delta\iota\alpha\beta\rho\omega\theta\epsilon\grave{\iota}\varsigma\ '\Lambda\lambda\epsilon\xi\alpha\nu\delta\rho o\varsigma\ \alpha\pi\omega\lambda\epsilon\sigma\epsilon\ \kappa\alpha\grave{\iota}\ K\alpha\lambda\lambda\iota\sigma\theta\epsilon\nu\eta\ \kappa\tau\lambda.$).

9 In view of 4:11, Belser, *ad loc.*, suggests Luke. Samples from the medical writings are given in Wettstein (Joannes Jacobus Wetstenius), *Novum Testamentum Graecum* II (Amsterdam: Ex Officiana Dommeriana, 1752), *ad loc.*

10 Cf. Galen, *De simpl. medicam. temp. et fac.* 9 (12, p. 179, Kühn): ". . . the dysenteric ulcers, before the ulcers become inclined to putrefy, it is customary among physicians to call such conditions 'pasturages' because the putrefaction grazes outwards towards the adjacent parts and corrupts them together with the part first affected." ($\tau\grave{\alpha}\varsigma\ \delta\upsilon\sigma\epsilon\nu\tau\epsilon\rho\iota\kappa\grave{\alpha}\varsigma\ \epsilon\lambda$-$\kappa\omega\sigma\epsilon\iota\varsigma\ \pi\rho\grave{o}\ \tau o\hat{\upsilon}\ \sigma\eta\pi\epsilon\delta o\nu\omega\delta\eta\ \gamma\epsilon\nu\epsilon\sigma\theta\alpha\iota\ \tau\grave{\alpha}\ \epsilon\lambda\kappa\eta,\ \kappa\alpha\lambda\epsilon\hat{\iota}\nu\ \delta'\ \epsilon\theta o\varsigma\ \epsilon\sigma\tau\grave{\iota}\nu\ \tau o\hat{\iota}\varsigma\ \iota\alpha\tau\rho o\hat{\iota}\varsigma\ \tau\grave{\alpha}\varsigma\ \tau o\iota\alpha\acute{\upsilon}\tau\alpha\varsigma\ \delta\iota\alpha\theta\epsilon\sigma\epsilon\iota\varsigma\ \nu o\mu\grave{\alpha}\varsigma\ \alpha\pi\grave{o}\ \tau o\hat{\upsilon}\ \nu\epsilon\mu\epsilon\sigma\theta\alpha\iota\ \tau\grave{\eta}\nu\ \sigma\eta\pi\epsilon\delta\delta\nu\alpha\ \pi\rho\grave{o}\varsigma\ \tau\grave{\alpha}\ \pi\lambda\eta\sigma\iota\alpha\sigma\alpha\nu\tau\alpha\ \mu\delta\rho\iota\alpha\ \sigma\upsilon\nu\delta\iota\alpha\phi\theta\epsilon\iota\rho o\upsilon\sigma\alpha\nu\ \alpha\upsilon\tau\grave{\alpha}\ \tau\hat{\omega}\ \pi\rho\omega\tau\omega\ \kappa\alpha\kappa\omega\theta\epsilon\nu\tau\iota$) [trans. by Ed.]; cf. also

■ **18** If one contests the unity of the description of the heretics in the Pastorals (see above pp. 65ff, the excursus to 1 Tim 4:3), one will try to relate 2 Tim 2:14, 17f to special occurrences in the life of the congregation.[11] But the sharpness of the criticism speaks decidedly against the assumption that the opponents are still legitimate authorities within the congregation. The thesis which is opposed here regarding the resurrection is best explained as a spiritualized teaching of Gnostics, a teaching which was already contested by Paul in 1 Cor 15.[12] To what degree the passage in the Acts of Paul[13] contributes to the clarification of this passage is debatable; the words there are spoken in opposition to the teaching of the semi-Gnostic Paul of the Acts of Paul, and are thus perhaps conditioned by that polemical situation. Moreover, this passage is absent from the Latin fragment of Brescia.[14]

■ **19** "Foundation" ($\theta\epsilon\mu\acute{\epsilon}\lambda\iota\sigma$) may refer to the cornerstone,[15] and "seal" ($\sigma\phi\rho\alpha\gamma\acute{\iota}s$) to the inscription on the stone which certifies it. But it is improbable that "foundation" refers to Christ, to the first generation, or to both. The group of images relating to housebuilding[16] is so commonly used in early Christianity that it is possible the metaphor in this case was not even recognized any more. Otherwise, one could mention *Herm. sim.* 9.4.2., where the ten stones upon the rock over the gate form the tower's foundation (of the "church" [$\grave{\epsilon}\kappa\kappa\lambda\eta\sigma\acute{\iota}\alpha$]); in *Herm. sim.* 9.15.4 they are explained as referring to the

"first generation" ($\pi\rho\acute{\omega}\tau\eta\ \gamma\epsilon\nu\epsilon\acute{\alpha}$). Of the two "inscriptions" of the "foundation," the first certainly depends upon the LXX (Num 16:5), the second probably so.[17] Yet the author is probably not quoting the LXX here, but early Christian poetry, whose language had been influenced by the Greek OT. This is indicated by the form of the second saying, perhaps also by the use of "knows" ($\grave{\epsilon}\gamma\nu\omega$) in the first. The latter was perhaps understood by the author, not mystically,[18] but in line with the conception of the church and of election.[19] *Odes of Sol.* 8.14f also points to the origin of the first saying in early Christian poetry: "For I do not turn away my face from them that are mine;/For I know them;/Before they came into being,/I took knowledge of them,/And on their faces I set my seal."[20] On the relation between the symbolism of building and the idea of election, see also the *Manual of Discipline*, (1 QS VIII, 4–8): "When these things come to pass in Israel, the Council of the Community shall be established in the truth as an everlasting planting. It is the house of holiness for Israel and the Company of infinite holiness for Aaron; they are the witnesses of truth unto Judgement and the chosen of Loving-kindness appointed to offer expiation for the earth and to bring down punishment upon the wicked. It is the tried wall, the precious cornerstone; its foundations shall not tremble nor flee from their place" [trans. Dupont-Sommer, *Essene Writings*, p. 91].[21] This text also

---

Plutarch, *Superst.* 3 (p. 165 E): "the passions feed savagely upon the flesh" ($\phi\lambda\epsilon\gamma\mu\sigma\nu\alpha\grave{\iota}\ \ldots\ \kappa\alpha\grave{\iota}\ \nu\sigma\mu\alpha\grave{\iota}\ \sigma\alpha\rho\kappa\grave{\sigma}s\ \theta\eta\rho\iota\acute{\omega}\delta\epsilon\iota s$).

11 Thus Michaelis, *Echtheitsfrage*, 117f, refers to the officers of the church, because people in the church are referred to as "hearers" of such disputations.

12 Justin, *Apol.* 1.26.4, writes concerning Menander: "who even convinced those who followed him that they would never die" ($\grave{\sigma}s\ \kappa\alpha\grave{\iota}\ \tau\sigma\grave{\nu}s\ \alpha\grave{\nu}\tau\tilde{\omega}\ \grave{\epsilon}\pi\sigma\mu\acute{\epsilon}\nu\sigma\nu s\ \grave{\omega}s\ \mu\eta\delta\grave{\epsilon}\ \grave{\alpha}\pi\sigma\theta\nu\acute{\eta}\sigma\kappa\sigma\iota\epsilon\nu\ \grave{\epsilon}\pi\epsilon\iota\sigma\epsilon$). Likewise, Irenaeus (*Adv. haer.* 1.23.5) writes concerning Menander: "for his disciples obtain the resurrection by being baptized into him, and can die no more, but never grow old and are immortal" (resurrectionem enim per id, quod est in eum baptisma, accipere eius discipulos, et ultra non posse mori, sed perseverare non senescentes et immortales) [trans. by Ed.]. Cf. also *De Resurrectione* (Letter to Rheginus) 45.23ff: "But then as the Apostle said, we suffered with him, and we went to heaven with him"; and 49.15f: "and already thou hast the Resurrection" (Malinine, ed.).

13 *Act. Pl.* 14 (Lipsius–Bonnet, 1, p. 245), "that it has already taken place in the children whom we have"

($\grave{\sigma}\tau\iota\ \grave{\eta}\delta\eta\ \gamma\acute{\epsilon}\gamma\sigma\nu\epsilon\nu$ (scil. $\grave{\eta}\ \grave{\alpha}\nu\acute{\alpha}\sigma\tau\alpha\sigma\iota s$) $\grave{\epsilon}\phi'\ \sigma\grave{\iota}s\ \grave{\epsilon}\chi\sigma\mu\epsilon\nu\ \tau\acute{\epsilon}\kappa\nu\sigma\iota s$).

14 See the excursus to 1 Tim 4:5, section 1. Further material can be found in Theodor Zahn, *Introduction to the New Testament* 2, tr. and ed. Melanchthon Williams and Charles Snow Thayer (New York: Charles Scribner's Sons, ³1917), sect. 37, n. 17.

15 See Dibelius–Greeven, *Kolosser, Epheser, Philemon*, on Eph 2:20.

16 Vielhauer, *Oikodome, passim.*

17 See also Isa 52:13: "Depart, depart . . . you who bear the vessels of the Lord" ($\grave{\alpha}\pi\acute{\sigma}\sigma\tau\eta\tau\epsilon\ \grave{\alpha}\pi\acute{\sigma}\sigma\tau\eta\tau\epsilon\ \ldots\ \sigma\grave{\iota}\ \phi\acute{\epsilon}\rho\sigma\nu\tau\epsilon s\ \tau\grave{\alpha}\ \sigma\kappa\epsilon\acute{\nu}\eta\ \kappa\nu\rho\acute{\iota}\sigma\nu$); Isa 26:13: "Thy name (alone) we acknowledge" ($\tau\grave{\sigma}\ \grave{\sigma}\nu\sigma\mu\acute{\alpha}\ \sigma\sigma\nu\ \grave{\sigma}\nu\sigma\mu\acute{\alpha}\zeta\sigma\mu\epsilon\nu$).

18 Here I diverge from the 2d German edition of this commentary. Cf. on this question *Corp. Herm.* 10:15: "For God is not ignorant with regard to man; on the contrary, he knows him very well and wishes to be known by him" ($\sigma\grave{\nu}\ \gamma\grave{\alpha}\rho\ \grave{\alpha}\gamma\nu\sigma\epsilon\tilde{\iota}\ \tau\grave{\sigma}\nu\ \grave{\alpha}\nu\theta\rho\omega\pi\sigma\nu\ \grave{\sigma}\ \theta\epsilon\acute{\sigma}s,\ \grave{\alpha}\lambda\lambda\grave{\alpha}\ \kappa\alpha\grave{\iota}\ \pi\acute{\alpha}\nu\nu\ \gamma\nu\omega\rho\acute{\iota}\zeta\epsilon\iota\ \kappa\alpha\grave{\iota}\ \theta\acute{\epsilon}\lambda\epsilon\iota\ \gamma\nu\omega\rho\acute{\iota}\zeta\epsilon\sigma\theta\alpha\iota$) [trans. by Ed.].

19 See Rudolf Bultmann, *TDNT* 1, p. 705.

112

contains an allusion to the OT: Isa 28:16.

If "the Lord knows his own" originally referred to the election of the church, it now refers to the chosen people within it. That corresponds to the shift in the conception of the church brought about by the emerging distinction between orthodoxy and heresy. The separation which occurred within Israel is repeated in the church (Schlatter). It becomes quite clear that the parenesis derives its fundamental motivation from the consciousness of election.

■ **20** The question as to why there are disloyal persons in the congregation at all is answered in v 20 by the image of vessels. This image appears without any prior preparation. It is probably influenced by Rom 9:21 and Wisd Sol 15:7. The introductory clause, to be sure, suggests an interpretation along the lines of 1 Cor 12:22f. The point would then be that the weaker members of the congregation should also be given the appropriate recognition. But the context speaks against this interpretation. We are not dealing with a problem of those who are less gifted, but with the seducers and the seduced. This interpretation is demanded by the context, but it is not expressed in verse 20's presentation of the image itself. The reason for this is that the point which such images originally had has been shifted toward a new meaning (see above at 1 Tim 1:1).

■ **21** This interpretation is confirmed here. The image is turned in an unmistakably parenetic direction: "even though these vessels for disreputable use ($\sigma\kappa\epsilon\acute{\nu}\eta$ $\epsilon\grave{\iota}\varsigma$ $\dot{\alpha}\tau\iota\mu\acute{\iota}\alpha\nu$) are present in the house, nevertheless be sure that you yourself remain a vessel for honorable use ($\sigma\kappa\epsilon\hat{\nu}o\varsigma$ $\epsilon\grave{\iota}\varsigma$ $\tau\iota\mu\acute{\eta}\nu$) by cleansing yourself of these ($\dot{\alpha}\pi\grave{o}$ $\tauo\acute{\nu}\tau\omega\nu$)." "These" ($\tauo\acute{\nu}\tau\omega\nu$) refers perhaps to the actions designated as "disreputable" ($\dot{\alpha}\tau\iota\mu\acute{\iota}\alpha$). But it is significant for the traditional character of the image that

the interpretation which, in view of 2:19, one would hope to find here is not expressed. It is not explicitly stated that the church must purify itself and rid itself of the false teachers.

■ **22** The personal parenesis of 2:15, which was interrupted by the statements about heretics and the church, is taken up again with a warning to Timothy against desires. It is a warning actually meant to apply to all youthful leaders of churches (see 1 Tim 4:12). The exhortation to virtue begins again with "uprightness" ($\delta\iota\kappa\alpha\iotao\sigma\acute{\nu}\nu\eta$) [see above at 1 Tim 6:11].

■ **23** "Uninstructed" ($\dot{\alpha}\pi\alpha\acute{\iota}\delta\epsilon\nu\tauo\varsigma$) in Epictetus means "the man who has not learned to think." It is used in *1 Clem.* 30:1, as well as here, in a general sense parallel to "stupid, senseless, foolish" ($\ddot{\alpha}\phi\rho\omega\nu$, $\dot{\alpha}\sigma\acute{\nu}\nu\epsilon\tauo\varsigma$, $\mu\omega\rho\acute{o}\varsigma$). Notice again the tendency of the polemic, as noted above on 1 Tim 1:6 and 6:20, which is directed against the form of the "false teaching," not against its actual content. This consistency in the manner of opposing the heresy is a strong argument against the individualizing interpretation[22] which would relate 2 Tim 2:23, but not 2 Tim 2:14ff, to members of the congregation.

■ **24** On "skillful in teaching" ($\delta\iota\delta\alpha\kappa\tau\iota\kappao\acute{\iota}$), see above on 1 Tim 3:2. The phrase "servant of the Lord" is reminiscent of "man of God" in the parallel passages (1 Tim 6:11; cf. 2 Tim 3:17).

■ **25** "Quarrels" ($\mu\acute{\alpha}\chi\alpha\iota$) and "to quarrel" ($\mu\acute{\alpha}\chi\epsilon\sigma\theta\alpha\iota$) in the preceding verses refer to opposition to the "false teachers." Thus "opponents" in this verse probably refers to the same people—at least primarily.[23] "Repentance" ($\mu\epsilon\tau\acute{\alpha}\nuo\iota\alpha$) is the return to the "truth," as the Pastorals understand it (see above on 1 Tim 2:3, 4). The "sin" which is presupposed by the word "repentance" was mentioned in v 23. The expression "grant repentance" ($\deltao\hat{\nu}\nu\alpha\iota$ $\mu\epsilon\tau\acute{\alpha}\nuo\iota\alpha\nu$) derives from Judaism.[24]

---

20 See Abramowski, "Der Christus der Salomooden", 44ff.

21 On the "foundation," see Anton Fridrichsen, "Neutestamentliche Wortforschung. Themelios, 1. Kor. 3, 11," *ThZ* 2 (1946): 316–17.

22 The reference is to the interpretation of Michaelis, *Echtheitsfrage*, on 1 Tim 2:18.

23 The clumsy sequence of the optative "he may grant" ($\delta\acute{\omega}\eta$) and the subjunctive "they might escape" ($\dot{\alpha}\nu\alpha\nu\acute{\eta}\psi\omega\sigma\iota\nu$) is not without parallel; see 2 Macc 9:24 ($\dot{\alpha}\pi o\beta\alpha\acute{\iota}\eta$ $\kappa\alpha\grave{\iota}$ $\pi\rho o\sigma\alpha\pi\acute{\epsilon}\lambda\theta\eta$); *P. Reinach* 17.15 (109 B.C.) ($\dot{\alpha}\pi o\kappa\alpha\tau\alpha\sigma[\tau\alpha]\theta\epsilon\acute{\iota}\eta-\tau\acute{\nu}\chi\omega\sigma\iota$). Since, however, such an optative would seem

strangely archaic (the case is different in Lk 3:15) the subjunctive $\delta\acute{\omega}\eta$ or $\delta\hat{\omega}$ ($\aleph$ 33) is preferable after all. See Moulton, *Prolegomena*, 55, 193; Blass–Debrunner, 370.3.

24 See *Sib.* 4.168f; cf. Joseph Thomas, *Le mouvement baptiste in Palestine et Syrie (150 av. J. C.–300 ap. J. C.)* (Gembloux [Belgium]: Duculot, 1935), 46, 52f.

It is used without the necessary implication that "repentance" must be understood strictly as a "gift."[25] Since the expression is common,[26] it is not advisable to assume literary dependence between the Pastoral Epistles and Pol. *Phil.* 11.4: "to these may the Lord give true repentance" (*quibus det dominus poenitentiam veram*). Nor can one prove on the basis of this passage any sort of libertinism of the Gnostics, who are here opposed.

■ **26** In "to escape," literally "to return to sobriety" (ἀνανήφειν), the image has receded into the background, as is shown by the continuation of the sentence. On the connection of this term with "repentance" (μετάνοια), cf. Ign. *Sm.* 9.1: "Moreover it is reasonable for us to return to soberness and . . . to repent towards God." (εὔλογόν ἐστιν λοιπὸν ἀνανῆψαι καὶ . . . εἰς θεὸν μετανοεῖν). On the "snares of the devil," see above on 1 Tim 3:7. "Captured" (ἐζωγρημένοι), because it comes directly after "snare" (παγίς), is surely meant as an explanation of the latter image. "By him" (ὑπ᾽ αὐ-τοῦ) then refers neither to God nor to the "servant of the Lord" (δοῦλος κυρίου), but rather to the devil. "To do his will" (εἰς τὸ ἐκείνου θέλημα) can be seen as continuing the thought "they might escape from the snare" (ἀνανήψωσιν ἐκ τῆς . . . παγίδος). But "captured" (ἐζωγρημένοι), then standing alone, would not completely explain the image of the snare. Therefore "to do his will" probably belongs to the participial clause ("since they have been captured") after all. "That one" (ἐκεῖνος) is then so weakened that it is almost equivalent to "he" (αὐτός). It is used here to avoid a repetition after "by him" (ὑπ᾽ αὐτοῦ). Both pronouns thus refer to the devil.

25 See Acts 5:31; 11:18; and, in addition, 17:30. Cf. Conzelmann, *Luke*, 100f. See also Wisd Sol 12:19 in comparison with 12:10. Cf. Johannes Behm, *TDNT* 4, pp. 976–1008, esp. 989ff.

26 See also *1 Clem.* 7.4; *Barn.* 16.9; *Herm. sim.* 8.6.1f.

3

Heretics are the Sinners of the Last Days

1   You should know that in the last days hard times will come. 2/ For men will be selfish and greedy, boastful, arrogant, blasphemers, disobedient to their parents, ungrateful, wicked, 3/ intolerant, intransigent, slanderers, without self–control, savage, not loving the good, 4/ traitors, reckless, puffed up, devoted to pleasure rather than devout, 5/ who appear to be religious but deny the power of religion. Avoid such people. 6/ Among them are those people who make their way into households and (with their talk) ensnare idle women who, overwhelmed with sins and driven by all kinds of desires, 7/ study continually but are never able to come to the recognition of the truth. 8/ Just as Jannes and Jambres opposed Moses, so also these people oppose the truth; their minds are corrupted and their faith does not pass the test. 9/ But they will not make further progress; for their folly will become plain to everyone, just as it was with their (Jannes' and Jambres') folly.

This is the section of the letter actually dealing with heretics. Its introduction shows such a great affinity with 1 Tim 4:1ff that one must regard both pericopes as variants of the same theme. That is altogether clear when one considers the characterization of the opponents in vss 8 and 9. The judgment will naturally be different if a fundamental distinction is made by the interpreter of these epistles between the polemic against heretics and the battle against notorious sinners.[1] The form of the presentation does not invite this interpretation. Motifs deriving from the form of the farewell address are more apparent here than in the parallel passage.[2]

■ **1** Vss 1–5 depict the corruption of the last days[3] in a long list of vices.[4] In v 1 the opponents attacked are explicitly identified with those sinners of the last days.

Such an identification was not necessary in 1 Tim 4:1; it was obvious. In the case of 2 Tim 3, it is a concomitant of the stylization of the whole epistle as a testament of Paul. The catalogue of vices is intended to be taken as a whole, since it is traditional, and is not meant to accuse the opponents of having committed any or all of the particular sins mentioned. Only v 5 seems an exception; on this see below.

■ **2–4** Notice the coupling of adjectives. It is not carried out consistently, but is achieved frequently by means of

---

1   Such a distinction is made by B. Weiss, *ad loc.*, and Michaelis, *Echtheitsfrage*; see above, pp. 65f, the excursus to 1 Tim 4:5, section 1.

2   See Johannes Munck, "Discours d'adieu", 155ff.

3   On this see the Commentary on Habakkuk from Qumran (1 QpHab II. 5ff); cf. Elliger, *Habakuk-Kommentar*, 168ff and 278f; see also Kuhn, "Die in Palästina gefundenen hebräischen Texte," 208f.

4   See Lietzmann, *Römer*, the excursus to Rom 1:31; Vögtle, *Tugend– und Lasterkataloge*, 15ff and 232ff; cf. above on 1 Tim 1:9.

assonance either at the beginning or at the end of words.[5] The list of vices is in many ways reminiscent of Rom 1:30f. On "intransigent" (ἄσπονδος) and "not loving the good" (ἀφιλάγαθος), see Bauer, *s.v.*; on the latter term also below on Tit 1:8. On "selfish" (φίλαυτος) see Aristotle.[6] On "savage" (ἀνήμερος), see Epict., *Diss.* 1.3.7: "and others (of us become like) lions, wild and savage and untamed" (οἱ δὲ λέουσιν (*scil.* ὅμοιοι γινόμεθα) ἄγριοι καὶ θηριώδεις καὶ ἀνήμεροι). On "reckless" (προπετής) see *1 Clem.* 1.1; the word occurs also several times in Epictetus. On "devoted to pleasure" (φιλήδονος) see the sayings of Epictetus in Stob., *Ecl.* 3.170 (169, Hense).

■ **5** Here the list of vices loses its traditional character; the following words thus contain a specific reproach against the heretics. On "appearance" (μόρφωσις, translated as "appear to be"), cf. Philo. *Plant.* 70 "for even now there are some who wear the appearance of piety, men who in a petty spirit find fault with the literal sense of the word, urging that it is irreligious and dangerous to speak of God as the portion of man" (ἐπεὶ καὶ νῦν εἰσί τινες τῶν ἐπιμορφαζόντων εὐσέβειαν, οἳ τὸ πρόχειρον τοῦ λόγου παρασυκοφαντοῦσι φάσκοντες οὔθ' ὅσιον οὔτ' ἀσφαλὲς εἶναι λέγειν ἀνθρώπου θεὸν κλῆρον) [Loeb modified]. See also Rom 2:20.

■ **6, 7** The opponents who have been spoken of as sinners are now depicted ironically. Their propaganda spreads primarily to women[7] with an unsavory past.[8] The reprimand that they do nothing but learn recalls the Stoic warning not to remain in the stage of learning.[9] Above all one is reminded of the repudiation of women who are eager to learn and ask questions in 1 Cor 14:35 and 1 Tim 2:11. From the latter passage we concluded that emancipation tendencies may be present. That agrees with the Gnostic spiritualism which must be presupposed on the opponents' part. It is precisely the philosophical-religious propaganda of syncretism, with its claim to supernatural authority, which seems to have found an audience among women.[10] A bad reputation clearly made little difference in such cases.[11] If one assumes a libertine tendency among the heretics, one could point to the "desires" which the author mentions here. But if he had wished to accuse his opponents of unchastity, he would probably have said it much more clearly.[12] Judging by the accounts of the conversion of women in the apocryphal acts of the apostles, the Gnostics instead brought such women to a strict personal asceticism. One may trace the preference of the Gnostics for this activity to repressed sexuality (Lütgert); but as far as their characterization is concerned, nothing is gained by doing so.[13]

■ **8** The subject is naturally "those who make their way into households" (ἐνδύνοντες, v 6), not "the idle women" (γυναικάρια). According to Jewish tradi-

---

5   This is, of course, difficult to imitate in a translation, but has been attempted in a few instances above, e.g. "intolerant, intransigent" [Ed.]. A good example of this stylistic technique in a catalogue is the long catalogue of vices in Philo, *Sacr AC.* 32 (reprinted also in Lietzmann, *Römer*, Appendix 2).

6   Cf. *Aristoteles*, ed. Bekker (Academia Regia Borussica: 1831ff), 4: *Index*, p. 818.

7   "Little" or "idle women" (γυναικάρια) is a mocking diminutive form, also used in Epictetus.

8   On "heap up," "overwhelm" (σωρεύω) see *Barn.* 4.6: "heaping up your sins" (ἐπισωρεύοντας ταῖς ἁμαρτίαις ὑμῶν).

9   See Musonius (pp. 22f, Hense) and Epict., *Diss.* 2.9.13: "That is why the philosophers admonish us not to be satisfied with merely learning, but to add thereto practice also and then training" (διὰ τοῦτο παραγγέλλουσιν οἱ φιλόσοφοι μὴ ἀρκεῖσθαι μόνῳ τῷ μαθεῖν ἀλλὰ καὶ μελέτην προσλαμβάνειν εἶτα ἄσκησιν). Cf. especially the ridicule which Epictetus (*Diss.* 1.29.35) pours on the young man who "weeps when the crisis calls" (καλέσαντος τοῦ καιροῦ) and says: "I wanted to keep on learning" (ἤθελον ἔτι μανθάνειν).

10 See Lucian, *Alex.* 6, and Irenaeus, *Adv. haer.* 1.13.3, writing on the Gnostic Marcus: "For he especially occupied himself with women, and among women, those who wore fine and purple garments and were the most wealthy" (μάλιστα γὰρ περὶ γυναῖκας ἀσχολεῖται καὶ τούτων τὰς εὐπαρύφους καὶ περιπορφύρους καὶ πλουσιωτάτας) [trans. by Ed.].

11 See Justin, *Apol.* 1.26.3 writing on Simon Magus: "And they call a certain Helen, who went about with him at that time and who had formerly been in a brothel, the First Thought, generated by him." (καὶ Ἑλένην τινά, τὴν περινοστήσασαν αὐτῷ κατ' ἐκεῖνο τοῦ καιροῦ, πρότερον ἐπὶ τέγους σταθεῖσαν, τὴν ὑπ' αὐτοῦ ἔννοιαν πρώτην γενομένην λέγουσι) [trans. by Ed.]. See also Irenaeus, *Adv. haer.* 1.23.2.

12 See Irenaeus, *Adv. haer.* 1.13.3; and the story of the lying prophets Ahab and Zedekiah, *Tanḥuma* ויקרא 134a (quoted in Billerbeck, 3, p. 659).

13 For further discussion, see the excursus to 1 Tim 4: 5.

tion,[14] Jannes and Jambres are the names of the magicians who argued against Moses before Pharaoh (Ex 7:8ff). No mention is made of these names in Philo (*Vit. Mos.* 1.91ff). A new attestation (and for the time being the earliest one) of this tradition occurs in *The Damascus Document* (CD V 17–19): "For formerly Moses and Aaron arose by the hand of the Prince of Light; but Belial raised up Jannes and his brother, in his cunning, when Israel was saved for the first time" [trans. by Dupont–Sommer, *Essene Writings*, p. 130]. Further, see Pliny, *Hist. Nat.* 30.2.11: "There is yet another branch of magic, derived from Moses, Jannes, Lotapes and the Jews, but living many thousand years after Zoroaster" (est et alia magices factio a Mose et Janne et Lotape ac Judaeis pendens, sed multis milibus annorum post Zoroastrem). See also Apuleius, *Apology* 90: "I am ready to be any magician you please—the great Carmendas himself or Damigeron or Moses of whom you have heard, or Jannes or Apollobex or Dardanus himself or any sorcerer of note from the time of Zoroaster and Ostanes till now" (ego ille sim Carmendas uel Damigeron uel his Moses uel Johannes uel Apollobex uel ipse Dardanus uel quicumque alius post Zoroastren et Hostanen inter magos celebratus est). See also Numenius as cited in Eusebius of Caesarea, *Preap. Ev.* 9, 8 (GCS 43, 1, ed. Karl Mras): "Next were Jannes and Jambres, sacred scribes of the Egyptians, men considered to be inferior to no one in magical ability, at the time when the Jews were being expelled from Egypt" (τὰ δ᾽ ἑξῆς Ἰαννῆς καὶ Ἰαμβρῆς Αἰγύπτιοι ἱερογραμματεῖς, ἄνδρες οὐδενὸς ἥττους μαγεῦσαι κριθέντες εἶναι, ἐπὶ Ἰουδαίων ἐξελαυνο-μένων ἐξ Αἰγύπτου) [trans. by Ed.].[15] The midrash *Tanḥuma*, commenting on Ex 32:1, relates: "and the two magicians of Egypt with them, and their names were Jonos and Jombros, who did all these works of magic before Pharaoh, as it is written in Exodus (7:11)" [Trans.].[16] See the *Evangelium Nicodemi* (*Acta Pilati A*) 5 (p. 239, Tischendorf): "And there were the servants of Pharaoh, and they also did signs not a few which Moses did, and the Egyptians held them as gods, Jannes and Jambres. And since the signs which they did were not from God, they perished themselves and those who believed in them." (καὶ ἦσαν ἐκεῖ ἄνδρες θεράποντες Φαραὼ Ἰαννῆς καὶ Ἰαμβρῆς, καὶ ἐποίησαν καὶ αὐτοὶ σημεῖα οὐκ ὀλίγα ἃ ἐποίει Μωυσῆς, καὶ εἶχον αὐτοὺς οἱ Αἰγύπτιοι ὡς θεοὺς, τὸν Ἰαννῆν καὶ τὸν Ἰαμβρῆν. καὶ ἐπειδὴ τὰ σημεῖα ἃ ἐποίησαν οὐκ ἦσαν ἐκ θεοῦ ἀπώλοντο καὶ αὐτοὶ καὶ οἱ πιστεύοντες αὐτοῖς) [trans. Hennecke–Schneemelcher 1, p. 456]. See also the *Mart. Pt. et Pl.* 34 (Lipsius–Bonnet 1, p. 148): "For just as the Egyptians Jannes and Jambres deceived Pharaoh and his army until they were drowned in the sea, so also etc." (καὶ ὥσπερ οἱ Αἰγύπτιοι Ἰαννῆς καὶ Ἰαμβρῆς ἐπλάνησαν τὸν Φαραὼ καὶ τὸ στρατόπεδον αὐτοῦ ἕως τοῦ καταποντισθῆναι ἐν τῇ θαλάσσῃ, οὕτως κτλ.) [Trans.].[17] There is no typology of the wilderness generation in the Pastoral Epistles; the reproach has parenetic significance.

■ **9** rounds out the preceding material by means of an encouraging look to the future.

---

14 See Theodoret (III, p. 689, Schulze): "from the unwritten teaching of the Jews" (ἐκ τῆς ἀγράφου τῶν Ἰουδαίων διδασκαλίας) [trans. by Ed.].

15 Cf. also Origen, *Cels.* 4.51 (GCS I, p. 324, Koetschau), on Numenius.

16 For the text of this midrash, see S. Buber, מדרש תנחומא (Wilna: 1885); for further literature, see Strack, *Introduction*, 336. According to the targum *Pseudo–Jonathan*, the magicians named here appear in Exod 1:15, 7:11, and Num 22:22 (as servants of Bileam). Cf. also Menachoth 85 a and the Shemoth Rabba on Exod 7:12 (See *The Midrash Rabbah*, gen. ed. H. Freedman, vol. 3, *Exodus*, ed. S. M. Lehrman [London: Soncino, 1939], p. 123f).

17 Further detailed Rabbinic quotations can be found in Billerbeck, 3, pp. 661ff; the Christian literature and attestations for the "Book of Jannes and Jambres" are found in Schürer, *A History of the Jewish People*, 2³, pp. 149f; cf. further Hugo Odeberg, *TDNT* 3, pp. 192f; Albrecht Oepke, *TDNT* 3, pp. 990f. On the occurrence of the names in pagan literature, see Joseph Bidez and Franz Cumont, *Les Mages hellénisés: Zoroaster, Ostanes et Hystaspe d'après la tradition grecque*, (Paris: Société d'éditions "Les Belles Lettres," 1938), pp. 11ff.

3

Summary Exhortation

10 But you have faithfully followed my teaching, my conduct, my resolve, faith, patience, love, endurance, **11/** persecutions and sufferings, which I encountered in Antioch, Iconium, and Lystra. Some of these I endured, and from all of them the Lord rescued me. **12/** But all those who want to lead a pious life in Christ Jesus will suffer persecution (in the same way). **13/** Bad people and sorcerers, however, will progress from bad to worse—"Deceived deceivers!"— **14/** But you must stand by these things which you have learned and by which you became convinced. And consider from whom you learned it, **15/** and (be aware of the fact) that ever since you were a child you have known the holy writings which enable you to have wisdom for salvation through the faith in Christ Jesus. **16/** Every scripture that is inspired by God is also salutary for teaching, for reproof, for improvement, and for education in righteousness, **17/** so that the man of God may be fit, and prepared for every good work.

4

1 I adjure you before God and Christ Jesus who will judge (the) living and (the) dead, and at his appearance and his kingdom: **2/** preach the word, stand by—whether you are expected or not—, reprove, threaten, admonish with all patience and instruction. **3/** For the time will come when they will not endure the sound teaching, but will gather together teachers after their own fancy, because their ears are itching (for their wisdom), **4/** and then they will turn their ears away from truth and turn to fables. **5/** But you must be sober in all things, endure in sufferings, do the work of the evangelist, fulfill your service! **6/** I (to be sure) am already sacrificed, and the time of my departure has come. **7/** I have fought the good fight. I have completed my course. I have remained faithful. **8/** Now the crown of righteousness is reserved for me which the Lord, the just judge, will bestow on me on that day—not only on me, but on all those who long for his appearance.

The concluding parenesis addressed to Timothy stresses once again the central ideas of the entire epistle: the sufferings of Paul[1] in 3:10f and 4:6–8, the fight against heresy in 3:13 and 4:3, 4, and the role of the tradition[2] in 3:14–17.

■ **10** "Conduct" (ἀγωγή) is the way in which one leads one's life.[3]

■ **11** The reference is to events like those reported in Acts 13:50; 14:2, 19. Paul's persecutions in Timothy's native country are listed. In a genuine Pauline epistle it would seem strange that the troublesome experiences which Paul and Timothy had had together are missing here (Acts 16 and 17)—although this is not to say that authenticity could be denied on this basis alone.

■ **12** The apostle's experience of suffering is applied to all Christians in the form of a general thesis. Thus the verse expresses the intention of these biographical allusions.

■ **13** "Deceived deceivers" is a common phrase.[4] Cf. above all Dio Chrysostom 4.33: "If, however, he falls in with some ignorant and charlatan sophist, the fellow will wear him out by leading him hither and thither, . . . not knowing anything himself but merely guessing, after having been led far afield himself long before by imposters like himself" (ἐὰν δὲ ἀγνοοῦντι καὶ ἀλαζόνι σοφιστῇ (scil. περιπέσῃ) καταρρίψει περιάγων αὐτὸν . . ., οὐδὲν αὐτὸς εἰδὼς ἀλλὰ εἰκάζων, καὶ πολὺ πρότερον αὐτὸς ὑπὸ τοιούτων ἀλαζόνων πεπλανημένος); 48.10: "and is it that you are the victims of deception now, or were you guilty of deception then?" (καὶ νῦν ἀπατώμενοι μᾶλλον ἢ τότε ἐξαπατῶντες;)); Philo, Migr. Abr. 83: "they are deceived while they think they are deceiving" (ἀπατᾶν δοκοῦντες ἀπατῶνται), referring to "those who use charms and enchantments, when they bring their trickery to play against the Divine Word" (ἐπαοιδοὶ καὶ φαρμακευταὶ ἀντισοφιστεύον-τες τῷ θείῳ λόγῳ) [Loeb modified]; Porphyr. Vit. Plot. 16: "they were deceiving them, though being themselves deceived" (ἐξηπάτων καὶ αὐτοὶ ἠπατημένοι); Augustine, Confessions 7.2: "those deceived deceivers" (deceptos illos et deceptores).[5] If, however, we are dealing with a common phrase consisting of two parts, then these two parts, "those who deceive" (πλανῶντες) and "those who are deceived" (πλανώμενοι), do not each designate a separate class of people. The familiar phrase refers as a whole rather to the "sorcerers" who have been seduced themselves, either by the devil (see 2 Tim 2:26) or by other sorcerers.

■ **14** The concept of tradition is first stressed by means of the expression "from whom you have learned" (παρὰ τίνων). In addition perhaps to Timothy's mother and grandmother (see 2 Tim 1:5), the reference is to his teachers, above all to Paul. Cf. Marcus Aurelius' reflection about himself (M. Ant. 1.1ff) in which he traces his own character traits to his forebears and teachers.

■ **15** The concept of tradition is, however, also emphasized with "ever since you were a child" (ἀπὸ βρέφους). To be sure, one cannot take the secondary clause "that you have known" (ὅτι οἶδας) as parallel with "consider" (εἰδώς), and therefore also directly dependent on the main clause "you must stand by those things"; rather, it must be subordinated to "consider" (εἰδώς): "consider first of all from whom you have learned, and secondly, how early you learned it." "Holy writings" (ἱερὰ γράμματα) is the name for the holy scriptures of the OT in Greek–speaking Judaism.[6] The lack of an article may be explained by the technical character of the

---

1   On these see above pp. 98ff, on 2 Tim 1:3–14.

2   On this see above pp. 98ff, 107f, on 2 Tim 1:3–14 and 2:1, 2.

3   See Ditt. Or. I, 223.15: "And you seem in general to conduct your life this way" (φαίνεσθε γὰρ καθόλου ἀγωγῆι ταύτῃ χρῆσθαι) [trans. by Ed.]; cf. ibid. 474.9; 485.3; P. Tebt. I 24.57; P. Par. 61.12; 63 col. 9.38; M. Ant. 1.6; 1 Clem. 47.6.

4   This has been demonstrated by Paul Wendland, "Miszellen. Betrogene Betrüger," Rheinisches Museum für Philologie 49 (1894): 309–10.

5   This passage need not be dependent on 2 Tim 3:13 [trans. of the last two passages above by Ed.].

6   See Philo, Vit. Mos. 2.292: "Such, as recorded by the Holy Scriptures, was . . . the end of Moses, king, lawgiver, high-priest, . . . prophet" (τοιαύτη δὲ καὶ ἡ τελευτὴ τοῦ βασιλέως καὶ νομοθέτου καὶ ἀρχιερέως καὶ προφήτου Μωυσέως διὰ τῶν ἱερῶν γραμμάτων μνημονεύεται); Josephus, Ant. 10.210: "let him take the trouble to read the book of Daniel which he will find among the sacred writings" (σπουδα-σάτω τὸ βιβλίον ἀναγνῶναι τὸ Δανιήλου. εὑρήσει δὲ τοῦτ' ἐν τοῖς ἱεροῖς γράμμασιν). See further Ditt. Or. I 56.36: "On the day on which the star of Isis rises, which is considered, because of the Holy Scriptures, to mark the new year" (τῆι ἡμέραι ἐν ἧι ἐπιτέλλει τὸ ἄστρον τὸ τῆς Ἴσιος, ἣ νομίζεται διὰ τῶν ἱερῶν γραμμάτων νέον ἔτος εἶναι) [trans. by Ed.].

expression.[7] The Greek word translated by "holy" (ἱερός) is used in this sense only here in the entire NT.[8]

■ **16** "Every scripture" (πᾶσα γραφή) means either "any passage of scripture"—then "scripture" (γραφή) is used as in Acts 8:35—or "every scripture"—in that case "scripture" (γραφή) takes the place of the singular of "writings" (γράμματα). The solemn word "scripture" does not necessarily require a determining attribute like "inspired by God" (θεόπνευστος). Yet the emphasis of the passage doubtless lies, not on the concept of inspiration, but on the usefulness of the inspired scriptures. For the question is here to what extent "holy writings" enable a man "to have wisdom." Thus "inspired by God" (θεόπνευστος) is perhaps to be taken attributively.[9] On the doctrine of inspiration in Judaism, see Josephus, *Ap.* 1.31ff; and, above all, the depiction of the "prophet possessed by God" (προφήτης θεοφόρητος) in Philo, *Spec. leg.* 1.65; 4.49.[10] In Christianity, see 2 Petr 1:21; Justin, *Apol.* 1.36; Athenagoras, *Suppl.* 9; Theophilus, *Autol.* 2.9. On the usefulness of scripture, see Epictetus *Diss.* 3.21.15 (on the Eleusinian mysteries): "Only thus do the Mysteries become helpful, only thus do we arrive at the impression that all these things were established by men of old time for the purpose of education and for the amendment of our life." (οὕτως ὠφέλιμα γίνεται τὰ μυστήρια, οὕτως εἰς φαντασίαν ἐρχόμεθα, ὅτι ἐπὶ παιδείᾳ καὶ ἐπανορθώσει τοῦ βίου κατεστάθη

πάντα ταῦτα ὑπὸ τῶν παλαιῶν).

■ **17** On "man of God" (ἄνθρωπος θεοῦ), see above on 1 Tim 6:11; on "good work" (ἔργον ἀγαθόν), see above on 1 Tim 2:10. The understanding of the scriptures (i.e. of the OT) which is transmitted by the tradition makes the leader of the congregation fit for the fight against the false teaching.

■ **4:1** After the doctrinal portion of 3:15–17, the parenesis is taken up again by means of a solemn entreaty. It is to be regarded as formulaic, as in 1 Tim 5:21, and is to an even greater extent kerygmatic in character.[11]

■ **2** "Stand by" (ἐπίστηθι), since it receives its tone only from the word–play "whether you are requested or not," literally "in season—out of season," (εὐκαίρως ἀκαίρως), can be taken in its original meaning. On the style of the parenesis (unconnected exhortations), cf. 1 Petr 5:10 and Plutarch.[12]

■ **3** On "sound teaching" (ὑγιαίνουσα διδασκαλία), see the excursus to 1 Tim 1:10. ἀκοή here has the meaning "ear"; see Acts 17:20.[13] On the expression "their ears are itching," see Clem. Alex., *Strom.* I, 3.22.5 (p. 15, Stählin): "Tickling and titillating in an unmanly fashion, I think, ears which are plagued with itching" (κνήθοντες καὶ γαργαλίζοντες οὐκ ἀνδρικῶς, ἐμοὶ δοκεῖν, τὰς ἀκοὰς τῶν κνήσασθαι γλιχομένων) [trans. by Ed.]. In 2 Tim 4:3, as in 1 Tim 4:1ff, it is obvious that the future which "Paul" predicts is already a present reality

---

7   This is corrected in the manuscripts in A C* ℵ. Cf. Philo, *Poster. C.* 158: "For it is said in the sacred books" (λέγεται γὰρ ἐν ἱεραῖς βίβλοις); *Rer. div. her.* 106 "in the sacred scripture" (ἐν ἱεραῖς γραφαῖς) [Loeb modified].

8   See Eduard Williger, *Hagios* (Giessen: Töpelmann, 1922), p. 96.

9   See also Theodore of Mopsuestia and Ambst. On "inspired by God" (θεόπνευστος), cf. Pseudo–Phocylides 129: "The doctrine of the divinely inspired wisdom is the best" (τῆς δὲ θεοπνεύστου σοφίης λόγος ἐστὶν ἄριστος) [trans. by Ed.]; Plutarch, *Moralia*, p. 904 F (variant θεοπέμπτους); *Sib.* 5.308 and 406 (Geffcken). Cf. Johannes Leipoldt, "Die Frühgeschichte der Lehre von der göttlichen Eingebung," *ZNW* 44 (1952–53): 118–45.

10 Cf. also *Rer. div. her.* 263ff. In this passage, in a reference to Plato (*Ion* 534 b), it is said that, in the prophet, human mental activity is replaced by the sole rulership of the divine spirit.

11 See above pp. 30f and 88f, on 1 Tim 1:17 and 6:13; cf. Lietzmann, "Symbolstudien" (2), p. 269. Cf. also *Act. Pt.* 1 (*Actus Vercellenses*) (Lipsius–Bonnet 1,

p. 46.1ff): "But the brethren besought Paul by the coming of our Lord Jesus Christ etc." (lucebant [perhaps urgebant?] autem fratres Paulum per adventum domini nostri Jesu Christi etc.); as well as the second article of the Apostles' Creed; see Ernst von Dobschütz, *Das Apostolicum in biblisch–theologischer Bedeutung*, Aus der Welt der Religion, Biblische Reihe (Giessen: Töpelmann, 1932), 32. On "appearance" (ἐπιφάνεια) see above p. 104, the second excursus to 2 Tim 1:10; on the "kingdom of Christ" see Bultmann, *Theology*, 1, p. 78.

12 1 Petr 5:10; Plutarch, *Lib. educ.* 16 (p. 12 C); see Almqvist, *Plutarch und das NT*, p. 127.

13 See also Hans Windisch, *Der Hebräerbrief*, HNT 14 (Tübingen: J. C. B. Mohr [Paul Siebeck], ²1931) on Heb 5:11; Liddell–Scott, s.v.

14 See above pp. 24f and 65f, the excursus to 1 Tim 1:10 and 1 Tim 4:5 (section 1c).

for the situation of the letters. For the enemies of future times who are named here are none other than the heretical opponents of the Pastoral Epistles; note the use of "fables" (μῦθοι) and the contrast to the "sound teaching" (ὑγιαίνουσα διδασκαλία).[14]

■ **4, 5** On "to turn to" (ἐκτρέπεσθαι), see above on 1 Tim 1:6. On "to be sober" (νήφειν), see *Corp. Herm.* 7.1: "Stop and be sober" (στῆτε νήψαντες).[15]

Vss 6–8 comprise the solemn conclusion of the parenesis.

■ **6** The words "I am sacrificed" (σπένδομαι) and "my departure" (ἀνάλυσις) are strongly reminiscent of Paul's epistle to the Philippians.[16] "Departure" is also used in *1 Clem.* 44.5 and by Philo to designate the end of life; cf. Philo, *Flacc.* 187: "at the final departure from life" (τὴν ἐκ τοῦ βίου τελευταίαν ἀνάλυσιν) [Loeb modified].

■ **7** follows upon v 6, which strongly reflects the awareness of impending death, like a triumphant proclamation which reviews the life of the apostle. It consists of three parallel clauses, of which two use images from the stadium, well–known from 1 Cor 9:24ff.[17] "To keep faith" (πίστιν τηρεῖν) is a fixed expression.[18] On "I have completed my course" (τὸν δρόμον τετέλεκα), cf. Virgil, *Aen.* 4.653, in which Dido says: "I have lived and accomplished the course which fortune appointed" (vixi et quem dederat cursum Fortuna peregi) [trans.

by Ed.].[19]

■ **8** "It is reserved for" (ἀπόκειται) is an expression which has almost become technical in edicts of commendation, in which recognition was bestowed on someone by oriental kings. It is perhaps originally connected with the fact that the names of those who received such honors were entered in the annals of the state.[20] This expression is reminiscent of the terminology of martyrdom. In accounts of martyrdom it appears first in the Martyrdom of Polycarp (cf. 17.1; 19.2), and celebrates the virtues of the martyrs in a typical Hellenistic fashion (as in 4 Macc).[21]

According to the tenor of the passage (see also 2 Tim 4:1), "appearance" (ἐπιφάνεια) is best understood as a reference to the parousia. The success of the apostolic life is described here in classic formulations. The sensibilities of modern scholars balk at having to deny the Pauline authorship of such passages as this; the "fragment hypothesis" finds support in such words. But one may still ask (without claiming that the answer decides the question of authenticity) whether Paul himself in such a situation would have spoken only of his success and not also of his weakness, whether he would have praised only *his* actions and not much rather *God's* action.

---

15 See also Dibelius, *Thessalonicher, Philipper*, on 1 Thess. 5:6.

16 Phil 2:17 and 1:23; see Dibelius, *Thessalonicher, Philipper*, on Phil 1:23 and 2:17.

17 See also 2 Tim 2:5; 1 Tim 6:11; cf. *BMI* III, 604, lines 7ff: "He competed in three contests and won the crown in two" (ἠγωνίσατο ἀγῶνας τρεῖς, ἐστέφθη δύω) [trans. by Ed.].

18 See Polybius 6.56.13 and 10.37.9; Josephus, *Bell.* 6.345 in the speech of Titus: "I gave pledges of protection to deserters, I kept the faith with them when they fled to me." (δεξιὰς αὐτομόλοις ἔδωκα, καταφυγοῦσι πίστεις ἐτήρησα); *BMI* III, 587ᵇ lines 5ff: "I have kept faith" (τὴν πίστιν ἐτήρησα); Ditt. *Or.* I, 339.46f: "Those who will keep the faith piously and righteously" (τοὺς τὴν πίστιν εὐσεβῶς τε καὶ δικαίως τηρήσοντας) [trans. by Ed.].

19 I am indebted to Günther Bornkamm for this reference.

20 See F. Pfister, "Zur Wendung ἀπόκειταί μοι ὁ τῆς δικαιοσύνης στέφανος," *ZNW* 15 (1914): 94–6. See also the inscription of Antiochus I of Commagene in Ditt. *Or.* I, 383.189ff: "Favor for their piety is reserved for them from gods and heroes" (οἷς ἀποκείσεται παρὰ θεῶν καὶ ἡρώων χάρις εὐσεβείας); Ditt. *Syll.* I, 22.15ff: "Therefore great favour is reserved for you in the king's household" ([δ]ιὰ ταῦτά σοι κεῖσεται μεγάλη χάρις ἐμ βασιλέως οἴκωι); Demophilus, *Similitudines* No. 22 (p. 6, Orelli): "For those who run in the foot races, there is reserved for them, at the finishing line, the prize of victory, and for those who have loved toils, at old age, the first prize for wisdom" (τοῖς μὲν σταδιοδρομοῦσιν ἐπὶ τῷ τέρματι τὸ βραβεῖον τῆς νίκης, τοῖς δὲ φιλοπονήσασιν ἐπὶ τῷ γήρους τὸ πρωτεῖον τῆς φρονήσεως ἀπόκειται); P. Par. 63, col. 9, line 47: "For a vengeance is reserved from God for those who have not preferred to live according to the best principles" (ἀπόκειται γὰρ παρὰ θ[εοῦ] μῆνις τοῖς μὴ κατὰ τὸ βέλτιστον [προαι]ρουμένοις ζῆν); Thucydides 1.120; Achilles Tatius 3.22 (p. 107, Hercher) [trans. in this footnote by Ed.].

21 On the "crown" see Ludwig Deubner, "Die Bedeutung des Kranzes im klassischen Altertum," *ARW* 30 (1933): 70–104; Karl Baus, *Der Kranz in Antike und Christentum* (Bonn: Hanstein, 1940).

4

Description of Paul's Situation

9   **Make every effort to come to me quickly. 10/ For Demas has left me, because he fell in love with this world, and he has gone to Thessalonica, Crescens to Galatia, Titus to Dalmatia; 11/ only Luke is staying with me. Get Mark and bring him with you, for I can make good use of his services. 12/ Tychicus I have sent to Ephesus.**

4:9-21 is made up of personal references and greetings.

■ **10, 11** The depiction of Paul deserted by almost everyone supplements 2 Tim 1:15. The picture is stylized: note the contradiction to v 21, a contradiction which is not to be brushed aside by literary critical manipulations (cf. Mk 13:13 and Lk 21:16). As a result, the motif of abandonment is characteristically complemented with the motif of support provided by the Lord (this concept was already intimated in 3:11). It is also typical of the writer that he places side by side a rebuke (for Demas), and a commendation (for Mark). Among the proper names which follow, Demas, Luke, and Mark recall the lists of greetings in the letters to the Colossians and to Philemon; but in the latter Demas is spoken of as being (still?) present, and Mark as absent (again?). In the Acts of Paul (12ff; Lipsius–Bonnet 1, pp. 244f) Demas, together with Hermogenes, is counted among the enemies of Paul. (Does this indicate dependence upon 2 Tim or reliance upon the tradition used by the Pastorals?) On the personal references in general, see below, the excursus to 2 Tim 4:21; on the "innuendo against Thessalonica," see Bauer.[1] At least later scribes (unless that is the original reading) assumed that Crescens was sent to Gaul.[2]

Moreover, even the better attested reading "Galatia" (Γαλατίαν) can be understood as referring to Gaul, if the context suggests it.[3] Therefore, the translation of 2 Tim 4:10 will depend upon the interpretation of the situation (see the excursus to 2 Tim 4:21). If Caesarea is meant to be conceived of as the place of composition, Galatia is more probable; if Rome, Gaul is preferable.[4] "Dalmatia" (Δαλματία) is the southern part of Illyria.[5] Perhaps it is essential for understanding the origin of this passage that the same area may be meant here, as the one Paul mentions in Rom 15:19.[6]

■ **12** It is impossible to conclude, on the basis of the reference to Ephesus, that Timothy is not thought of as being in Ephesus at this time (nor does 2 Tim 1:18 allow such a conclusion). Paul also mentions the city by name in 1 Cor, which was written in Ephesus (1 Cor 15:32 and 16:8; but see below on 2 Tim 4:19).

---

1   See Bauer, *Orthodoxy and Heresy*, 74f.

2   See the reading "Gaul" (Γαλλίαν) in ℵ C Eus Epiph instead of "Galatia"; this tradition may be reflected also in the *Act. Pl.* 1 (Lipsius–Bonnet 1, p. 104), where Titus, who is coming from Dalmatia, and Luke (not Crescens) are mentioned as coming from Gaul (but the Latin text has "Galilee"!). On Titus see below pp. 153f, the excursus to Tit 3:14, section 3. On the substitution of Luke for Crescens, see Theodor Zahn, *Geschichte des neutestamentlichen Kanons* (Erlangen and Leipzig: Deichert, 1890–92), 2, p. 888.

3   Cf. *Monumentum Ancyranum* 6.20 (in: KIT 29f): "From Spain and Galatia" (ἐξ Ἱσπανίας καὶ

Γαλατίας, also 13.20; 14.4f); 16.1f: "From Spain and Galatia and from the Dalmatians" (ἐξ Ἱσπανίας καὶ Γαλατίας καὶ παρὰ Δαλματῶν). Further examples can be found in Zahn, *Introduction*, 2, section 33, n. 8.

4   See Theodoret (III, p. 694, Schulze).

5   See Theodor Mommsen, *Römische Geschichte* (Berlin: Weidmann, ²1856–57), 5, pp. 19f; *CIL* III, part 1, pp. 271, 279ff; on the extension of the concept Illyria, see Weber, *Hadrianus*, p. 55.

6   See below pp. 127f, the second excursus to 2 Tim 4:21, section 2.

4

13 When you come, bring the coat that I left in Troas with Carpus, and also the books, especially the parchments. 14/ Alexander the coppersmith did me a great deal of harm—the Lord will give him (his) recompense according to his deed!—15/ you should also be on your guard against him, because he resisted our words very much.

■ **13** "Coat" (φαιλόνης) is a word that has been formed by inversion from the Greek word φαινόλης (is there a connection with the Latin word "cloak" (*paenula*)?).[7] But now we also know the word and its diminutive, in the form attested here, from the papyri.[8] One should not try to interpret the word as a reference to the leather case for papyrus scrolls (διφθέρα).[9] Is there a connection between the reference to the coat which was left behind in Troas and the march which Paul made on foot from Troas to Assos, which is mentioned in Acts 20:13? The "parchments" (μεμβράναι—a Latin loan word) is perhaps a reference to scrolls.[10] By "books" the author means these "parchments" (μεμβράναι) and other things, hence perhaps also books of papyri. The usual writing material (even for the writers of the NT) was still papyrus at that time.[11]

■ **14** "Alexander" ('Αλέξανδρος) is usually identified with the man mentioned in 1 Tim 1:20. In that case, the person in question clearly had not yet been "handed over to Satan."[12]

It cannot be determined with certainty whether the author himself had heard of an apostate Christian by this name, or if this is simply an allusion to Acts 19:33f.[13] Is "the Lord will give him his recompense" (ἀποδώσει κτλ.) perhaps a Jewish curse formula formed on the analogy of Ps 61:13 and Pr 24:12? Cf. the wish expressed in v 16, where the use of the optative already points to formulaic language.[14]

---

7 On the derivation of the Latin word from the Greek, see Blass–Debrunner 32.30. On the inversion see G. B. Winer, *Grammatik des neutestamentlichen Sprachidioms*, 1867; rev. P. Schmiedel, 1894ff, sect. 5.18; James Hope Moulton and W. F. Howard, *A Grammar of New Testament Greek* 2: *Accidence and Word-Formation* (Edinburgh: T. & T. Clark, 1929), pp. 70, 106 and 155. On the meaning "coat" for φαινόλης and φαινόλιον see *P. Oxy.* III, 531.14; IV, 736.4; VI, 936.18f; XII, 1584.7, 8; XIV, 1737.9, 15; *P. Giess.* I, 10.21; 79, col. IV 2f; *P. Hamb.* 10.19.

8 See *BGU* III, 816.23f: "and he did not pay the price of the coats" (καὶ τὴν τιμὴ[ν τ]ῶν φαι[λο]νίων οὐκ ἔδωκε); *P. Oxy.* VI, 933.29f: "if it is no trouble to you, find out from Antinoos, whether he bought the coat for your child, and if not, buy it" (ἐάν σοι ἀβαρὲς ᾖ [πεύθου] παρὰ 'Αντινόου εἰ ἠγόρασεν τῷ παιδίῳ σου τὸ φαινόλιον, εἰ δ[ὲ μὴ ἀγό]ρασον); *P. Giess.* I, 12.2ff: "You sent me in good condition the warp and woof for the coats" (ἔπεμψας μοι ὑγιῶς τὸν στήμονα καὶ τὴν κρόκην τῶν φαιλωνίων). The fact that the word was common in this form is demonstrated by its appearance in bills and lists; see *P. Fay.* 347: φελονῶν; *P. Gen.* 80.14: φ[ε]λόνιον. The word also occurs as פלייונא in the Talmud (see Billerbeck 3, 666) [trans. in this footnote by Ed.].

9 See Chrysostom (XI, p. 721, Montfaucon): "but some say it is the box where the books were kept" ·

(τινὲς δέ φασι τὸ γλωσσόκομον, ἔνθα τὰ βιβλία ἔκειτο) [trans. by Ed.].

10 Do these scrolls include perhaps the Greek OT? See Theodoret (III, p. 695, Schulze): "He called the scrolls 'parchments,' for that is what the Romans call skins (prepared for writing). In former times they had the divine scriptures in rolls, and even up to the present time the Jews have them in this form" (μεμβράνας τὰ εἰλητὰ κέκληκεν· οὕτω γὰρ 'Ρωμαῖοι καλοῦσι τὰ δέρματα. ἐν εἰλητοῖς δὲ εἶχον πάλαι τὰς θείας γραφάς, οὕτω δὲ καὶ μέχρι τοῦ παρόντος ἔχουσιν οἱ 'Ιουδαῖοι) [trans. by Ed.].

11 On the relation between scroll and codex see Karl Preisendanz, "Zur Papyruskunde," *Handbuch der Bibliothekswissenschaft* 1, ed. G. Leyh (Wiesbaden: Harrassowitz, ²1950), 163ff; Joachim Jeremias, "Der gegenwärtige Stand der frühchristlichen Papyrologie," *ThLZ* 75 (1950): 55–8; C. C. McCown, "Codex and Roll in the New Testament," *HTR* 34 (1941): 219–50.

12 On the relation between the two epistles in general see above p. 71, the excursus to 1 Tim 4:14, section 2.

13 But cf. below pp. 126ff, the two excursi to 4:21. On Acts 19:33f, see Ernst Haenchen, *Die Apostelgeschichte* KEK 3 (Göttingen: Vandenhoeck & Ruprecht, ⁶1968), *ad loc.*

14 Cf. Radermacher, *Grammatik*, p. 164f.

4   **Personal Information
about Paul**

16   **At my first defense no one stood by me,
but everyone had deserted me—may it
not be counted against them!—17/ but
the Lord stood by me and gave me
strength—that through me the preaching might be proclaimed far and wide,
and that all nations might be able to
hear it—and thus I was rescued from the
lion's mouth. 18/ The Lord will (henceforth) rescue me from every evil act,
and he will give me safe conduct into his
heavenly kingdom. Glory be to him for
ever and ever! Amen.**

■ **16–18** The traditional interpretation of this passage[15] is that Paul, now in his second Roman imprisonment, is looking back to the first one and to his successful liberation. The "lion" from which he was rescued would then be Nero. According to this assumption, the apostle would have visited the eastern provinces again during the interval between the two imprisonments (see 2 Tim 4:13, 20). In this case, however, Timothy would have known about the release. Moreover, reading these verses, one has the impression that Paul is still in the same period of imprisonment in which the "first defense" took place. For, after all, he is narrating his fate in order to enjoin Timothy to come as soon as possible—perhaps even before an anticipated second defense. It is therefore more probable to understand "defense" (ἀπολογία) as referring only to a portion of one and the same legal process against Paul, especially if one assumes that the apostle's situation is that of a first or second Roman imprisonment (note, however, that the Pastorals themselves know of only one imprisonment). In that case, "lion" refers to the imperial power.[16] But whoever thinks that this epistle, or a portion of the epistle, points to a Caesarean setting, will be reminded of the hearing in Acts 23:1ff, and even of the appearance of the Lord in Acts 23:11.

If that is possible, the final clause in v 17 would refer to the promise given in Acts 23:11 "you must be a witness also in Rome" (καὶ εἰς Ῥώμην μαρτυρῆσαι). The description of Paul, as one who has been abandoned by all, would reflect what the author thinks about the attitude toward Paul in the primitive Christian community in Palestine. "Lion" could be taken figuratively— not necessarily influenced by the language of the OT;[17] see the comparison of the soldiers with leopards in Ign. *Rom.* 5.1.[18] The ethos of suffering which permeates the whole epistle (see above on 2 Tim 1:3–14) comes once again into play in the impressive connection between information, prayerful petition, and thanksgiving, as well as in the prospect of victory in v 18.

---

15   This interpretation goes back as far as Eusebius, *Hist. eccl.* 2.22.2, 3, and Theodoret (III, p. 695f, Schulze).

16   See Josephus, *Ant.* 18.228: "the lion is dead" (τέθνηκεν ὁ λέων), a reference to the death of Tiberius.

17   One might think of Ps 21:22: "save me from the mouth of the lion" (σῶσόν με ἐκ στόματος λέοντος).

18   For further discussion of the situation in general, see below, the excursus to 4:21.

4

Greetings and Valediction

19   Greet Prisca, Aquila, and the family of Onesiphorus. 20/ Erastus remained in Corinth. I had to leave Trophimus behind in Miletus, because he was sick. 21/ Make every effort to come before the winter. Eubulus, Pudens, Linus, Claudia, and all the brothers here send their greetings.

22   The Lord be with your spirit. Grace be with you.

■ **19–21** bring the final greetings of the letter. The family of Onesiphorus is believed by some scholars to have resided in Ephesus; the basis for this assumption is 2 Tim 1:18. According to the Acts of Paul, Onesiphorus lives in Iconium.[1] It is perhaps from this source that manuscripts 181 and 460 have inserted the three names Lectra, Simmias, and Zenon into the text. But the insertion was made mechanically after "Aquila" so that "Lectra, his wife" (Λέκτραν τὴν γυναῖκα αὐτοῦ) seems to refer to Aquila. He and his wife would be present in Rome according to Rom 16:3—if that chapter belongs to the Epistle to the Romans. The author might, however, have known of a new journey to Asia Minor, or—what is more probable—he may have presupposed, on the basis of Acts 18:19, 26, that the couple was living in Ephesus. According to Acts 19:22 Paul sent Erastus ahead to Macedonia with Timothy. It is not known whether this Erastus is identical with the city accountant of Corinth mentioned in Rom 16:23. According to Acts 20:4, Trophimus belongs with Tychicus among those who were sent out to make the collection. According to Acts 21:29, he was with Paul in Jerusalem. K. Erbes[2] has attempted to resolve the contradiction between the latter passage

and 2 Tim 4:20 in favor of Acts. But there are other explanations for the contradiction. For example, one might take "left behind" (ἀπέλιπον) as the third person ("he left behind")—but that is impossible in this context. Or one might change Μιλήτῳ (Miletus) to Μελίτῃ (Malta), thereby alluding to what took place on the journey to Rome. In that case Trophimus would not have been mentioned in Acts 27:2.[3] The fact that the Roman poet Martial names a Claudia and a Pudens is unimportant since the names are common. Irenaeus (*Adv. haer.* 3.3.3.) asserts that this Linus was the "bishop" of Rome. This would be probable only if this name, known from Greek mythology, were really so unusual as is often believed. Against this assumption is the fact that Martial calls one of his fictitious individuals *Linus*.[4] Another consideration is the inscriptions,[5] which are, after all, more or less random, and hence ought to be weighed heavily in an assessment of how common the names were. That the names are in part Latin proves nothing with respect to the idea that the Pastorals were written in Rome. There is great support for the assumption that Roman names were common in the East.[6]

---

1   See the *Act. Pl.* 2 (Lipsius–Bonnet 1, p. 236), in which it says of him: "(he) went out with his children Simmias and Zeno and his wife Lectra to meet Paul" (ἐξῆλθεν σὺν τοῖς τέκνοις αὐτοῦ Σιμμίᾳ καὶ Ζήνωνι καὶ τῇ γυναικὶ αὐτοῦ Λέκτρᾳ εἰς συνάντησιν Παύλου) [trans. Hennecke–Schneemelcher 2, p. 353].

2   "Zeit und Ziel der Grüsse Röm 16, 3–15 und der Mitteilungen 2 Tim 4, 9–21," *ZNW* 10 (1909): 207ff.

3   For further discussion see the next two excursi below pp. 126ff. On ancient and modern legends which have been attached to the names given in 4:21, see

Zahn, *Introduction* 2, section 33, n. 2.

4   On this point, see the edition of Martial by Friedländer, 2, pp. 373ff. The passages from Martial are: 1.75.1; 2.38.1; 54.1; 4.66.1; 7.10.1; 95.4; 11.25.2; 12.49.1.

5   See *CIG* IV, 8518 p. 261.53; *IG* XIV, 2276.8ff; *CIL* V, 2119; 2528; 3699. On a very doubtful Linus inscription see K. Erbes, "Das Alter der Gräber und Kirchen des Paulus und Petrus in Rom. Eine historisch–antiquarische Untersuchung," *ZKG* 7 (1883): 20.

6   Cf. the indices of the collections of inscriptions mentioned above, or simply compare the names in Rom

The Situation of 2 Timothy

On the basis of 2 Tim 1:17, with less certainty on the basis of 4:16f (see above), and with even less certainty on the basis of 4:6ff (where "Paul" expresses his readiness for death), ancient and modern scholars have considered Rome as the place of composition of 2 Tim. For the most part this thesis is based, especially if the authenticity of the epistle is assumed, on a postulated *second Roman imprisonment* of Paul. This imprisonment is usually placed after a second stay in the East and a second visit to the mission stations in Greece and Asia Minor.[7] But the assumption of a second Roman imprisonment and of a journey to Spain before that imprisonment can be based on *1 Clem.* 5:7 (as well as on the *Muratorian Canon* 38f), only if one includes in that hypothesis the second assumption that the apostle had left the East forever at the time of the first (and probably only) journey to Rome, which is mentioned in Acts 27f. Acts 20:25 and the scanty information about a journey to Spain in general prove that the apostle never again returned to the East. If, therefore, the hypothesis that 2 Tim was written in Rome is based upon the hypothesis of a second imprisonment, the latter is in danger of being automatically rejected along with the former. If they are accepted, it is difficult to situate the writing of 1 Tim and Tit—since the Pastorals themselves know of only one imprisonment.

2 Tim 4:13, 17 make it improbable, though perhaps not impossible, that the epistle belongs to the *"first" imprisonment* (if we assume authenticity). The reference to the evangelization of "all the nations," ($\pi\acute{\alpha}\nu\tau\alpha$ $\tau\grave{\alpha}$ $\acute{\epsilon}\theta\nu\eta$) which is to be made possible by the success of the first defense, must refer to the plans for a journey to Spain. It is rather strange that the coat ($\phi\alpha\iota\lambda\acute{o}\nu\eta s$) and the books ($\beta\iota\beta\lambda\acute{\iota}\alpha$) should have been stored with Carpus for such a long time—about three years. But the hypothesis in question is entirely impossible in light of 4:20. According to Acts 20, Trophimus was left behind in Miletus by Paul at the time of the events reported in

that chapter; according to 1 Tim 4:20, he is lying there as a sick man, years later. Timothy, who is in Ephesus or somewhere nearby, is pictured as knowing nothing about this fact as yet; he only discovers it through a letter from Paul, who is in Rome!

On the other hand, all the personal information in 2 Tim 4:10ff appears to speak for *Caesarea as the place of composition* (while Ephesus seems to be the residence of the addressee). Consider the place names: the apostle's assistants have travelled to Dalmatia, Thessalonica, Ephesus and Galatia (as 4:10 would then naturally be explained); the addressee is in Asia Minor; Paul stopped in Corinth, Troas and Miletus along his way—all this agrees with the route attested in Acts 20f. According to the account in Acts the stay in Miletus was not long before. The reference to the coat left in Troas, according to 2 Tim 4:13, can be connected with the report of the journey on foot to Assos in Acts 20:13. Moreover, there is a good correspondence between Acts 23:1–10, 11 and 2 Tim 4:16f. The list of names in 4:21 (see above) does not provide an argument against the Caesarean hypothesis. But perhaps Timothy's participation in Paul's journey to Jerusalem, apparently implied by Acts 20:4, does supply such an argument, for it would make notices such as 2 Tim 4:20 superfluous. Most of all, however, the mention of Rome in 2 Tim 1:17 seems to exclude the possibility of locating the letter in Caesarea. If one is unwilling to take refuge in improbable assumptions (see above on 2 Tim 1:17), the advocate of authenticity may still take flight into areas about which we know nothing, i.e. to periods in Paul's life which cannot be accounted for (e.g., the hypothesis of a trip to the East after the first Roman imprisonment, see above).

If one holds that the Pastorals are pseudonymous, then it is best to assume that the author simply made mistakes. Perhaps he was also incorrect in presuming that Aquila and Prisca were in Ephesus (see above on 4:19; on 4:20 see the next excursus). It is quite possible that in his statements about Onesiphorus in 2 Tim 1:17, the author

---

16:21ff; one should also recall the role of the Roman army. On this whole question see C. Wessely, "Die lateinischen Elemente in der Gräzität der ägyptischen Papyrusurkunden," *Wiener Studien* 24 (1902): 99–151.

7 See 2 Tim 4:9ff. Michaelis holds this opinion, see *Echtheitsfrage*, 153ff; cf. *ibid.*, 140ff, the review and criticism of the dating by L. Davies (*Pauline Read-*

justments [London, 1927]); George Duncan (*St. Paul's Ephesian Ministry* [London: Hodder & Stoughton, 1929]); P. N. Harrison, *The Problem*; Heinrich Lisco (*Vincula Sanctorum* [Berlin: Schneider & Co., 1907]); and W. Hartke (*Die Sammlung und die ältesten Ausgaben der Paulusbriefe*, Unpub. Diss. [Bonn: 1917]). See also Spicq, pp. LXXVff and 398ff.

did not consider the fact that, according to 2 Tim 4, Paul had not yet visited Rome at all. Naturally the author did not have the sequence of events in Paul's life (reconstructed by the modern historian) as clearly in mind as does a theologian today, though he was familiar with Acts and some of the Pauline epistles.

The attitude of the Acts of Paul is also instructive for understanding these contradictions. If, as is probable, only *one* journey of Paul is presupposed in this work, then the imprisonment in Philippi it reports is identical with the one described in Acts 16. At the time of that arrest, Paul had not yet been in Corinth. Nevertheless, the (apocryphal) Epistle of the Corinthians to Paul (which, according to the Acts of Paul, is addressed to the apostle being held captive in Philippi!) presupposes Paul's visit in Corinth, and so does the apostle's letter in response! It is clearly inconceivable for the author of the Acts of Paul that a time existed in the ministry of the great founder of the Corinthian church, in which he had not yet founded the church in Corinth. Thus the author of the Pastorals, defying all chronological sequence, could have put 2 Tim 1:17 in the mouth of Paul, under the dominant influence of the picture of his hero residing in Rome, even though he writes 2 Tim 4:9ff in order to give the impression that the epistle was composed in Caesarea. It is also conceivable that in this case the author purposely modified what was a well–known situation.[8] If that is so, the author may have written 2 Tim 1:19 quite deliberately in order to alter the usual picture of Paul's imprisonment in Caesarea.

Finally, an advocate of the fragment hypothesis may regard the last part of 2 Tim 4 as a fragment of a genuine Pauline epistle from Caesarea.[9] For the argument against this hypothesis, see above the Introduction to the present commentary, section 1.[10]

Information About Persons

The strongest basis for all positions which assert the authenticity of the present text of the Pastoral Epistles, or of some portions of them, is provided by the information about persons. Therefore, whoever holds, on the basis of the arguments given in the Introduction, that the Pastorals are non–Pauline, must try to explain the purpose of the inclusion of such information. In general, it must first be noted that whoever could compose fictitious letters could also compose fictitious greetings and personal references. Furthermore, in an age rich in pseudonymous writings, one need not postulate any special craftiness nor an ethically questionable character on the part of the creator of such fictitious information. But the abundance of personal references in 2 Tim is perhaps best explained by the fact that several motifs came together in such a way as to require the insertion of such notices (see below, especially sections 3, 4, and 5 of the following considerations).

1. It must be said first of all that certain statements can be considered authentic, even if they do not come from Paul's own hand. Thus, what is reported in 2 Tim 4:20, as distinct from the conflicting information in Acts 21:29, is perhaps historically correct (see above, on 2 Tim 4:20). It is also quite possible that the author was referring to historical facts when he specially honored Onesiphorus in 2 Tim 1:16ff, or cast blame upon certain heretics in 2:17 (see also 1 Tim 2:20). These facts may belong to the life of Paul or, what is perhaps more probable, to a somewhat later time even though they are otherwise unknown to us. It is indeed unlikely that all this information about persons was simply invented by the author (see also below, sections 2 and 3); they are probably supported by correct or false (see below, section 2) tradition. Indeed, the fragment hypothesis wants to emphasize this particular point; the problem is, that thereby it creates new difficulties.[11]

2. At the time of the composition of the Pastoral Epistles, an interest in the story of the apostle's life (see above on 1 Tim 1:16 and 2 Tim 1:3, 5) obviously existed already. Thus it seems plausible that the formation of legends about Paul had already begun, legends like those

8   See above pp. 15f, the excursus to 1 Tim 1:3.

9   See K. Erbes, "Zeit und Ziel," 121ff, 195ff, and P. N. Harrison, *The Problem*, 121ff (with reference to 4:16–18a).

10   See Spitta's treatment of the passage, which he considers genuine, in his article "Über die persönlichen Notizen im zweiten Briefe an Timotheus," *ThStKr* 51, 1 (1878): 582–607.

11   On the fragment hypothesis see above p. 4, the Introduction, section 1.

attested in the Acts of Paul. In these apocryphal Acts, legendary accounts are particularly attached to those places in the tradition of Paul's journeys which received less attention in the canonical book of Acts, such as Iconium. In 2 Tim 1:15 and 4:10 names are mentioned which also appear in the Acts of Paul. Perhaps even the list in 2 Tim 4:21 derives from the influence of legends, as might the notice regarding the mission of Titus in Dalmatia in 2 Tim 4:10 (see above). This latter notice may be a legendary expansion of Rom 15:19 (Illyria). The assertion that the legend–making process had such an influence becomes more credible if one takes into consideration the use of Paul's image in parenetic and dogmatic formulations (see below, section 5).

3. Finally, some of the information may have been created by conjecture. It is possible that the author knew of the Erastus in Corinth and identified him with the apostle's assistant (see 2 Tim 4:20). Perhaps he took the Ephesian Jew Alexander from Acts 19:33 and transformed him into a "coppersmith," a member of a guild closely related to that of Demetrius the "silversmith" ($\dot{\alpha}\rho\gamma\upsilon\rho\kappa\dot{o}\pi\sigma$) of Acts 19:24.[12] He probably also knew that Aquila and his wife had once stayed in Ephesus, and that Onesiphorus had visited Paul in Rome, and used both data without regard to chronology (2 Tim 1:17; 4:19; see also the preceding excursus).

4. The information about persons in pseudonymous epistles serves, in some instances, as proof of the (fictitious) authorship; see, for example, 1 Petr 5:12, 13. In other instances, they are intended as a description of the situation in which the epistle is supposed to have been composed; see, for example, Eph. 6:21f. In the process by which information is adapted for these purposes, situations can be modified to such a degree that it is impossible to identify them with certainty. This is illustrated again by the Acts of Paul, which (perhaps consciously) slightly changes the references from 2 Tim 4:10.[13] In the same way, the author of 2 Tim uses the information about persons from the Epistles to the Colossians and to Philemon only partially and freely. He also uses the information from the canonical book of Acts about the journey to Jerusalem, but he seems to vary and to correct it insofar as it relates to Trophimus. The occurrence of similar processes in other pseudonymous works proves that it is not a question of an individual writer's craftiness, but of a common technique of pseudonymous writers in general.[14]

5. But what gives the situation presupposed in 2 Tim its special importance and justifies the extensive presentation of information about persons is the special character of this "epistle." Its purpose is to portray Paul as the model of patient endurance in suffering, and thereby of the Christian life in general (see the general rule in 3:12). One can understand this intention by seeing this portrait of Paul in the context of the typical transitional passages of the other two epistles. This portrait is used to confirm the validity of the teaching which is presented (faith, church order, and parenesis). This purpose is also served by the picture of the abandoned prisoner and the description of his exemplary attitude; this picture is enhanced by the addition of information about other persons. The wonderful ethos of the final portion, which expresses the sense of vocation in suffering felt by the apostle and missionary, has caused some interpreters to defend this epistle, or at least the last portion of it, against the suspicion of inauthenticity. But it is meaningless to assert that such passages are too "true" to have been "invented"—how many scenes which truly represent the nearness of death, both in ancient and modern literature, have after all been "invented"? Such a consideration proves nothing. But if the personal element in 2 Tim is valued in the proper way, especially for its significance for church history (see above, section 2), it will no longer be hard to believe that the "epistle" is not Pauline, despite the personal information it contains.

■ 22 The concluding greeting resembles the greetings in the Epistles to the Galatians, Philippians, and Philemon.

---

12 The same designation "the coppersmith" ($\dot{o}$ $\chi\alpha\lambda$-$\kappa\epsilon\dot{\upsilon}s$) is given to Hermogenes in the *Act. Pl.* 1 (Lipsius–Bonnet 1, p. 235).

13 See the *Martyrdom of the Holy Apostle Paul* 1 (Lipsius–Bonnet 1, p. 104): "There were awaiting Paul at Rome, Luke from Gaul and Titus from Dalmatia" ($\mathring{\eta}\sigma\alpha\nu$ $\delta\dot{\epsilon}$ $\pi\epsilon\rho\iota\mu\dot{\epsilon}\nu\nu\tau\epsilon s$ $\tau\dot{o}\nu$ $\Pi\alpha\hat{\upsilon}\lambda\nu$ $\dot{\epsilon}\nu$ $\tau\hat{\eta}$ $\dot{P}\dot{\omega}\mu\eta$ $\Lambda\nu\kappa\hat{\alpha}s$ $\dot{\alpha}\pi\dot{o}$ $\Gamma\alpha\lambda\lambda\iota\hat{\omega}\nu$ $\kappa\alpha\dot{\iota}$ $T\dot{\iota}\tau\sigma s$ $\dot{\alpha}\pi\dot{o}$ $\Delta\alpha\lambda\mu\alpha\tau\dot{\iota}\alpha s$)

[trans. Hennecke–Schneemelcher 2, p. 383].

14 On the problem see Frederik Torm, *Die Psychologie der Pseudonymität im Hinblick auf die Literatur des Urchristentums* (Gütersloh: Bertelsmann, 1932).

Titus

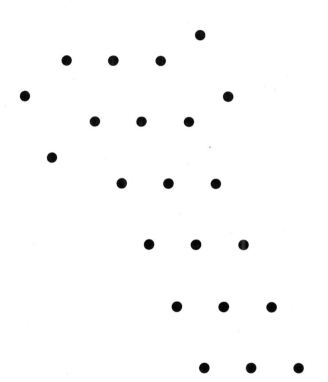

Outline

Initial greeting, 1:1–4.

Titus must install "presbyters" on Crete, 1:5, 6; in order to give a basis for this request, a church order for bishops is appended which also mentions the opponents, 1:7–9. There are many such opponents, especially on Crete, 1:10–16.

Church order in the form of lists of rules for the household, 2:1; for the old men, 2:2; the old and the young women, 2:3–5; the young men, for whom Titus should be a model, 2:6–8; and the slaves, 2:9, 10. The basis for these directions is found in the history of salvation, 2:11–15.

Conclusion of the church regulation with general exhortations, 3:1, 2, which are based on the history of salvation, 3:3–7. Renewed exhortation and warning about the heretics 3:8–11. Assignments, greetings, and the concluding greeting 3:12–15.

1

Initial Greeting

1 Paul, servant of God and apostle of Christ Jesus—according to the faith (which those possess who are) chosen by God, and according to the recognition of truth, as it corresponds to our religion, 2/ on the basis of the hope of eternal life; God, who cannot lie, has promised this to us before time began, 3/ but in his own time he has revealed his word in the proclamation with which I have been entrusted, according to the commission of God our savior—4/ to Titus, his true child in the common faith: grace and peace from God the father and Christ Jesus our savior.

This is a long prescript. Its structure may well be analyzed by analogy with the other Pastoral Epistles.

■ **1, 2a** V 2 doubtless corresponds to "according to the promise of life" ($\kappa\alpha\tau'$ $\dot{\epsilon}\pi\alpha\gamma\gamma\epsilon\lambda\dot{\iota}\alpha\nu$ $\zeta\omega\hat{\eta}s$) in 2 Tim 1:1. In that case "on the basis of the hope etc." ($\dot{\epsilon}\pi'$ $\dot{\epsilon}\lambda\pi\dot{\iota}\delta\iota$ $\kappa\tau\lambda.$, see below on 3:7), which is parallel to the two expressions with "according to" ($\kappa\alpha\tau\dot{\alpha}$) in the other epistles, must be taken as a third predicate of "apostle" ($\dot{\alpha}\pi\dot{o}\sigma\tau o\lambda os$). Thus the Christian religion for which the "apostle" works in his ministry is characterized by means of three expressions: as the faith of those who have been chosen,[1] as the "recognition of truth" ($\dot{\epsilon}\pi\dot{\iota}\gamma\nu\omega\sigma\iota s$ $\dot{\alpha}\lambda\eta\theta\epsilon\dot{\iota}\alpha s$),[2] and finally as "hope" ($\dot{\epsilon}\lambda\pi\dot{\iota}s$), in a way analogous to that of 2 Tim 1:1.

■ **2b, 3** What follows is a description of salvation based on the pattern of the contrast between "then" and "now," a pattern which was popular in preaching.[3] The motif of the "commission" ($\dot{\epsilon}\pi\iota\tau\alpha\gamma\dot{\eta}$), which was used in 1 Tim 1:1 to explain the title of apostle, appears here at the end of a relative clause reminiscent of 1 Tim 1:11. "He who cannot lie" ($\dot{\alpha}\psi\epsilon\upsilon\delta\dot{\eta}s$) is also used by the Greeks to designate gods and divine things. See Plato, *Resp.* 2.382e: "From every point of view, the divine and the divinity are free from falsehood" ($\pi\dot{\alpha}\nu\tau\eta$ $\dot{\alpha}\rho\alpha$ $\dot{\alpha}\psi\epsilon\upsilon\delta\dot{\epsilon}s$ $\tau\dot{o}$ $\delta\alpha\iota\mu\dot{o}\nu\iota\dot{o}\nu$ $\tau\epsilon$ $\kappa\alpha\dot{\iota}$ $\tau\dot{o}$ $\theta\epsilon\hat{\iota}o\nu$); see also 383b (in a quotation from Aeschylus): "that Phoebus' divine mouth could not lie" ($\tau\dot{o}$ $\Phi o\dot{\iota}\beta o\upsilon$ $\theta\epsilon\hat{\iota}o\nu$ $\dot{\alpha}\psi\epsilon\upsilon\delta\dot{\epsilon}s$ $\sigma\tau\dot{o}\mu\alpha$) [trans. by Ed.]; compare this with Ign. *Rom.* 8.2, where it is said of Christ that he is "the mouth which cannot lie, by which the Father has spoken truly" ($\tau\dot{o}$ $\dot{\alpha}\psi\epsilon\upsilon\delta\dot{\epsilon}s$ $\sigma\tau\dot{o}\mu\alpha$, $\dot{\epsilon}\nu$ $\dot{\phi}$ $\dot{o}$ $\pi\alpha\tau\dot{\eta}\rho$ $\dot{\epsilon}\lambda\dot{\alpha}\lambda\eta\sigma\epsilon\nu$ $\dot{\alpha}\lambda\eta\theta\hat{\omega}s$). But see also Wisd Sol 7:16: "a knowledge of the things that does not lie" ($\tau\hat{\omega}\nu$ $\dot{o}\nu\tau\omega\nu$ $\gamma\nu\hat{\omega}\sigma\iota\nu$ $\dot{\alpha}\psi\epsilon\upsilon\delta\hat{\eta}$).[4] On "in its own time" ($\kappa\alpha\iota\rho o\hat{\iota}s$ $\dot{\iota}\delta\dot{\iota}o\iota s$), see above on 1 Tim 2:6. Tit 1:3 is the passage in the Pastorals which most clearly expresses the inclusion of the "word" (which is again immediately linked with the office of Paul) in the process of revelation and its actualization. It corresponds to the style of this schema that God, himself, is directly referred to as the one who enacts the work of salvation.

■ **4** The greeting here, in contrast to 1 and 2 Tim, is in only two parts, as in the genuine Pauline epistles.[5] On "true child" ($\gamma\nu\dot{\eta}\sigma\iota o\nu$ $\tau\dot{\epsilon}\kappa\nu o\nu$), see above on 1 Tim 1:2; on "savior" ($\sigma\omega\tau\dot{\eta}\rho$) see above, the excursus to 2 Tim 1:10.

---

1 "The chosen ones" is a self–designation of Christians in Rom 8:33; Mk 13:20ff and parallels; 2 Tim 2:10; *1 Clem.* 1:1; and frequently in the Shepherd of Hermas.

2 See above p. 41, on 1 Tim 2:4. The expression is more closely defined by the term "piety", "religion" ($\epsilon\dot{\upsilon}\sigma\dot{\epsilon}\beta\epsilon\iota\alpha$), as is "teaching" ($\delta\iota\delta\alpha\sigma\kappa\alpha\lambda\dot{\iota}\alpha$) in 1 Tim 6:3; cf. 1 Tim 2:2.

3 It has been analyzed above p. 99, on 2 Tim 1:9f. Cf. Bultmann, *Theology* 1, p. 106; Nils Astrup Dahl,

"Die Theologie des Neuen Testaments," *ThR* N.S. 22 (1954): 38; *idem*, "Formgeschichtliche Beobachtungen," 3ff.

4 Cf. Philo, *Omn. prob. lib.* 46; *Deus immut.* 61; a hermetic saying in Stobaeus calls that which is "bodiless" ($\dot{\alpha}\sigma\dot{\omega}\mu\alpha\tau o\nu$) "that which cannot lie" ($\dot{\alpha}\psi\epsilon\upsilon\delta\dot{\epsilon}s$) (I, 274, Wachsmuth; III, 55, Nock).

5 In the manuscripts A $\mathfrak{K}$ pl, "mercy" ($\dot{\epsilon}\lambda\epsilon os$) is added as in the other Pastorals.

5

Installation of Presbyters
and Regulations for the Bishop

5 **I have left you in Crete so that you might
set right what remains and install
presbyters in each city according to my
directions (which I gave) to you.
6/ (Such a man should be) without reproach, the husband of one wife, (and
should) have children who are believers
and who cannot be accused of loose
living and disobedience. 7/ For a bishop,
as the householder of God, should be
without reproach, not arrogant, not
irascible, not given to wine or brawling,
nor fond of dishonest gain. 8/ But he
should be devoted to hospitality and to
what is good, prudent, just, pious,
self-controlled; 9/ he should be concerned with the preaching that is
reliable with respect to the teaching, so
that he may be able to give instructions
in the sound teaching and to convict
the opponents.**

The section that begins in v 5 maintains the style of a
letter. It suggests the situation and introduces the question of heresy. A description of the duties of the bishop
is included. On the situation see below, the excursus
to Tit 3:14; on the expression "to set right what remains,"
cf. Philo, *Flacc.* 124: "that you will amend what remains
for amendment" ($\pi\epsilon\rho\grave{\iota}\ \tau\hat{\eta}s\ \tau\hat{\omega}\nu\ \lambda\epsilon\iota\pi o\mu\acute{\epsilon}\nu\omega\nu\ \acute{\epsilon}\pi\alpha\nu o\rho$-
$\theta\acute{\omega}\sigma\epsilon\omega s$). In this passage the titular use of "presbyter" is
unambiguous.[1]

■ **6** On "the husband of one wife" ($\mu\iota\hat{\alpha}s\ \gamma\upsilon\nu\alpha\iota\kappa\grave{o}s$
$\grave{\alpha}\nu\acute{\eta}\rho$), see above, on 1 Tim 3:2. It is noteworthy that,
according to this passage, it is the apostle's assistant who
must install the presbyters, whereas in 1 Tim the existence
of the congregation and its offices is presupposed. But
it is not possible to draw the conclusion with respect to the
historical situations that Tit represents less developed
conditions than 1 Tim.[2] Rather, Tit gives a concrete
example; once the basic presuppositions have been
described in 1 Tim, this last epistle shows the bearer of

the tradition in action. The word $\pi\iota\sigma\tau\acute{o}s$ means "believing" as in 1 Tim 6:2. The existence of the Christian
family is presupposed; cf. 1 Tim 3:4. Nor in this case
can one speak of a development.[3]

■ **7–9** This "epistle" was also intended to be used as a
regulation. This is demonstrated not only by the chapters
that follow, but already in these verses. Without any
regard to a particular situation, they reproduce in modified form the same schema that was given in 1 Tim 3:2ff.[4]
But the variations do not reveal a tendency in any particular direction. The abrupt beginning of the statute and
the sudden appearance of "bishop" ($\grave{\epsilon}\pi\acute{\iota}\sigma\kappa o\pi o s$) as a
title (and in the singular!) provide strong support for the
interpolation hypothesis.[5] But these observations can
also be explained if one assumes that Tit 1:7–9 quote a
traditional regulation, upon which both 1 Tim and Tit
perhaps depend.[6] On the other hand, the commentator
who believes he can find an interpolation here, one which
is intended to bring in the monarchial episcopate, will

---

1   The translation given by Jeremias, *ad loc.*, "to in-
    stall older men," is not possible linguistically.
2   On this point the present edition contradicts the
    2d German edition of this commentary by Martin
    Dibelius.
3   On the ideal of a Christian upbringing, see above,
    p. 40, the second excursus to 1 Tim 2:2.
4   See above pp. 50f, the excursus to 1 Tim 3:1.

5   On this hypothesis, see above p. 56, the excursus
    to 1 Tim 3:7, section 2.
6   On the question of dependence upon traditional
    materials, see above p. 5ff, Introduction, section 2.

have to supply the following between vss 6 and 7: "for the bishop (ἐπίσκοπος) comes from among the presbyters and the bishop should be" etc. The variations on the schema in 1 Tim 3:1ff and Tit 1:7ff may be illustrated by the following chart.[7]

Tit	1 Tim
without reproach	irreproachable
(the husband of one wife 1:6)	the husband of one wife
hospitable	hospitable
devoted to what is good	? respectable
self–controlled	? sober *
(children who are believers 1:6)	children who are obedient *
prudent	prudent *
concerned with the preaching?	able to teach
just	
pious	
not arrogant	gentle
not irascible	peaceable
not given to wine	not given to wine
not given to brawling	not given to brawling
not fond of dishonest gain	not greedy
(children who are believers 1:6)?	able to govern his own house well
	not newly converted

Tit	1 Tim
ἀνέγκλητος	ἀνεπίλημπτος
(μιᾶς γυναικὸς ἀνήρ 1:6)	μιᾶς γυναικὸς ἀνήρ
φιλόξενος	φιλόξενος
φιλάγαθος	? κόσμιος
ἐγκρατής	? νηφάλιος *

(τέκνα ἔχων πιστά 1:6)	τέκνα ἔχων ἐν ὑποταγῇ *
σώφρων	σώφρων *
ἀντεχόμενος τοῦ πιστοῦ λόγου?	διδακτικός
δίκαιος	
ὅσιος	
μὴ αὐθάδης	ἐπιεικής
μὴ ὀργιλος	ἄμαχος
μὴ πάροινος	μὴ πάροινος
μὴ πλήκτης	μὴ πλήκτης
μὴ αἰσχροκερδής	ἀφιλάργυρος
(τέκνα ἔχων πιστά 1:6)?	τοῦ ἰδίου οἴκου καλῶς προϊστάμενος
	μὴ νεόφυτος

■ **7** Paul refers to himself as "householder of God" (οἰκο-νόμος θεοῦ) in 1 Cor 4:1. "Arrogant" (αὐθάδης) occurs in the OT in Gen 59:3, 7 and Pr 21:24; but in the NT it is found only here and in 2 Petr 2:10.[8]

■ **8** The linking of "devoted to hospitality" and "devoted to what is good" (φιλόξενος and φιλάγαθος) is derived from the same rhetorical motifs which have been observed in the catalogues of vices.[9] "Love of what is good" (φιλαγαθία) appears frequently in the honorary inscriptions. It is also mentioned by itself as a quality worthy of honor.[10] Moreover, in Asia Minor φιλάγαθος also became the title of an office in the associations.[11]

■ **9** To translate ἀντέχεσθαι as "to hold fast"[12] would be very weak. It is, therefore, perhaps better to translate it as "to be concerned with something"; λόγος should then be translated as "preaching," as in 1 Tim 5:17.[13] Here the ability to teach, which 1 Tim 3:2 only recom-

---

7   The asterisk indicates parallels in Onosander (for the text, see pp. 158ff, Appendix 3). See also above pp. 50f, the excursus to 1 Tim 3:1. In Onosander as in 1 Tim, it is often a question only of qualities corresponding to those referred to in Tit, not of identical predicates.

8   For the other predicates, see on 1 Tim 3:2ff; cf. Vögtle, *Tugend– und Lasterkataloge*, pp. 52ff and 239ff.

9   See Philo, *Sacr. AC.* 20ff (which is also cited in Lietzmann, *Römer*, Appendix 2).

10   See Ditt. *Or.* I, 146.1ff: "The assembly of the Lycians stationed (?) on the island (honors) Diasthenes, the kinsman of the king, on account of his devotion to what is good" (Τὸ κοινὸν τῶν ἐν τῆι νήσωι | τασσομένων Λυκίων Διασθένη, | τὸν συγγενῆ τοῦ βασιλέως, | φιλαγαθίας ἕνεκεν) [trans. by Ed.]; see also 148.3; 163.4; Ditt. *Syll.* III, 1101.9; *Inscr. Priene*

107.10, 16; on the adverb (φιλαγάθως), see Ditt. *Syll.* II, 762.13; Ditt. *Or.* I, 339.27, 68.

11   See *IPE* II, pp. 60–4 and 438–43.

12   See the formula "We hold fast and will hold fast to the rights which remain to us" (τῶν ὑπόντων ἡμεῖν δικαίων πάντων ἀντεχόμεθα καὶ ἀνθεξόμεθα) in *P. Oxy.* IX, 1203.29ff, and similarly *P. Strassb.* 74.17ff [trans. by Ed.].

13   On ἀντέχεσθαι in this meaning, cf. Jer 2:8: "those who are concerned with the law" (οἱ ἀντεχόμενοι τοῦ νόμου); and *P. Par.* 14.22: "not concerned with any right" (οὐθενὸς δικαίου ἀντεχόμενοι). On the relation of the office of "bishop" to the teaching office, see above pp. 54f, the excursus to 1 Tim 3:7, section 1 [trans. in this footnote by Ed.].

mends, seems to be required. The reason for this is perhaps not so much for the sake of the worship service; the following clause shows an interest in the bishop's authority over against Christians and heretics. With this in mind, the phrase "(reliable) with respect to the teaching" ($\kappa\alpha\tau\grave{\alpha}$ $\tau\grave{\eta}\nu$ $\delta\iota\delta\alpha\chi\acute{\eta}\nu$) seems to refer to the ecclesiastical tradition which the bishop is expected to represent (see 2 Tim 2:1f and 3:14f). In that case the meaning "believing" for $\pi\iota\sigma\tau\acute{o}s$ is redundant; rather, chiefly because of the idea of tradition (cf. 2 Tim 2:2!), the meaning "reliable" is suggested. To what a great extent this and the following clauses were regarded as statutes is proven by the addenda of miniscule 460 here and after v 11,[14] which clearly seek to satisfy the need for the treatment of specific cases by the apostle.

---

14 Minuscule 460 reads: "Not to appoint bigamists, not even as deacons; nor should they have wives who are married for the second time. Such should not approach the altar to administer the sacrament. The rulers who are unjust judges or robbers or liars or unmerciful, he must reprove as a servant of God;" in v 11: "Silence the children who mistreat and beat their own parents; reprove and admonish them like a father to children." The Greek text is given in the apparatus of Nestle's edition of the NT [trans. by Ed.].

1   Against Heretics in Crete

10   For there are many insubordinate men,
       foolish talkers and deceivers, especially
       those of the circumcision; 11 / these
       must be silenced. For they ruin entire
       families and teach what is not becoming
       for the sake of dishonest gain. 12 / In
       fact one of them said, (speaking) as
       their own prophet,
           "Cretans are mostly liars / brutes and
           loitering gluttons."
13   This testimony is true! Therefore admon-
       ish them strictly that they may come
       to the sound faith 14 / and not follow
       Jewish fables and commandments
       of men who turn their back on the truth.
       15 / Everything is pure for those who
       are pure, but for those who are defiled
       and who do not believe, nothing is
       pure, but their mind and conscience
       are defiled. 16 / They claim to know
       God, but deny him with their works,
       abominable as they are, and disobedient
       and useless for any good deed.

What follows, as well as 3:9, is similar to the controversy with the heretics in the other Pastoral Epistles. On "foolish talkers" (ματαιολόγος), see 1 Tim 1:6; on "for dishonest gain" (αἰσχροῦ κέρδους χάριν), 1 Tim 6:5; on "turning their back to the truth" (ἀποστρεφόμενοι τὴν ἀλήθειαν), see 2 Tim 2:18; "everything is pure" (πάντα καθαρὰ κτλ.), 1 Tim 4:4; and on "they are defiled" (μεμίανται κτλ.), 1 Tim 4:2. "They ruin entire families" (οἴκους ἀνατρέπουσιν) recalls what is related in 2 Tim 3:6 about the false teachers. "What is not becoming" (ἃ μὴ δεῖ) is related to the description of the "widows who are busybodies" (χῆραι περίεργοι) in 1 Tim 5:13.

But this section is to be distinguished in two ways from the heresy polemic in the other Pastoral Epistles. Cretan characteristics are mentioned (1:12), and the Jewish origin of the opponents is stressed (1:10, 14). The two motifs might belong together, for the mention of Jews might also be intended to give the writing local color. The Jews of Crete were, according to Josephus,[1] victims of the false Alexander; a Jewess from Crete was the last wife of Josephus.[2] It is hard to say why the author chose to give more local color to this passage than to other pas-

sages in the Pastorals.[3] But even though we do not know to what extent we are justified in drawing conclusions about the heretics of the Pastorals in general from these local references, this passage probably indicates that the entire heretical movement had something to do with Judaism.[4]

■ 10   "Deceiver" (φρεναπάτης) is attested in *P. Grenf.* 1.1.10 (2d century B.C.): "The deceiver who hitherto was presumptuous and who said that sexual desire was not the cause of my loving, did not bear very well the injustice that befell." (ὁ φρεναπάτης ὁ πρὸ τοῦ μέγα φρονῶν καὶ ὁ τὴν κύπριν οὐ φάμενος εἶναι τοῦ ἐρᾶν μοι αἰτίαν οὐκ ἤνεγκε λίαν τὴν τυχοῦσαν ἀδικίαν) [trans. by Ed.]; cf. also the occurrence of the verb φρεναπατᾶν in Gal 6:3.

■ 11   The phrase "for the sake of dishonest gain" (αἰσχροῦ κέρδους χάριν) is paralleled by 1 Tim 6:5, but might also have been meant to contribute to the passage's local color. In that case, cf. Polybius 6.46: "So much in fact do sordid love of gain and lust for wealth prevail among them, that the Cretans are the only people in the world in whose eyes no gain is disgraceful" (καθόλου θ' ὁ περὶ τὴν αἰσχροκέρδειαν καὶ πλεονεξίαν

---

1   *Ant.* 17.327 and *Bell.* 2.103.
2   See *Vit.* 76. Other attestations are 1 Macc 15:23 (mentions the Jewish population in Gortyn, Crete); the epistle of Agrippa in Philo, *Leg. Gaj.* 282; cf. also

Tacitus, *History* 5.2.
3   See below pp. 150f, the excursus to Tit 3:14, section 3.
4   See above pp. 66f, the excursus to 1 Tim 4:5, section 3 a.

τρόπος οὕτως ἐπιχωριάζει παρ' αὐτοῖς ὥστε παρὰ μόνοις Κρηταιεῦσι τῶν ἀπάντων ἀνθρώπων μηδὲν αἰσχρὸν νομίζεσθαι κέρδος). On the variant reading in the text of this verse see above, on 1:9.

■ **12** "Their" (αὐτῶν) with "own" (ἴδιος) here, as in other instances,[5] proves that the word "own" (ἴδιος) has been weakened, and hence requires an auxiliary pronoun.[6] Epimenides (see below), who composed the quotation that follows, is probably considered a prophet by the author of the Pastorals, because of the correctness of his testimony. But it is possible that the author wished to characterize the Epimenides, whom Cicero (*Divin.* 1.18, sec. 34) counts among those who "forecast the future while under the influence of mental excitement, or of some free and unrestrained emotion" (concitatione quadam animi aut soluto liberoque motu futura praesentiunt). If this is the case, the following passage from Aristotle becomes very important: *Rhet.* 3.17 (p. 1418.23): ". . . the past, which is already known, even by diviners, as Epimenides the Cretan said; for he used to divine, not the future, but only things that were past but obscure" (τὸ γεγονὸς ὃ ἐπιστητὸν ἤδη καὶ τοῖς μάντεσιν ὡς ἔφη Ἐπιμενίδης ὁ Κρής· ἐκεῖνος γὰρ περὶ τῶν ἐσομένων οὐκ ἐμαντεύετο, ἀλλὰ περὶ τῶν γεγονότων μέν, ἀδήλων δέ). On the origin of the hexameter[7] see Clement of Alexandria, *Strom.* 1.59.2; it is said there that some persons include Epimenides of Crete as one of the seven wise men: "whom the apostle Paul cites in the letter to Titus when he says" (οὗ μέμνηται ὁ ἀπόστολος Παῦλος ἐν τῇ πρὸς Τίτον ἐπιστολῇ, λέγων οὕτως [the hexameter follows]). See also Jerome: "but this verse is said to be found in the oracles of the poet Epimenides of Crete" (dicitur autem iste versiculus in Epimenidis Cretensis poetae oraculis reperiri) [Trans.].[8] According to this testimony, the verse comes from a book

entitled the *Theogony* or the *Chresmoi*.[9] It has been suggested that this book might be ascribed to a Cretan priest who lived shortly before the Persian war and called himself Epimenides—possibly after the Attic hero—and about whose life many incredible legends have sprung up.[10]

The verse seems to be formed in imitation of Hesiod, *Theog.* 26: "Shepherds dwelling in the fields, base reproaches (upon you), nothing but gluttons!" (ποιμένες ἄγραυλοι, κάκ' ἐλέγχεα, γαστέρες οἶον) [trans. by Ed.]. It has been imitated by Callimachus, *Hymnus in Iovem* 8f (cited in Athenagoras, *Suppl.* 30): "Cretans are always liars. For a tomb, O Lord, Cretans build for you; but you did not die, for you are forever" (Κρῆτες ἀεὶ ψεῦσται· καὶ γὰρ τάφον, ὦ ἄνα, σεῖο | Κρῆτες ἐτεκτήναντο· σὺ δ'οὐ θάνες· ἐσσὶ γὰρ αἰεί) [trans. by Ed.]. Theodore of Mopsuestia (II, p. 243, Swete) is referring to the derivation of this verse from Callimachus when he writes: "Those who have composed books against Christian teachings have said in them that the blessed Paul agrees with the voice of the poet and witnesses in his behalf, namely that he (the poet) had spoken rightly on behalf of Zeus concerning the Cretans . . . But he (Paul) neither agrees with the poem nor with the voice of the poet; rather, he only uses the poet's voice as a proverb, as if by chance and since people at that time were using the expression" (οἱ κατὰ τῶν χριστιανικῶν συντάξαντες δογμάτων ἐνταῦθα ἔφασαν καὶ τὸν μακάριον Παῦλον ἀποδέχεσθαι τὴν τοῦ ποιητοῦ φωνὴν καὶ ἐπιμαρτυρεῖν αὐτῷ, ὡς ἂν δικαίως ταῦτα ὑπὲρ τοῦ Διὸς περὶ Κρητῶν εἰρηκότι . . . οὐ γὰρ τὸ ποίημα οὐδὲ τὴν τοῦ ποιητοῦ ἀποδέχεται φωνήν, ἀλλ' ὡς παροιμίᾳ τῇ τοῦ ποιητοῦ φωνῇ χρησάμενος, τυχὸν καὶ τῶν τότε τῇ φωνῇ κεχρημένων) [trans. by Ed.].[11]

5   Examples have been collected by W. Kuhring, *De praepositionum graec. in chartis egypt. usu quaestiones selectae*, Unpub. Diss. (Bonn: 1906), p. 13.

6   Moulton, *Prolegomena*, 87–90, mentions as a characteristic parallel a passage in *BGU* IV, 1110.8, where αὐ(τῆς) has been written over the words τῷ ἰδίῳ γάλακτι for the sake of clarity.

7   The quotation in 1:12 is an hexameter. The German original of this commentary, as well as the present edition, attempt to reproduce the hexameter in their translations [Ed.].

8   Hieronymus, *Commentaria in epistulam ad Titum* 7 (p. 707, Vallarsi).

9   The fragments are collected in Hermann Diels ed., *Fragmente der Vorsokratiker* (Zürich: Weidmann, ¹¹1964), 1, p. 31ff; translated by Kathleen Freeman as *Ancilla to the Pre–Socratic Philosophers* (Oxford: B. H. Blackwell, 1956), pp. 9ff. On the sources for the life of Epimenides see Diels, *op. cit.*, pp. 27ff.

10   Otto Kern, "Epimenides," in Pauly–Wissowa, VI, col. 173–78. Whether this hexameter belongs to this or to another work of Epimenides has been settled by Pohlenz, "Paulus und die Stoa," 101ff; see also below.

11   Theodoret also derives this verse from Callimachus; cf. Theodoret (III, p. 701, Schulze). On the further

The assertion that the Cretans are liars is, according to the Hymn of Callimachus to Zeus and other writings, based on the fact that they claim to have the grave of Zeus on their island.[12] *Anthologia Palatina* VII, 275: "But on the land they raised me a lying tomb. What wonder! since 'Cretans are liars,' and even Zeus has a tomb there." (τὸν ψεύσταν δέ με τύμβον ἐπὶ χθονὶ θέντο. τί θαῦμα; Κρῆτες ὅπου ψεῦσται, καὶ Διός ἐστι τάφος). Cf. Lucian, *Philopseudes* 3: "The Cretans exhibit the tomb of Zeus and are not ashamed of it" (εἰ Κρῆτες μὲν τοῦ Διὸς τάφον δεικνύοντες οὐκ αἰσχύνονται); Lucian, *Timon* 6: "Unless indeed the tale is true that the Cretans tell about you and your tomb in their island" (εἰ μὴ ἀληθῆ ἐστι τὰ ὑπὸ Κρητῶν περὶ σοῦ καὶ τῆς ἐκεῖ ταφῆς μυθολογούμενα); Theodoret (III, p. 701, Schulze): "But the poet called the Cretans liars because of the matter of the tomb of Zeus" (ἀλλ' ὁ μὲν ποιητὴς διὰ τὸν τοῦ Διὸς τάφον τοὺς Κρῆτας ὠνόμασε ψεύστας) [trans. by Ed.].[13] It is interesting that in the source of the Isho'dad commentary on Acts,[14] the Epimenides verse quoted in Tit 1:12 is combined with the Callimachus quotation and Acts 17:28. There the eulogy of Minos, the son of Zeus, is quoted: "The Cretans carve a tomb for thee, O holy and high! Liars! Evil beasts and slow bellies; for thou art not dead for ever; thou art alive and risen; for in thee we live and are moved, and have our being."[15]

After the seriousness of the situation in Crete has been explained, together with the bad tendencies of the Cretans—untruthfulness, coarseness (κακὰ θηρία), love of pleasure—further warnings are made.

■ **13** On "strictly" (ἀποτόμως), see 2 Cor 13:10;[16] on "to be sound" (ὑγιαίνειν), see above pp. 24f, the excursus to 1 Tim 1:10.

■ **14** On the Jewish question, see above on Tit 1:10ff. The emphasis upon the "commandments of men" (ἐντολαὶ ἀνθρώπων, cf. Col 2:8 and perhaps Tit 1:22) might justify the suspicion that the term "Jewish" ('Ιουδαϊκοί) refers to method rather than to origin.[17] In that case "fable" (μῦθος) lacks any special emphasis or force (see 1 Tim 1:4); otherwise the term might recall Jewish angel worship or some related phenomenon. "Turn one's back to" (ἀποστρέφεσθαι) is used as in 2 Tim 1:15.

■ **15** The first "pure" (καθαρός) is to be understood in the same sense as 1 Tim 4:4; "everything is pure" (πάντα καθαρά) is the equivalent of "nothing is to be rejected" (οὐδὲν ἀπόβλητον)—a statement to which enlightened persons of all countries subscribe as against cultic asceticism regarding food. In Rom 14:20 this view is presupposed as the opinion of enlightened Christians in Rome. The adoption of this maxim by Christian congregations as valid for themselves was perhaps conditioned by a saying of Jesus (Lk 11:41).[18] In Tit 1:15 this principle is not restricted for the sake of the "weak" brothers, i.e. the ascetics, as is the case in Paul. Rather, by means of the addition of "for the pure" (τοῖς καθαροῖς), it is pointed particularly against the ascetic tendencies of the opponents: for us everything which you forbid (1 Tim 4:3) is pure, for we are "pure," but you are "defiled." In this polemical use of the sentence, the author plays with the various levels of meaning that the

consequences of this derivation, see Pohlenz, "Paulus und die Stoa."
12 See Rohde, *Psyche*, 130f.
13 Cf. also Ovid, *Amores* 3.10.19: "and the Cretans are not wholly false" (nec fingunt omnia Cretes); and *Ars amatoria* 1.298: "Crete . . . cannot deny this, liar though she be" (quamvis sit mendax, Creta negare potest). On the word κρητίζειν meaning "to lie" see Plutarch, *Aemilius Paulus* 23 (II, p. 63, Sintenis); *Lysander* 20 (II, p. 404, Sintenis); Zenobius 4.62 (I, p. 101, von Leutsch).
14 Ed. Margaret Dunlop Gibson, *The Commentaries of Isho'dad of Merv*, Introduction by James Rendel Harris, Horae Semiticae 10–11 (Cambridge: The University Press, 1913), 4–5; see 4, p. 39 of the Syriac text.
15 The conclusions drawn from this passage by Harris (Introduction to Gibson, *op. cit.*, 4, p. XIIff; 5,

p. XIVff), by Theodor Zahn (*Die Apostelgeschichte des Lukas*, Kommentar zum Neuen Testament, ed. Theodor Zahn, 5; 1, 2 [Leipzig and Erlangen: Deichert, 1922, 1927] on Acts 17:28) and by Kirsopp Lake (*The Beginnings of Christianity* Part I, *The Acts of the Apostles*, ed. F. J. Foakes–Jackson and Kirsopp Lake, 5 [London: Macmillan, 1933], 247ff) have been refuted by Pohlenz, "Paulus und die Stoa," who shows that the confusion goes back to an error of Chrysostom. See also Martin Dibelius, *Studies in the Acts of the Apostles*, ed. Heinrich Greeven, tr. Mary Ling (London: SCM Press, 1956), pp. 48ff, and the correction in p. 153, n. 37.
16 Cf. Lietzmann–Kümmel, *Korinther*, on 2 Cor 13:10.
17 See above pp. 66f, the excursus to 1 Tim 4:5, section 3a; cf. Lohse, *Colossians, Philemon*, on Col 2:8; 2:22.
18 J. Horst, "Die Worte Jesu über die kultische Reinheit und ihre Bearbeitung in den evangelischen Be-

terms "pure" and "defiled" have. The second "pure" (καθαρός) refers to ethical purity; the third "nothing is pure" (οὐδὲν καθαρόν) refers again to cultic purity. Then, where one would expect "nothing is pure, but the creation of God has become defiled for them" (οὐδὲν καθαρόν, ἀλλὰ τὸ κτίσμα θεοῦ αὐτοῖς μεμιαμμένον), the thought again shifts toward the ethical by the introduction of the terms "mind" (νοῦς) and "conscience" (συνείδησις). The opponents are accused of raising their ascetic demands with a sinful purpose. They are thus criticized more severely than the ascetics in 1 Cor 8:7. For the latter, their consciences were said to be defiled if they did what they could not justify in their consciences; here the demand for ascetic practice itself is held as proof that their consciences are already defiled.[19]

The author of the Pastorals is not alone in stressing the ethical component of this concept. Seneca, *Epistulae Morales* 98.3, writes that "the evil man turns everything to evil" (malus omnia in malum vertit). But the entire thought complex finds a parallel in Philo, *Spec. leg.* 3.208f: "Everything else too, he says, that the unclean person touches must be unclean, being defiled by its participation in the uncleanness. *This pronouncement may be thought to include a more far-reaching veto, not merely stopping short with the body but extending its inquiry to matters of temperament and characteristics of the soul.* For the unjust and impious man is in the truest sense unclean. No thought of respect for things human or divine ever enters his mind. He puts everything into chaos and confusion, so inordinate are his passions and so prodigious his vices, and thus every deed to which he sets his hand is reprehensible, changing in conformity with the worthlessness of the doer. For conversely all the doings of the good are laudable, gaining merit through the virtues of the agents in accordance with the general law that the results of actions assimilate

themselves to the actors" (ἔστω δέ, φησίν, ἀκάθαρτα καὶ τὰ ἄλλα ὅσων ἂν ὁ ἀκάθαρτος προσάψηται, μετουσίᾳ τοῦ μὴ καθαροῦ μιαινόμενα [cultic]. **καθολικωτέραν δ᾽ ἀπόφασιν ὁ χρησμὸς οὗτος ἔοικέ πως δηλοῦν, οὐκ ἐπὶ σώματος αὐτὸ μόνον ἱστάμενος, ἀλλὰ ἤδη καὶ τρόπους προσδιερευνώμενος ψυχῆς.** ἀκάθαρτος γὰρ κυρίως ὁ ἄδικος καὶ ἀσεβής, ὅτῳ μήτε τῶν ἀνθρωπίνων μήτε τῶν θείων αἰδώς τις εἰσέρχεται, πάντα φύρων καὶ συγχέων διά τε τὰς ἀμετρίας τῶν παθῶν καὶ τὰς τῶν κακιῶν ὑπερβολάς, ὥστε ὧν ἂν ἐφάψηται πραγμάτων πάντ᾽ ἐστὶν ἐπίληπτα τῇ τοῦ δρῶντος συμμεταβάλλοντα μοχθηρίᾳ· καὶ γὰρ κατὰ τοὐναντίον αἱ πράξεις τῶν ἀγαθῶν ἐπαινεταί, βελτιούμεναι ταῖς τῶν ἐνεργούντων ἀρεταῖς, ἐπειδὴ πέφυκέ πως τὰ γινόμενα τοῖς δρῶσιν ἐξομοιοῦσθαι). Yet one must not overlook the fact that the passage from Philo is an interpretation of prescriptions for purity (Num 19:22), whereas Tit 1:15 is a polemic against such regulations.

■ **16** contains a reproach similar to that found in 2 Tim 3:5. Here we may relate "denying God" to the opponents' negative position toward God's creation; compare 1 Tim 4:4. "Disobedient" (ἀπειθεῖς) can be interpreted in the same way: they are disobedient to God. "Abominable" (βδελυκτοί) may have an especially ironic note:[20] these persons who find "abomination" everywhere are themselves "abominable." The conclusion asserts their total uselessness; cf. similar formulas in Tit 3:1; 2 Tim 3:17; and in Plutarch.[21]

---

richten," *ThStKr* 87 (1914): 449, assumes that even Rom 14:20 is a quotation of this saying and that Tit 1:15 also alludes to it.

19 On the concept of conscience see above pp. 18ff, the excursus to 1 Tim 1:5.

20 B. Weiss, *ad loc.*

21 Plut., *Lib. Educ.* 7 (p. 4 B): "(but any) slave (whom they find) to be a wine–bibber and a glutton, and useless for any kind of business . . ." (ἀνδράποδον οἰνόληπτον καὶ λίχνον, πρὸς πᾶσαν πραγματείαν ἄχρηστον); see Almqvist, *Plutarch und das NT*, p. 127; on the ethical judgment about the heretics, see above p. 67, the excursus to 1 Tim 4:5, section 3 b.

2 Regulations for Men, Women, Slaves

1 But as for you, proclaim what is proper to the sound teaching. 2/ Old men should be sober, dignified, prudent, sound in faith, love, (and) endurance. 3/ In the same way old women: priestly in their conduct, not given to gossip nor to a great deal of drinking, teachers of all good things. 4/ Then they can advise the young women to love their husbands and children, 5/ to live prudently and in sincerity, to fulfill their household duties well and to obey their husbands, that God's word may not be blasphemed (as a result of their behavior). 6/ In the same way exhort the young men to conduct their lives prudently 7/ in all respects; and show yourself to be an example through good works, pure and dignified as a teacher, 8/ with irreproachable, sound preaching, so that the opponent may be converted, if he cannot say anything bad about us. 9/ Slaves should obey their masters in all respects, they should be well-pleasing and should not contradict them. 10/ They should not pilfer anything, but show that they are entirely faithful and worthy, so that they are a credit to the teaching of God, our savior, in every way.

■ **1** A personal appeal introduces regulations which are presented in the form of rules for the household.[2] It is significant that Tit 2:2ff is not formulated as a sequence of imperatives, as is usually the case in these rules for the household, but primarily as a series of adjectives (with "to be" [$\epsilon\hat{\iota}\nu\alpha\iota$]). As a result, the section looks more like a catalogue of duties than a list of rules for the household. In external features it is therefore related to the regulations for bishops and deacons in 1 Tim 3:2ff (see also Tit 1:7ff). The infinitive "to be" ($\epsilon\hat{\iota}\nu\alpha\iota$) does not have the force of an imperative, but is subordinated to "proclaim," or "it is proper," or an implicit "exhort" ($\lambda\acute{\alpha}\lambda\epsilon\iota$, $\pi\rho\acute{\epsilon}\pi\epsilon\iota$, or $\pi\alpha\rho\alpha\kappa\acute{\alpha}\lambda\epsilon\iota$) from 2:1; nor are the infinitives in vss 4f and 6 independent.[3]

■ **2** On "sober" ($\nu\eta\phi\acute{\alpha}\lambda\iota\sigma$) see above on 1 Tim 3:3.

The early Christian triad "faith, love, endurance" is connected with "sound" ($\acute{\upsilon}\gamma\iota\alpha\acute{\iota}\nu\epsilon\iota\nu$).[4] "Endurance" ($\acute{\upsilon}\pi\sigma\mu\sigma\nu\acute{\eta}$) appears here instead of "hope" ($\acute{\epsilon}\lambda\pi\acute{\iota}\sigma$), as in Ign. *Pol.* 6.2.

■ **3** "Conduct," "attitude," "constitution" ($\kappa\alpha\tau\acute{\alpha}\sigma\tau\eta\mu\alpha$) is probably used in a broad sense as in 3 Macc 5:45, and as "deportment" ($\kappa\alpha\tau\alpha\sigma\tau\sigma\lambda\acute{\eta}$) is used in 1 Tim 2:9 (see above). The word refers to an inner "bearing," as in *Ep. Ar.* 210: ". . . of piety" (. . . $\tau\hat{\eta}\sigma$ $\epsilon\acute{\upsilon}\sigma\epsilon\beta\epsilon\acute{\iota}\alpha\sigma$) and 278: ". . . of virtue" (. . . $\tau\hat{\eta}\sigma$ $\acute{\alpha}\rho\epsilon\tau\hat{\eta}\sigma$). It refers to external bearing in Josephus, *Bell.* 1.40: "The city was just recovering its hallowed constitution" ($\lambda\alpha\mu$-$\beta\alpha\nu\sigma\acute{\upsilon}\sigma\eta\sigma$ $\delta\grave{\epsilon}$ $\acute{\alpha}\rho\tau\iota$ $\tau\grave{\sigma}$ $\acute{\iota}\epsilon\rho\grave{\sigma}\nu$ $\kappa\alpha\tau\acute{\alpha}\sigma\tau\eta\mu\alpha$ $\tau\hat{\eta}\sigma$ $\pi\acute{\sigma}\lambda\epsilon\omega\sigma$)

1 On "sound doctrine" ($\acute{\upsilon}\gamma\iota\alpha\acute{\iota}\nu\sigma\upsilon\sigma\alpha$ $\delta\iota\delta\alpha\sigma\kappa\alpha\lambda\acute{\iota}\alpha$) and "sound in faith" ($\acute{\upsilon}\gamma\iota\alpha\acute{\iota}\nu\epsilon\iota\nu$ $\tau\hat{\eta}$ $\pi\acute{\iota}\sigma\tau\epsilon\iota$, v 2), see above pp. 18ff, the excursus to 1 Tim 1:10.

2 On this point, see von Campenhausen, "Polykarp," 229ff. On the significance of the rules for the household, see Dibelius–Greeven, *Kolosser, Epheser, Philemon*, excursus to Col 4:1; Lohse, *Colossians, Philemon*, on Col 4:1ff.

3 See Blass–Debrunner, 389.

4 See Dibelius, *Thessalonicher, Philipper*, on 1 Thess 1:3; Lietzmann–Kümmel, *Korinther*, on 1 Cor 13:13; and see the bibliographical study by Harald Riesenfeld, "Étude bibliographique sur la notion biblique d' ΑΓΑΠΗ; surtout dans 1 Cor. 13," *Con. Neot.* 5 (1941): 1ff; Günther Bornkamm, "The More Excellent Way (1 Cor 13)," *Early Christian Experience*,

[Loeb modified]; [5] Ditt. *Or.* II, 669.3f: "Taking all fore-thought to persevere in the constitution appropriate to the city" (πᾶσαν πρόνοιαν ποιούμενος τοῦ διαμένειν τῷ προσήκοντι καταστήματι τῆς πόλεως) [trans. by Ed.]. The following passage (as does Tit 2:3) seems to refer to both external and internal bearing; Ign. *Tr.* 3.2: "in the person of your bishop, whose very demeanour is a great lesson, and whose meekness is a miracle [or, possibly, "is his power"], and I believe that even the godless pay respect to him" (ἐν τῷ ἐπισκόπῳ ὑμῶν, οὗ αὐτὸ τὸ κατάστημα μεγάλη μαθητεία, ἡ δὲ πρᾳ-ότης αὐτοῦ δύναμις· ὃν λογίζομαι καὶ τοὺς ἀθέους ἐντρέπεσθαι). "Priestly" (ἱεροπρεπής) can have the general meaning "holy," as in Philo, *Abr.* 101 and *Decal.* 60. But the peculiar nuance of the parallel passage, 1 Tim 2:10, must be taken into account: "Christian women are holy women" (see above). Accordingly, Tit 2:3 may also be understood as a demand placed on older women to achieve a kind of "priestly" dignity. [6]

The following verses warn against vices which should be avoided by the Christian as a matter of course. That the warning is still presented, even though it would seem superfluous, is explained by the consideration that both the rules for the household and the list of virtues frequently use traditional material. [7] "Teacher of all good things" (καλοδιδάσκαλος), which occurs here for the first time, seems unusual at first, in light of the position

taken in 1 Tim 2:12. But it is explained by what follows.

■ 4 The older women are supposed to remind the young-er ones of their duties; this is their task by virtue of age, not by virtue of an office. The assumption of an "official" function is not possible because of the structure of this regulation, i.e., according to age groups. [8] "Advise" (σωφρονίζειν) is used in the sense of "to admonish" (νουθετεῖν). [9] The following injunction for the younger women is thus embedded in that for the older ones. That this is only an external feature is shown by the fact that the regulations for the young men are separate. In fact, all the regulations for the members of the congregation are disguised this way in the Pastorals: as regulations which are handed over to the apostle's assistant! The regulation for young women corresponds to what is expected of the young widows in 1 Tim 5:14. "Love of husbands" (φιλανδρία) and "love of children" (φιλοτεκνία) are praised in the literature [10] and in the inscriptions as womanly virtues. [11]

■ 5 Another virtue, named after those quoted above in some of these passages, is "prudent" (σώφρων). Note the use of "prudence" (σωφροσύνη) in 1 Tim 2:9. The virtue referred to by "with modesty" (μετὰ αἰδοῦς) in the latter passage is reproduced here by "in sincerity" (ἁγνός). "To fulfill their household duties" (οἰκουρ-γούς) could stand alone without a laudatory epithet; cf. the use of "to govern the house" (οἰκοδεσποτεῖν) in

p. 186f.

5 What is meant is the reinstitution of the divine wor-ship in Jerusalem by Judas Maccabaeus.

6 Regarding this narrower meaning of the word, see the inscription in Paul François Foucart, *Des asso-ciations religieuses chez les Grecs* (Paris: Klincksieck, 1873), p. 240, No. 66.3, 13: "in a priestly manner and zealous for honor" (ἱεροπρεπῶς καὶ φιλοδόξως, referring to religious accomplishments); Ditt. *Syll.* II, 708.23f: "in processions of priestly dignity" (πομπαῖ[ς ἱε]ροπρεπέσιν); C. Michel, *Recueil d'in-scriptions grecques* (Brussels, 1900), p. 163, line 21 (re-ferring to offerings); *Inscr. Priene* 109.215f: "he marched at the head in a priestlike manner" (προε-πόμπευσεν . . . ἱεροπρεπῶς) [preceding trans. by Ed.]; on the extension of the meaning of the term, note how it is used in Philo, *Omn. prob. lib.* 75 "they have shown themselves especially devout in the serv-ice of God, not by offering sacrifices of animals, but by resolving to become like priests in their minds" (θεραπευταὶ θεοῦ γεγόνασιν, οὐ ζῷα καταθύοντες, ἀλλ' ἱεροπρεπεῖς τὰς ἑαυτῶν διανοίας κατασκευά-ζειν ἀξιοῦντες) [Loeb modified].

7 See Weidinger, *Die Haustafeln*, 54.

8 Theodoret (III, p. 703, Schulze): "He referred in this manner to women who were aged, not to those who had been deemed worthy of some official func-tion" (τὰς γεγηρακυίας οὕτως ὠνόμασεν, οὐ τὰς λειτουργίας τινὸς ἠξιωμένας) [trans. by Ed.].

9 See Gerhard, *Phoinix*, 35ff.

10 Apart from 4 Macc 15:4ff, note the use of these terms especially in Plutarch, *passim*.

11 As examples of the inscriptions about women, see *CIG* II, 1812.2; 2384.7; III, 3813.1; *Bulletin de Cor-respondance Hellenique* 22 (1898): 496.9; *ibid.*, 23 (1899): 301 No. 29.8; 25 (1901): 88 No. 210.4; N. Müller and N. A. Bees, *Die Inschriften der jüdischen Katakomben am Monteverde zu Rom* (Leipzig: 1919), No. 7 (φιλόταικνος); moreover, see *Inscr. Perg.* II, 604ff, "To the most sweet woman who loved her husband and her children." (τῇ γλυκυτάτῃ [γ]υ-ναικὶ φιλάνδρ[ῳ] καὶ φιλοτέκνῳ) [trans. by Ed.].

1 Tim 5:14. But since the general predicate "good" (ἀγαθάς) would then stand alone at the end of the list, and since the meaning "benevolent"[12] cannot be derived from the context (as is the case in 1 Petr 2:18), the two words οἰκουργούς and ἀγαθάς should be taken together and translated "fulfill their households duties well."[13]

The entire list of duties here is written in view of the opponents. This motif can be felt throughout.[14] It is symptomatic of the way in which the church tries to find its bearings in the world, and is thus a typical feature of the concept of "good Christian citizenship." This concept must be understood in the context of a transformed self–understanding of the church. The formation of Christian moral conduct with a view to the surrounding world also implies a demarcation from the Gnostic movement, and in turn demands the preservation of the tradition in a new situation.

■ **6, 7** Since the duties of the young men are included under the single infinitive "to be prudent" (σωφρονεῖν), it seems appropriate to connect it with "in all respects" (περὶ πάντα) from v 7. On "example" (τύπος), see above on 1 Tim 4:12.[15] The addressee assumes, as far as age is concerned, a position among the members of the congregation similar to that held by Timothy, according to 1 Tim 5:1f. In reality, therefore, the exhortations directed to him still belong to the regulations for young men, and the fact that they appear in the disguise of exhortations to Titus does not change their general character; see above on Tit 2:4. ἀφθορία (here translated as "pure") means "innocence," as is shown by Justin's use of the adjective ἄφθορος. In *Apol.* 1.15.6, he uses it in the sense "chaste"; in *Dial.* 100.5, it describes Eve before the fall. The fact that it is seldom used as a noun appears to have occasioned the textual variants:

"freedom from envy" (ἀφθονίαν) in P32 G; or "integrity" (ἀδιαφθορίαν) in ℵ al. Even "incorruptibility" (ἀφθαρσίαν), which was added to the end of the verse in ℵ pm, could originally have been a variant of ἀφθορίαν.

■ **8** On "sound" (ὑγιής) see above pp. 18ff, the excursus to 1 Tim 1:10. On "irreproachable" (ἀκατάγνωστος) see *IG* XIV, 2139.3: "blameless, irreproachable, unreviled" (ἄμεμπτος, ἀκατάγνωστος, ἀλοιδόρητος).[16] The accusatives are still dependent upon "show yourself to be . . ." (παρεχόμενος). On the purpose clause "so that . . .," (ἵνα), see v 5.

■ **9, 10** form a regulation for slaves; see above on 1 Tim 6:1. "Well pleasing" (εὐάρεστος) is used here, as in Rom 12:2, without being closely defined, and is not to be supplemented by a specific object such as "to God" (θεῷ). It is in the emphasis placed upon such purely social values[17] that the originally secular character of the parenesis is shown.[18] Paul was able to adopt ethical material from secular sources because of the structure of his theology. The Pastoral Epistles also base their ethics of Christian citizenship on the concept of revelation (see the following verses).

"God the savior" (θεὸς σωτήρ) does not refer to Christ; cf. the formulaic usage of "God the savior" elsewhere in the Pastorals, and see above pp. 100ff, the excursus to 2 Tim 1:10. That a reference to Christ is missing is perhaps a further indication of the pre–Christian origin of the list of rules for the household. On the genitive "the teaching of . . .," cf. 2 Tim 1:8.

12 See the Vulgate reading, *benignas*; and Lock, *ad loc.*
13 It follows from this interpretation that the reading οἰκουργούς is to be preferred to the Koine reading οἰκουρούς ("to stay at home"). On the use of οἰκουργός as a noun see Moulton–Howard, p. 274.
14 See Tit 2:8, 10; cf. above on 1 Tim 3:6, 7.
15 On ἑαυτὸν παρέχεσθαι ("to show oneself to be something") see J. Rouffiac, *Recherches sur les caractères du Grec dans le NT d'après les inscriptions de Priene* (Paris: 1911), p. 52.
16 Cf. also 2 Macc 4:47; *CIG* II, 1911ᵇ 5 (2d century A.D.); furthermore, *P. Giess.* I, 56.15 (where it stands beside "blameless" [ἀμέμπτως]). ἀκατάγνωστος and ἀνεπίλημπτος are synonyms; cf. Liddell-Scott, *s.v.*
17 The case is different in Col 3:23 and Eph 6:6.
18 See Dibelius, *Thessalonicher, Philipper*, on Phil 4:8. Cf. the inscriptions from Nisyros found in *Mitteilungen des deutschen archäologischen Instituts, Athenische Abteilung* 15 (1890): 134.11f: "pleasing in all regards" (γενόμενον εὐάρεστον πᾶσι); and especially *Inscr. Priene* 114.15: "well–pleasing in the expenditures of the office of gymnasiarch" (γενηθεὶς δὲ εὐάρεσ[τος] ἐν τοῖς τῆς γυμνασιαρχίας ἀναλώμασιν) [trans. by Ed.].

2   Conduct Based on the
History of Salvation

11   For the grace of God has appeared, bringing salvation to all men, 12/ and it
educates us to renounce godlessness
and worldly desires, and to lead a
prudent, upright, and pious life in this
age. 13/ Because we await the blessed
hope and the appearance of the glory of
the great God and of our savior Christ
Jesus: 14/ he gave himself for us, in
order to redeem us from all injustice and
to consecrate us for himself as his
special people who are eager for good
works.—15/ In this way you must teach,
exhort, and reprove with all impressiveness; no one should look down on you.

This section provides a basis in the history of salvation not only for the regulation for slaves, but also for the entire list of rules for the household. The possession of the grace of salvation should result in "leading a prudent, upright, and pious life" ($\sigma\omega\phi\rho\acute{o}\nu\omega\varsigma$ $\kappa\alpha\grave{\iota}$ $\delta\iota\kappa\alpha\acute{\iota}\omega\varsigma$ $\kappa\alpha\grave{\iota}$ $\epsilon\dot{\upsilon}\sigma\epsilon\beta\hat{\omega}\varsigma$ $\zeta\hat{\eta}\nu$). The Christianization of the rules for the household[1] is illustrated in the later texts, which base these rules upon the Christian faith.[2] The use of the kerygma as a motivating force for the parenesis is a pattern that had been created even before Paul. Paul provided the theological foundation for this pattern, and his thought, naturally, had its aftereffects, even if the relationship between indicative and imperative which he defined was modified.[3] What is presented in Tit 2:12 as the content of the Christian life is almost identical with "the ideal of Greek ethics."[4] Of the four cardinal virtues only "courage" ($\dot{\alpha}\nu\delta\rho\epsilon\acute{\iota}\alpha$) is missing. See Ditt. *Or.* I, 339.47f: "Those who have kept the faith piously and righteously" ($\tau o\grave{\upsilon}\varsigma$ $\tau\grave{\eta}\nu$ $\pi\acute{\iota}\sigma\tau\iota\nu$ $\epsilon\dot{\upsilon}\sigma\epsilon\beta\hat{\omega}\varsigma$ $\tau\epsilon$ $\kappa\alpha\grave{\iota}$ $\delta\iota\kappa\alpha\acute{\iota}\omega\varsigma$

$\tau\eta\rho\acute{\eta}\sigma o\nu\tau\alpha\varsigma$); *Inscr. Magn.* 162.6: "Living prudently and in modesty" ($\zeta\acute{\eta}\sigma\alpha\nu\tau\alpha$ $\sigma\omega\phi\rho\acute{o}\nu\omega\varsigma$ $\kappa\alpha\grave{\iota}$ $\kappa o\sigma\mu\acute{\iota}\omega\varsigma$) [trans. by Ed.]. Cf. also above pp. 39ff, the second excursus to 1 Tim 2:2.

On the particular words by which salvation is described here, see below. Instead of the epiphany of Christ,[5] this passage speaks of the epiphany of grace. This is consistent with the prescript (Tit 1:1ff, "the revelation of the word"). In general, in the Pastoral Epistles the actualization of the salvation event is a part of the fixed content of the kerygmatic statements.[6] To be sure, there is no concept of hypostatization;[7] rather the character of the revelation as word is further elaborated, as is the case in 1:3 (cf. 3:4). One can see the basis for this in Paul (of which the author is quite aware: see Tit 3:5); one can also see its modification. In Paul the accent is placed upon justification, here upon education in the faith.[8]

Even the word "to educate" ($\pi\alpha\iota\delta\epsilon\acute{\upsilon}\epsilon\iota\nu$) shows an

---

1   Dibelius–Greeven, *Kolosser, Epheser, Philemon,* excursus to Col 4:1; Lohse, *Colossians, Philemon,* on Col 4:1ff.
2   This is partly the case even in Eph 5:22ff, but it is especially clear in 1 Petr 2:18ff.
3   On this see Bultmann, *Theology* 1, pp. 203ff.
4   Eduard Meyer, *Ursprung und Anfänge des Christentums,* 3, p. 396.
5   See above p. 104, the second excursus to 2 Tim 1:10.
6   See Windisch, "Zur Christologie," 213ff. In fact a myth of such a revelation existed in Gnosticism, see *Odes of Sol.* 33.
7   Here the present edition differs with the 2d German edition of this commentary.
8   See Gilles P:son Wetter, *Charis; ein Beitrag zur Geschichte des ältesten Christentums* (Leipzig: Hinrichs, 1913), pp. 55ff.
9   See 1 Cor 11:32 and 2 Cor 6:9; also *1 Clem.* 56.2, which contains copious quotations of OT passages. Cf. also 1 Tim 1:20 and Heb 12:5ff.

important change in meaning from the usage in the genuine Pauline epistles. Paul uses the word in its LXX meaning, "to discipline through punishment."[9] But here the word is used in its actual Hellenic sense, which contrasts the "uninstructed" (ἰδιώτης) with the one who "is educated" (πεπαιδευμένος).[10] On the use of the word in Jewish contexts, cf. *Ep. Ar.* 287, where it is said of the "lovers of learning" (φιλομαθεῖς) that "these are beloved by God, for they have educated their minds toward what is excellent" (οὗτοι γὰρ θεοφιλεῖς εἰσι πρὸς τὰ κάλλιστα πεπαιδευκότες τὰς διανοίας) [trans. by Ed.]. This concept is already applied to Christ in the congregational prayer of *1 Clem.* 59.3: "through Jesus Christ . . . through him have you taught us, made us holy, and brought us to honour" (διὰ Ἰησοῦ Χριστοῦ . . . , δι' οὗ ἡμᾶς ἐπαίδευσας, ἡγίασας, ἐτίμησας). Tatian used the word very characteristically in *Or. Graec.* 42: "I Tatian, adherent of a foreign philosophy, have composed this book, I who was born in the land of the Assyrians, but afterward was educated first in your beliefs, and then in those which I now profess to proclaim" (ὁ κατὰ βαρβάρους φιλοσοφῶν Τατιανὸς συνέταξα, γεννηθεὶς μὲν ἐν τῇ τῶν Ἀσσυρίων γῇ, παιδευθεὶς δὲ πρῶτον μὲν τὰ ὑμέτερα, δεύτερον δὲ ἅτινα νῦν κηρύττειν ἐπαγγέλλομαι) [trans. by Ed.].

"Worldly" (κοσμικός) is used here, just as "world" (κόσμος) is often used, with a pessimistic nuance; cf. *2 Clem.* 17.3: "and let us not be dragged aside by worldly lusts" (μὴ ἀντιπαρελκώμεθα ἀπὸ τῶν κοσμικῶν ἐπιθυμιῶν). Note the use of "desire of the flesh" (ἐπιθυμία [τῆς] σαρκός) in Gal 5:16 and Eph 2:3.

■ **13** "Blessed" (μακάριος) designates the sphere of the "hope" (ἐλπίς), the object of hope. It is debated whether the divine predicate in this passage ("our great God and savior") is applied to Jesus, or whether a distinction is made between the "great God" and the "savior Jesus Christ." The formulation of the expression itself speaks for the former alternative. The subordination of Christ to God, which is consistently retained precisely in the "epiphany passages" of the Pastoral Epistles, supports the latter alternative.[11] The fact that the title "savior" (σωτήρ) is applied to Christ does not prove that the designation "God" is also given to him. We have here a level of Christological development which corresponds to that in the Lucan writings: transfer of the soteriological functions from God to Christ, while maintaining clear subordination.[12]

■ **14** The formulation is primarily influenced by Ex 19:5 (see Deut 14:2): "You shall be for me a special people, distinct from all the nations" (ἔσεσθέ μοι λαὸς περιούσιος ἀπὸ πάντων τῶν ἐθνῶν). The same influence is seen in 1 Petr 2:9f; cf. also *1 Clem.* 64: "who chose out the Lord Jesus Christ, and us through him for 'a special people' " (ὁ ἐκλεξάμενος τὸν κύριον Ἰησοῦν Χριστὸν καὶ ἡμᾶς δι' αὐτοῦ εἰς λαὸν περιούσιον) [Loeb modified]. On "consecrate" (καθαρίζειν) see Heb 9:14. It is most characteristic of the origin of Christian cultic language that the honorary title of the people of Israel, which was adopted by the Christians from the LXX, is placed here between a Hellenistic soteriological statement and an equally Hellenistic conclusion. For the word "eager for" (ζηλωτής), used in contexts similar to Tit 2:15, derives from the terminology of the inscriptions.[13] The Hellenistic Jewish–Christian genesis of the entire context is clear.[14]

The Soteriological Terminology of Titus 2:11–14 and 3:4–7

1. In the two excursus to 2 Tim 1:10, it was demonstrated that the Pastorals prefer terms which had long been common in the hieratic language of the Greeks, but which at the time of these epistles had received a new tone and new weight through the emperor cult. These two passages in Titus bear this hieratic stamp perhaps more clearly than any other passage in the Pastoral Epistles. For the concept of "the God who appeared" (θεὸς ἐπιφανής)—represented here by the term "appearance" (ἐπιφάνεια)—and of the "savior" (σωτήρ)

---

10 For documentation see Liddell–Scott, *s.v.*, and other lexica; see also the text given below in Appendix 4.

11 See Windisch, "Zur Christologie," 226; Jeremias, *ad loc.*

12 See Conzelmann, *Luke*, 170ff. On this particular verse in Tit, see A. W. Wainwright, "The Confession 'Jesus is God' in the New Testament," *SJT* 10 (1957): 274ff.

13 See, for example, Ditt. *Or.* I, 339.90: "eager for the best" (ζηλωταὶ τῶν καλλίστων); similarly *Inscr. Priene* 110.11f; cf. Ditt. *Syll.* II, 717.33; 756.32; 714.46; but also Philo, *Migr. Abr.* 62. "Eager" (ζηλωτής) is used with περί ("for") in *1 Clem.* 45.1 and Pol. *Phil.* 6.3.

14 Cf. also the following excursus; on the concepts and the terminology, see above p. 43 on 1 Tim 2:6.

is still further elaborated by terms belonging to the same constellation of concepts. "The grace that brings salvation" (σωτήριος χάρις): "bringing salvation" (σωτήριος)[15] is used in religious terminology both in cultic[16] and spiritual[17] contexts. "Grace" (χάρις) in this context does not recall the grace of God of which Paul writes, but rather the "graces" of the epiphanous gods in their manifestations (as they are praised, e.g., in the cult of the ruler).[18] What is meant in Tit 2:11 by the phrase "bringing salvation to all men" (σωτήριος πᾶσιν ἀνθρώποις) is expressed in the inscriptions by "the common savior of human life" (κοινὸς τοῦ ἀνθρωπίνου βίου σωτήρ), or something similar.[19] "Blessed hope" (μακαρία ἐλπίς, see above on 1 Tim 1:11) and "great God" (μέγας θεός) belong to the same category of expressions. Divinities coming from the East frequently received the attribute "great" (μέγας).[20] Thus the word was also used as a title for the regent in the cult of the ruler, since that cult was influenced by the East.[21] The expression had already

been appropriated by Hellenistic Judaism (see section 2 below). "The greatest God" (ὁ μέγιστος θεός) is common in Josephus, and "the greatness of God" (μεγαλειότης τοῦ θεοῦ) occurs in Aristobulus and Josephus,[22] as well as Lk 9:43 and 1 Clem. 24.5. The "greatness" (μεγαλειότης) of Christ is attested in 2 Petr 1:16. "Loving kindness" (φιλανθρωπία) is the one virtue typical of the ruler.[23] "Loving kindness" and "generosity" (φιλανθρωπία and χρηστότης) are often mentioned together.[24] Both words are also found in the LXX. In this context it is significant that they are both used to refer to God[25] and that "loving kindness" (φιλανθρωπία) is commonly mentioned as a virtue of the ruler.[26]

Thus the terms under discussion, including "savior" (σωτήρ) and "appearance" (ἐπιφάνεια), prove to be, first of all, quite clearly part of the higher Koine, and secondly, technical terms from Hellenistic cults, especially from the cult of the ruler. More important is the fact that there is a close relationship in tone. If one is

---

15 See Wisd Sol 1:14; 3 Macc 6:31; 7:18 (codex Venetus); 4 Macc 12:6 (according to codex S); 15:26.

16 On σωτήρια θῦσαι, see Ditt. Syll. I, 384.23; 391.22; Or. I, 4.43; as well as Amos 5:22.

17 Corp. Herm. 10.15 (I, 120, Nock): "This is the only saving thing for men, the knowledge of God" (τοῦτο μόνον σωτήριον ἀνθρώπῳ ἐστίν, ἡ γνῶσις τοῦ θεοῦ) [Trans.].

18 See Ditt. Syll. II, 798.7ff about Caligula: "But those who enjoy the fruits of the abundance of immortal grace are in this respect greater than former generations, for they shared an inheritance from their fathers, while these, by the grace of Gaius Caesar, by sharing the administration with such gods have become kings; and the graces of gods are as different from mortal inheritance as is the sun from night or incorruptibility from mortal nature" (οἱ [δὲ] τῆς ἀθανάτου | χάριτος τὴν ἀφθονίαν καρπούμενοι, ταύτηι τῶν πάλαι μείζονες, ὅτι οἱ μὲν παρὰ πατέρων διαδοχῆς ἔσχον, οὗτοι | δ' ἐ[κ] τῆς Γαΐου Καίσαρος χάριτος εἰς συναρχίαν τηλικούτων θεῶν γεγόνασι βασιλεῖς, θεῶν δὲ χάριτες τούτῳ διαφέρου|σιν ἀνθρωπίνων διαδοχῶν, ᾧ ἢ νυκτὸς ἥλιος καὶ τὸ ἄφθαρτον θνητῆς φύσεως). Antiochus I of Commagene says at the beginning of his great inscription (Ditt. Or. I, 383.9f), that he "wrote down the works of his own grace for eternity" (ἔργα χάριτος ἰδίας εἰς | χρόνον ἀνέγραψεν αἰώνιον) [trans. in this footnote by Ed.].

19 See Ditt. Syll. II, 760.7; BMI IV, 894.6f; cf. Ditt. Or. II, 669.7: (about Galba) "from the benefactor who shone forth upon us for the salvation of the

whole race of men" (παρὰ τοῦ ἐπιλάμψαντος ἡμεῖν ἐπὶ σωτηρίᾳ τοῦ παντὸς ἀνθρώπων γένους εὐεργέτου) [trans. by Ed.].

20 This has been documented in the extensive collection of materials by Bruno Müller, ΜΕΓΑΣ ΘΕΟΣ, Dissertationes philologicae Halenses 21 (1913), 281ff.

21 Ibid., 389ff.

22 See Adolf Schlatter, Wie sprach Josephus von Gott? (Gütersloh: Bertelsmann, 1910), 18f and 21.

23 See Ditt. Or. I, 90.12; 139.20; Syll. II, 888.101; Harold Idris Bell, Jews and Christians in Egypt (London: Quaritch, 1924), 1912.81; further attestations are given in Preisigke, 2, p. 692 (with a reference to "Your loving kindness" [ἡ σὴ φιλανθρωπία] in petitions directed to the emperor and the governor); see also 3, pp. 201f.

24 See Philo, Jos. 176; Josephus, Ant. 10.163; Onosander, Strategikos 381 (p. 112, Schwebel); further references in Wettstein, Novum Testamentum Graecum, ad loc.

25 "Loving kindness" (φιλανθρωπία) is found in Musonius (p. 90.12, Hense); "kindly" (φιλάνθρωπος) in Philo, Virt. 77; "generosity" (χρηστότης) in the LXX; Josephus, Ant. 20.90; Rom 2:4; 11:22.

26 See, e.g., Inscr. Magn. 18.17; 201.2; Ditt. Or. I, 90.12; 139.20; 168.12, 46; see Wendland, "Σωτήρ," p. 345, note 2. Cf. also Dg 9.2 "the time came which God had appointed to manifest his generosity and power—O the excellence of the kindness and love of God!" (ἦλθε δὲ ὁ καιρὸς ὃν θεὸς προέθετο λοιπὸν φανερῶσαι τὴν ἑαυτοῦ χρηστότητα καὶ δύναμιν—ὦ

familiar with the lofty, stylized manner in which the emperor was honored as a god in the inscriptions,[27] he will sense that it is the same language being spoken both there and here.[28]

2. The manner in which these terms are introduced indicates quite clearly that the author is aware that he is not saying something new, but is passing on what he has received. The importance of this style for the language of the church from the time of the Apologists on, makes it difficult to imagine that the author of the Pastorals introduced this kind of language into Christian literature singlehandedly. Since the other cultic expressions in the Pastorals (see above on 1 Tim 1:17 and 2:10) apparently derive from the usage of the Judaism of the Diaspora, these formulas may, by analogy, be said to have come to the author of the Pastorals through the same process. The passages quoted above from Greek Jewish texts confirm this. Thus, one exegetical difficulty is eliminated: a cluster of related expressions, but applied to different persons, God and Christ, can be explained; cf. the "epiphany" of the "savior" God, viz. Christ.[29] Hence the variation of meaning in the use of other expressions in the Pastorals is also explained. For instance "grace" ($\chi\acute{\alpha}\rho\iota\varsigma$) in Tit 2:11 means divine power, whereas in 3:7 it is used in a Pauline sense. "Bringing salvation" ($\sigma\omega\tau\acute{\eta}\rho\iota\sigma\varsigma$) in 2:11 refers to the power of grace, while "he saved" ($\check{\epsilon}\sigma\omega\sigma\epsilon\nu$) in 3:5 refers to salvation through baptism. The expressions are already formulaic and are used without any attempt to relate them to each other. There is no conscious reflection upon the relationship between the titles given to God and to Christ. Finally, the fact, which is especially obvious in Tit 2:14 and 3:5, that ideas of a completely different nature and origin could be combined with those discussed in this excursus (see above on Tit 2:14) is explained if the latter

expressions were not formulated *ad hoc*.

3. The passages in question are also of special importance in deciding the question of authenticity. First of all, we may state that in the "accepted" epistles, Paul uses the linguistic material discussed here to a very limited extent. The statistics on "savior" ($\sigma\omega\tau\acute{\eta}\rho$),[30] even if only accidental, are nevertheless symptomatic. Even more important, however, is a second observation. It is precisely the history of salvation experience of the Christian which Paul describes in a completely different style. His soteriological language remains original, despite all dependence upon Jewish and pre–Pauline Christian tradition. The Pastorals speak in the lofty style used by the Greek world and occasionally even by Greek-speaking Judaism. Insofar as a lofty style of language can become commonplace, it has done so here. One should not be deceived by the fact that the language of the Pastoral Epistles (and, for example, that of the 2nd Epistle of Peter as well, which is related to it)[31] seems relatively unique within the NT.

One solution to the problem raised by this contradiction is to resort to the explanation that Paul's language went through a development. But this argument cannot stand. If the Pastoral Epistles could be dated at the beginning of his activity, then (purely from a linguistic standpoint) a progression might seem conceivable: a progression from the common language of Hellenistic Judaism to a more original way of speaking. But the situation presupposed in the Pastorals makes it impossible to do this. The mission, the congregations, the teaching, the heresies—all these things show that the great missionary step into the pagan world was not made only recently. Thus there remains only one possible assumption for anyone who considers the epistles Pauline. That is the assumption that Paul changed his original manner

---

$\tau\hat{\eta}\varsigma$ $\dot{\upsilon}\pi\epsilon\rho\beta\alpha\lambda\lambda o\acute{\upsilon}\sigma\eta\varsigma$ $\phi\iota\lambda\alpha\nu\theta\rho\omega\pi\acute{\iota}\alpha\varsigma$ $\kappa\alpha\grave{\iota}$ $\dot{\alpha}\gamma\acute{\alpha}\pi\eta\varsigma$ $\tau o\hat{\upsilon}$ $\theta\epsilon o\hat{\upsilon}$) [Loeb modified]. See also Just. *Dial.* 47.5: "The generosity and loving kindness of God and his richness without measure consider him who repents from his sins ... as just and innocent" ($\dot{\eta}$ $\gamma\grave{\alpha}\rho$ $\chi\rho\eta\sigma\tau\acute{o}\tau\eta\varsigma$ $\kappa\alpha\grave{\iota}$ $\dot{\eta}$ $\phi\iota\lambda\alpha\nu\theta\rho\omega\pi\acute{\iota}\alpha$ $\tau o\hat{\upsilon}$ $\theta\epsilon o\hat{\upsilon}$ $\kappa\alpha\grave{\iota}$ $\tau\grave{o}$ $\check{\alpha}\mu\epsilon\tau\rho o\nu$ $\tau o\hat{\upsilon}$ $\pi\lambda o\acute{\upsilon}\tau o\upsilon$ $\alpha\dot{\upsilon}\tau o\hat{\upsilon}$ $\tau\grave{o}\nu$ $\mu\epsilon\tau\alpha\nu o o\hat{\upsilon}\nu\tau\alpha$ $\dot{\alpha}\pi\grave{o}$ $\tau\hat{\omega}\nu$ $\dot{\alpha}\mu\alpha\rho\tau\eta$-$\mu\acute{\alpha}\tau\omega\nu$ ... $\dot{\omega}\varsigma$ $\delta\acute{\iota}\kappa\alpha\iota o\nu$ $\kappa\alpha\grave{\iota}$ $\dot{\alpha}\nu\alpha\mu\acute{\alpha}\rho\tau\eta\tau o\nu$ $\check{\epsilon}\chi\epsilon\iota$) [trans. by Ed.]. See also S. Lorenz, *De progressu notionis* $\phi\iota\lambda\alpha\nu\theta\rho\omega\pi\acute{\iota}\alpha\varsigma$, Unpub. Diss. (Leipzig, 1914), especially pp. 42f.

27 See, e.g., Appendices 8–12 in Wendland, *Hellenistische Kultur*, 409ff, where the evidence is collected.

28 See Meyer, *Ursprung und Anfänge des Christentums* 3, p. 396; F. Bilabel, "Aegyptische Thronbesteigungsurkunden," in *Festschrift Cimbria* (Dortmund: Friedrich Wilhelm Ruhfus, 1926), 63ff.

29 The transfer of the divine title belongs here as well, if Tit 2:13 is to be taken in this sense (see above).

30 See above pp. 100ff, the excursus to 2 Tim 1:10.

31 See Ernst Käsemann, "An Apologia for Primitive Christian Eschatology," *Essays on New Testament Themes*, SBT 41 (Naperville: Allenson, 1964), 181ff.

of speaking in his old age and adopted more worldly expressions, to express precisely those thoughts which form the very center of his Christianity. Whoever is unwilling to accept this assumption (and if I may say so, it is an extremely hazardous one) will deny the Pauline authorship of these epistles.

■ **15** "With all impressiveness" (μετὰ πάσης ἐπιταγῆς) is to be regarded as a heightened form of "by command" (κατ' ἐπιταγήν) as found in 1 Cor 7:6. Theodoret (III, p. 706, Schulze) paraphrases the expression thus:

"It is necessary to teach and to admonish with confidence" (σὺν παρρησίᾳ διδάσκειν καὶ ἐπιτιμᾶν ἔνθα δεῖ) [trans. by Ed.]. On the concluding exhortation see above on 1 Tim 1:18–20.

3   General Exhortations Based on History of Salvation

1   **Admonish them to be subject to magistrates and authorities, to be obedient, to be prepared for every good work, 2/ not to defame anyone, to be peaceable (and) kind (and) to show all gentleness to all men. 3/ Once we too were (caught) in foolishness, disobedience, and error, slaves to all kinds of desires and lusts, spending our lives in malice and envy, hateful (to others) and hating one another. 4/ But when the generosity and loving kindness of God our savior appeared, 5/ he saved us, not because of the works of righteousness we had done, but according to his mercy through the bath of rebirth and renewal, (as it is worked by) the holy spirit, 6/ which he richly poured out over us through Jesus Christ our savior; 7/ thus, justified by his grace we should become heirs, as we hope for eternal life. 8a/ The word stands firm!**

■ **1, 2** contain exhortations of a more general nature which are introduced by the demand for obedience to those in authority. This commandment, to which the author refers briefly, was extensively treated by Paul in Rom 13:1ff as an independent unit of the parenesis. In 1 Petr 2:13ff, it already has its place at the beginning of the rules for the household.[1] "To be obedient" ($\pi\epsilon\iota\theta\alpha\rho\chi\epsilon\hat{\iota}\nu$) can be used in an absolute sense.[2] "Prepared for every good work" ($\pi\rho\grave{o}s\ \pi\hat{a}\nu\ \check{\epsilon}\rho\gamma o\nu\ \dot{a}\gamma\alpha\theta\grave{o}\nu\ \check{\epsilon}\tau o\iota\mu os$) is used as in *1 Clem.* 2.7.[3] "To show all gentleness . . ." ($\pi\hat{a}\sigma\alpha\nu\ \dot{\epsilon}\nu\delta\epsilon\iota\kappa\nu\acute{\nu}\mu\epsilon\nu os\ \kappa\tau\lambda.$) is a conventional expression; cf. Jude 3 and 2 Petr 1:5.[4]

■ **3–7** speak of the state of the reader with regard to salvation, before and after becoming a Christian. Note that the author includes himself in this characterization. In the comparison of Tit 3:3–7 with Rom 6:17f; 1 Cor 6:9–11; Col 3:7, 8; Eph 2:2ff; *2 Clem.* 1.6–8, a significant similarity in the train of thought is apparent. Such a presentation of a person's past before becoming a Christian,[5] followed by a description of his condition as a Christian, was one of the most common topics of early Christian preaching. The turning point was described either from the standpoint of the mission or that of the history of salvation. If the former, the conversion was stressed; if the latter, the appearance of Christ, as is the case here (see also Gal 4:4). A direct literary dependence of any of these passages upon one another is unlikely in view of their differences in wording. Only the pattern was transmitted by the parenetic tradition.

In Tit 3:3ff, however, the formula "the word stands firm" ($\pi\iota\sigma\tau\grave{o}s\ \dot{o}\ \lambda\acute{o}\gamma os$)[6] indicates that these sentences were derived from the tradition. That the passage is based on a particular schema also explains the use of the first person plural. To be sure, the passage is not of a uniform character; terms described in the excursus to Tit 2:14 stand side by side with terms used by Paul.[7] Apparently the author supplemented these traditional soteriological statements with Pauline interpretations,

---

1   See above p. 37f, the first excursus to 1 Tim 2:2.
2   It is so used in the law from Pergamon, Ditt. *Or.* II, 483.70f: "and if private persons are not obedient in this fashion . . ." ($\dot{\epsilon}\grave{a}\nu\ \delta\grave{\epsilon}\ \mu\eta\delta'\ o\check{\nu}\tau\omega\ \pi\epsilon\iota\theta\alpha\rho\chi\hat{\omega}|\sigma\iota\nu\ o\dot{\iota}\ \dot{\iota}\delta\iota\hat{\omega}\tau\alpha\iota\ \kappa\tau\lambda.$) [trans. by Ed.].
3   See also Tit 1:16.
4   Similar expressions are found in *P. Giess.* I, 56.14; 79, col. II.7; Ditt. *Or.* II, 669.3 (cited at Tit 2:2);

Ep. Ar. 190, and many other passages.
5   "We were" or "you were" ($\check{\eta}\mu\epsilon\nu$ or $\check{\eta}\tau\epsilon$) and a catalogue of vices were common features of such a presentation.
6   See below on Tit 3:8 and above pp. 28f, the excursus to 1 Tim 1:15.
7   See Tit 3:5, 7, and above, the excursus to Tit 2:14 section 3.

which stand out, even stylistically, as pure prose.

Again, as in Tit 2:11 and 2:13, the subject of the epiphany is the personified power of revelation, although one may not yet speak of hypostatization. Again the salvation is made a present reality, in this case by the reference to the sacrament and the explicit statement of the consequences of salvation.

■ **3** "Hateful" (στυγητός) is found only here in the entire NT, but it is attested also in *1 Clem.* 35.6; 45.7; and in Philo, *Decal.* 131.

■ **4** On the terminology of this verse, see the excursus to Tit 2:14.

■ **5** As in 2 Tim 1:9 (see above), righteousness by works is here repudiated; such expressions have been taken over from Paul. They, in the meantime, had themselves become part of the tradition, as is shown by their use in the Epistle to the Ephesians (2:5, 8; 3:12) and *1 Clem.* 32.4. "Bath" (λουτρόν) refers to baptism, as in Eph 5:26. The event connected with baptism is called "rebirth" (παλιγγενεσία), although it is not said how this rebirth is effected.

Rebirth

1. Philo (*Vit. Mos.* 2.65) and *1 Clem.* 9.4 use the word "rebirth" (παλιγγενεσία) in a cosmological sense (after the Flood); Josephus (*Ant.* 11.66), in a national sense; and Matthew (19:28), in a messianic–eschatological sense. One may also compare the Stoic use of the word: rebirth of the cosmos. Between these meanings of the word on the one hand, and the mystical sense to be discussed below on the other hand, is the intermediate definition which equates "rebirth" (παλιγγενεσία) with "reincarnation" (μετενσωμάτωσις). This definition seems to be presupposed in Nemesius,[8] and possibly Plutarch as well.[9]

In Tit 3:5, the parallel "of renewal etc." (ἀνακαινώσεως κτλ.) makes clear what is expected from the "bath of rebirth." The understanding of baptism as rebirth expressed in Tit 3:5ff is similar to that of Rom 6:4 and Jn 3:3, 5; cf. also 1 Petr 1:3, 23. The understanding of rebirth common to these passages is analogous to certain concepts of the mysteries. It is an understanding related to the image of baptism as death or burial, but it is not elaborated further here. It seems that "bath of rebirth" (λουτρὸν παλιγγενεσίας) as a term for baptism was well known and frequently used by the author of the Pastorals and in his congregations. That Paul did not use the word "rebirth" in the genuine epistles, was emphasized by Albert Schweitzer as a fact of the highest importance; he takes it as an indication that for Paul the new state of life is attained only through a real dying and rising with Christ; therefore it cannot be expressed by a different and, in this case, purely symbolic term such as rebirth.[10] It is an open question, however, whether terms like this one in common Christian usage still suggested a specific type of experience or event. Completely different expressions are frequently used for the same thing as early as the second and third Christian generations. Such a state of affairs speaks against such an assumption.[11] But the very frequency and currency of these terms might support the thesis that the Christians adopted them from some other source.

2. Although the word is not unknown in Judaism, there is no real analogy to its usage in Tit 3:5. The comparison between a proselyte and a newborn child is not analogous.[12] The thought–world of the mysteries seems to provide better parallels.[13] Here "rebirth" can designate the life after death, as in a passage from Philo that derives from some unknown source, Philo, *Cher.* 114: "What of it after death? But then we who are here joined to the

---

8   See Nemesius, *De natura hominis* 2 (p. 51, Matthaei) "For Kronios in his work 'On Rebirth' (that is his term for 're-incarnation')" (Κρόνιος μὲν γὰρ ἐν τῷ Περὶ παλιγγενεσίας—οὕτω δὲ καλεῖ τὴν μετενσωμάτωσιν) [trans. by Ed.].

9   Plutarch, *Is. et Os.* 72, p. 379 e. Cf. Reitzenstein, *Mysterienreligionen*, 262.

10 Albert Schweitzer, *The Mysticism of Paul the Apostle*, tr. William Montgomery (London: Adam & Charles Black, 1953), 13ff.

11 See Adolf von Harnack, *Die Terminologie der Wiedergeburt und verwandter Erlebnisse in der ältesten Kirche*, TU 42, 3–4, (Leipzig: Hinrichs, 1918–19), pp. 97ff.

Von Harnack, however, does not assume that these terms were derived from a non–Christian source.

12 See Windisch–Preisker, *Katholische Briefe*, excursus to 1 Petr 2:2.

13 See Bauer, *s.v.*

body, creatures of composition and quality, shall be no more, but shall go forward to our rebirth, to be with the unbodied, without composition and without quality" (μετὰ τὸν θάνατον; ἀλλ' οὐκ ἐσόμεθα οἱ μετὰ σω-μάτων σύγκριτοι ποιοί, ἀλλ' εἰς παλιγγενεσίαν ὁρμήσομεν οἱ μετὰ ἀσωμάτων ἀσύγκριτοι ποιοί).[14] But the mysteries also mediate a new birth which takes place in this life; see Apuleius, *Met.* 11.21 (p. 283, Helm): "considering that it was in her power (that of the goddess) both to damn and to save all persons, and that the tak-ing of such orders was like to a voluntary death and a difficult recovery to health: and if anywhere there were any at the point of death and at the end and limit of their life . . . it was in her power by divine providence to make them, as it were, new–born and to reduce them to the path of health." (nam et inferum claustra et salutis tutelam in deae manu posita ipsamque traditionem ad instar voluntariae mortis et precariae salutis celebrari, quippe cum transactis vitae temporibus iam in ipso finitae lucis limine constitutos: . . . numen deae soleat eligere et sua providentia quodam modo renatos ad novae reponere rursus salutis curricula).[15] It is clear that the term rebirth is closely connected with the transfer of vital powers in the cult. Cf. further the great Parisian magical papyrus (the so–called "Mithras Liturgy") in Preis. *Zaub.* 499ff: "But if it seem good to you to hand me over once more to the birth that is immortal" (ἐὰν δὲ ὑμῖν δόξῃ μεταπαραδῶναί με τῇ ἀθανάτῳ γενέσει); "O Lord, in being born again I die, as I increase and as I have increased I come to an end, born through the birth which generates life and departed into death I go my way . . ." (κύριε, παλινγενόμενος ἀπογίγνομαι αὐξό-μενος καὶ αὐξηθεὶς τελευτῶ, ἀπὸ γενέσεως ζωογόνου γενόμενος εἰς ἀπογενεσίαν ἀναλυθεὶς πορεύομαι) [trans. by Ed.].

For further clarification one may refer to the Hermetic "Secret discourse on rebirth" (λόγος ἀπόκρυφος περὶ παλιγγενεσίας) in *Corp. Herm.* 13; in 13.3 Hermes responds to Tat's request, "show me in detail the manner of rebirth" (διάφρασόν μοι τῆς παλιγγενεσίας τὸν τρόπον) by answering: "I cannot say anything but this; as I see in myself something, an immaterial vision pro-duced by the mercy of God, I both have gone forth from myself into an immortal body, and I am no longer who I was, but have been born in the mind" (οὐκ ἔχω λέ-γειν, πλὴν τοῦτο· ὁρῶν † τι † ἐν ἐμοὶ ἄπλαστον θέαν γεγενημένην ἐξ ἐλέου θεοῦ καὶ ἐμαυτὸν ἐξελή-λυθα εἰς ἀθάνατον σῶμα, καὶ εἰμι νῦν οὐχ ὁ πρίν, ἀλλ' ἐγεννήθην ἐν νῷ) [Trans.].

"Renewal etc." (ἀνακαίνωσις κτλ.) describes the same process with a different expression. It is the divine "spirit" (πνεῦμα) which creates man anew, see Col 3:10.[16]

3. Therefore, some relationship in conception and ter-minology seems to exist between the Hellenistic and the Christian "rebirth," as Tertullian, *Bapt.*, affirms. Never-theless, one ought not underestimate the differences. Notice, e.g., the difference in the presentation of the so–called "Mithras Liturgy": there "the perishable na-ture of mortals" (φθαρτὴ βροτῶν φύσις), the "human psychic power" (ἀνθρωπίνη ψυχικὴ δύναμις)[17] must stand still, "that I may be reborn in thought and that the sacred spirit may breathe upon me" (ἵνα νοήματι μεταγεν[ν]ηθῶ καὶ πνεύσῃ ἐν ἐμοὶ τὸ ἱερὸν πνεῦμα).[18] But in the Christian concept, there is no ecstasy "for a brief time" (πρὸς ὀλίγον), but a new and lasting life in the spirit, which furthermore does not require a renewal of such a rebirth, as does the mystery described by Apuleius (*Met.* XI). Nor is that life available only within a special mystical Christian group; it is the state of

---

14 Cf. Joseph Pascher, ἡ βασιλικὴ ὁδός (Paderborn: Schöningh, 1931), *passim*, especially pp. 246ff and 252; see also pp. 259ff for a discussion of the relation between cosmology and soteriology. Joseph Dey, ΠΑΛΙΓΓΕΝΕΣΙΑ, *ein Beitrag zur Klärung der religions-geschichtlichen Bedeutung von Tit 3.5*, NTAbh 17, 5, (Münster: Aschendorff, 1937), 34f, however, holds a different opinion.

15 See also *CIL* VI, 510.17ff: "Reborn forever by the sacrifice of a bull and a ram" (tauro-bolio criobo-lioq[ue] in aeternum renatus); Dey, ΠΑΛΙΓΓΕΝΕ-ΣΙΑ, 99 and 73f, doubts the value of these two pas-sages as evidence.

16 The genitive "of the spirit" (πνεύματος) is there-fore not an objective, but a causative genitive; in Rom 12:2 and *Herm. vis.* 3.8.9: "the renewal of your spirits" (ἡ ἀνακαίνωσις τῶν πνευμάτων ὑμῶν) it is an objective genitive. Moreover, since "rebirth" (παλιγγενεσία) unlike "renewal" (ἀνακαίνωσις) needs no explanation, it belongs perhaps only to the latter substantive (against Spicq, *ad loc.*).

17 Preis. *Zaub.* IV, 533 and 523f. The phrases are syn-onymous.

18 Preis. *Zaub.* IV, 508ff.

salvation which is available to all. This fact points to a process in which mystical expressions were adopted and modified in common usage.[19] Therefore two points of difference exist between the concept of rebirth in the mysteries and the understanding of this term in the passage under discussion. Tit 3:5 knows nothing of ecstasy, but only of the lasting power of a new life. Rebirth is thus not solely available to certain individual mystics, but is the fundamental event and experience of all Christians.[20]

■ **7** As far as the words are concerned, the passage is reminiscent of the genuine Pauline epistles. But one might ask whether the act of justification itself is actually meant, or rather a life which is righteous by virtue of grace (as substantiation for the latter alternative, see above on Tit 2:11–14). But one cannot decide with certainty how the author interpreted what for him was already a traditional expression. It might seem surprising that the text

does not say "heirs of eternal life" ($\kappa\lambda\eta\rho o\nu\acute{o}\mu o\iota \ \zeta\omega\tilde{\eta}s$ $a\iota\omega\nu\acute{\iota}o\upsilon$). The explanation is perhaps to be found in Tit 1:2. From this passage it can be inferred that "hope for eternal life" ($\grave{\epsilon}\lambda\pi\grave{\iota}s \ \zeta\omega\tilde{\eta}s \ a\iota\omega\nu\acute{\iota}o\upsilon$) constitutes a formulaic entity in itself; therefore, it cannot be divided into its constituent parts, but is simply joined to "heirs" ($\kappa\lambda\eta\rho o\nu\acute{o}\mu o\iota$) by means of "according to" ($\kappa a\tau\acute{a}$).

■ **8a** The phrase "the word stands firm" ($\pi\iota\sigma\tau\grave{o}s \ \grave{o}$ $\lambda\acute{o}\gamma os$)[21] is best understood here as a formula of affirmation, not as a quotation formula, even though the preceding statement about the appearance of salvation employs fixed traditional sentences. It is precisely as such stylized tradition that the formula affirms the passage.

---

19   Dibelius–Greeven, *Kolosser, Epheser, Philemon,* excursus to Eph 4:16, section 4.

20   See also the following literature: Paul Gennrich, *Die Lehre von der Wiedergeburt* (Leipzig: Deichert, 1907), who denies non–Christian influence; Richard Reitzenstein, *Die Vorgeschichte der christlichen Taufe* (Leipzig: Teubner 1929); Windisch–Preisker, *Katholische Briefe,* excursus on 1 Petr 2:1–10 and 1 Jn 3:9; V. Jacono, "La ΠΑΛΙΓΓΕΝΕΣΙΑ in S. Paolo e nell'-ambiente pagano," *Biblica* 15 (1934): 369ff; Dey, ΠΑΛΙΓΓΕΝΣΙΑ, which contains comprehensive presentation of the material and calls attention to the wide, unspecific usage of the word; on the latter point see Friedrich Büchsel, *TDNT,* 1, pp. 686–89;

Rudolf Bultmann, *The Gospel of John,* tr. G. R. Beasley-Murray (Philadelphia: Westminster Press, 1971), p. 135, n. 4; Joseph Ysebaert, *Greek Baptismal Terminology* (Nijmegen [Netherlands]: Dekker & Van de Vegt, 1962), pp. 87ff; Erik Sjöberg, "Wiedergeburt und Neuschöpfung im palästinischen Judentum," *ST* 4 (1951–52): 44–85; Carl–Martin Edsman, "Schöpfung und Wiedergeburt: Nochmals Jac. 1:18," in *Spiritus und Veritas. Festschrift für K. Kundsin,* ed. Auseklis (Eutin [Germany]: Ozolins Buchdruckerei, 1953), 43–55.

21   On the significance of this phrase, see above pp. 28ff excursus on 1 Tim 1:15.

3   Exhortations and Warning about Heretics

8b   About all this you must speak firmly, in order that (all) those who have put their confidence in God learn to be concerned with good works.
That is good and beneficial for men.
9/ But avoid foolish investigations about genealogies, quarrels, and disputes about the law, because they are useless and fruitless. 10/ Reject a factious person after warning him once or twice, 11/ since you know that such a person is (hopelessly) perverted and has condemned himself through his sin.

The ideal of an active piety is described once more, in this instance in sharp contrast to the heresy which for all practical purposes did not produce good works. The heresy was attacked in the same way in Tit 1:10ff. As in that passage, there are a great many reminiscences here of polemics against heretics in the other Pastorals: "investigations" (ζητήσεις, 1 Tim 1:4; 6:4; 2 Tim 2:23); "foolish" (μωράς) is also found in the latter passage; "genealogies" (γενεαλογίαι, 1 Tim 1:4); "quarrels" (ἔρις, 1 Tim 6:4); "fights," "disputes" (μάχαι, 2 Tim 2:23; cf. also 2:14 and 1 Tim 6:4); in the case of "disputes about the law" (μάχαι νομικαί), one is reminded of the statements in 1 Tim 1:8f (see above, p. 22). The controversy here might also be about ascetic (not specifically Jewish) commandments, but see above on Tit 1:10ff and the excursus to 1 Tim 4:3, section 3a. On "avoid" (περιΐστασθαι), see 2 Tim 2:16; on "fruitless" (μάταιος), 1 Tim 1:6; on "reject" (παραιτεῖσθαι), 1 Tim 4:7 and 2 Tim 2:23.

■ **8b** The verb προΐστασθαι is here used in the sense of "to be concerned with," "to care for";[1] see also Epictetus, *Diss.* 3.24.3: (referring to God as) "the one who provides for us and cares for us like a father" (τὸν κηδόμενον ἡμῶν καὶ πατρικῶς προϊστάμενον) [trans. by Ed.]. "Those who put their confidence in God" (οἱ πεπιστευκότες θεῷ) corresponds perhaps to "our people" (ἡμέτεροι) in v 14, and is therefore a name for the Christians. It might seem surprising that no relationship to Christ is indicated by this name, but cf. what was said on 1 Tim 2:10 about "reverence for God" (θεοσέβεια).

■ **10** "Factious" (αἱρετικός, "heretical") is not a "Christian" word. It is found in Pseudo–Plato, *Def.* 412a, in the meaning "able to choose," parallel to "careful to avoid" (εὐλαβητικός); also in Hierocles[2] where the

adverb is also attested as synonymous with "exercising a choice" (ἐκλεκτικῶς). But Paul had already used the word "faction" (αἵρεσις) in a pejorative sense in 1 Cor 11:19 and Gal 5:20. In the latter passage it appears without any explanation in the middle of a catalogue of vices, after "disputes" (ἐριθεῖαι) and "dissensions" (διχοστασίαι). This meaning is by no means suggested by the usage of the word in the LXX. In light of these facts one must assume that this pejorative sense was not first created by Paul. It is, therefore, not at all certain that the meaning "factious," which is presupposed in Tit 3:10 for the adjective (αἱρετικός), was created by the Christians. But it remains a question whether the word here alludes only to the divisions implied in Tit 1:11, or whether it indicates membership in sects.

■ **11** "One who has condemned himself" (αὐτοκατάκριτος) is attested in a fragment from Philo: "Reproach no one for misfortune . . . lest, if you be caught by the same, you be found self–condemned by your conscience" (μηδενὶ συμφορὰν ὀνειδίσῃς . . . μήποτε τοῖς αὐτοῖς ἁλοὺς αὐτοκατάκριτος ἐν τῷ συνειδότι εὑρεθῇς).[3] It is clear what it means here. If the person being exhorted still does not listen, error becomes sin; that which was "involuntary" (ἀκούσιον) becomes "voluntary" (ἑκούσιον).[4] Such a person has spoken his own judgment by his refusal to listen.

---

1   Cf. Dibelius, *Thessalonicher, Philipper,* on 1 Thess 5:12.

2   *Hierokles' Ethische Elementarlehre nebst den bei Stobäus erhaltenen ethischen Exzerpten aus Hierokles,* ed. H. von Arnim and W. Schubart, Berliner Klassikertexte 4 (Berlin: Weidmann, 1906), pp. 40f (9.5ff).

3   The passage is taken from John of Damascus and can be found in Philo's *Fragmenta* (II, 652, Mangey) [trans. by Ed.].

4   On this point see Philo, *Spec. leg.* 1.227 and 235.

3

Assignments and Greetings

12 **When I send Artemas or Tychicus to you, make every effort to come to me in Nicopolis; because I have decided to spend the winter there. 13/ Equip Zenas the lawyer and Apollos well for the winter journey so that they lack nothing. 14/ Our people should learn anyway to take care of the necessities of life through good works, so that they do not lead an unproductive life.**

■ **12, 13** On these vss, see also the following excursus. It is improbable that νομικός refers, as it does in the gospels, to a (former) rabbi, because for the Pastorals "teacher of the law" (νομοδιδάσκαλος), as it is used in 1 Tim 1:7, has another meaning and not a good one. The term must, therefore, refer to a jurist.[5] "To equip well etc." (σπουδαίως προπέμπειν) means, as the dependent clause "so that . . ." (ἵνα) shows, "to provide them well with everything and so send them on their way."[6] The dependent clause is almost consecutive, although the expression of intention is not completely excluded.[7]

■ **14** On "to take care of" (προΐστασθαι), see above on v 8. The clause is, in any case, a generalization of the preceding verse. It means either that all Christians should learn from the "equip well . . ." (σπουδαίως προπέμπειν); or (as Lock interprets it) that our people too (like the pagans, and in order to show them that we are not "unproductive" [ἄκαρποι]) should learn to contribute with good works "to the necessities of life" (εἰς τὰς ἀναγκαίας χρείας). The primary emphasis lies on the last phrase, which naturally refers to material needs. These words often have this meaning in popular philosophy;[8] see Diodorus Siculus 1.34.11: "Many other plants, capable of supplying men with the necessities of life, grow in Egypt in great abundance" (πολλὰ δὲ καὶ ἄλλα τὰ δυνάμενα τὰς ἀναγκαίας χρείας παρέχεσθαι τοῖς ἀνθρώποις, δαψιλῆ φύεται κατὰ τὴν Αἴγυπτον);

Philo, *Decal.* 99: "every man being a partaker of mortal nature and needing a vast multitude of things to supply the necessaries of life" (ἀνθρώπων δ' ἕκαστος ἄτε θνητῆς φύσεως μετέχων καὶ μυρίων ἐνδεὴς ὢν πρὸς τὰς ἀναγκαίας τοῦ βίου χρείας); *Inscr. Priene* 108.80: "(he gave him a sum of money) for the necessities of life" (εἰς χρείας ἀναγκαίας ἔδωκεν) [trans. by Ed.].

The Situation of the Epistle to Titus

1. From Tit 1:5 one can conclude that Paul had been with Titus in Crete, and that they had either founded Christian congregations there, or had found them already in existence. These congregations are still in need of organization, all the more so in view of the rise of heresy on the island (1:10ff and 3:9ff). It is Titus' task to do this work of organization; it is the task of the epistle to guide him in this assignment. Paul plans to spend the winter in Nicopolis, but at the time of the composition of the epistle, he is obviously not there yet. A number of cities by the name of Nicopolis can be eliminated on the basis of their location or the time of their founding,[9] but the following cities still come under consideration: a) Nicopolis in Cilicia[10] may be considered eligible only under certain presuppositions regarding the time of composition of Titus. Moreover, because of its location, it does not seem suitable for winter quarters. b) Nicopolis

---

5   On the use of the word in this sense see *BGU* I, 326.22; 361 col. 3.2; III, 2.15; *Inscr. Magn.* 191.4 with note; Epict., *Diss.* 2.13.6–8.

6   See Windisch–Preisker, *Katholische Briefe*, on 3 Jn 6; Theodore of Mopsuestia (II, p. 256, Swete): "with sufficient money" (cum sumptu sufficienti).

7   See *P. Lond.*, III, p. 212, lines 12ff: "Taking as many cupfuls of lentils as will suffice" (λαβὼν κοτύλας

τ[ό]σας φακῶν ἵνα ἀρκέσ[η] ἡ[μ]ῖν) [trans. by Ed.].

8   See Wendland, "Philo und die kynisch–stoische Diatribe," 10; Gerhard, *Phoinix*, 122.

9   See Zahn, *Introduction* 2, section 35, n. 3.

10 See Strabo 14.5.19, and Ptolemy 5.7.7.

in Thrace, now Nikopoli.[11] But the city was founded by Trajan. Did the author of the Pastorals overlook this fact, assuming that he wrote even later? At least it is more probable to think of c) Nicopolis in Epirus,[12] the city of Epictetus' activity.[13] There was a change in the province to which the city belonged.[14] The reference to Zenas and Apollos implies that "these are those by whom he (Paul) wrote, sending them to him (Titus)."[15] According to the Acts of Paul 2 (Lipsius–Bonnet 1, p. 236), Zenon is the name of a son of Onesiphorus. It is possible that a connection exists between him and the Zenas mentioned here. Apollos is the man known from Acts and 1 Cor.[16] Tychicus (see 2 Tim 4:12), or an otherwise unknown Artemas, is supposed to arrive perhaps some time after the epistle itself to relieve Titus.

2. It seems credible that Paul was once in Nicopolis and Epirus. However, one can point out that the winter stay there was only planned; we have no evidence that it was carried out. It is more difficult to find a time in Paul's life for the stay in Crete. The so–called second missionary journey—starting from Cilicia or, better, from Corinth— has been suggested by some scholars. But was Titus already in Paul's company at this time and did Titus already know Apollos? Paul's visit in Corinth between the writing of 1 and 2 Cor (such a visit must be assumed on the basis of 2 Cor) has also been used to support the assumption of a stay in Crete, but such a visit could only have been a short detour. It seems more probable to assume that Paul and Titus were in Crete at the time of Acts 20:3. In that case, the epistle to Titus would have been composed during Paul's return journey to the North (consider the location of Nicopolis!). The only possible objections to this reconstruction would be that, according to Acts 20:4, Tychicus went with Paul to Jerusalem, and that the author of Acts would probably not have omitted such an important occurrence as the evangelization of Crete. As the last possibility, then, there remains the time after the first Roman imprisonment; but against such an assumption, see the first excursus to 2 Tim 4:21.

3. If the theory is adopted that Titus, like the other Pastoral Epistles, is non–Pauline, it follows that here as well as elsewhere,[17] a known situation—in this case Acts 20:3—was used as a point of departure by the Pastorals' author. He may have been either more or less informed about that situation than the author of Acts, or he may have deliberately altered it. As far as the personal references are concerned, the basic considerations given in the second excursus to 2 Tim 4:21 apply here as well. Some possible connections with the Pauline legend are indicated above.[18] The reference to Nicopolis may also have originated in a similar context: Rom 15:19 probably occasioned a legendary expansion of Paul's travels into the northwestern part of the Balkan peninsula; cf. also the note on Titus in 2 Tim 4:10.

If the situation indicated in the Epistle to Titus can be explained on the basis of the assumption of inauthenticity, this explanation does not in itself provide conclusive proof for that assumption. Such proof must rather be sought in the reason for the epistle's composition. Paul left Titus behind to organize the congregations. Must he now send him even the most elementary directions about this in written form—directions such as the list of duties for the bishop and rules for the household? The same applies to the instruction regarding the heresies, assuming that Paul himself witnessed their rise in Crete. If, however, he knew about them only through Titus,[19] what purpose has the characterization of the heresies in 1:10ff? The artificiality of the occasion for the letter is obvious. Because of this artificiality and other considerations (see above pp. 1ff of the Introduction), the following

---

11 See Ptolemy 3.11.7; and cf. Theodoret (III, p. 709, Schulze).

12 Dio C., 50.12.3–5; 51.1.3; Strabo 7.7.5; 10.2.2.

13 See Aulus Gellius, *Noctes atticae* 15.11.5: "And it was at that time that the philosopher Epictetus also withdrew from Rome to Nicopolis because of that senatorial decree" (qua tempestate Epictetus quoque philosophus propter id senatusconsultum Nicopolim Roma decessit); cf. Suidas: "he settled in Nicopolis in New Epeirus" (ἐν Νικοπόλει τῆς νέας Ἠπείρου ᾤκησε).

14 Zahn, *Introduction* 2, section 35, n. 3.

15 Per hos scripsit ad eum mittens eos, Theodore of Mopsuestia (II, p. 256, Swete).

16 On Apollos, see Acts 18:24; 19:1; 1 Cor 1:12; 3:4–6, 22; 4:6; 16:12.

17 See above pp. 15f and 126f, the excursus to 1 Tim 1:3 and 2 Tim 4:21.

18 See section 1 of the present excursus on the discussion of the name Zenas. Cf. Onesiphorus in 2 Tim 1:16ff and 4:19.

19 But observe that, as in the other Pastoral Epistles, there is nothing to suggest a mutual exchange of letters; indeed, the style of writing practically excludes a previous letter by Titus to Paul.

hypothesis is quite probable: the author wanted to invest congregational regulations, which were already practiced in part, with the authority of the apostle and to direct them against the heretics.

But it is precisely at this point that the question must be asked, why an epistle to Titus was necessary *after* the first epistle to Timothy, or vice versa. The answer is implied by the situation indicated by Tit. The letter does not deal with congregations which were already organized, but with congregations which needed to be organized. Consequently Tit is not concerned primarily with the duties of church officers, but rather with duties pertaining to families. 1 Tim is thus intended mainly for the leader of the congregation, while Titus is written primarily for the missionary. Therefore, each epistle can with equal right claim its place beside the other in the canon of the NT. Of course, no conclusions as to the sequence of the epistles can be drawn from their purposes.

In conclusion, it should be emphasized again that the hypotheses put forth here and in the related excursus should be regarded as tentative. But the duty of the exegete, once he has declared a work "inauthentic," is to set out to answer the question why these "epistles" were written, and why they were written in their present form.

3 Concluding Greeting

15   **All those who are with me send their greetings to you. Greet those who love us in
faith. Grace be with you all.**

In the formulation of the greeting addressed to "those
who love us in faith" (φιλοῦντες ἡμᾶς ἐν πίστει), some
scholars see an explicit exclusion of the heretics, who
are only remembered in the more inclusive final greeting.
But it may merely be a conventional expression, Christianized by the phrase "in faith" (ἐν πίστει).[1] The
following serve as examples of such a conventional expression: *P. Giess.* I, 12.7ff: "I visit your wife and all those
who love you" (ἐπισκοποῦμαι τὴν σὴν σύνβιον καὶ
τοὺς φιλοῦντάς σε πάντας); *P. Greci e Latini* 94.10ff:
"Greet Terens and all those who love you" (ἄσπασαι

Τερεῦν καὶ τοὺς φιλοῦντάς σε πάντας). *BGU* III,
814.39. Cf. also the related formula: "Greet all those to
whom we are well disposed, each by name" ([ἄσπαζε]
οὓς ἡδέως ἔχομεν κατ' ὄνομα) in *P. Oxy.* IX, 1218.12.
[preceding translations by Ed.].

---

1   On the Christianization of the proem, see Dibelius,
Thessalonicher, Philipper, the excursus to 1 Thess 1:2.

Appendices
Bibliography
Indices

Appendices

1. Isocrates, Ad Nicoclem 40 and 41 (See the Introduction, 2.).

40. Καὶ μὴ θαυμάσῃς, εἰ πολλὰ τῶν λεγομένων ἐστίν, ἃ καὶ σὺ γιγνώσκεις· οὐδὲ γὰρ ἐμὲ τοῦτο παρέλαθεν, ἀλλ' ἠπιστάμην, ὅτι τοσούτων ὄντων τὸ πλῆθος καὶ τῶν ἄλλων καὶ τῶν ἀρχόντων οἱ μέν τι τούτων εἰρήκασιν, οἱ δ' ἀκηκόασιν, οἱ δ' ἑτέρους ποιοῦντας ἑωράκασιν, οἱ δ' αὐτοὶ τυγχάνουσιν ἐπιτηδεύοντες. 41. ἀλλὰ γὰρ οὐκ ἐν τοῖς λόγοις χρὴ τούτοις (τῶν ἐπιτηδευμάτων) ζητεῖν τὰς καινότητας, ἐν οἷς οὔτε παράδοξον οὔτ' ἄπιστον οὔτ' ἔξω τῶν νομιζομένων οὐδὲν ἔξεστιν εἰπεῖν, ἀλλ' ἡγεῖσθαι τοῦτον χαριέστατον, ὃς ἂν τῶν διεσπαρμένων ἐν ταῖς τῶν ἄλλων διανοίαις ἀθροῖσαι τὰ πλεῖστα δυνηθῇ καὶ φράσαι κάλλιστα περὶ αὐτῶν

"And do not be surprised that in what I have said there are many things which you know as well as I. This is not from inadvertence on my part, for I have realized all along that among so great a multitude both of mankind in general and of their rulers there are some who have uttered one or another of these precepts, some who have heard them some who have observed other people put them into practice. 41. But the truth is that in discourses of this sort we should not seek novelties, for in these discourses it is not possible to say what is paradoxical or incredible or outside the circle of accepted belief; but rather, we should regard that man as the most accomplished in his field who can collect the greatest number of ideas scattered among the thoughts of all the rest and present them in the best form."

2. Pseudo–Isocrates, Ad Demonicum 44

44. Καὶ μὴ θαυμάσῃς, εἰ πολλὰ τῶν εἰρημένων οὐ πρέπει σοι πρὸς τὴν νῦν παροῦσαν ἡλικίαν· οὐδὲ γὰρ ἐμὲ τοῦτο διέλαθεν· ἀλλὰ προειλόμην διὰ τῆς αὐτῆς πραγματείας ἅμα τοῦ τε παρόντος βίου συμβουλίαν ἐξενεγκεῖν καὶ τοῦ μέλλοντος χρόνου παράγγελμα καταλιπεῖν. τὴν μὲν γὰρ τούτων χρείαν ῥᾳδίως εἰδήσεις, τὸν δὲ μετ' εὐνοίας συμβουλεύοντα χαλεπῶς εὑρήσεις. ὅπως οὖν μὴ παρ' ἑτέρου τὰ λοιπὰ ζητῇς, ἀλλ' ἐντεῦθεν ὥσπερ ἐκ ταμιείου προφέρῃς, ᾠήθην δεῖν μηδὲν παραλιπεῖν, ὧν ἔχω σοι συμβουλεύειν.

"Do not be surprised that many things which I have said do not apply to you at your present age. For I also have not overlooked this fact, but I have deliberately chosen to employ this one treatise, not only to convey to you advice for your life now, but also to leave with you precepts for the years to come; for you will then readily perceive the application of my precepts, but you will not easily find a man who will give you friendly counsel. In order, therefore, that you may not seek the rest from another source, but that you may draw from this as from a treasure house, I thought that I ought not to omit any of the counsels which I have to give you."

3. Onosander, De imperatoris officio 1 [1] (ΠΕΡΙ ΑΙΡΕΣΕΩΣ ΣΤΡΑΤΗΓΟΥ)

1. Φημὶ τοίνυν αἱρεῖσθαι τὸν στρατηγὸν οὐ κατὰ γένη κρίνοντας, ὥσπερ τοὺς ἱερέας, οὐδὲ κατ' οὐσίας, ὡς τοὺς γυμνασιάρχους, ἀλλὰ σώφρονα, ἐγκρατῆ, νήπτην, λιτόν, διάπονον, νοερόν, ἀφιλάργυρον, μήτε νέον μήτε πρεσβύτερον, ἂν τύχῃ καὶ πατέρα παίδων, ἱκανὸν λέγειν, ἔνδοξον. [2]

1. I believe, then, that we must choose a general, not because of noble birth as priests are chosen, nor because of wealth as the superintendents of the gymnasia, but because he is temperate, self–restrained, vigilant, frugal, hardened to labour, alert, free from avarice, neither too young nor too old, indeed a father of children if possible, a ready speaker, and a man with a good reputation.

---

[1] Pp. 11ff in the edition by Schwebel. The work was also edited by Köchly, Leipzig, 1860.

[2] In this introduction the catalogue of virtues contributes little that is especially appropriate for the "general" (στρατηγός). For this very reason (as Wettstein has remarked), it resembles the list of duties for

2. α'. σώφρονα μέν, ἵνα μὴ ταῖς φυσικαῖς ἀνθελκόμενος ἡδοναῖς ἀπολείπῃ τὴν ὑπὲρ τῶν μεγίστων φροντίδα·

3. β'. ἐγκρατῆ δέ, ἐπειδὴ τηλικαύτης ἀρχῆς μέλλει τυγχάνειν· αἱ γὰρ ἀκρατεῖς ὁρμαὶ προσλαβοῦσαι τὴν τοῦ δύνασθαί τι ποιεῖν ἐξουσίαν ἀκατάσχετοι γίγνονται πρὸς τὰς ἐπιθυμίας·

4. γ'. νήπτην δέ, ὅπως ἐπαγρυπνῇ ταῖς μεγίσταις πράξεσιν· ἐν νυκτὶ γὰρ ὡς τὰ πολλὰ ψυχῆς ἠρεμούσης στρατηγοῦ γνώμη τελειοῦται·

5. δ'. λιτὸν δέ, ἐπειδὴ κατασκελετεύουσιν αἱ πολυτελεῖς θεραπεῖαι δαπανῶσαι χρόνον ἄπρακτον εἰς τὴν τῶν ἡγουμένων τρυφήν·

6. ε'. διάπονον δέ, ἵνα μὴ πρῶτος τῶν στρατευομένων, ἀλλ᾽ ὕστατος κάμνῃ.

7. ϛ'. νοερὸν δέ. ὀξὺν γὰρ εἶναι δεῖ τὸν στρατηγὸν ἐπὶ πᾶν ἄττοντα δι᾽ ὠκύτητος ψυχῆς κατὰ τὸν Ὅμηρον "ὡσεὶ πτερὸν ἠὲ νόημα."
πολλάκις γὰρ ἀπρόληπτοι ταραχαὶ προσπεσοῦσαι σχεδιάζειν ἀναγκάζουσι τὸ συμφέρον·

8. ζ'. ἀφιλάργυρον δέ· ἡ γὰρ ἀφιλαργυρία δοκιμασθήσεται καὶ πρώτη· τοῦ γὰρ ἀδωροδοκήτως καὶ μεγαλοφρόνως προΐστασθαι τῶν πραγμάτων αὕτη παραιτία· πολλοὶ γὰρ, κἂν διὰ τὴν ἀνδρίαν ἀσπίσι πολλαῖς καὶ δόρασιν ἀντιβλέψωσιν, περὶ τὸν χρυσὸν ἀμαυροῦνται· δεινὸν γὰρ πολεμίοις ὅπλον τοῦτο καὶ δραστήριον εἰς τὸ νικᾶν·

9. η'. οὔτε δὲ νέον οὔτε πρεσβύτερον, ἐπειδὴ ὁ μὲν ἀλόγιστος, ὁ δ᾽ ἀσθενής, οὐδέτερος δ᾽ ἀσφαλής, ὁ μὲν νέος, ἵνα μή τι διὰ τὴν ἀλόγιστον πταίσῃ τόλμαν, ὁ δὲ πρεσβύτερος, ἵνα μή τι διὰ τὴν φυσικὴν ἀσθένειαν ἐλλείπῃ . . .

12. θ'. πατέρα δὲ προύκρινα μᾶλλον, οὐδὲ τὸν ἄπαιδα παραιτούμενος, ἐὰν ἀγαθὸς ᾖ· ἐάν τε γὰρ ὄντες τύχωσιν νήπιοι, ψυχῆς εἰσιν ἰσχυρὰ φίλτρα περὶ τὴν εὔνοιαν ἐξομηρεύσασθαι δυνάμενα στρατηγὸν πρὸς πατρίδα . . .

13. ι'. λέγειν δ᾽ ἱκανόν· ἔνθεν γὰρ ἡγοῦμαι τὸ μέγιστον ὠφελείας ἵξεσθαι διὰ στρατεύματος· ἐάν τε γὰρ ἐκτάττῃ πρὸς μάχην στρατηγός, ἡ τοῦ λόγου παρακέλευσις τῶν μὲν δεινῶν ἐποίησε κατα-

2. The general must be temperate in order that he may not be so distracted by the pleasures of the body as to neglect the consideration of matters of the highest importance.

3. He must be self-restrained, since he is to be a man of so great authority; for the licentious impulses, when combined with the authority which confers the power of action, become uncontrollable in the gratification of the passions.

4. Vigilant, that he may spend wakeful nights over the most important projects; for at night, as a rule, with the mind at rest, the general perfects his plans.

5. Frugal, since expensive attendance upon the luxurious tastes of commanders consumes time unprofitably and causes resources to waste away.

6. Hardened to labour, that he may not be the first but the last of the army to grow weary.

7. Alert, for the general must be quick, with swiftness of mind darting at every subject—quick, as Homer says, 'as a bird, or as thought.' For very frequently unexpected disorders arise which may compel him to decide on the spur of the moment what is expedient.

8. Free from avarice; for this quality of freedom from avarice will be valued most highly, since it is largely responsible for the incorruptible and large-minded management of affairs. For many who can face the shields and spears of a host with courage are blinded by gold; but gold is a strong weapon against the enemy and effective for victory.

9. Neither too young nor too old; since the young man does not inspire confidence, the old man is feeble, and neither is free from danger, the young man lest he err through reckless daring, the older lest he neglect something through physical weakness . . .

12. I should prefer our general to be a father, though I would not refuse a childless man, provided he be a good man. For if he happens to have young children, they are potent spells to keep his heart loyal, availing to bind him to the fatherland . . .

13. A ready speaker; for I believe that the greatest benefit can accrue from the work of a general only through this gift. For if a general is drawing up his men before battle, the encouragement of his words makes them

the bishop in 1 Tim 2 and Tit 1. After the introduction, there follows a commentary which treats the individual qualities as they relate to the specific theme of the treatise. It would not be difficult to write an analogous commentary to 1 Tim 3, except of course it would sound quite different.

φρονεῖν, τῶν δὲ καλῶν ἐπιθυμεῖν . . . 16. οὐδὲ χωρὶς στρατηγοῦ οὐδεμία πόλις ἐκπέμψει στρατόπεδον, οὐδὲ δίχα τοῦ δύνασθαι λέγειν αἱρήσεται στρατηγόν.

17. ια΄. **τὸν δ᾽ ἔνδοξον**, ὅτι τοῖς ἀδόξοις ἀσχάλλει τὸ πλῆθος ὑποταττόμενον· οὐθεὶς γὰρ ἑκὼν ὑπομένει τὸν αὑτοῦ χείρονα κύριον ἀναδέχεσθαι καὶ ἡγεμόνα. 18. πᾶσα δ᾽ ἀνάγκη τὸν τοιοῦτον ὄντα καὶ τοσαύτας ἀρετὰς ἔχοντα τῆς ψυχῆς, ὅσας εἴρηκα, καὶ ἔνδοξον εἶναι.

despise the danger and covet the honour; . . . 16. No city at all will put an army in the field without generals nor choose a general who lacks the ability to make an effective speech.

17. The general should be a man of good reputation, because the majority of men, when placed under the command of unknown generals, feel uneasy. For no one voluntarily submits to a leader or an officer who is an inferior man to himself. 18. It is absolutely essential, then, that a general be such a man, of such excellent traits of character as I have enumerated, and besides this, that he have a good reputation.

4. Lucian, Salt. 81 (Pantomimus)[1]

ὅλως δὲ τὸν ὀρχηστὴν δεῖ πανταχόθεν ἀπηκριβῶσθαι, ὡς εἶναι τὸ πᾶν εὔρυθμον, εὔμορφον, σύμμετρον, αὐτὸ αὑτῷ ἐοικός—ἀσυκοφάντητον, ἀνεπίληπτον, μηδαμῶς ἐλλιπές, ἐκ τῶν ἀρίστων κεκραμένον, τὰς ἐνθυμήσεις ὀξύν, τὴν παιδείαν βαθύν, τὰς ἐννοίας ἀνθρώπινον μάλιστα. ὁ γοῦν ἔπαινος αὐτῷ τότ᾽ ἂν γίγνοιτο ἐντελὴς παρὰ τῶν θεατῶν, ὅταν ἕκαστος τῶν ὁρώντων γνωρίζῃ τὰ αὑτοῦ, μᾶλλον δὲ ὥσπερ ἐν κατόπτρῳ τῷ ὀρχηστῇ ἑαυτὸν βλέπῃ καὶ ἃ πάσχειν αὐτὸς καὶ ἃ ποιεῖν εἴωθε. . . . ἀτεχνῶς γὰρ τὸ Δελφικὸν ἐκεῖνο τὸ Γνῶθι σεαυτὸν ἐκ τῆς θέας ἐκείνης αὐτοῖς περιγίγνεται· καὶ ἀπέρχονται ἀπὸ τοῦ θεάτρου ἅ τε χρὴ αἱρεῖσθαι καὶ ἃ φεύγειν μεμαθηκότες καὶ ἃ πρότερον ἠγνόουν διδαχθέντες.

"In general, the dancer should be perfect in every point, so as to be wholly rhythmical, graceful, symmetrical, consistent,—unexceptionable, impeccable, not wanting in any way, blent of the highest qualities, keen in his ideas, profound in his culture, and above all, human in his sentiments. In fact, the praise that he gets from the spectators will be consummate when each of those who behold him recognizes his own traits, or rather sees in the dancer as in a mirror his very self, with his customary feelings and actions. . . . Really, that Delphic monition 'Know thyself' realises itself in them from the spectacle, and when they go away from the theatre they have learned what they should choose and what avoid, and have been taught what they did not know before."

---

1 Vol. 2, p. 149f, ed. Sommerbrodt. There is some doubt concerning the authenticity of this work. Lucian relates certain professional qualities to a greater number of general traits in his description of the perfect dancer. The description is unusual because the requirement of general human qualities is derived in an original way from the requirements of an occupation. (In the text I have separated the special from the general traits by means of a dash.)

Bibliography

1. Commentaries
(listed in order of their first publication)

Weiss, Bernhard
  Die Briefe Pauli an Timotheus und Titus, KEK 11
  (Göttingen: Vandenhoeck & Ruprecht, [7]1902).
von Soden, H(ermann)
  *Die Briefe an die Kolosser, Epheser, Philemon. Die
  Pastoralbriefe, etc.* Handcommentar zum Neuen
  Testament 3 (Freiburg i. B. and Leipzig: J. C. B.
  Mohr [Paul Siebeck], [2]1893).
Wohlenberg, Gustav
  Die Pastoralbriefe, etc., Zahn's Kommentar zum
  Neuen Testament 13 (Leipzig: Deichert, [4]1923).
Belser, J. E.
  *Die Briefe des Apostel Paulus an Timotheus und Titus
  übersetzt und erklärt* (Freiburg i. B.: Herder, 1907).
Ramsey, W. M.
  "A Historical Commentary on the Epistles to
  Timothy," *Expositor*, ser. 7, vol. 7 (1909): 481–94;
  vol. 8 (1909): 1–21, 167–85, 264–82, 339–57,
  399–416, 557–668; vol. 9 (1910): 172–87, 319–33,
  433–40; ser. 8, vol. 1 (1911): 262–73, 356–75.
Köhler, F.
  *Die Pastoralbriefe, Die Schriften des NT für die
  Gegenwart erklärt*, ed. Wilhelm Bousset and Wil-
  helm Heitmüller (Göttingen: Vandenhoeck &
  Ruprecht, [3]1917).
Brown, E. F.
  The Pastoral Epistles (Philadelphia and London:
  Westminster Press and Methuen, 1917).
Parry, R. St. John
  *The Pastoral Epistles: with Introduction, Text and
  Commentary* (Cambridge: Cambridge University
  Press, 1920).
Lock, Walter
  *A Critical and Exegetical Commentary on the Pastoral
  Epistles*, ICC (Edinburgh and New York: T. & T.
  Clark, 1924).
von Häring, Theodor
  *Die Pastoralbriefe und der Brief des Apostels Paulus
  an die Philipper* (Stuttgart: Calwer Verlag, 1928).
Meinertz, Max
  Die Pastoralbriefe übersetzt und erklärt, Die Heilige
  Schrift des NT 8 (Bonn: Hanstein, [4]1931).
Schlatter, Adolf
  *Die Kirche der Griechen im Urteil des Paulus: Eine
  Auslegung seiner Briefe an Timotheus und Titus*
  (Stuttgart: Calwer Verlag, [2]1958).
Falconer, Robert
  The Pastoral Epistles (Oxford: Clarendon Press,
  1937).

Scott, Ernest Findlay
  The Pastoral Epistles, The Moffatt NT Commen-
  tary (London: Hodder & Stoughton, 1936).
Easton, Burton Scott
  *The Pastoral Epistles: Introduction, Translation, Com-
  mentary and Word Studies* (London: SCM, 1948).
Spicq, Ceslaus
  Saint Paul: Les Épîtres Pastorales, Études Bibliques
  (Paris: Gabalda, [4]1969).
Boudou, P. Adrien
  Les Épîtres Pastorales (Paris: Beauchesne et ses
  Fils, 1949–50).
Freundorfer, Joseph
  Die Pastoralbriefe, Das Neue Testament übersetzt
  und erklärt (Regensburg: Pustet, [3]1959).
Jeremias, Joachim, and Strathmann, Hermann
  *Die Briefe an Timotheus und Titus. Der Brief an die
  Hebräer* NTD 9 (Göttingen: Vandenhoeck &
  Ruprecht, [8]1963).
Ambroggi, P. de
  Le Epistole Pastorali di S. Paolo a Timoteo e a Tito,
  La Sacra Biblia (Torino: Marietti, 1953).
Simpson, E. K.
  *The Pastoral Epistles: The Greek Text with Intro-
  duction and Commentary* (London: Tyndale Press,
  1954).
Brox, N.
  Die Pastoralbriefe, Regensburger Neues Testament.
  (Regensburg: F. Pustet, [4]1969).
Guthrie, Donald
  *The Pastoral Epistles: An Introduction and Com-
  mentary*, The Tyndale New Testament Commen-
  taries (Grand Rapids, Mich.: Eerdmans, 1957).
Barrett, C. K.
  The Pastoral Epistles in the New English Bible,
  The New Clarendon Bible (New York and Lon-
  don: Oxford University Press, 1963).
Kelly, J. N. D.
  The Pastoral Epistles. I Timothy. II Timothy. Titus,
  Harper's New Testament Commentaries (New
  York and Evanston, Ill.: Harper & Row, 1964).
Holtz, G.
  Die Pastoralbriefe, Theologischer Handkommentar
  zum Neuen Testament 13 (Berlin: Evangelische
  Verlagsanstalt, 1965).
Hanson, A. T.
  The Pastoral Letters, The Cambridge Bible Com-
  mentary on the New English Bible (New York
  and London: Cambridge University Press, 1966).
Dornier, P.
  Les Épîtres Pastorales, Sources Bibliques (Paris:
  Gabalda, 1969).

161

2. Select Monographs and Articles
(alphabetically)

Adler, N.
"Die Handauflegung im NT bereits ein Buß-
ritus? Zur Auslegung von I Tim. 5,22," *Neutestamentliche Aufsätze, Festschrift für Prof. Josef
Schmid zum 70. Geburtstag*, ed. J. Blinzler, O. Kuss
and F. Mussner (Regensburg: Pustet, 1963), 1–6.

Allan, John A.
"The 'In Christ' Formula in the Pastoral Epistles," *NTS* 10 (1963): 115–21.

Baldensperger, G.
" 'Il a rendu témoignage devant Ponce Pilate',"
RHPR 2 (1922): 1–25.

Barton, J. M. T.
" 'Bonum certamen certavi . . . fidem servavi'
(2 Tim. 4,7)," *Biblica* 40 (1959): 878–84.

Bartsch, Hans–Werner
*Die Anfänge urchristlicher Rechtsbildungen: Studien
zu den Pastoralbriefen* (Hamburg: Herbert Reich,
1965).

Baur, Ferdinand Christian
*Die sogenannten Pastoralbriefe des Apostels Paulus
aufs neue kritisch untersucht* (Stuttgart and Tübingen: Cotta, 1835).

Bover, José M.
" 'Fidelis sermo'," *Biblica* 19 (1938): 74–9.

Brox, N.
"Zu den persönlichen Notizen der Pastoralbriefe," *BZ* 13 (1969): 76–94.

Bruston, C.
"De la date de la première Épître de Paul à
Timothée," *EThR* 5 (1930): 272–76.

Bultmann, Rudolf
"Pastoralbriefe," *RGG²* IV, col. 993–97.

von Campenhausen, Hans
"Polykarp von Smyrna und die Pastoralbriefe"
in *Aus der Frühzeit des Christentums* (Tübingen:
J. C. B. Mohr [Paul Siebeck], 1963), 197–252.

Dey, J.
ΠΑΛΙΓΓΕΝΕΣΙΑ: *Ein Beitrag zur Klärung der religionsgeschichtlichen Bedeutung von Titus 3, 5*, NTAbh
17, 5 (Münster: Aschendorff, 1937).

Dibelius, Martin
"'Επίγνωσις ἀληθείας," *Botschaft und Geschichte* 2
(Tübingen: J. C. B. Mohr [Paul Siebeck], 1956),
1–13.

von Dobschütz, Ernst
"Die Pastoralbriefe (zu Gösta Thörnell, Pastoralbrevens Äkthet)," *ThStKr* 104 (1932): 121–23.

Ellis, E. E.
"The Problem of Authorship: First and Second
Timothy," *Review and Expositor* 56 (1959): 343–54.

Erbes, K.
"Zeit und Ziel der Grüsse Röm. 16, 3–15 und
der Mitteilungen 2 Tim. 4, 9–21," *ZNW* 10
(1909): 207 ff.

Foerster, Werner
"Εὐσέβεια in den Pastoralbriefen," *NTS* 5
(1959): 213–18.

Frey, Jean–Baptiste
"La signification des termes μόνανδρος et *univira*," *RechSR* 20 (1930): 48–60.

Galtier, P.
"La Réconciliation des Pécheurs dans la Première Épître à Timothée," *RevSR* 39 (1951): 316–
20.

Grayston, K. and G. Herdan,
"The Authorship of the Pastorals in the Light
of Statistical Linguistics," *NTS* 6 (1959): 1–15.

Grossow, W.
"Epiphania in de pastorale brieven," *Nederlandse
katholieke stemmen* 49 (1953): 353 ff.

Hanson, A. T.
Studies in the Pastoral Epistles (London: S.P.C.K.,
1968).

Harrison, P. N.
"Important Hypotheses Reconsidered. III. The
Authorship of the Pastoral Epistles," *ExpT* 67
(1955): 77–81.

Harrison, P. N.
"The Pastoral Epistles and Duncan's Ephesian
Theory," *NTS* 2 (1956): 250–61.

Harrison, P. N.
The Problem of the Pastoral Epistles (London: Oxford University Press, 1921).

Hilgenfeld, A.
"Die Hirtenbriefe des Paulus; neu untersucht,"
ZWTh 40 (1897): 1–86.

Holtzmann, Heinrich Julius
Die Pastoralbriefe kritisch und exegetisch bearbeitet
(Leipzig: Wilhelm Engelmann, 1880).

Holzmeister, U.
"Si quis episcopatum desiderat, bonum opus
desiderat," *Biblica* 12 (1931): 41–69.

Jacono, V.
"La ΠΑΛΙΓΓΕΝΕΣΙΑ in S. Paolo e nell' ambiente
pagano," *Biblica* 15 (1934): 369 ff.

Käsemann, Ernst
"Das Formular einer neutestamentlichen Ordinationsparänese," *NT Studien für Bultmann*, pp.
261–68.

Kittel, Gerhard
"Die γενεαλογίαι der Pastoralbriefe," *ZNW* 20
(1921): 49–69.

Klöpper, D. A.
"Zur Christologie der Pastoralbriefe (1. Tim.
3, 16)," *ZWTh* 45 (1914): 339–61.

Koch, Klaus
"Das Lamm, das Ägypten vernichtet: Ein Fragment aus Jannes und Jambres und sein geschicht-
licher Hintergrund," *ZNW* 57 (1966): 79–93.

Kühl, E.
Die Gemeindeordnung in den Pastoralbriefen (Berlin:
Besser'sche Buchhandlung, 1885).

Kuss, Otto
"Jesus und die Kirche im Neuen Testament II,"

ThQ 135 (1955): 150 ff.

Lattey, Cuthbert
"Unius uxoris vir (Tit. 1, 6)," *Verbum Domini* 28 (1950): 288–90.

Loewe, R.
Ordnung in der Kirche im Lichte des Titus (Gütersloh: Der Rufer, 1947).

Loewe, Hugo
Die Pastoralbriefe des Apostel Paulus in ihrer ursprünglichen Fassung wieder hergestellt (Köln: C. Roemke und Cie., 1929).

Lütgert, Wilhelm
Die Irrlehrer der Pastoralbriefe, BFTh 13, 3 (Gütersloh: Bertelsmann, 1909).

Maehlum, H.
Die Vollmacht des Timotheus nach den Pastoralbriefen, Theologische Dissertationen 1 (Basel: F. Reinhardt, 1969).

Maier, Friedrich
Die Hauptprobleme der Pastoralbriefe Pauli, Biblische Zeitfragen III, 12 (Münster in Westfalen: Aschendorff, 1911).

Manfold, W.
Die Irrlehrer der Pastoralbriefe (Frankfurt: Völcker, 1856).

Maurer, Christian
"Eine Textvariante klärt die Entstehung der Pastoralbriefe auf," *ThZ* 3 (1947): 321–37.

Mayer, Hans Helmut
Über die Pastoralbriefe (Göttingen: Vandenhoeck & Ruprecht, 1913).

Michaelis, Wilhelm
Pastoralbriefe und Gefangenschaftsbriefe. Zur Echtheitsfrage der Pastoralbriefe, NF 1, 6 (Gütersloh: Bertelsmann, 1930).

Michaelis, Wilhelm
"Pastoralbriefe und Wortstatistik" *ZNW* 28 (1929): 69–76.

Michel, Otto
"Grundfragen der Pastoralbriefe" in *Auf dem Grunde der Apostel und Propheten, Festgabe für Theophil Wurm*, ed. Max Loeser (Stuttgart: Quell-Verlag, 1948), 83–99.

Moule, C. F. D.
"The Problem of the Pastoral Epistles: A Reappraisal," *Bulletin of the John Rylands Library* 47 (1965): 430–52.

Müller–Bardorff, Johannes
"Zur Exegese von I. Timotheus 5, 3–16" in *Gott und die Götter, Festgabe für Erich Fascher* (Berlin: Evangelische Verlagsanstalt, 1958), 113–33.

Nauck, Wolfgang
Die Herkunft der Verfassers der Pastoralbriefes, Unpub. Diss. (Göttingen: 1950).

Oates, W. E.
"The Conception of Ministry in the Pastoral Epistles," *Review and Expositor* 56 (1959): 388–410.

Phister, F.
"Zur Wendung ἀπόκειταί μοι ὁ τῆς δικαιο-

σύνης στέφανος," *ZNW* 15 (1914): 94–6.

Rohde, J.
"Pastoralbriefe und Acta Pauli," *Studia Evangelica* V, ed. F. L. Cross, TU 103 (Berlin: Akademie-Verlag, 1968), 303–10.

Schleiermacher, Friedrich
Sendschreiben an J. C. Gaß: Über den sogenannten ersten Brief des Paulos an den Timotheos (Berlin: Realschulbuchhandlung, 1807); reprinted in *idem, Sämtliche Werke* I, 1 (1836), pp. 221 ff.

Schmid, Josef
Zeit und Ort der paulinischen Gefangenschaftsbriefe; mit einem Anhang über die Datierung der Pastoralbriefe (Freiburg i.B.: Herder, 1931).

Schulze, W. A.
"Ein Bischof sei eines Weibes Mann . . . Zur Exegese von 1. Tim. 3, 2 und Tit. 1, 6," *Kerygma und Dogma* 4 (1958): 287–300.

Spicq, Ceslaus
"La philanthropie hellénistique, vertu divine et royale (à propos de Tit. III, 4)," *StTh* 12 (1958): 169–91.

Spicq, Ceslaus
"Si quis episcopatum desiderat," *RSPT* 29 (1940): 316–25.

Spicq, Ceslaus
"St. Paul et la loi des dépôts." *RB* 40 (1931): 481–502.

Spitta, F.
"Über die persönlichen Notizen im zweiten Briefe an Timotheus," *ThStKr* 51, 1 (1878): 582–607.

Stenger, W.
"Der Christushymnus in 1 Tim. 3, 16. Aufbau-Christologie-Sitz im Leben," *Trierer Theologische Zeitschrift* 78 (1969): 33–48.

Strobel, August
"Schreiben des Lukas? Zum sprachlichen Problem der Pastoralbriefe," *NTS* 15 (1968–69): 191–210.

Thörnell, Gösta
Pastoralbrevens Aekthet (Uppsala: Svenskt arkiv för humanistika avhandlingar, 1931).

Torm, F.
"Über die Sprache in den Pastoralbriefen," *ZNW* 18 (1917–18): 225–43.

Wendland, Paul
"Miszellen: Betrogene Betrüger," *Rheinisches Museum für Philologie* 49 (1894): 309–10.

Windisch, Hans
"Sinn und Geltung des apostolischen *Mulier taceat in ecclesia* (Die Frau schweige in der Gemeinde)," *Christliche Welt*, 1930, col. 411–25 [Continued under the title] "Noch einmal: *Mulier taceat in ecclesia*; Ein Wort zur Abwehr und zur Klärung," col. 837–40.

Windisch, Hans
"Zur Christologie der Pastoralbriefe," *ZNW* 34 (1935): 213–38.

Indices*

1. Passages

a / Old Testament and Apocrypha

Gen
59:3, 7	133

Ex
7:8ff	117
19:15	143

Num
19:22	138

Deut
14:2	143
32:15	100(16)

Judg
3:9, 15	100
12:3	100

1 Kings
10:19	100(16)

1 Chr
16:35	100(16)

LXX 1 Esdras
6:9ff	37

LXX Est
15:2D, 2	37

Neh
19:27	100

Est
3:13B2	39(24)

Jdth
9:11	100(16)

Tob
7:12	13(7)

1 Macc
15:23	135(2)

2 Macc
3:11	36(15)

Ps
21:22	124(17)

Prov
21:24	133

Job
1:21	85(10)

Sir
25:24	47(23)
36:19	30(18)

Mal
1:11	45

Isa
26:13	112(17)
52:13	112(17)
58:8	81

Jer
2:8	133(13)

LXX Bar
1:10ff	37
4:22	100

Wisd Sol
7:6	85(11)
7:16	131
13:1ff	27
13:6ff	27
15:7	113
16:7ff	100(16)

b / Old Testament Pseudepigrapha and Other Jewish Literature

Baba Batra
91a	17

Berakoth
60b	30(18)

CD
13.7–11	57(47)
IV, 15.17ff	54
V, 17–19	117

Deus Imm.
26	26

1 En
48.7	101

Ep. Ar.
140	87
175	36(15)
250	25
287	143

Joseph and Aseneth
8.10	88(10)

Josephus

Ant.
1.272	30(18)
3.231ff	27
10.210	119(6)
10.278	26
11.66	148
14.24	30(18)
15.375	39(29)
17.327	135(1)
18.228	124(16)

Ap.
1.31ff	120
2.190	26

Bell.
1.40	139
2.103	135(1)
2.126	45(10)
5.380	44(2)
6.102	68
6.345	121(18)

Philo

Abr.
101	140
202	25
223	25
275	25

Cher.
36	24
114	148

Conf. ling.
43	39(24)
93	102

Decal.
60	140
99	152

Det. pot. ins.
10	24
65	92

Flacc.
49	37(18)
124	132
187	121

Fragmenta
II, 652, Mangey	151(3)

Fug.
55	74(11)

Gig.
61	87

Leg. all.
3.27	102

Leg. Gaj.
5	26

Migr. Abr.
83	119

Omn. prob. lib.
75	140(6)

Plant.
70	116

Praem. Poen.
13	29(12)

Rer. div. her.
206	42(44)
263ff	120(10)
285	39(24)

* Numbers in parentheses following page citations for this volume refer to footnotes.

d / Early Christian Literature and the Ancient Church

Acts of Paul

2	153
5	65
12	122

Acts of Peter

20	90(27)

Acts of the Scilitan Martyrs

3 and 6	90

Act. Pl.

1	122(2)
2	125(1), 128(12)
12, 14	66(15)
14	112(13)

Act. Pt.

1	120(11)

Asc. Isa.

11.23	62

Athenag.
Suppl.

13.2	44(2)
37.1	38(22)

Augustine
Conf. 7.2   119

Barn.

4.12	81
5.9	30(14)

Chrysostom (Montfaucon)

XI, 590	45(10)
666	99
693	88
721	123(9)

1 Clem.

2.3	45(3)
2.7	147
5.4	89
5.7	3, 89
20.4	43(52)
24.5	144
29.1	44(2)
32.4	148
42.4	56
44.1	56
59.3	143
59.4	38(21)
60.2	39(26)
61	38
62.1	39(29)
64	143

2 Clem.

1.6–8	147
17.3	143
19.1	72(15)
20.5	102

Clement of Alexandria
Exc. Theod.

12.3	90(26)

Paed.

1.8.69	17
3	17
70, 1	17

Quis div. salv.

42	16, 56(46)

Strom.

1.59.2	136
3.9.64	49(32)
I, 3.22.5	120

Ps. Clem. Hom.

13.16	46

Const. Ap.

2.28	78(19)

Dg.

9.2	144(26)
9.6	102
11.3	61

Didache

7–10	5, 6
10	6
11–13	6
13	78(19)
14	5, 6
14.2ff	45
15	5
15.1	55
15.1, 2	6
15.4	45

Eusebius
Hist. eccl.

2.22.2, 3	124(15)
5.20.4	24

Praep. Ev.

9, 8	117

Evangelium Nicodemi
Acta Pilati A

5	117

Herm.
Mand.

6.1.2	87(1)
11.1.17	87(1)

Sim.

1.6	84
2.6	35(5)
9.4.2	112
9.10.6	32(3)
9.15.4	112
9.27.2	54(33)

Vis.

2.4.3	75
3.8.9	149(16)

Hieronymus
Commentaria in epistulam ad Titum   136(8)

Ignatius
Eph

10	38(21)
10.1	35(3)
14.2	46

Tr

3.2	140

Rom

5.1	124
8.2	131

Phld

2.2	21(37)
7.1	21(37)
8.2	22(37), 62

Sm

9.1	114

Irenaeus
Adv. haer.

1, Preface 1	17
1, Preface 2	17
1.13.3	116(10)
1.23.5	112(12)
1.24.2	49
3.3.3	125

Justin
Apol.

1.14.4	36(11)
1.17.3	36
1.26.3	116(11)
1.26.4	112(12)
1.41.2	30
47.5	145(26)

Dial.

3.3	24

Mart. Pt. et Pl.

34	117

Martyrdom of the Holy Apostle Paul

1	128(13)

Odes of Sol.

4.8	80
7.13	30
8.14ff	112
8.23	82
9.13	41
19.10ff	61
31.5	62
33	142(6)
41.9ff	42(46)
41.12	102

2. Greek Words

4. Modern Authors

In the design of the visual aspects of *Hermeneia,* consideration has been given to relating the form to the content by symbolic means.

The letters of the logotype *Hermeneia* are a fusion of forms alluding simultaneously to Hebrew (dotted vowel markings) and Greek (geometric round shapes) letter forms. In their modern treatment they remind us of the electronic age as well, the vantage point from which this investigation of the past begins.

The Lion of Judah used as a visual identification for the series is based on the Seal of Shema. The version for *Hermeneia* is again a fusion of Hebrew calligraphic forms, especially the legs of the lion, and Greek elements characterized by the geometric. In the sequence of arcs, which can be understood as scroll-like images, the first is the lion's mouth. It is reasserted and accelerated in the whorl and returns in the aggressively arched tail: tradition is passed from one age to the next, rediscovered and re-formed.

"Who is worthy to open the scroll and break its
seals . . ."
Then one of the elders said to me
"weep not; lo, the Lion of the tribe of David,
the Root of David, has conquered,
so that he can open the scroll and
its seven seals."
Rev. 5:2, 5

To celebrate the signal achievement in biblical scholarship which *Hermeneia* represents, the entire series will by its color constitute a signal on the theologian's bookshelf: the Old Testament will be bound in yellow and the New Testament in red, traceable to a commonly used color coding for synagogue and church in medieval painting; in pure color terms, varying degrees of intensity of the warm segment of the color spectrum. The colors interpenetrate when the binding color for the Old Testament is used to imprint volumes from the New and vice versa.

Wherever possible, a photograph of the oldest extant manuscript, or a historically significant document pertaining to the biblical sources, will be displayed on the end papers of each volume to give a feel for the tangible reality and beauty of the source material.

The title page motifs are expressive derivations from the *Hermeneia* logotype, repeated seven times to form a matrix and debossed on the cover of each volume. These sifted out elements will be seen to be in their exact positions within the parent matrix. These motifs and their expressional character are noted on the following page.

Horizontal markings at gradated levels on the spine will assist in grouping the volumes according to these conventional categories.

The type has been set with unjustified right margins so as to preserve the internal consistency of word spacing. This is a major factor in both legibility and aesthetic quality; the resultant uneven line endings are only slight impairments to legibility by comparison. In this respect the type resembles the hand written manuscript where the quality of the calligraphic writing is dependent on establishing and holding to integral spacing patterns.

All of the type faces in common use today have been designed between 1500 A.D. and the present. For the biblical text a face was chosen which does not arbitrarily date the text, but rather one which is uncompromisingly modern and unembellished so that its feel is of the universal. The type style is Univers 65 by Adrian Frutiger.

The expository texts and footnotes are set in Baskerville, chosen for its compatibility with the many brief Greek and Hebrew insertions. The double column format and the shorter line length facilitate speed reading and the wide margins to the left of footnotes provide for the scholar's own notations.

Kenneth Hiebert, Designer

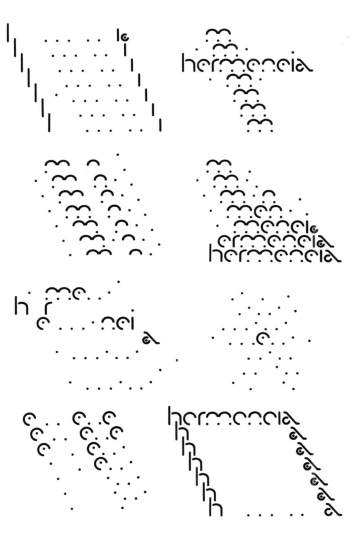

Category of biblical writing,
key symbolic characteristic,
and volumes so identified

**1
Law
(boundaries described)**
  Genesis
  Exodus
  Leviticus
  Numbers
  Deuteronomy

**2
History
(trek through time and space)**
  Joshua
  Judges
  Ruth
  1 Samuel
  2 Samuel
  1 Kings
  2 Kings
  1 Chronicles
  2 Chronicles
  Ezra
  Nehemiah
  Esther

**3
Poetry
(lyric emotional expression)**
  Job
  Psalms
  Proverbs
  Ecclesiastes
  Song of Songs

**4
Prophets
(inspired seers)**
  Isaiah
  Jeremiah
  Lamentations
  Ezekiel
  Daniel
  Hosea
  Joel
  Amos
  Obadiah
  Jonah
  Micah
  Nahum
  Habakkuk
  Zephaniah
  Haggai
  Zechariah
  Malachi

**5
New Testament Narrative
(focus on One)**
  Matthew
  Mark
  Luke
  John
  Acts

**6
Epistles
(directed instruction)**
  Romans
  1 Corinthians
  2 Corinthians
  Galatians
  Ephesians
  Philippians
  Colossians
  1 Thessalonians
  2 Thessalonians
  1 Timothy
  2 Timothy
  Titus
  Philemon
  Hebrews
  James
  1 Peter
  2 Peter
  1 John
  2 John
  3 John
  Jude

**7
Apocalypse
(vision of the future)**
  Revelation

**8
Extracanonical Writings
(peripheral records)**